Sacrifice Imagined

Sacrifice Imagined

Violence, Atonement, and the Sacred

Douglas Hedley

continuum

Continuum International Publishing Group
80 Maiden Lane, New York, NY 10038
The Tower Building, 11 York Road, London SE1 7NX

www.continuumbooks.com

Library of Congress Cataloging-in-Publication Data

A catalog record of this book is available from the Library of Congress

ISBN: 978-1-4411-1003-9 (hardcover)
ISBN: 978-1-4411-9445-9 (paperback)

Typeset by Pindar NZ, Auckland, New Zealand
Printed in the United States of America

Contents

For Margaret Barker

Acknowledgments

I am very grateful to the Arts and Humanities Research Council (AHRC) for awarding me a term of funded sabbatical leave in 2008, and my college, Clare, and the Faculty of Divinity for research leave. I am also grateful to the Fellows of Clare Hall for providing such a warm welcome during my research leave.

Some of the ideas in this text were presented to the European Society for the Philosophy of Religion meeting at Oslo in 2008. I am very grateful to Marius Timmann Mjaaland, Jan Rohls, Allen Brent, Hans Peter Grosshans, Mark Wynn, Geoffrey Rowell, Catherine Pickstock, Peter Harland, John Cottingham, Werner Beierwaltes, Roger Scruton and Jacob Sherman. Walter Schweidler is to be thanked for an invitation to the Hermann and Marianne Straniak Foundation Symposium, "Sacrifice between Life and Death," at the Katholische Akademie in Weingarten. Also thank you to Pierpaolo Antonello for inviting me to a Girard Colloquium at St. John's College in Cambridge, and to Johannes Zachhuber in Oxford for inviting me to "The Political Dimension of Sacrifice" conference in Oxford. Parts were read to the D Society in Cambridge and the Philosophy Department of Liverpool. Material was read at the University of Geneva, and I am grateful to Richard Swinburne and others there for their comments. Sarah Coakley kindly invited me to speak at her Faith and Passions Colloquium at Wolfson College, Cambridge. George Wilkes invited me to speak to his seminar on religion and conflict at St. Edmund's College, Cambridge.

I am very grateful for the very helpful staff of the University Library and the Divinity Faculty Library at Cambridge. Dave Goode was an enormous help with computing. I am also deeply indebted to the help and suggestions of Sarah Hutton, James Vigus, Dan Davies, Alain Wolf, Wilhelm Schmidt-Biggemannn, Ranja Knøbl, Siegbert Peetz, Sylvana Chrysakopoulou and thanks to Carolina Armenteros and Richard Lebrun for help with Maistre. I wish to thank the late and much missed Emile Perreau-Saussine, who died so tragically, and Vittorio Montemaggi for our discussions of Vico and Dante. I wish to thank Giles Waller, Ian Cooper, and Adrian Poole for much stimulating discussion.

Thanks to Ingolf Dalferth, Ann Loades and David Brown, Brian Hebblethwaite, George Watson, Richard Meade, Charles Moseley, Tim Mawson, Christopher Hamilton, David Leal, Rémi Brague, John Milbank, Charles Taliaferro, Stephen Clark, Wayne Hankey, Torrance Kirby, John Kenney, Kevin Corrigan, Anthony O' Hear, David Leech, Russell Re Manning, David Grumett and Benedikt Aigner, and Christian Hengstermann. Vincenzo Vergiani and Julius Lipner helped me with Sanskrit world, I have profited immensely from my undergraduate and postgraduate students at Cambridge Divinity Faculty. Especial thanks to Marco Andreacchio for providing some Vico translations and some notes for chapter three, and Russell Hillier and Thomas Simpson for specific suggestions. Geoff Dumbreck was of enormous help with index and he tirelessly read through the entire manuscript. Thanks to Harris Naqvi at Continuum for taking the project on.

Earlier versions of parts of chapters have already appeared in print:

'Between Enlightenment and Idealism: Reflections on G.B. Vico's Theological Imagination', *Der Gott der Vernunft*. (Tubingen: Mohr Siebeck, 2009), eds. Lauster, J. and Oberdorfer, B., pp. 111-123.

'Sacrifice and At-one-ment: Joseph de Maistre and Cudworth's Types and Shadows Admired', *International Journal for the Study of the Christian Church*, 9: 282-94

'Imagining the Unimaginable: Reflections upon the Concept of Sacrifice', in Walter Schweidler (ed.), *Opfer in Leben und Tod, Ergebnisse und Beiträge der Hermann und Marianne Straniak-Stiftung* (Weingarten: Akademia), pp. 71-82

'For God's Sake? Why Sacrifice?' *Neue Zeitschrift für Religionsphilosophie*, 50: 296-312

Alyssa has made the world seem much more hospitable and less sacrificial.
    The book is dedicated to Margaret Barker. She introduced me as a boy to the Greek tongue and to the world of the Hebrews and their Temple. With characteristic generosity, she came to Cambridge on the day of my interview for a lectureship in Divinity and showed me her *alma mater*. I was inspired by her support and encouragement on that day and have been ever since.

Prologue

[W]e still live in what is essentially, although in derivative
rather than direct manifestations, a Biblical culture, and readily
mistake our hereditary ways of organizing experience for the
conditions of reality and the universal forms of thought.

M. H. Abrams

But life, the highest representation of the Idea in Nature is
just this: to sacrifice itself and to become Spirit. (Aber das
Leben, die höchste Darstellung der Idee in der Natur ist nur
dies, sich aufzuopfern und zum Geiste zu werden.)

G. W. F. Hegel

Varieties of sacrifice

Religion remains. Notwithstanding the secularization thesis of Weber, it seems
a strikingly prominent part of the contemporary world. This phenomenon has
generated the alarm, frustration, and puzzlement of the cultured despisers of
religion. Religion is frequently identified as the source of the violence of current political conditions and oppression and injustice in apparently advanced
societies. Sacrifice serves as a focal point of such criticisms, implicitly or
explicitly. The idea of sacrifice seems to distil the ignorance, superstition,
violence, and cruelty of true religion: from the intolerance of monotheism
to the bloodletting of savage polytheists; offerings and bribes to barbarous
deities or the holy cruelty of destroying one's enemies in God's name.

Throughout the centuries, such critics have poured scorn upon the idea
of sacrifice, which they have targeted as an index of the irrational and
wicked in religious practice. Lucretius saw the sacrifice of Iphigenia as an
instance of the evils perpetrated by religion. But even religious reformers
like Xenophanes or Empedocles rail against "bloody sacrifice."[1] What kind
of God can demand sacrifice?

Yet the language of sacrifice persists in a secular world.[2] Nor does
its secularized form seem much more appealing. One need only think

---

1 Chrysakopoulou, S. (2003) "Théologie versus physique dans la poésie présocratique
 de Xénophane à Empedocle," (doctoral thesis). Paris: Sorbonne, pp. 318–28.
2 See the useful selection by Carter, C. (2003) *Understanding Religious Sacrifice: A Reader.*
 London and New York: Continuum.

of the appalling and grotesque cult of sacrifice in numerous totalitarian regimes of the twentieth century. The perversion of the jihad in radical Islam in contemporary Europe would provide another somber instance. In the last few years throughout Europe, we have seen the revival of a classical Enlightenment atheism, a movement that, far removed from Nietzsche's pathos for the Death of God, pursues a vigorous and relentless policy of *Écrasez l'infâme!* Indeed, contemporary polemicists like Dawkins and Hitchens wish to emphasize precisely the sacrificial dimension of Christianity: not just false but also nasty! The modern cultured despisers of religion are the self-confessed descendants of Hume and Voltaire. Religion is the product of the period of ignorance in the superstitious and terrified fearful infancy of humanity, and is the crude attempt to face the natural human longing for knowledge, consolation, and emotional support.

How can one strive to defend the concept of sacrifice against such cultured despisers? I think we need to start by reflecting upon why the slaughter of an animal, say, makes holy — *sacra facere*? The root meaning of "sacrifice" has a basis in ritual practice, as its Latin etymology suggests. Though in common parlance it communicates a giving up or rejection, the word as we are going to understand it signifies the substitution — or more, perhaps sublimation — of an item or interest for a higher value or principle. St. Augustine speaks of the outward symbol of the true sacrifice of spiritual offering that God requires in the altar of the heart — a sacrifice of humility and praise.[3] The metaphor works because his audience was familiar with the literal sense of the term.

Three phases of sacrifice: ancient, first millennium, and Enlightenment

Our culture possesses an inherited concept of sacrifice, largely from Christianity and the Greco-Roman world. The near sacrifice of Isaac by Abraham or the sacrifice of Iphigenia by Agamemnon (though she is spirited away in one major version) are instances. The death of Jesus Christ is understood by the Gospel writers as a sacrifice and St. Paul enjoins Christians to become living sacrifices. Yet we have to be scrupulous about distinguishing between the literal and the figurative. Sacrifice is a universal component of the human imaginary, but sacrifice in the strict ritual sense is generally limited to ancient or archaic societies.

Sacrifice was immensely important within the Greco-Roman world, but Judaism and Christianity marked the end of that kind of literal sacrifice. Animal sacrifice was part of the expected behavior of the Roman citizen, a contribution to the sustaining order of the universe. When Christians refused to submit to Imperial power and offer sacrifices to him, they seemed to be challenging the very cosmic order supported by the sacrificial system.[4] Whereas animal sacrifice was a fundamental part of the ritual

3   Augustine. (1984) *On the City of God.* Harmondsworth: Penguin, p. 379.
4   Heyman, George. (2007) *The Power of Sacrifice: Roman and Christian Discourses in Conflict.* Washington, DC: Catholic University of America Press.

method of attaining communion between the Divine and the human in the Greco-Roman world, the destruction of the Temple in AD 70 meant that animal sacrifice disappeared in Judaism.

One might note the argument of Guy Stroumsa concerning the end of public sacrifice.[5] Christianity rejected the sacrifices of both the Jews and the "Pagans." The religion of the Rabbis, like Christianity, was a radical transformation of sacrifice.[6] The period between Christ and Mohammed was an age of transition that prepared for the great metaphysical theologies of medieval Islam and Christendom. But another key date is that of the destruction of the First Temple of Jerusalem in 587 BC. As Margaret Barker has emphasized, the religion of the ancient Hebrews, out of which Christianity and Rabbinic Judaism emerged, was a religion divided and traumatized by the destruction of the First Temple and the exile in Babylon. Hence, although sacrifice finally disappeared from Judaism after AD 70, there was much debate about true and valid sacrifice that emerged out of the collapse of the old Temple order. The imagery of the book of Revelation is incomprehensible without this background.[7]

However, the potency of the figurative meaning of sacrifice did not end there. Throughout its history, Christianity has been fascinated by the idea of sacrifice, and the battles of the Reformation are incomprehensible without reference to it. Much of this debate is about the levels of the symbolic, figurative and literal. Luther can speak of the "monstrum impietatis" and Calvin bemoans the "Sacrilege execrable."[8] Yet, as Hildebrand observes, "the sacrificial altar disappears in the Reformation; the scriptural altar . . . remains, and with it true eucharistic worship."[9]

The real shift occurs with Socinianism. Protestants and Catholics argued about the extent of sacrifice. The second article of the 39 Articles of the Church of England asserts Christ to be a "sacrifice, not only for original guilt, but also for all actual sins of men."[10] In the wake of Faustus Socinus and his *De Jesu Christo servatore* of 1578, the Socinians rejected the idea of Christ's death as sacrifice for the sins of humanity as unjust and incompatible with Divine goodness. The role of Christ as Messiah is guaranteed by his resurrection, but he is effective for believers through his example of perfect dedication to God.[11] The impact of Socinianism upon later theology can barely be overemphasized.

In the early modern period, in philosophy and theology, we have the development of a radical critique of sacrifice *tout court*. Philosophers of "self

5 Stroumsa, Guy G. (2005) *La Fin Du Sacrifice : Les Mutations Religieuses De L'antiquité Tardive.* Paris: Odile Jacob.
6 Klawans, Jonathan. (2006) *Purity, Sacrifice and the Temple: Supercessionism in the Study of Ancient Judaism.* Oxford: Oxford University Press.
7 Barker, M. (1996) *The Revelation of Jesus Christ.* T&T Clark.
8 Hildebrand, F. (1967) *I Offered Christ: A Protestant Study of the Mass.* London: Epworth Press, p. 35.
9 Hildebrand, *I Offered Christ*, p. 91.
10 Church of England. (2009) Book of Common Prayer. Cambridge: Cambridge University Press, p. 612.
11 Miller, G. (ed.) (2003) *Theologische Realenzylkopaedie.* Berlin: De Gruyter, p. 30ff.

preservation" such as Machiavelli, Hobbes, and Spinoza have criticized the very idea of sacrifice. The key question is no longer just whether the relationship between literal and figurative sacrifice is one of continuity or rupture. It is now: has sacrifice hitherto "imagined" become unimaginable? Is the very language of sacrifice a barbaric vestige of antiquated cruelty and superstition? As Girard observes in his own terminology: "[T]he phrase 'modern world' seems almost like a synonym for the sacrificial crisis."[12] If we take that to mean the problem that post-Enlightenment European culture confronts in the legacy of sacrificial language, then Girard's point is most apt.

Plato and Kant produce an account of self-sacrifice as an index of the freedom of the agent to pursue the good. They both explicitly use the language of ethical sacrifice to express the sublime power of a transcendent goodness. Both envisage the reception of the power in terms of a dualism of a phenomenal and noumenal, sensible and intelligible, domain. Both envisage the good life in metaphysical terms as proper subordination of the former to the latter. Both present the fulfillment of that good life as a life of sacrifice. A good example is one of the seminal discussions of sacrifice in modern philosophy: Kierkegaard's *Fear and Trembling*. The title itself points to that experience of the nonrational *Schaudern* of Goethe and Otto. Abraham is famously silent in Kierkegaard's account: he cannot conceptualize his experience. For Kierkegaard — and I think this is a plausible interpretation of the position presented in *Fear and Trembling* — it is the fact of transcendence, of the "absolute relation to the absolute" that justifies the idea of sacrifice. This, of course, makes any rational-ethical justification impossible. Kierkegaard's idea of the teleological suspension of the ethical is highly suggestive and problematic.[13] It challenges any cozy domestication of religion — like Arnold's famous "morality touched with emotion". But Kierkegaard's rejection of an identification of religion with the ethical has the unwelcome effect of furnishing warrant for fanaticism.

Sacrifice and imagination

Sacrifice Imagined is the second volume in a trilogy — the first is *Living Forms* of the Imagination; the third, *The Iconic Imagination*. Let me emphasize that my interest is in sacrifice "imagined." My primary concern is not in the anthropological or sociological phenomenon of sacrifice.[14] The distinguished French scholar Marcel Detienne famously considers sacrifice as merely a political and sociological phenomenon. Others have doubted whether any rational explanation for such an irrational activity can be given.[15]

There is considerable literature consisting of anthropological approaches

12   Girard, R. and Gregory, P. (2005) *Violence and the Sacred*. London: Continuum, p. 199.
13   See Rudd, Anthony. (1993) *Kierkegaard and the Limits of the Ethical*. Oxford: Clarendon Press.
14   Hedley, Douglas. (2008) *Living Forms of the Imagination*. London: T&T Clark.
15   Henninger, Joseph. (1987) "Sacrifices," in Mircea Eliade (ed.), *Encyclopedia of Religion*. New York: Macmillan.

to sacrifice, a body that has developed since the late nineteenth century.[16] The starting point is often seen as the English anthropologist Edward Burnett Tylor, who published his *Primitive Culture: Researches in the Development of Mythology, Philosophy, Religion, Language, Arts and Custom* in 1871. Tylor is the source of gift theories of sacrifice. Tylor defines sacrifice as "a gift made to a deity as if he were a man."[17] This most primitive level of sacrifice looks like a bribe. However, Tylor believes that sacrifice evolves to higher stages. The second stage is that of the homage, in which there is often a shared meal. The third stage is one of "abnegation." Notwithstanding this evolutionary modification, the core paradigm of sacrifice in Tylor is utilitarian. The sacrificer offers a gift for a favor from the god: sacrifice is a form of a crude or even economic "do ut des". Marcel Mauss's observation is that the gift paradoxically entails obligation. A gift seems freely given; the value of the gift seems based upon the benefit accrued. However, Mauss observes in human societies that a gift generates a reciprocal relationship between giver and receiver. Mauss noted the intense rivalry induced by gift exchange in Pygmy groups in the Andaman Islands.

William Robertson Smith, in his *Religion of the Semites* of 1881, attacked this idea of sacrifice as gift and replaced it with the idea of sacrifice as primarily the sacrificial meal as an "act of communion." He argues that sacrifice is prior to any idea of property. The item, animal, or victim sacrificed was already deemed holy and not the property of the sacrificer. The sacrificial act was not the offering of a gift to the god or gods but a mystical meal that cemented the communion between the worshipers and the unseen Divine realm.

Many commentators have objected to any strict opposition between gift and communion theories of sacrifice. H. Hubert and M. Mauss, in their great work *Sacrifice: Its Nature and Function*, view sacrifice as the means of *mediation* between the profane and the sacred. They do not explore the origins of sacrifice.[18] Freud's theories of religion emerge out of the works of anthropological exploration of religion through theories of sacrifice, exemplified by Robertson Smith or the French anthropologists. Freud provides an explanation of the origins of sacrifice in his comparison of savage and contemporary society in his *Totem and Taboo* of 1913: "the beginnings of religion, morals, society and art converge in the Oedipus complex."[19] It is here that he develops his highly speculative theory of the death of the primordial father by the horde. All religion is grounded in the guilt generated by this highly ambivalent relation to the primal father. The totem is a surrogate for the primal horde father and the sacrificial killing of the totem constitutes as repetition of the primal killing.

The totemic system was, as it were, a covenant with their father, in which he promised them everything that a childish imagination may expect from

16 Strenski, Ivan. (2003) *Theology and the First Theory of Sacrifice*. Leiden: Brill.
17 Burnett Tylor, Edward. (1871) *Primitive Culture*, vol. 2, p. 328.
18 Hubert, H. and Mauss, M. (1964) *Sacrifice: Its Nature and Function*, W. D. Halls (trans.) Chicago: University of Chicago Press.
19 Freud, Sigmund. (1961) *Totem and Taboo*, Strachey (trans.) London: Routledge, p. 156.

a father — protection, care, and indulgence — while on their side they undertook to respect his life (that is to say, not to repeat the deed which had brought destruction on their real father).[20] Freud draws explicitly upon Robertson Smith: the holy mystery of sacrificial death "is justified by the consideration that only in this way can the sacred cement be procured which creates or keeps alive a living bond between worshippers and their god".[21]

Freud's theory of patricide is an odd reversal of the more familiar Abrahamic-Christian sacrificial filicide. It sees culture generally as grounded in the sacrifice of raw and dangerous instincts and religion as an Oedipal illusion generated by wish fulfillment. In his recent book *Battling to the End*, René Girard accuses anthropologists in general of colluding with psychoanalysis.[22] Girard considers anthropologists as falsely viewing prohibitions as directed against sex. The real problem, according to Girard, is not sex but violence. Prohibitions are best seen as directed against mimetic rivalries, within which sexuality often plays a role. The core problem, in Girard's eyes, lies in the mimetic rivalry that is a relentless mechanism of violence. For Girard, the lack of sacrifice in contemporary culture is a kind of problem: without this mechanism societies are much more susceptible to violence. Girard thinks he has discovered the origins of sacrifice in relation to the mechanism of violence. Like Freud, he is offering a grand theory of the origins of sacrifice, which draws upon anthropology but which attempts to provide an account of the origins of sacrifice.

Walter Burkert's *Homo Necans* (1983) and Girard's *La Violence et Le sacré* (1972) represent a momentous period in the literature on sacrifice. Among the manifold and wildly incompatible theories of sacrifice, Girard and Burkert produce clear explanations of the nature of sacrifice.

We are the only religious animals. This should not be surprising as we are peculiar animals in other respects. Since we have emerged from lower organisms, it seemed perplexing even to Darwin that we should be uniquely cognitive: why trust any human beliefs, convictions, or values much more than a monkey's? Hence, as I argued in the preceding volume, the implausibility of methodological naturalism lies in the fact that it limits knowledge to the domain explored by physics. In the physical sciences we can imagine structures of an invisible ordered universe in stark contrast to the manifest image of reality. But it seems puzzling that minds *so* good at knowing complex facts should have emerged as a by-product or epiphenomena of scanning equipment. If the existence of a complex body of knowledge, based upon reason, is puzzling for this reason, perhaps we should not be surprised by the uniquely religious nature of human animals. Yet, if the weakness of naturalism lies in its failure to explain reason, the great problem of theism is evil. This book does not try to answer the problem of evil, but endeavors to explore some aspects of the inherited topics of suffering, violence, and atonement as sacrifice imagined.

20 Freud, *Totem and Taboo*, p. 144.
21 Freud, *Totem and Taboo*, p. 137.
22 Girard, R. (2010) *Battling to the End: Conversations with Benoit Chantre*, Mary Baker (trans.). East Lansing: Michigan State University Press, p. 62.

The contemporary concentration on personal religion, and the historic separation of Church and State, means that many Western cultures like the US or France can engender a rather innocuous and deracinated "bourgeois" religion. To compare the private religion of the secular West with the five-yearly decapitation of thousands of buffalo in Nepal in honor of the Hindu goddess Gadhimai is instructive. Is it not "real" religion as puzzling as it is grim and bloody? In the ancient Greek world "sacrifices" or *ta hiera* were literally holy things, and our English word has its roots in *sacra facere*, making holy. Why is such violence or killing holy?

M. H. Abrams rightly insisted that we underestimate the Romantic legacy: we still inhabit its imaginary even if the rationalists and proponents of "science" rail against quaint or pernicious illusions of ancestors. The Romantics did consciously attempt to re-inhabit and re-imagine those traditions of medieval Europe discredited or abandoned by the "Enlightenment." The Romantics also highlighted darker and morbid qualities of experience: Medusa and Satan. Many images of evil in the contemporary mind are of Romantic provenance. Perhaps, as Goethe and Eliot thought, this is the morbid and decadent side of the Romantics. Or perhaps the Romantics were more attuned to this "crooked timber of humanity" than their enlightened forbears. In this volume I wish to examine the somber aspect of the inherited Western religious imagination: the world as an arena of sacrifice. Philosophers may argue about evidences for or against the existence of God; Coleridge rightly insisted that a man must rather feel his want and develop a self-knowledge of his need of Christianity. But that "want" and "need" will scarcely emerge within the immanent frame of contemporary secularism! It is not that God or the soul are rationally implausible to many contemporary minds; materialism is philosophically a problematic creed: the existence of mental items may be denied by eliminative materialism and "explained" by non-reductive physicalism, but there is little consensus among contemporary philosophers about the status of the mental. Rather, the traditional "objects" of metaphysical and religious faith cannot furnish any imaginative grip on the reflective and serious critic.

The Christian language of sacrifice only makes sense within a context of the Fall and salvation. It is only intelligible if we recognize contingency and "fallenness" of the world, its nature as Divine gift, and the joy and the suffering it entails; and love as the form in which we accept sacrifice and suffering as a "making sacred" — a redemptive path. If, in *Living Forms of the Imagination*, I stressed the more positive role of the imagination, in this work I wish to explore the darker dimension of human existence, the sense of "Fallenness." One does not require the clinic evidence of The Milgram Experiment, psychoanalytic lucubration of the lurid scenes of European Tragedy, or reports from Rwandan genocide to expound a picture of the Fall. Virtue in the greatest philosophers is depicted as the strenuous attempt to ascend towards goodness, and such thinkers as Plato or Kant naturally used the language of sacrifice to express such a vision.

Girard is a most important figure in this respect because he provides a remarkable vision of a "fallen" society. Violence for Girard is endemic in human society. The sacred is not a construction that emerges out of certain social relations. Rather, the sacred produces particular social structures. So far, Girard is incisive and illuminating. In his theory, God is not the sacred but, rather, violence. This leads to an odd distortion in his theory, notwithstanding its many merits. Although we shall argue against Girard's view that the sacred is identified with violence, he is right to highlight a dimension of religion that even many of its critics overlook.

We are the only animals who shape our environment, and we use our imagination to do so. An ancient historic culture such as England provides a striking example of this shaping activity, which included horticulture, ritualized hunting, and political, economic, and agricultural innovations. Many of these activities are far removed from mere survival; indeed, they often spring from leisure and wealth. The magnificent rural fabric of hedges, fields, cottages, and church spires of the English landscape is at least in part a product of a certain ingenious and fractious tribe. But so too are the motorways, the "functional" civic architecture, and drab conurbations. The shaping imagination has its burdens as well as its glories.

The shaping imagination is particularly potent in literature. Shakespeare is the modern Homer. It is often Shakespeare mediated by Schlegel, Verdi, or Delacroix, but Shakespeare nonetheless. To think of jealousy today in twenty-first-century Berlin, Rome, or London is to have "in mind" *Othello*; ambition just *is Macbeth*. Just as the ancient Hellenes brooded over the images furnished by the epic Ionic poet (whoever or whatever the real identity of the author/s), so too the minds and imaginations of modern Europeans have been forged by the singular genius of the Elizabethan dramatist. Much of the Christian Neoplatonic exitus-reditus model of life has seeped into our bloodstream through the great Stratford bard. If Darwin thought there was more to *homo sapiens* than natural selection, why shouldn't we?

Two philosophers play a central role in my narrative: Vico and Maistre. Vico is a good place to start since he is a thinker who rejects the Cartesian starting point of hyperbolic skepticism. He is illuminating on the precariousness of human existence and the importance of institutions and laws. We have to recognize the importance of struggle and hardship involved: mankind is both limited and free. Human liberty is a victory over circumstances. Virtue is a necessary condition of society, unlike those from Machiavelli and Marx who see money or power as the key.

I often think of Giambattista Vico walking the streets of Naples, a town with a Greek name, with its rich layers of Roman Norman-Viking, Swabian, and Saracen conquests. The medieval university where he taught was also where Thomas Aquinas taught, Federico Secundo. In Vico's age it was one of the most cultured and intellectually vibrant cities, and perhaps the most rebellious and tempestuous city in Europe. Vico had a deep sense of layers of culture and the fragility of culture's hold on the beast that lies in human nature. He was acutely aware of the dynamic and creative role of strife in human society, and its capacity to overspill into grim terror. There is another respect in which Vico is Platonic: his denial of the "tragic view of life." Plato's rejection of tragedy as an art form was clearly linked to his sense that the pervading pessimism of the tragic poets would subvert both society and metaphysics. Vico's view of both society and metaphysics is very different from Plato, but he shares the anti-tragic stance. Vico's life appeared tragic. He was born in relative poverty and suffered a serious accident as a child, and his schooling was irregular. As a scholar he was condemned to obscurity: he failed to win promotion and was largely ignored by his intellectual contemporaries outside Naples. Even his funeral was marked by a squabble among the pallbearers. But Vico's work is an attack upon what one might call the tragic view of life, the position of his great Stoic contemporary Shaftesbury.

Maistre is a darker figure than Vico, but one of his successors in stressing the symbolic, agonistic, and violent dimension of human existence. Joseph-Marie, Comte de Maistre (1753–1821) was a Savoy diplomat of French stock in the service of the Kingdom of Sardinia as ambassador to Russia (1803–1817) and in Turin (1817–1821). The Savoyard philosopher was an outstanding apologist for the Counter-Revolution. This is the man described as

> a fierce absolutist, a furious theocrat, an intransigent legitimist, apostle of a monstrous trinity composed of Pope, King and Hangman, always and everywhere the champion of the hardest, narrowest and most inflexible dogmatism, a dark figure out of the Middle Ages, part learned doctor, part inquisitor, part executioner.[23]

A trenchant critic of the French Revolution, he viewed it as the apotheosis of the atheism and philosophical empiricism of the Enlightenment. For Maistre, the core of Enlightenment ideology was the denial of God, the view of morality as essentially secular, and the belief in the inevitability of progress. Traumatized by the horrors of the French Revolution, he develops Vico's thought that civilization exists wherever one finds an altar. The so-called "friend of the executioner," a savage critic of Enlightenment optimism that has been misinterpreted as the avowal of violence and irrationalism. Isaiah Berlin saw Maistre as the earliest fashioner of the fascist "vision" of the universe.[24] In his *Soirées de St Pétersbourg*, Maistre develops a theodicy, which is, at the same time, a theory of redemption: evil reveals God's plan for mankind, which is the expiation of guilt through vicarious suffering (represented by the shedding of blood in sacrifice, and more remotely in execution and war). Yet this is not the whole theory:

> *Y a-t-il quelque chose de plus certain que cette proposition: tout a été fait par et pour l'intelligence?* (Is there anything more certain than the proposition that everything has been made by and for intelligence?)[25]

23 Faguet, Emile. (1899) *Politiques et moralists du dix-neuvieme siècle*. Paris, p. 1. See Isaiah Berlin's introduction in Maistre, Joseph Marie. (1994) *Considerations on France*, Richard Lebrun (trans.). Cambridge: Cambridge University Press, p. xi.

24 Berlin, Isaiah. (1953) *The Hedgehog and the Fox: An Essay on Tolstoy's View of History*. New York: Simon & Schuster, p. 1.

25 Maistre, Joseph de. (1993) *St Petersburg Dialogues; or, Conversations on the Temporal Government of Providence*. Montreal: McGill-Queen's University Press, p. 383.

It strikes me that any philosopher who proposes that the universe is grounded in and made is a very unlikely precursor of the fascist "vision." Indeed, it may be more accurate to view Maistre as a prophet of the paradoxical cruelty of "secular" ideologies. We can dispose of the proto-fascist label easily. Yet Maistre remains, many would suggest, a morally questionable figure. Does he not rejoice in suffering, draconian punishment, and violence? Is he not the embodiment of a grotesque militarism that is such a shameful legacy of the Christian tradition? If that challenge is correct, then the famed eloquence of Maistre's pen is put to the service of a cruel philosophy. My answer is twofold. First, the challenge confuses the descriptive with the normative. Maistre is describing the violence of the world as it appears to him. His perception may be false, but that is quite different from advocating such suffering and violence. Second, Maistre's universalism, as we shall see, constitutes a critique of the cruelty of the Augustinian type of theology.

Maistre is a controversial writer but one of great and limpid genius. Maistre was much admired by German Romanticism: Schelling's Munich friend Franz von Baader greatly admired Maistre's opus maximum, the *St Petersburg Dialogues*. In Russia, the influence of the Savoy count's metaphysical reflections on crime and punishment was profound. Dostoevsky was known as the "Russian Maistre." More recent views, however, like that of Berlin, who presents Maistre as a proto-fascist, are often deeply distorting, and amount to confusing the description of horrors with their advocacy. Maistre makes this thought explicit: mankind's proper relation to the physical cosmos is a sacrificial rite, a "making sacred." Through sacrifice, the hidden seed of the Divine is brought out of potentiality into actuality. As such, the renunciation of the will, the sacrifice of self for an absolute good must remain an integral element of human self-realization. Maistre, with Burke the most eloquent polemicist against Enlightenment, saw himself as the inheritor of the great philosophical inheritance of Europe and the relentless adversary of the trivialization and banalization of Western philosophy in so-called "philosophes" like Voltaire. Yet Maistre was no mere polemicist: he was an astute reader of Plato and the Platonic tradition, and his reflections upon the relevance of the concept of sacrifice reflect his deep immersion in the European philosophical canon. Maistre is much less coy than Kant about the theological dimension of his philosophy of suffering, of *régénération dans le sang*. And Maistre is more inclined to provoke and shock. But the ethics of both philosophers is shaped by an anthropology of emotions in an asymmetrical, even agonistic, relationship with reason.

As philosophers or theologians we want "to save the appearances." The erosion or elision of value from ontology generates absurdity. The classic instance is that of determinism. If determinism were correct, then the choice of the theory of determinism itself would not be a free act but, rather, a necessary effect of particular causes. If so, it cannot be better or worse, qua theory, than indeterminism, which is equally produced by necessary causes. One of the theological influences behind this work is Origen, with his sense of human existence as both a grim struggle and a festival of joy. It was Origen, hero of Erasmus, the sanguine Cambridge Platonists and the gloomy Maistre, the Alexandrian who saw freedom as the key component of Christian anthropology. But for a substantial freedom of agency within a theistic metaphysics — that is, a subject capable of recognizing objective and transcendent values in a fallen world and acting in accordance with them — sacrifice is unavoidable. I draw particularly upon Cudworth's fine *A Treatise of Freewill* and his exploration of agency through an employment of Origen's idea of the ruling principle or "To Hegemonikon."

If we accept responsibility and freedom, we cannot avoid the depressing facts of human behavior: the irrationality, superstition, the wars, the plunder, and exploitation. The Alexandrian-Florentine-humanistic tradition — that tradition of letters that spawned the modern "humanities" — contains a range of attempts to understanding and describe the paradoxes and burden of human freedom: from Adam and Eve to contemporary politics.

The language of sacrifice, in particular, only makes sense within a sacramental context. This is the reason why the language of politicians who talk about making sacrifices because the ecological crisis or in the prosecution of wars is so puzzling. We have inherited another imaginary, that of modern secular ethics from Hobbes to Habermas, which has expunged the archaic idea of the "sacrificium."

Closely linked to the sacramental is the Platonic hierarchy of being. Unity is superior to plurality: soul to body, eternity to time, reason to the passions. The sense of the holy is linked to the awareness of difference between human and Divine. Many of the critics of the idea of sacrifice are anti-Platonic and so is Nietzsche's odd retrieval of sacrifice, where sacrifice is an expression of the Will to Power and not the slave morality that encourages sacrifice of self for the sake of metaphysical values. Nietzsche is very telling in this reversal of the idea of sacrifice. The increasing emphasis upon individual freedoms and rights and the *horizontal* web of beliefs and commitments: dimension of family, friends, and contracts has been combined in occidental culture with an erosion of *vertical* sense of a mediated transcendent *order*, where this order is the basis of non-contractual obligations, duties to elders, priests, or rulers seem increasingly odd or archaic in contemporary Western society.

The defense of such a hierarchy of being is deferred to the third volume of this trilogy. To reiterate, this book is not about sacrifice *per se* but, rather, sacrifice imagined. It is sacrifice imagined because, in the absence of a developed anthropology of sacrifice, our concern here is with the inherited *imaginary* of sacrifice: why a certain cluster of images and narrative continue to interest and engage, especially in popular culture. Whether in General Gordon or Captain Oates, Nelson Mandela or Martin Luther King, Jr., the power of sacrifice is evident.

Is this merely the power of propaganda? The Christian answer must be no. Sacrifice imagined is not the ritual slaughter of livestock, but the participation in the life of He who bodied forth the love of God the Father. We are made in the image of God but are far removed from his likeness. The realization of that likeness, the participation of the indwelling Christ, is a *sacra facere*, a making holy and an offering of a living sacrifice in His image.

Sacrifice is primordially linked with the very human experience of the "sacred" and the often puzzling, sometimes terrifying instances of offerings to God. But this culminates in the self-offering or sacrifice of the Divine in and through humanity, the unveiling of the Divine essence, of an eternal love in the depths of the Godhead.

There are two immediate objections. First, if "dying to live" is so fundamental, then this can be used to exonerate atrocities. Theologically, it can be used as part of a repellent justifications of the ways of God to man. Politically, it can be used to rationalize scapegoating activities; for example, the Tutsi by the Hutu in the appalling Rwandan genocide. The first objection, that sacrifice becomes the ideological instrument of repression and oppression, theological or political, bears much force, not least because of some of the repugnant secular usages of sacrificial language in the Western tradition. However, the insight of Maistre was that language of sacrifice only *becomes* dangerous within the utopian context. The French Revolution and, indeed, many of the violent and murderous *sans culottes* of the twentieth century who emerged out of the break-up of the old European dynastic empires; from the millions who died of famine in the Ukraine in 1933 through collectivization, the Nazi-Soviet pact, which Stalin claimed was "cemented in blood," the Holocaust and beyond to Pol Pot and Ceausescu. *Utopian* ideologies of society designated a scapegoat like the Jews or the kulaks or the bourgeoisie as the necessary stage in the transformation into the ideal state. Thus, for Maistre, the French Terror was a grotesque and wicked travesty of sacrifice, a grim celebration of violence justified by an unattainable secular political ideal. Within Christianity, Maistre opines, the sense of human frailty and limits prevents such a perversion of sacrifice. Maistre is a polemicist and, notwithstanding his genius, prone to exaggeration. But Cudworth's more general point that "Pure Falsehood is pure Non-Entity, and could not subsist alone by it self [sic], wherfore [sic] it always twines up together about some Truth"[26] obtains. We should not be surprised to find the truth of sacrifice is often entwined with distortions and errors.

The technological success of the scientific revolution and the Industrial Revolution may lead to an oversanguine estimate of human progress and possibility. The language of sacrifice properly belongs to an imaginary that accepts both the reality of the transcendent and its normative force and the imperfect nature of the created order. From a certain secular perspective, the language of imperfection or "Fallenness" is deeply puzzling.

The second main objection is that creation would seem to be determined and not free, if it is seen as a primordial sacrificial act. Against the second objection, we shall offer the following consideration. If not merely goodness but love is the law of Divine being, the first objection can be rejected summarily. Meister Eckhart puts the point in characteristically paradoxical terms:

I will never give thanks to God for loving me, because He cannot help it, whether he would or not: His nature compels Him to it. I will give him

26   Cudworth, R. (1642) *A Discourse Concerning the True Notion of the Lords Supper*, London, p. 2.

thanks because by his goodness He cannot cease to love me.[27]

Voluntaristic theologies of an inscrutable Divine will are often identified with theism, especially Christian theism, but a Christian Neoplatonist can happily dissent from these traditions, and appeal to a theology grounded in the Divine essence as goodness. Cudworth is adamant on this point:

> God is therefore God, because he is the highest and most perfect Good and Good is not therefore Good, because God out of an arbitrary will of his would have it so. Whatsoever God doth in the World, he doth it as it is suitable to the highest Goodnesse; the first Idea, and fairest Copy of which is his own essence . . . God who is absolute goodnesse, cannot love any of his Creatures & take pleasure in them, without bestowing a communication of his Goodness and likeness upon them.[28]

There are related metaphysical issues concerning Divine perfection and freedom, which will be addressed in the next volume. But briefly, the answer lies in the Divine love that is self-limiting. God is not merely limited by the laws of logic but by His very nature. In St. John, the God of the Greeks, the God who creates the world as an image of himself because he is without envy, and this is the language of mimesis and generosity of Plato's *Timaeus*, becomes the God who offers one perfect and sufficient sacrifice. The genius of St. John, like that of St. Paul, is not to reject the pagan mind but to deepen its insight through their own forceful minds and what we Christians can only think of as inspiration more Divine than poetical, providential rather than philosophical.

For reasons given here it is the thesis of this book that we should not be won over by those secular despisers of religion of tender-minded Christians who advocated a radical break with the language of sacrifice. Here we shall plead for continuity between even the crass and ritual elements of ancient sacrifice to the most sublime aspects of a genuinely spiritual religion. Rather than a rupture between the archaic and pagan sacrificial and the contemporary Christian worldview, we shall stress the continuity. A key to this is our emphasis upon the symbolic imagination. Christianity does not shirk the terrors of our experience. Its struggle against temporal evil is not, like that of the ancient or modern Stoic, to resist and reject but to transform and overcome.

It is a mistake to associate the symbolic with fantasy or illusion. A culture like ours, which is so proud of its ideological materialism as "scientific," is prone to a false alternative between crude literalism and the figurative. Thus, it is assumed, sacrifice can only be violence or some vague moralism. In this book, I wish to argue for the polyvalence of the language of sacrifice. Its symbolic power lies in its capacity to resonate with the psyche at various different levels, while conveying truths. Perhaps, as Walter

---

27 Eckhart (1996) *Sermons and Treatises*, vol II, p. 197.
28 Cudworth, Ralph. (1647) *A Sermon Preached before the House of Commons*, March 31, pp. 26–7.

14 *Sacrifice Imagined*

Burkert suggests, it reminds us of our evolutionary hunter-gather past. Perhaps, as Freud and Girard aver, it reflects the guilty tensions and raw envy camouflaged and disguised by human civilization. This recognition need not be incompatible with the affirmation of self-control and discipline as genuine forms of sacrifice sublimated. Nor need this moral dimension of sacrifice be incompatible with the worship and celebration of the sacred that sacrifice in the form of banquet and feast entails.

The Cambridge Platonist John Smith entitled his first sermon "On the True Way or Method of attaining to Divine Knowledge."[29] He begins by claiming that the mode of rationality proper to theology includes emotion and will. This knowledge of God is not to be confused with mere definitions and syllogisms but enlightens, heats, and enlivens. Smith consciously employs striking imagery of the circulation of the blood and gardening, or cultivation, to convey the practical and transforming energy of this intellectual vision of God. The attaining of knowledge of the intelligible has an ineluctable aesthetic and moral component:

> How sweet and delicious that Truth is which holy and heaven born Souls feed upon in their mysterious converses with the Deity, who can tell but they that tast it? When *Reason* once is raised by the mighty force of the Divine Spirit into a converse with God, it is turned into *Sense*: That which before was onely Faith well built upon sure Principles, (such as our *Science* may be) now becomes *Vision* . . . a blissful, steady, and invariable sight of him.[30]

Only those who strive to be godlike can understand divinity. Smith speaks of spiritual cognition as a form of sensation: God is discerned by "touch." Divine things are to be comprehended more readily by a "Spiritual Sensation" than by a "Verbal description," or mere Speculation[31]. Here Smith is consciously drawing upon Plotinus for whom ultimately nondiscursive experience of the presence of the Divine is superior to any conceptual articulation.[32] The vision, he says, "is hard to put into words."[33] Plotinus is a rationalist in the Hellenic tradition, but we should not confuse this with Baconian or Cartesian "rationalism." Plotinus is very interested in the limits and fringes of rational discourse, which he understands as states of ecstasy. Smith is deeply influenced by Plotinus's stress upon the experiential dimension of cognition. The true method of knowing is based upon a

> true Efflux from the Eternal light, which, like the Sun-beams, does not only enlighten, but heat and enliven; and therefore our Saviour hath in his *Beatitudes* connext Purity of heart with the Beatifical Vision. And as

29 Smith, John. (1978) *Select Discources*. New York and London: Garland, p. 199.
30 Smith, *Select Discourses*, pp. 16–17.
31 Smith, *Select Discourses*, pp. 2.
32 Plotinus. (1989) *Enneads* (revised edn.) 6.9(9)4.
33 Plotinus, *Enneads*, 6.9(9)10, 20.

the Eye cannot behold the Sun . . . unless it be *Sunlike* . . . so neither can the Soul of man behold God . . . unless it be *Godlike*.[34]

Smith's emphasis upon inner light as purified rationality consists in the combination of the doctrine of the agent intellect with the medieval mystical doctrine of the scintilla (spark) or the apex mentis (peak of the mind) Here we find explicitly the Plotinian doctrine of the "center" of the soul of *Ennead* 6.9.8 whereby the highest point of the human mind is its immanent Divinity and salvation is the realization of this essential or true nature. The idea of the "infant Christ" is employed by Smith as the Christian theological construal of this Plotinian doctrine. Smith, as a late Renaissance Platonist, is perfectly aware of the pedigree of his doctrine that "like can only be known by like" and his related theological doctrine that salvation consists in the realization of the soul's true nature. Smith writes:

> The true Metaphysical and Contemplative man, . . . who running and shooting above his own *Logical* or *self rational* life, pierceth into the *Highest Life* . . . endeavours the nearest Union with the Divine Essence . . . as Plotinus speaks; knitting his owne centre, if he have any, unto the centre of Divine Being. . . . This life is nothing else but God's own breath within him, and an *Infant-Christ* (if I may use the expression) formed in his Soul, who is in a sense . . . the *shining forth of the Father's* glory. But yet we must not mistake, this knowledge is but here in its Infancy . . . here we can see *but in a glass*, and that *darkly* too. Our own *Imaginative* Powers, which are perpetually attending the highest acts of our soul, will be breathing a grosse dew upon the pure Glasse of our Understandings, and so sully and besmear it, so that we cannot see the Image of the Divinity sincerely in it. But yet this knowledge being a true heavenly fire kindled from God's own Altar, begets an undaunted Courage in the Souls of Good men . . .[35]

Here in this passage we see a very characteristic combination of St. Paul and Plotinus. Like Plotinus, Smith wants to give some account of the spiritual exercises, the huge effort — moral and spiritual — demanded by the true philosophical life.

The goal of this simplification and purification is the inexpressible and hence supralinguistic state of union with Divine. Pierre Hadot, thinking of Plato's *Phaedrus*, has spoken of the "ontological value of the spoken word"; this living and animated discourse was not principally intended to transmit information, but to produce a certain psychic effect in the reader or listener. Thus the "propositional element" was not the most important element of ancient philosophical teaching, and Hadot has frequently cited Victor Goldschmitt's formula . . . that ancient philosophical discourse

---

34 Smith, *Select Discourses*, p. 2.
35 Smith, *Select Discourses*, pp. 20–1.

intended to "form more than to inform."[36] But this formation within the Platonic school meant a strict ascetic discipline. John Smith is referring to this Plotinian motif when he says:

> We should endeavour to polish and shape our Souls into the dearest resemblance of him (sc. God) . . . according to that Pattern which we behold in the Mount of a holy Contemplation of him . . . and preserve that Heavenly fire of the Divine Love and Goodness (which issuing forth from God centres it self within us . . .) . . . always alive and burning in the Temple of our Souls, and to sacrifice our selves back again to him.[37]

Such is "Divine life" rather than a "Divine science" — it being something to be understood by a "spiritual sensation than by any verbal description." This life is based upon the indwelling Christ. For Smith this "becoming like God" is the educing of the "infant Christ" within the soul. The infant Christ is the theological aspect of the metaphysical doctrine of the "core self" in Plotinus. But note the reference to the "heavenly fire kindled from God's own Altar." The space of the *transforming* vision is the Temple. Smith draws upon the medieval mystical (or Neoplatonic) idea of "spark" of the soul or "apex mentis." If we are to think of sacrifice as the reigniting of the spark of the soul, then we need to consider this idea of a soul center kindled at the Divine altar, and its return to its source – transformed into the "likeness" of God.

The conception of the first principle that Christian theology inherited (albeit modified) from Plotinus is of the supreme One in terms of a vision of the structure of reality as a hierarchy of unified manifolds: intellect soul and material world. The primary unity in manifold is Intellect: this presupposes a principle of unity that is not many or multiple. No qualities or properties, not some-thing. The One is not a possible object of knowledge: we must go away in silence and enquire no more.[38] For Neoplatonic philosophy generally, its goal was the transformation of lives not system building in the narrow sense. This is not because the search for the One is an illegitimate barren enterprise. Mere armchair speculation is empty: through this aporetic thinking about the One, the soul goes around the One. The soul is both kept at a distance from its "object" and driven closer. Hence there is no pure cognition of the Divine. The striving for moral excellence is path to knowledge understanding (the Lord is nigh unto them that are of broken heart (Ps. 34.19), fear of God is the beginning of wisdom (Prov. 1.7)) This idea is both biblical and Platonic.

The narrative of the covenant of God with Abraham or the new Covenant established by Christ through his sacrificial death and resurrection seems to have little obvious relation to the God of classical theism, the *ens*

36 Davidson, A. (1995) "Introduction: Pierre Hadot and the spiritual phenomenon of ancient philosophy," in Hadot, P. *Philosophy as a Way of Life: Spiritual Exercises from Socrates to Foucault*. Oxford: Blackwell, p. 19.
37 Smith, *Select Discourses*, p. 157.
38 Plotinus. (1989), *Ennead*, 6.8.11.

necessarium, esse ipsum of the scholastics, or *causa sui* of Plotinus and Descartes. Are we caught between the "metaphysical horror"[39] of a sterile and abstract Absolute of the philosophers or the jejune anthropomorphisms of scripture? The language of sacrifice is on the tongues of those philosophers who sought the appearance of the Divine in the Jerusalem Temple and who viewed the God of Abraham as breaching of any sterile Divine aseity through the Divine self-duplication in the symbolism of the "birth of Christ" in the soul.

Meister Eckhart (1260–1327/8) employs the image of the Temple as the spiritual locus of the vision of the Divine. Eckhart inherited the henological Neoplatonism of Plotinus indirectly through Proclus, Avicenna, and Maimonides. The two key ideas of his philosophy are unity and "Bild" (image). In his account of this speculative Temple tradition, Henry Corbin employs the Coleridgean-Schellingian concept of the tautegory.[40] The tautegory does not hide that which it symbolises (as some "other") but discloses through itself or, rather, corresponds enigmatically with its transcendent referent. For Corbin, the imagery of the Temple within the traditions of the book, or the Abrahamic traditions, depends upon this Platonic correspondence between the noetic and the physical cosmos.

In *Living Forms*, I referred to Hölderlin's remarkable meditations upon the Last Supper and the figure of Christ on the eve of the crucifixion. Hölderlin identifies Christ with both Dionysus or Bacchus the wine god who is dismembered and who was often seen with the Christian tradition as a typological prefiguring of Christ. As we explain in our account of Schelling and Creuzer, Hölderlin is not merely indulging in learned allusion or fanciful analogies. The Swabian poet avers that the great sacrifice at the heart of the Christian Faith generates the energy of renewal. The poem tells us that Divine work, *göttliches werk*, is like the sower's seed or the glowing iron in the furnace or the lava in Mount Etna, the effect of the Divine life is abundance and expansion, and the task of the Christian is participation in this expansion of the Divine work and, specifically, the imitation of the life of Christ out of the riches and energy of the Spirit:

> *So hätt ich Reichtum*
> *Ein Bild zu bilden, und ähnlich*
> *Zu schaun, wie er gewesen, den Christ.*

> (Thus I would have riches
> To make an image of his image
> In contemplating the Being of Christ.)[41]

---

39 See Kolakowski, Leszek. (1988) *Metaphysical Horror*. Oxford: Blackwell.
40 See Hedley, D. (2008) *Living Forms of the Imagination*. New York: Continuum, pp. 121ff and 140ff.
41 Hölderlin. (1966) *Poems and Fragments*, Michael Hamburger (trans.). London: Routledge, p. 472

The poet's message is one of liberation and transformation. The vision of Christ crucified and risen is the transforming contemplation of the Divine nature, the Christ seen by the beloved disciple in Patmos and the very God of whom St. Paul was preaching to the reflective Athenians, the living image, not merely of the unknown deity of the philosophers but the God in whom we live and move and have our being.[42] René Girard is quite right to emphasize the "deeply Christian" dimension of Hölderlin, though we will disagree with Girard's view of the German poet's appropriation of Dionysus.

Girard faces a problem when he tries to unravel the Apocalyptic dimension of Christianity. In his searing depiction and critique of mimetic violence, Girard views Christian Apocalyptic as an interruption into history: the revelation of nonviolence. What Girard fails to recognise is the Temple (i.e sacrificial) nature of Apocalyptic theology. What else can we make of the Lamb of Revelation 5.6: "as it had been slain." His overwhelmingly negative view of sacrifice and his construal of sacrifice in terms of the scapegoat means that he cannot attribute sufficient weight to the imagery of Temple in the book of Revelation, any more than he can do justice to the text of the Hebrews.[43]

The core image of *Living Forms of the Imagination* was that of the chariot. The corresponding figure in this work is that of the Temple. Sacrifice remains a force in our culture even though it is sacrifice spiritualized. The same applies to the Temple. The Jerusalem Temple is the symbolic meeting point of the terrestrial and the spiritual, the material and the heavenly. It is vision of heaven and an image of longing and hope in the midst of suffering and doubt and in a world that seems to exhibit so much cruelty and discord. It is an image of that transcendent beauty that Dostoevsky maintains will save the world.

---

42   Acts 17.28.
43   Girard, *Battling to the End*, pp. ix–xv.

1

The Theophanic Imagination: "Making Sacred" and the Sublime

To think is to speculate with images.

Bruno

Das ausschliessend Eigenthumlich der Absolutheit ist, das
sie ihrem Gegenbild mit dem Wesen von ihre Selbstandigkeit
verleiht. Dieses in-sich selbst-sein, diese eigentlich und
wahre Realitaet des Angeschauten, ist Freiheit.
(The exclusive particularity of the Absolute is that it offers its
counter-image independence. This independent existence,
the proper and real reality of observed, is freedom.)

Schelling

Shut your eyes and awake to another way of
seeing, which everyone has but few use.

Plotinus

In this chapter we consider the status of mankind's involvement or participation in the process of "making sacred" — an involvement in the sacrificial rite — as coexisting with the activity of God. The physical cosmos bears within it its own logos or creative essence, but these Divine energies cannot be realized without the corresponding human contribution. The role of the imagination employed in this process is outlined. The locus of this perception of the Divine within the Israelite prophetic tradition was the Temple, as the point of correspondence between the finite cosmos and the mind of God.

Plato and Aristotle both saw wonder as the inspiration of philosophy. And the love of a beautiful and intelligible universe, and the source or principle (*arche*) "that moves the sun and other stars" has inspired much traditional metaphysics. Indeed, one could argue that philosophy is itself chimerical if the universe is a brute absurdity. If consciousness and freedom, the soul and responsibility are systematic illusions, or perhaps at best the epiphenomena of a deterministic universe, these are metaphysical positions and not the simple inferences from scientific facts. More fundamentally still, is there an uncreated necessary Being, the source of the vast contingent cosmos and the realm of becoming? Is there a transcendent Mind beyond the flux of fleeting thoughts, intentions, and aspirations? Plato and Aristotle claim that the answer is yes! The imagination of this transcendent uncreated reality has inspired the greatest poetry from the Upanishads to the Sufi mystics, Dante, Wordsworth, and Eliot.

Sir William Jones, the great Sanskritist, believed that the subtle theology of ancient India "induced many of the wisest among the Ancients,

and some of the most enlightened among the Moderns, to believe, that
the whole Creation was rather *energy* than a *work*, by which the Infinite
Being, who is present at all times and in all places, exhibits to the minds
of his creatures a set of perceptions".[1] It is a doctrine of original uncreated
oneness, of *māyā* as the fall into deception and multiplicity, and of a return
to oneness where only God is perceived.

False philosophical extremes continue to trouble serious Christian
theology. One extreme consists of a crude essentialism and the other might
be deemed loosely nominalism. According to the first, God can be grasped
as an object of intellectual inquiry. Theology is not possible if its supreme
object is viewed as an entity that can be captured as an item among others:
si comprehendis non est Deus. However, equally corrosive is the second
option, the nominalism that insists that our abstract names and predicates
are universal expressions for a *de facto* plurality of discrete concrete items.
The denial of abstract universals infects theology with a radical and unten-
able skepticism. The proper balance must consist in a balance between
the proper respect for the limits of conceptual definition and sufficient
epistemological optimism. Imagination constitutes the inward light of the
soul. If faith is the substance of things hoped for, the evidence of things not
seen, then these objects cannot be seen by the physical organs or deduced
rationally. If God is beyond thought and language, then imagination is
necessary for theology. As Wordsworth insists,

> This spiritual love acts not nor can exist
> Without imagination, which, in truth,
> Is but another name for absolute power
> And clearest insight, amplitude of mind,
> And Reason in her most exalted mood.[2]

Love is the means by which the deepest nature of reality is revealed. The
very reason for the world's existence is love: the *bonum diffusivum sui* of
God. Imagination is an inward light that can be identified with rationality
in its most sublime function. Philosophy is etymologically the love of wisdom, not wisdom itself. Notwithstanding the power of specific arguments
for the existence of God or the nature of the soul, the key to the knowledge
of God is that joy of experience of the Divine presence by a living soul that
Wordsworth describes as "spiritual love." Already in book 2 of *The Prelude*
Wordsworth writes:

> Wonder not/
> If high the transport, great the joy I felt
> Communing in this sort through earth and heaven
> With every form of creature, as it looked
> Towards the Uncreated with a countenance

1   See Urs App. (2009) 'William Jones's Ancient Theology', *Sino-Platonic Papers*, 191, July
    2009, p. 21.
2   Wordsworth, William (1970) *The Prelude*, 6. Stephen C. Gill (ed.) Oxford: Clarendon, p. 104.

Of adoration, with an eye of love.[3]

Christian theology, in particular, should be partial to the claims of the imagination, notwithstanding the dangers of idolatry and superstition. Even in an age of disenchantment, the mysterious but central doctrine of the *imago Dei* must mean that there is a special and unique link between the human being and God. This doctrine is reinforced by the doctrine of the incarnation. In a political world where "rights" and "human dignity" are so momentous, it is ironic that we fail to see those "fire darting steeds,"[4] the horses of the Titan Helios, the sun God, in the movement of the sun from East to West: we know the sunset to be an illusion because it is the earth, not the sun, that is moving; a fact that any rational and educated mind knows since Copernicus. Thus, not only is nature rendered devoid of meaning but also human agency seems redundant: the product of mechanical processes that we are incapable of understanding; we are thus robots deluded by the belief in freedom. As the sense of the cosmos as meaningful has been eroded by the scientific revolution of the seventeenth century, so too the belief in human freedom seems battered. A deterministic and scientistic view of human nature, however, leaves out the role of ideas upon the events of history. The etymology of words often sheds light upon the history of philosophy. Any philosophy overlooks, at its peril, the important of history and tradition for

> a creature who not prone
> And brute as other creatures, but endued
> With sanctity of reason, might erect
> His stature, and upright with front serene
> Govern the rest, self-knowing, and from thence
> Magnanimous to correspond with heaven.[5]

Modern theology is embarrassed about immanence. For various reasons, philosophy in both the analytic and the continental traditions tends to conceive of God as an entirely transcendent. Continental philosophers have been so concerned about Heidegger's critique of "onto-theology" that any retrieval of God-talk is almost paralyzed by the fear of collapsing into reification of the Divine. Analytic philosophers have been traditionally more concerned by the objections of Humean and Kantian provenance. The predominant model, is, however, that of a *deus absconditus* — that is, a radically transcendent agent.

One of the major problems with the emphasis upon Divine transcendence is that it is open to Schellenberg's objection. Schellenberg claims that hiddenness of God is an argument for atheism.[6] A good God would have

---

3   Wordsworth, *The Prelude*, 2.
4   Pindar. *Olympian Ode* 7.71.
5   Milton, (1971) *Paradise Lost*, Alaistair Fowler (ed.). London: Longmans, p. 388.
6   Schellenberg, J. L. (1993) *Divine Hiddenness and Human Reason. Cornell Studies in the Philosophy of Religion*. Ithaca, NY; London: Cornell University Press.

provided adequate evidence of his existence. Clearly, however, there exist many who would like to believe in God but who sincerely lack the requisite evidence. Any serious theology must be able to provide examples of the experience of God.[7]

If the presence of God is described in terms of the goodness, truth, and beauty of the world, this has many attractions to the philosophical theist. Yet human experience is deeply perplexing and troubling what about death and suffering?

Environment, shaping, and shaped?

Animals are shaped by their environment; we are makers of our own milieu. The evolution of the long neck of the giraffe is a striking instance of a genetic adaptation to the environment. Clearly humans also adapt to their environment via their genetic inheritance. Tibetans, for example, have developed a distinct physiological adaptation to high altitude. The Tibetan can naturally withstand conditions at high altitude that would be intolerable for other human beings. However, much more characteristically human is the capacity to shape the environment rather than be shaped by it. The town or city is a good example of how human beings structure their immediate environment. The town provides amenities and protection from predators. Yet the architecture of the city is an imaginative structure. The forms of building and the ornamental designs, the "concrete music"[8] of even the most functional architecture constitutes a distinctive and imaginative representation of reality, one that varies enormously between different human cultures.

The shaping imagination of human beings — evident in, for example, the city — has a positive and a negative dimension. The environmental crisis is an example of the destructive power of the human imagination. This Promethean or Faustian energy, lamented in the book of Job, or by Tolkien in *The Lord of the Rings*, is the capacity of human technical process to put "nature on the rack" and wars and pollution and ugliness and cruelty of much contemporary civilization exhibits this negative shaping energy of the human mind. The scientific and industrial revolutions of the early Modern period have greatly enhanced this characteristic of *homo sapiens*.

As makers, humans are intensely aware of the impact of this creative imagination, and the great myths explored this theme long before the seventeenth century. Our special place in the created order as creative beings brings special responsibilities and burdens. The normative is fused with an obligation that precedes any conscious agreement.

7   I take the theology of David Brown to be a paradigm of this in *God and Enchantment of Place: Reclaiming Human Experience* (Oxford: Clarendon, 2004).
8   Schelling, F. W. J. (1989) *The Philosophy of Art*, D. W. Stott (ed. and trans.). Minneapolis: University of Minnesota, p. 166.

The ambivalence of the normative

Plato's cave is a graphic imaginative expression of the epistemic, ontological, and axiological gap between appearance and reality. What we take to be reality is suffused with illusion. Knowledge, for Plato, is linked to a process of liberation from ignorance, a process that he sees as an ascent. The idea of the sacred is tied to the sense of gulf of rupture between value and empirical reality. This odd tension between the axiological (the sense of value in the world) and the *kakurgic* (the tendency towards needless suffering and destruction) provides a puzzling rift in human experience.

Consider the battle of Mers-el-Kébir in July 1940 when the Royal Navy destroyed most of the French fleet, killing 1,297 men. Britain and France were recent allies. Since France had agreed an armistice with Nazi Germany, Britain was concerned that the considerable French fleet in this port would be employed by the Germans and Italians to isolate Britain from its empire and thus gain easy victory. British and French relations were poisoned by the act, especially between Churchill and de Gaulle. Yet it is clear why Britain considered this unavoidable, and it might be argued that in its draconian horror it displayed a resolve to continue war with Germany and Italy. However horrendous, this attack on allied forces can be understood and justified, notwithstanding its moral perplexity. This is an example of the problem of "dirty hands." There is often no way of avoiding some degree of evil in human action. As Arjuna emphasizes to Krishna in the chariot, inertia is potentially as destructive as reckless violence. One important aspect of sacrifice is the ambiguity of the holy in human experience. Among the Aztecs, notoriously the cruelest exponents of a sacrificial religion, the leaders of enemy peoples would be spared in warfare and treated with respect until their ritual execution.[9] This ambiguous dimension of the sacred as the *mysterium tremendum* and the ambivalence of sacrifice has been noted by manner of the great writers on the subject, from Maistre to Girard.

Many reflective minds are struck by the fact we find these contradictions odd in the first place. If Schopenhauer's relentless pessimism were correct as an account of the world, then there would be little sense of the oddity of discord between good and evil: the paradoxical nature of the created order as both grounded in the Divine order and yet rent asunder from its source. Schopenhauer's sense that human beings attend to illness and pain and happiness is merely the cessation of discord and misery and the ultimate reality is both grim and absurd, cannot furnish much basis for the wonder that has provoked so much philosophy. Equally Hume's "'Tis not contrary to reason to prefer the destruction of the whole world to the scratching of my finger," though based upon very different premises, has the same result.[10]

Schopenhauer's nemesis, Hegel, seemed to go to the opposite extreme

---

9 See the works of Carter, J. *Understanding Religious Sacrifice*, p. 167.
10 Hume, D. (1978) *A Treatise of Human Nature* (2nd edn.). Oxford: Clarendon Press, p. 3, §3.

when he encompasses negativity within the dialectical process; as did his pupil, Marx, in the assumption that the amelioration of conditions in the world is a matter of metaphysical necessity (a position, ironically, empirically disproved the effects of Marxism in the last century). Such optimism tends further to minimize the reality of suffering in humans and the rest of the both extremes of pessimism and optimism are implausible. The right approach is some *via media*. This is a world in which physical laws tend to encourage life and consciousness and thus creatures, who are servants and not mere slaves of "ethical realities."[11] Yet there can be no serious denial of the real cost of such freedom. A magical realm in which evil failed and robust goodness was superfluous would hardly be an ethical domain at all. A moral life without struggle is hardly worth aspiring to, and almost all the great spiritual traditions of mankind insist upon this. Yet equally the degree of innocent suffering, waste, and destruction is deeply troubling to any but the most cynical observer.

The puzzles of such a combination of good and evil drive the mind towards a transcendent absolute, that is supreme unity, but also constitutes the values of truth, beauty, and goodness. Here my model is that of the anti-volutarism of Cudworth and his insistence that the nature of God is prior to the will of God.

What the odd combination of good and evil reveals is a world fallen, a domain that is divorced from God. The sacrament is the means by which the "fallenness" and division of the created order can be overcome.

Imagination or fantasy

It is within the context of this rift between value and the experience of evil that I wish to place the theophanic imagination. It is an iconic imagination because the images as icons point in an enigmatic manner to a transcendent reality. Much of the Enlightenment critique of religious is a critique of the misuse of imagination. Religion on this account is a dangerous fantasy. For Pascal, imagination is characteristically *"cette maitresse d'erreur et de faussete"* — "this mistress of falsehood and error."[12] In *Living Forms of the Imagination*, I argued that Theism's espousal of an invisible transcendent God is compatible with the idea that images can be enigmatic signs of the transcendent. Plato's myths offer an illustration of this. Gibbon noted that a pagan philosopher of Antiquity

who considered the system of polytheism as a composition of human fraud and error, could disguise a smile of contempt under the mask of devotion, without apprehending that either the mockery or the compliance would expose him to the mockery of the invisible, or as he conceived them, imaginary powers.[13]

11   Leslie, John. (1979) *Value and Existence*. Oxford: Basil Blackwell, p. 39.
12   Pascal, Blaize. (1976) *Pensées*, Philippe Sellier (ed.). Paris: Mercure de France, §78.
13   Gibbon, Edward. (1993) *The Decline and Fall of the Roman Empire*, vol. 6. H. R.

Christian writers, however, saw the pagan deities "in a much more odious and formidable light" as "the authors, the patrons, and the objects of idolatry." But Gibbon's word can be misleading. Indeed, the oldest and most venerable critique of religious belief, from Xenophanes to Feuerbach, is an argument about fantasy. Religious belief is based upon the human propensity to project its interests and longing upon the cosmos. The development of philosophical theology, in the strict sense, from the idea of an invisible and intelligible deity as the transcendent and supreme being reinforced the fantasy argument.

Another, if rather cynical, view of religion, from Epicurus to Hume, is the idea that it is grounded in fear and fantasy. Is this fair? Consider this characteristically eloquent passage from Hume:

> We are placed in this world, as in a great theatre, where the true springs and causes of every event are entirely concealed from us; nor have we either sufficient wisdom to foresee, or power to prevent those ills, with which we are continually threatened. We hang in perpetual suspense between life and death, health and sickness, plenty and want; which are distributed amongst the human species by secret and unknown causes, whose operation is oft unexpected, and always unaccountable. These *unknown causes*, then, become the constant object of our hope and fear; and while the passions are kept in perpetual alarm by an anxious expectation of the events, the imagination is equally employed in forming ideas of those powers, on which we have so entire a dependance [sic]. Could men anatomize nature, according to the most probable, at least the most intelligible philosophy, they would find, that these causes are nothing but the particular fabric and structure of the minute parts of their own bodies and of external objects; and that, by a regular and constant machinery, all the events are produced, about which they are so much concerned. But this philosophy exceeds the comprehension of the ignorant multitude, who can only conceive the *unknown causes* in a general and confused manner; though their imagination, perpetually employed on the same subject, must labor to form some particular and distinct idea of them. The more they consider these causes themselves, and the uncertainty of their operation, the less satisfaction do they meet with in their researches; and, however unwilling, they must at last have abandoned so arduous an attempt, were it not for a propensity in human nature, which leads into a system, that gives them some satisfaction. There is a universal tendency among mankind to conceive all beings like themselves, and to transfer to every object, those qualities, with which they are familiarly acquainted, and of which they are intimately conscious. We find human faces in the moon, armies in the clouds; and by a natural propensity, if not corrected by experience and reflection, ascribe malice or goodwill to every thing that hurts or pleases us.[14]

Trevor-Roper (ed.). London: David Campbell, p. 15.
14   Hume, David. (1993) *Dialogues Concerning Natural Religion*, J. C. A. Gaskin (ed.). Oxford: Clarendon, p. 140f.

Hume's argument against religion depends upon the analysis of this supposedly deep-rooted instinct of fear and capacity for delusion among human beings. Yet if there is a constructive use of imagination in science and other domains of rationality, and perhaps the sense of the "holy" is not a fact about our projections but, rather, a quality or property that human beings recognize.

The sacred

What is the "sacred"? It is often contrasted with the profane. In the popular imagination the sacred or the holy is associated with a sacred place and a time: a temple, a festival, or perhaps a place that seems to evoke awe. The Latin root of the English word "sacred" is instructive in its proximity to mystery. The root *sacer* was used in *sacramentum* (originally a military oath; later something to be kept sacred) and then as the translation of Greek *mysterion* (despite the existence of *mysterium*).

I wish to suggest that the concept of the sublime can give us a key to the "sacred." In order to do so, I wish to consider the seminal work of Rudolf Otto, *Das Heilige* (1917). This is a much maligned classic, more reported than read. Doubtless, in the heady days of Dialectical Theology it appeared rather bland as theology; with the rise of "Religious Studies" it appeared either as a version of the consensus gentium argument for religion or as armchair science of religion. Yet Otto was a philosopher and theologian, not an anthropologist (though widely traveled and with great knowledge of world religions). We can allay some of the more crass objections. The sense of the holy described by Otto cannot be dismissed with a rudimentary knowledge of logic, anthropology, sociology, and psychology. I wish to suggest that there is some profit in his unashamedly philosophical approach to the subject and that this may illuminate the subject of the conference.

Rudolf Otto produced an eloquent, powerful defense of the holy as an autonomous sphere in human consciousness rather than as primitive and false philosophy, morality tinged with emotion, or consoling poetic fancy. Otto, as a good Kantian, rejects attempts to explain the human in terms of the subhuman, the employment of the sciences of nature to the study of man. His first book, *Religion and Naturalism*, was an attack on naturalistic attempts to explain religion. His is describing a uniquely human sense of wonder, and I think any attempt to explain that wonder experienced by self-conscious agents in the world cannot be reduced to evolutionary instincts or pressures towards social cohesion.

Both the "sublime" and the "holy" are associated with the feeling of wonder in self-conscious language users. Awareness of wonder is an instance of the point made so eloquently in recent philosophy by Charles Taylor: we are self-understanding creatures and merely causal descriptions of behavior are phenomenologically woefully inadequate and philosophically question begging. We might bracket off his account from theories of the sacred that derive religion from psychological or sociological categories.

I shall mention just two: Durkheim and Boyer. In Durkeim's *Les formes élémentaires de la vie religieuse* (*The Elementary Forms of Religious Life,* 1912), he defines religion in terms of a dichotomy between the sacred and the profane. Durkheim's approach is sociological: religion is about the cohesion of the social group. It is striking that his work was based on the totemism of certain Australian aborigines. Boyer, in his *Religion Explained* (2001) tries to give an account of belief systems and rituals in terms of what he terms cognitive constraints with their basis in evolutionary development of human beings. Boyer claims that religious ideas are based upon innate structure of the mind and in particular certain inferential capacity evident in non religious domains like ethics. Religion is a by-product of evolution. Again his work is based upon a primitive tribal religion, that of the Fang people. Durkheim's is a sociological explanation of religion; Boyer's is biological and cognitive. The first ignores human self-consciousness in favor of the dynamics of group behavior. In the second, religious thought is understood in terms of "information processing."[15] The information-processing model is a descendant of Enlightenment materialism of D'Holbach and LaMettrie: the mind is essentially a computional mechanism, which at best registers solely a factual input divested of any (subjective) evaluations.

The success of the rational procedures developed since the seventeenth century is evident in the great success of modern science. The question remains about the scope of the procedural method. Can it be extended to the fabric of the mind itself? Language shapes a uniquely human consciousness, and that there is an irreducibility of human consciousness to the subhuman.

Otto employs for his motto the lines from Goethe's *Faust* (part 2, act 1, scene 5):

> *Das Schaudern ist der Menschheit bestes Teil.*
> *Wie auch die Welt ihm das Gefuehl verteuere,*
> *Ergriffen fulht er tief das Ungeheure.*

These lines are very difficult to translate. *Schaudern* is cognate with the English shudder. *Ungeheuer* has connotations of massive scale and the uncanny. *Ergriffen* is literally a state of being grasped. It means that awe is the best part of mankind, even if not valued by the world, it is grasped in the depths by the sense of the numinous. But I don't know how to translate it into poetry. The difficulty is to find words that resonate in a similar manner.

> Awe is the best of man: howe'er the world's
> Misprizing of the feeling would prevent us,
> Deeply we feel, once gripped, the weird Portentous.

Furthermore, that linguistic interpretation is inseparable from evaluation.

---

15   Taylor, Charles. (1995) *Philosophical Arguments*. Cambridge, MA; London: Harvard University Press, p. 63.

If language were a neutral picturing device, a representation of a set of bare facts, translation might be a problem of technique. But words imply and suggest a range of values. Furthermore, any great modern language is inseparable from the poetry and myths of the race. Consider the influence of the Book of Common Prayer and the King James Bible and Shakespeare upon modern English. This is a pervaded sense of wonder that is lost to an age characterized by the "barbarism of calculation." Vico in particular links the sublime to the more primitive poetic mentality, the mind of a Dante or a Homer. For our culture it is often associated with scripture, and in English with the King James translation.

The Jerusalem Temple as the paradigm sublime

As Henri Corbin has described in detail the paradigmatic place of what he calls the *mundus imaginalis*, the psychic domain within which the super-sensible is experienced via epiphanies, theophanies, or dreams is the Jerusalem Temple. Let us consider Isaiah's experience in the Temple:

> In the year that King Uzziah died I saw the Lord sitting upon a throne, high and lifted up, and his train filled the Temple. Above him stood the seraphim: each one had six wings; with twain he covered his face, and with twain he covered his feet, and with twain he did fly. And one cried unto another, and said, Holy, holy, holy, is the LORD of hosts: the whole earth is full of his glory. And the foundations of the thresholds were moved at the voice of him that cried, and the house was filled with smoke, Then said I, Woe is me! For I am undone; because I am a man of unclean lips, and I dwell in the midst of a people of unclean lips: for mine eyes have seen the King, the LORD of hosts. Then flew one of the seraphim unto me, having a live coal in his hand, which he had taken with the tongs from off the altar: and he touched my mouth with it, and said, Lo, this hath touched thy lips; and thine iniquity is taken away, and thy sin is purged.[16]

The prophet is aware of his own unworthiness in the Temple. The idea of purification of the lips of Isaiah is emphasized by Otto in his use of the prophet's encounter with God.[17] The sublime is traditionally an experience of boundless grandeur and immensity of nature, at once conveying danger and inspiring awe or worship: an experience with evidently religious implications. The sublime has the capacity to transport the soul to "rise above what is mortal." Otto notes affinity between the sublime and the numinous. The sublime and the numinous are "at once daunting, and yet singularly attracting." The experience "humbles" same time "exalts us,"

---

16   Isa. 6.1–7.
17   Otto, Rudolf. (1928) *The Idea of the Holy: An Inquiry into the Non-Rational Factor in the Idea of the Divine and its Relation to the Rational* (revised edn.), John W. Harvey (trans.). London: Oxford University Press, p. 50.

arouses fear and joy. Both resist conceptual unfolding (*unauswickelbar*).

The sublime "exhibits the same peculiar dual character as the numinous; it is at once daunting and yet singularly attracting in its impress upon the mind. It humbles and at the same time exalts us, circumscribes and extends us beyond ourselves; on the one hand releasing in us a feeling analogous to fear and, on the other; rejoicing us." Otto had a particular interest in the experience of the prophet Isaiah in the Temple. This forms an instance of the sublime,

> a mode of expression, by way of "grandeur" or "sublimity," is found on higher levels, where it replaces mere "terror" and "dread." We meet it in an unsurpassable form in the sixth chapter of Isaiah, where there is a sublimity alike in the lofty throne and sovereign figures of God, the skirts of his raiment "filling the temple" and the solemn majesty of the attendant angels about Him. While the element of "dread" is gradually overborne, the connection of "the sublime" and "the holy" becomes firmly established as a legitimate schematization and is carried on into the highest forms of religious consciousness — a proof that there exists a hidden kinship between the numinous and the sublime, which is something more than a merely accidental analogy, and to which Kant's *Critique of Judgement* bears distant witness.[18]

Yet Otto does not regard the term "sublime" as coextensive with the "Holy." In *The Holy*, Otto notes that "Religious feelings are not the same as aesthetic feelings and the 'sublime is definitely an aesthetic category as the beautiful,' however widely they may differ."

The opposite of the sublime is not quite the profane, but the idea is clearly charged with a religious dimension. Temples, cathedrals, mountains, and waterfalls are sublime. The sublime can help us to understand the Holy or the sacred because art, as Tillich notes aptly, is the barometer of culture: the spirit of culture expressed in art. That is to say that though art expresses religion, it cannot shape it. There is an asymmetry: religion is the more primordial dimension of human experience. Otto himself writes: In the arts nearly everywhere the most effective means of representing the numinous is "the sublime."[19]

The Platonic sublime

Otto links the idea of the Holy quite explicitly to the Platonic tradition, and especially Plato,

> who grasps the object of religion by quite different means than those of conceptual thinking, viz. by the "ideograms" of myth, by "enthusiasm" or inspiration, "*erôs*" or love, "mania" or the divine frenzy. He abandons the attempt to bring the object of religion in one system of knowledge

---

18 Otto, *The Idea of the Holy*, p. 63.
19 Otto, *The Idea of the Holy*, p. 68.

with the object of "science" (ἐπιστήμη), i.e., reason, and it becomes something not less but greater thereby; while at the same time it is just this that allows the sheer non rational aspect of it to be so vividly felt by Plato, and indeed vividly expressed as well as felt. No one has enunciated more definitely than this master-thinker that God transcends all reason, in the sense that He is beyond the powers of our conceiving, not merely beyond the powers of our comprehension.[20]

The subtitle of Otto's *The Holy* is *An Inquiry into the Non-Rational Factor in the Idea of the Divine and its Relation to the Rational.* Otto was not part of the widespread vitalism of the period, largely emanating from Kierkegaard and Nietzsche, and evident in his younger colleague Heidegger. Otto stresses the significance of reason in religion. He means by the "rational" the idea of the Divine as clearly grasped by the powers of understanding and within the domain of customary and recognizable definitions. However, Otto asserts that "Beneath this sphere of clarity and lucidity, we go on to maintain, there lies a hidden depth, inaccessible to our conceptual thought which we in so far term 'non-rational'."[21]

One interesting aspect of the sublime is that it does not fit with the general phenomenon of secularization in Western culture. In fact its popularity dovetails with the process of secularization. It begins in the seventeenth century and reaches a peak in the Romantic period, roughly contemporaneous with the great revolutions. If the sense of the beauty of the cosmos has a Platonic lineage, so too is the mood of the awe that accompanies experiences of transcendence:

> Of aspect more sublime; that blessed mood,
> In which the affections gently lead us on
> Until, the breath of this corporeal frame
> And even the motion of human blood
> Almost suspended, we are laid asleep
> In body, and become a living soul:
> While with an eye made quiet by the power of harmony
> and the deep power of joy,
> We see into the life of things.[22]

The Sublime was ostensibly an English discovery, both in the literal sense of English exploration of the Alps during the "Grand Tour" and those mountains that filled their minds with "agreeable horror," and the literary exploitation of Boileau's translation of Longinus (1674). This tradition of John Dennis, Shaftesbury, and Addison can be traced to the Cambridge Platonist Thomas Burnet and his *Theoria sacra telluris* (1671).[23]

---

20 Otto, *The Idea of the Holy*, p. 95.
21 Otto, *The Idea of the Holy*, p. 58.
22 Wordsworth, William. (1936) Complete Poetical Works, E. de Selincourt (ed.). Oxford: Oxford University Press, p. 164.
23 Jakob, Michael. (2005) *Paesaggio E Letteratura, Giardini E Paesaggio.* Firenze: Leo S. Olschki, pp. 116–19.

As a concept, the sublime, as the awe-inspiring object of the imagination that is too exalted (sublimis!) for comprehension, has a striking history. The text attributed to Longinus was not referred to in antiquity and there is no evidence that it was read until the Renaissance, and it was not until Boileau's text of 1674 that it became a very popular work in Europe, especially evident in the aesthetics of Burke and Kant. But it also declined in significance through the wane of Romanticism. If Turner, Friedrich, and Delacroix, in their depictions of storms and terrors and lonely spectators, were supremely sublime artists, Biedermeier was certainly not. The realism of the novels of Balzac, Dickens, and Zola seem to represent a loss of the sublime that persisted into the following century alongside the loss of the Platonic mood of transcendence characteristic for so many of the Romantic artists.[24] Twentieth-century artists like Rothko and Newman employ the term, but their versions of the sublime are much modified or reduced.

Longinus's *On the Sublime* is a largely rhetorical text about the style and feeling of sublimity. The unknown author discusses the importance of grandeur or elevation in relation to the moral role of literature. While referring to Plato, he observes that

> Nature has distinguished man, as a creature of no mean or ignoble quality. As if she were inviting us rather to some great gathering, she has called us into life, into the whole universe, there to be spectators of all that she has made and eager competitors for honour; and she has therefore from the first breathed into our hearts an unconquerable passion for whatever is great and more Divine than ourselves. Thus within the scope of human enterprise. There lie such powers of contemplation and thought that even the whole universe cannot satisfy them, but our ideas often pass beyond the limits that enring us.[25]

The idea of an elevation of the mind that transcends habitual human nature and, indeed, the physical cosmos is evidently Platonic, whether or not Longinus himself is a Middle Platonist.

The sublime is nonrational in this sense. The sublime presents the mind with the limits of our powers of comprehension, the failure to represent the transcendent. With the 1756 publication of Edmund Burke's seminal work *Philosophical Inquiry into the Origin of Our Ideas on the Sublime and Beautiful* the concept becomes a core idea in Western thought. Burke claims that terror and pain are experienced in the face of the sublime. The sublime is contrasted with the more tranquil experience of beauty. Burke identifies the sublime with immense objects or places. Burke observes:

> The passion caused by the great and sublime in nature, when those causes operate most powerfully, is Astonishment; and astonishment is

---

24 Whether postmodern retrievals of the sublime as in Lyotard represent a reversal of this general decline of the "sublime" is far from clear.

25 Longinus. (1927) "On the sublime," W. Hamilton Fyfe (trans.). *Aristotle: The Poetics; Longinus: On the Sublime; Demetius: On Style*. London: William Heinemann.

that state of the soul, in which all its motions are suspended, with some degree of horror. In this case the mind is so entirely filled with its object, that it cannot contain any other, nor by consequence reason on that object which employs it.[26]

When Kant takes up the idea of the sublime, both in his *Early Observations on the Feeling of the Beautiful and the Sublime* (1763) and in his seminal *Critique of Judgement* (1790), he evinces not just the fashionable language of the day but also much of the Platonic strand underlying it:

Now, in the immensity of nature and in the insufficiency of our faculties to take in a standard proportionate to the aesthetical estimation of the magnitude of its *realm*, we find our own limitation, although at the same time in our rational faculty we find a different, non sensuous standard, which has that infinity itself under it as a unity, in comparison with which everything in nature is small, and thus in our mind we find a superiority to nature even in its immensity. And so also the irresistability of its might, while making us recognize our own (physical) impotence, considered as beings of nature discloses to us a faculty of judging independently of and a superiority over nature, on which in based a kind of self preservation entirely different from that which can be attacked and brought into danger by external nature. Thus humanity in our person remains unhumiliated, though the individual might have to submit to this dominion. In this way nature is not judged to be sublime in our aesthetical judgements in so far as it excites fear, but because it calls up that power in us (which is not nature) of regarding as small the things of life about which we are solicitous (goods, health, and life) and of regarding its might (to which we are no doubt subjected in respect of these things) as nevertheless without any dominion over us and our personality to which we must bow where our highest fundamental propositions, and their assertion or abandonment, are concerned.[27]

The Platonic sublime has its clear counterpart in Kant's view that physical grandeur inspires a sense of the unique power of human beings as agents in the noumenal world, conforming to laws of pure reason. Hepburn writes:

Objects are sublime because they raise the forces of the soul. The huge energies of nature trigger a self-discovery Even the awesome thought of God as sublime does not crush or humiliate the soul Rather, the quality of révérence, Achtung, in the sublime, is an intimation of our transempirical activity, as free, rational and moral beings.[28]

26 Burke, Edmund. (1998) *A Philosophical Enquiry into the Origins of our Ideas of the Sublime and the Beautiful*, Adam Phillips (ed.). Oxford: Oxford University Press, p. 53.
27 Kant, Immanuel. (1951) *Critique of Judgement* (2nd edn.), J. H. Bernard (trans.). New York: Hafner, §28. cf. the dynamical and mathematical sublime in §23–4 and §29.
28 Hepburn, R. (2001) "Life and life-enhancement as key concepts of aesthetics," in *Reach of the Aesthetic*. Aldershot: Asgate, p. 67.

In this sense, this Kantian "quickening" of the soul through the sublime belongs to a Platonically inspired theodicy. The sublime represents for Kant transcendence over those sensuous components that constitute mankind as a causally determined part of nature. The pressure placed upon the imagination by the sublime induces an awareness of humanity's supersensible nature.

> The beautiful prepares us to love disinterestedly something, even nature itself; the sublime prepares us to esteem something highly even in opposition to our own (sensible) interest.[29]

In this sense, it belongs to a Platonically inspired theodicy. However weak the traditional arguments for Divine existence, Kant has no desire to shake off theism. And the sublime becomes a most apt expression of the elevation of the human spirit to the Divine, which pure practical reason cannot assume but emphatically implies. However much we may suffer as puny, physical creatures, rational spirits can raise themselves to an awareness of a higher vocation. At this point Kant is vehemently opposed to the radical French (or Dutch!) Enlightenment, which dissolved freedom into necessity and the soul into an exclusivement material item within a world without Providence, however coy his own metaphysical commitments may be. R.W. Hepburn's remark is apposite for Kant: "central to sublimity — at least common to many of its diverse forms — is the idea of a grave difficulty or threat being transformed (through free and sustained effort) into an austere but valued experience." Kant himself observes:

> What is it in me that makes it so that I can sacrifice the most inner allurements of my drives and all the desires that proceed from my nature to a law that promises me no advantage as a replacement and threatens no loss if it is transgressed: indeed, a law that I honor all the more inwardly the more strictly it bids and the less it offers in return? The question stirs up the entire soul through astonishment over the greatness and sublimity of the inner disposition of humanity and at the same time the imprenetrability of the secret that it conceals . . . One cannot become tired of directing one's attention toward it and admiring in oneself a power that yields to no power of nature.[30]

Wordsworth certainly did not read Kant but he had the advantage of the proximity of Coleridge. *The Prelude* is a poem that bears the indelible mark of their friendship and Coleridge's influence upon his friend. The poem contains a number of experiences, "spots in time," that confirmed Wordsworth in his vocation to become a poet. The culminating experience is one recalled from his student period when ascending Mount Snowdon. He wished to observe the sun rising but had a rather surprising experience instead.

29 Kant, I. *Critique of Judgement*, 5: 267.
30 Kant, I. (1993) "On a newly arisen superior tone in philosophy,"in Peter Fenves, *Raising the Tone of Philosophy*. Baltimore: Johns Hopkins Press, pp. 51–81, p. 68.

Walking through clouds, he is suddenly confronted with the moon. This constitutes one of the classic expressions of the experience of the sublime:

> A meditation rose in me that night
> Upon the lonely Mountain when the scene
> Had pass'd away, and it appear'd to me
> The perfect image of a mighty Mind,
> Of one that feeds upon infinity,
> That is exalted by an underpresence,
> The sense of God, or whatsoe'er is dim
> Or vast in its own being, above all
> One function of such mind had Nature there
> Exhibited by putting forth, and that
> With circumstance most awful and sublime.[31]

The Prelude was only published in 1850. Even though it is now held to be Wordsworth's masterpiece, it was largely unknown to the Romantics. Yet the *Lyrical Ballads*, starting with Coleridge's tormented character in "The Rime of the Ancient Mariner" and finishing with Wordsworth's "Tintern Abbey," contained a great paean to

> a sense sublime
> Of something far more deeply interfused,
> Whose dwelling is the light of the setting suns,
> And the round ocean and the living air,
> And the blue sky, and in the mind of man:
> A motion and a spirit, that impels
> All thinking things, all objects of thought,
> And rolls through all things.[32]

It is striking that a work which contained so much emphasis upon ordinary life should start and end with powerful archetypal poems of sublime experience. The mariner and his torments is an image, familiar to ancient Platonists, of the journey of the soul. Tintern Abbey, a popular ruin on the "Sylvan Wye"' in that period, represents a holy place where the soul can be restored. As in a Caspar David Friedrich landscape, the symbolic is carefully lodged within a representation of a stark but sublime natural world.

Burke and Kant use specific instances of the physical landscape that evoke reverence and awe. Friedrich's magnificent landscapes, luminous but opaque seascapes, and means for generated this mood of transcendence and response of wonder and awe:

> A savage place! As holy and enchanted
> As e'er beneath a waning moon was haunted

---

31 Wordsworth, W. *The Prelude*, p. 231.
32 Wordsworth, W. (1970) "Tintern Abbey." *Wordsworth, Complete Poetical Works*, S. Gill (ed.). Oxford: Clarendon, p. 230–31.

By a woman wailing for her demon lover.[33]

Caspar David Friedrich's paintings often employ partially obscured figures gazing towards a seemingly infinite expanse. The Rückenfigur bids the observer to join the vision of the inscrutable, eluding comprehension. The wonder that is evoked by the sublime presupposes value. Raw pessimism might generate Sartrean nausea or anxiety about the world's absurdity, but hardly wonder. The question is whether this value can be linked to the sacred as emanating from God. Philosophers like R.W. Hepburn have claimed that for historical reasons theistic ideas have impregnated the "sacred" in the West, "whether we like it or not, and no matter whether the sacred was or was not older than God or the gods."[34]

Wonder and self-consciousness

At least since Xenophanes anthropomorphism has been leveled at religious belief. Yet what kind of anthropos is being projected? Boyer consciously employs a projection theory to explain religion. But he is obviously indebted to a computational model of the mind. But consider the contrast with the doleful utterance of the chorus in Sophocles' *Antigone* (332):

πολλὰ τὰ δεινά· κοὐδὲν ἀνθρώπου δεινότερον πέλει.

Otto notes that the adjective δεινός designates the numinous energy, power, and awe that Sophocles is drawing upon when he says that, "much is awesome or terrible, but nothing more so than man." Let us call this the numinous dimension of personality.

We can try to explore this sense of the inscrutable and numinous dimension of personality with reference to Jung. Jung was deeply influenced by Otto's account of the numinous. It is, for Jung,

a dynamic agency of effect not caused by an arbitrary act of will. On the contrary, it seizes and controls the human subject, who is always rather its victim than its creator. The numinosum — whatever its cause may be — is an experience of the subject independent of his will . . . either a quality belonging to a visible object or the influence of an invisible presence that causes a particular alteration of consciousness.[35]

The phenomenon produces unusual experiences and emotions in the "victim." Jung says that such numinous experiences "have become sanctified and congealed in a structure of doctrines or rituals." On his own theory,

---

33   Samuel Taylor Coleridge (1772–1834), British poet. *Kubla Khan; or, A Vision in a Dream* (l. 12–16). Poems, John Beer (ed.) London: Dent (1993), p. 199.
34   Hepburn, R. W. (2001) "Restoring the sacred: sacred as a concept of aesthetics", in *The Reach of the Aesthetic*. Ashgate: Aldershot, p. 127.
35   Jung, *Jung: Selected Writings*, p. 201.

the archetypes are numinous. He argued that the "legendary heroes of mankind" sons of God give expression to the numinous force of personality that strikes the masses as supernatural. Hence Jung considers the deification of Christ or the Buddha is an instance of the value placed on the ideal of personality.[36] Jung writes:

> The Age of Enlightenment, which stripped nature and human institutions of gods, overlooked the God of terror who dwells in the human soul. If anywhere, fear of God is justified in the face of the overwhelming supremacy of the psychic.[37]

The mystical Sinai

The sense of the numinous power of personality provided a basis for theism and it has good scriptural roots. One of the most striking accounts of the experience of the numinous is in the third chapter of Exodus, the account of Moses's encounter with God, the I AM THAT I AM:

> And the angel of the LORD appeared unto him in a flame of fire out of the midst of a bush: and he looked, and behold, the bush burned with fire, and the bush was not consumed. And Moses said I will turn aside now, and see this great sight, why the bush is not burnt. And the LORD saw that he turned aside to see, God called unto him out of the midst of the bush, and said Moses, Moses. And he said here am I. And he said, Draw not nigh hither: put thy shoes from off thy feet, for the place whereon thou standest is holy ground. Moreover he said, I am the God of Abraham, the God of Isaac, and the God of Jacob. And Moses his face; for he was afraid to look upon God.[38]

This passage resonates with the combination of fear and reverence in the face of the numinous. The burning bush represents vividly the *mysterium tremendum* of Deity, but Moses must keep his distance and remove his shoes. The place is holy. When Moses asks for the name of God, the reply is: I AM THAT I AM.

We have in this paradigmatic and historically momentous passage a striking testimony to the numinous force of the personal. What Wordsworth calls "The perfect image of a mighty Mind." The problem with Otto is, though it is *mysterium tremendum et fascinans*, it is the *tremendum* that dominated, the awe (the wrath of the God of the Old Testament). *Fascinans* should convey the realm of love and grace, but this is somewhat underdeveloped in Otto. Yet rather than God as the "other" we require the sense of the "not other," *non aliud*. If we are looking at the roots of high religion, then it must be located in a sense of communion and communication

36 Jung, *Selected Writings*, p. 205.
37 Jung, *Selected Writings*, London, 1983, p. 201.
38 Exod. 3.2-6.

notwithstanding the apparently incommensurable gulf between the finite mind and the transcendent. It is perhaps no accident that Kant should have tied subjectivity and the experience of the sublime so closely. Hence his emphasis upon "our personality to which we must bow where our highest fundamental propositions, and their assertion or abandonment, are concerned."[39]

The fact of phenomenal experience, the domain of subjectivity, is not just the "hard problem of consciousness"[40] in the sense that it is not clear how "hard science" might explain phenomenal experience but experience of wonder is inextricably linked to self-consciousness and the depths of personality. If finite subjectivity were readily explicable, the argument that God is merely the projection of the human agent upon a cosmic landscape might be feasible. But subjectivity, notwithstanding the valiant efforts of eliminative materialism and identity theorists, is far from readily intelligible. Some distinguished philosophers like Nagel think that any progress is very far off; others like McGinn think it a forlorn hope. If human consciousness is a genuine mystery, the theistic hypothesis of attempt to ground it in the Divine mind seems no less attractive than the agnostic materialism of McGinn or the appeal to the brute givenness of mind in a philosopher like Chalmers.

Consider the painting of Caspar David Friedrich in which the intense heightening of subjectivity is aroused by the landscape. His notorious altarpiece *Cross in the Mountains* (1820) was defended by Gerhard von kügelgen:

> Friedrich's originality should be all the more welcome to us, since it presents us with a form of landscape painting previously less noticed, in which within its very peculiarity, is revealed a spirit striving after truth.[41]

If we think of the point of communion as "personal," then we must be careful to retain this numinous dimension of the uniquely human. It is thus not surprising that between anthropologists who prefer to analyze religion in very remote and archaic cultures where subjectivity is more latent rather than articulate. And perhaps that theist would wish to claim that the highest forms of religion are those where the Godhead is perceived and encountered as absolute subjectivity: I AM THAT I AM. This is, perhaps, an answer to Philo's question in Hume's *Dialogues*, "What particular privilege has this little agitation of the brain which we call thought, that we must make it the model of the whole universe?"[42] We might reply with Aristotle, that though the intellect be perhaps small in bulk, "in power

39   Kant, *Critique of Judgement*, §28, p. 101.
40   Chalmers, D. (1995) "Facing up to the problem of consciousness," *Journal of Consciousness, Studies* 2, (3): 200–19.
41   Körner, Joseph Leo. (1990) *Caspar David Friedrich and the Subject of Landscape*. New Haven, CT: Yale University Press, p. 112.
42   Hume, David. (1993) *Principal Writings on Religion Including Dialogues Concerning Natural Religion and the Natural History of Religion*, J. C. A. Gaskin (ed.). Oxford: Oxford University Press, p. 50.

and value it far surpasses all the rest" (εἰ γὰρ καὶ τῷ ὄγκῳ μκρον ἐστι· δυνάμι καὶ τιμιότητι πολύ μᾶλλον πάντων ὑπερέχει.).[43] The conception of the "little agitation of the brain" resonates with many contemporary views of mind as over-elaborated scanning equipment. Consciousness, for many of the contemporary critics of religion, is — like religion itself — a puzzling by-product of evolution rather than one of its most prized productions. Perhaps there is a sublime terror as well as wonder in sensing the mind is a conduit to the archetypal and intelligent ground of the universe, a feeling both humbling and exalting, the very sentiment of Wordsworth's *The Prelude*: "The perfect image of a mighty Mind."

Of course, Otto's account of this dimension of human consciousness and culture is a long way from providing any justification for theistic belief. But the idea of the Holy, the numinous intimation of a personal ground of Being, in such experiences of the sublime is far from mere crude anthropomorphism; it is, rather, a momentous and recurring theme in the human imagination. Plato and Aristotle both saw wonder as the inspiration of a philosophy that fired the love of a beautiful and intelligible universe, predicated upon the source or principle (arche) "that moves the sun and other stars." Indeed, one could argue that philosophy is itself chimerical if the universe is a brute absurdity. If consciousness and freedom, the soul and responsibility are systematic illusions, or perhaps at best the epiphenomena of a deterministic universe, these are metaphysical positions and not the simple inferences from scientific facts. More fundamentally still, is there an uncreated necessary Being, the source of the vast contingent cosmos and the realm of becoming? Is there a transcendent Mind beyond the flux of fleeting thoughts, intentions, and aspirations? *Nil admirari* say the Stoics. But the sublime wonder of this transcendent uncreated reality has inspired the greatest religious poetry from the Upanishads to the Sufi mystics, Dante, Wordsworth, or Eliot.

The regenerate imagination

In *Living Forms of the Imagination*, I argue that the imagination is best thought of as the capacity to exist both in the immediate and the imagined reality. This feature of *homo imaginans* (man imagining) should not be confused with fantasy or delusion. Imagination has etymological links with *imaginari* (to imagine, conceive, or picture mentally) and *imago* (likeness). Given this etymological history, it is natural to think of imagination in terms of a capacity for analogy. As such it is the basis for thinking about absent or occluded realities. Analogy operates by employing some likeness between two items, events, or situations. Indeed, the failure to employ imagination on the basis of perceived likeness is often the basis of cruelty and injustice. The incapacity to imagine genuine likenesses between perceived and unperceived instances in the case of inductive reasoning would lead to rational collapse.

---

43   Aristotle. (1976) *Ethics*, J. K. A. Thompson (ed.). Harmondsworth: Penguin, 117b 13-33.

Fantasy, by way of contrast with imagination, is often consider the capacity merely to entertain, or, more particularly, to confuse appearances with reality. Fantasy is rooted in the Greek Φαντᾱσία (*phantasia*), which is cognate with verbs of appearance (φαίνεσται, *phainesthai*, to appear) or appearing (φαίνειν, *phainein*, to show). This etymological sense of fantasy as linked to appearance rather than reality, with deception or illusion, is captured neatly by the Renaissance humanist Shakespeare. In the first scene of *Hamlet*, Marcellus the guard asks whether the ghost has appeared and Horatio says "'tis but our fantasy." Superstition and fanaticism are often the fruits of fantasy. Emerson is characteristically eloquent on the point:

> It is a problem of metaphysics to define the province of Fancy and Imagination. The words are often used, and the things confounded. Imagination respects the cause. It is the vision of an inspired soul reading arguments and affirmations in all Nature. Of that which it is driven to say. But as soon as this soul is released a little from its passion, and at leisure plays with resemblances and types, for amusement and not for its moral end, we call its action Fancy ... Fancy amuses; imagination expands and exalts us.[44]

To "see" a tree is also to imagine its three-dimensional nature, including those parts phenomenologically hidden to the specific observer. To observe an artifact, say a building like a Gothic cathedral, is to engage, perhaps unconsciously, with the "world" embodied by the building — for example, gargoyles, saints, and angels.[45] The world that we in fact experience includes many imaginative constructs: elements of myth, legend, and fiction as well as theories provided by scientific thought that pervade our experience of the phenomenal world. Consider a walk on the Cornish coastline. Who cannot think of Arthur and Merlin, Tristan and Isolde, pirates or smugglers, while contemplating the lush vegetation and the company of seabirds visiting the Cornish coasts? And we are used to accepting the powerful sway of the imagination over our minds. Indeed, a foreign traveler with an appetite for light opera on such a Cornish sojourn might be pleasantly surprised to discover that Penzance is a real place — and not merely the imaginary abode of fantastical pirates of Gilbert and Sullivan!

Imagination is a dimension of human thinking that is often defined in terms of the analogous employment of images or concepts in terms of memories, possibilities, or plans. These need not be images as such; they can be touches, tastes, or smells. Yet the paradigm of an image that can be drawn from memory or projected into the future in daydreams or plans can serve as a useful starting point. The practical employment of such imaginative powers in remembering incidents or planning actions, and of course creative

44 Emerson, Ralph Waldo. (1971) "Poetry and Imagination," *The Collected Works of Ralph Waldo Emerson*. Cambridge, MA: Belknap Press, p. 14.
45 See Wynn, Mark. (2009) *Faith and Place: An Essay in Embodied Religious Epistemology*. Oxford: Oxford University Press.

in literature, the arts, and natural science, depends upon the use for such uniquely human powers. Socrates was a thinker who demanded strict definitions if not rigid formulas from his interlocutors; yet Plato presents Socrates contemplating the nature of morality and justice and producing a picture of the righteous man in the well-ordered state. Indeed, he contrasts this picture with its opposite image — that of the tyrant. Socrates's greatest pupil was a rationalist, and yet one who used "likely tales" or myths at the most decisive points of his dialogues, such the analogy of the cave in *The Republic* or the myth of the chariot in the *Phaedrus*. These imaginative stories are not fantasies. In Plato, they are governed by *logos* or reason. And they are necessary when we attempt to climb out of the cave that is the realm of appearances.

Various philosophers from Meinong to David Lewis have developed theories of imaginary worlds. Russell's theory of descriptions is an explicit attempt to raze such ontological extravagances. The imaginary is the counterpart to the "real" and as such is as an essential part of human experience. An imagined item does not have to be "at hand" to be a forceful presence. But imagination, like memory, vastly increases the scope of human experience. Lacking imagination and memory mankind would dwell in a constricted *hic et nunc*. Not only would poetry or history be unlikely without imagination but also experimental science would be impossible since it extends decisively beyond the immediate scope of the senses.

As we have insisted, imagination is not necessarily a creative or cognitive process. Indeed, sometimes imagination is thought of primarily in terms of hallucination. The ability of the human mind to creatively employ images copied or derived from sensible experience in memory, to entertain suppositions or projections, or to make hypotheses and imaginative plans has long intrigued philosophers. Yet is not philosophical speculation about the imagination an outrageous instance of piling Pelion on Ossa? The emphasis upon lucid and rigorous argument, and, perhaps less admirably, the scrupulously "everyday" style of analytic philosophy, marks a conscious aversion to any literary or imaginative mode in philosophy. However, this is somewhat paradoxical: philosophy involves a creative employment of words in order to explore the relation between the self-conscious mind and the phenomena that it encounters. Bacon's fine definition of allegorical poetry as that "which represents intellectual things to the senses"[46] can be expanded to express the general significance of the imagination in religion and science. Much of the Enlightenment critique of religion is a critique of the misuse of imagination. Against a host of contemporary cultured despisers of religion, reason must be employed to expunge dangerous fantasy. I would wish to argue for the constructive use of, in Baudelaire's apposite phrase, "La Reine des Facultés." I will not try to offer a definition of the word and I will conform to conventional usage. Perhaps in philosophical reflection, there is a proper place for scouring an idea within the tradition of thought, sometimes an idea that has been variously named. Especially since the idea of imagination has generally lost much of its prestige and currency. Heidegger pointedly refuses to use the term imagination (*Einbildungskraft*)

---

46   Bacon, *Advancement of Learning*, Book 2, chapter XIII.

in his theory of art.[47] Ryle, in his *The Concept of Mind*, devotes a chapter to the idea, but only to demolish notion of a "special Faculty of Imagination, occupying itself single-mindedly in fancied viewings and hearings."[48] The post-structuralists, notwithstanding their post-Heideggerian critiques of truth as *adaequatio rei et intellectus*, do not appeal to imagination.

Given the paucity of material in more contemporary discussions, it is necessary to consider some of the ideas and assumptions of past thinkers. In our thoughts about the idea of imagination we shall operate like Isis in the story of Isis and Osiris, where the goddess collects the scattered parts of her husband. We are compelled to draw upon the rich tradition of philosophical reflection about this remarkable dimension of the human mind from Plato to Nicholas of Cusa, Vico, or the Romantics.

History, imagines, and human agency

Ancient and primordial images suffuse the modern mind, whether it is aware of these or not.[49] Though contemporary culture tends to diminish the significance of the historical, one philosopher in the modern period who resolutely challenged this ahistorical dimension of modern thought, and who identified it with the legacy of Descartes, was Giambatista Vico (1668–1744). One must consider the role of Vico in challenging the idea of a knowledge that comprises of clear and distinct ideas, *l'esprit de géométrie*. Vico's critique of Cartesianism requires a strong philosophical theory of tradition. Vico's view of history is dominated by the concept of the *ricorsi*, the cycles of history, the view of history that we tend to associate with (disreputable) historians like Spengler and Toynbee. Through the idea of *ricorsi*, we can see Vico interpreting historical events through poetic archetypes, and to see the facts of history as part of an intelligible structure:

> The poetic speech which our poetic logic has helped us to understand continued for a long time into the historical period, much as great and rapid rivers continue far into the sea keeping sweet the waters borne on by the force of their flow.[50]

Donald Phillip Verene has laid great emphasis upon imagination in Vico, and especially the idea of *universali fantastici* or imaginative universals.[51] Vico also uses the terms *caratteri poetici* and *generi fantastici*. These several formulations of the same idea constitute a key element in Vico's thought: how human beings create society and thereby move from the stage of

47   Heidegger, Martin. (1950) *Holzwege*. Frankfurt am Main: V. Klostermann, p. 60.
48   Ryle, Gilbert. (1949) *The Concept of Mind*. Harmondsworth: Penguin, p. 244.
49   Mali, Joseph. (1992) *The Rehabilitation of Myth: Vico's "New Science."* Cambridge: Cambridge University Press.
50   Vico, Giambattista. (1999) *New Science: Principles of the New Science Concerning the Common Nature of Nations* (3rd edn.), David Marsh (trans.). London: Penguin, §412.
51   Verene, Donald Phillip. (1981) *Vico's Science of Imagination*. Ithaca, NY: Cornell University Press.

beasts to men. It is, for Vico, through "fantasia" that we can appreciate how we can understand even the most alien of societies. Hence, amid the apparently "deplorable obscurity" of the ancient nations, we can find intelligible patterns. Among the very muddle of history, we can find materials for metaphysics.

One manner of conceiving these imaginative universals, or poetic characters, is as poetic archetypes that lie somewhere between (both conceptually and historically) Plato's ideas and Jung's archetypes. The use of Jungian language here is deliberate. One could, indeed, see Vico as a stage between Plotinus and Jung in European intellectual historical history — and the Platonic tradition in particular.[52] Jung's archetypes are a refashioning of Platonic forms within contemporary culture. Indeed, Jung is quite explicit in his autobiography about the Neoplatonic debt, through the influence of the great Romantic Neoplatonist, friend, and contemporary of Hegel, Friedrich Creuzer (1771–1858), upon his thought. Jung writes:

> I came across Friedrich Creuzer's *Symbolik und Mythologie der alten Völker* — and that fired me! I read like mad, and worked with feverish interest through a mountain of mythological material . . . I was as if I were in an imaginary madhouse and were beginning to treat and analyse all the centaurs, nymphs, gods and goddesses in Creuzer's book as though they were my patients.[53]

The idea of analyzing mythic beasts and minor deities makes one wonder about Jung's own sanity! Yet this episode in Jung's personal history is most illuminating. Creuzer was, among other things, the great translator of Neoplatonic texts of German Romanticism.

Creuzer thought the key to myth was not buried in history or some naturalistic explanation, but in the symbolic power of the myths. Such power, according to Creuzer, must be intuited. Creuzer belongs to that tradition of "philosophers saving myths," in the language of Luc Brisson, by turning those myths into the expressions of intelligible realities. For all his metaphysical coyness, Jung's crucial disagreement with Freud came over the interpretation of a myth — Oedipus. They famously disagreed over the question of incest. Freud took the issue quite literally and Jung, in my opinion quite correctly, pointed to the absurdity of the literal view, and pointed instead to the symbolic dimension of incest contained in countless myths and cosmogonies. In this respect, Jung was following Creuzer and the Neoplatonic legacy.

If Creuzer is the link to Jung, we should recall that it was Ficino who translated the Neoplatonists on myth and Hesiod and Hermetic writings into Latin (Vico knew little Greek). Thus Vico could draw upon this Neoplatonic tradition in the wake of Ficino, albeit cautiously because

---

52   See Hillman, J. (1975) "Plotino, Ficino and Vico," in *Loose Ends*. Dallas, TX: Spring Publications, pp. 146–69.

53   Jung, C. G. (1963) *Memories, Dreams, Reflections*, Aniela Jaffé, Richard Winston, and Clara Winston (eds.). London: Collins and Routledge & Kegan Paul, p. 158.

of the Counter-Reformation. As for so many post-Reformation thinkers, Platonism became a semi-guilty refuge from the arid scholasticism of high Protestant and Catholic orthodoxies. Rather than concentrate upon logic, Renaissance Platonists were concerned with articulating man's place in relation to God and the rest of creation. Ficino or Pico's view of man as the apex of God's world contrasts starkly with Plotinus and the Neoplatonists, but it had a clear Neoplatonic lineage. I would wish to see Vico as a Christian humanist within this Renaissance tradition.[54] His thoughts about human society are not so much proto-sociology as implicit theology. When Goethe, Herder, or Hamann read Vico, they were reading a man with roots in the Christian humanism of the Italian Renaissance.

The fact that Vico is using the practices of the pagans as an index of Providence reveals his proximity to the humanists. Though he is critical of various forms of "ancient theology," the ritual practices and myths of the pagans cannot be dismissed as mere idolatry and vice.

For Vico, the understanding of agency in the present must involve an awareness of the continuing significance of the past. Donald Phillip Verene has laid great emphasis upon imagination in Vico, and especially upon the idea of *universali fantastici* or imaginative universals.[55] Vico also uses the terms *caratteri poetici* and *generi fantastici*. These several formulations of the same idea constitute a key element in Vico's thought: how human beings create society and thereby move from the stage of beasts to men. It is, for Vico, through imagination that we can appreciate how we can understand even the most alien of societies. Hence, amid the apparently "deplorable obscurity" of the ancient nations, we can find intelligible patterns. Among the muddle of history, we can find materials for metaphysics. From the vantage point of a perspective like that of Vico, we can turn to reflect upon the impact of the "imaginary" on actions and events in history.

Take, for example, the impact of "atheism" upon human history. The first great high point of atheism in modern culture was the French Revolution, a development deeply influenced and shaped by philosophical ideas. Indeed, we might consider not just the atheism of the French Revolution but also its other, related ideas. The year 1789 is a nodal point for occidental culture since the ideas of the French Enlightenment were put into practice in France and much of Europe in the wake of the revolutionary wars.

The great sterile beauty of Versailles became a mausoleum of the grandeur and futility of *Ancien Régime*, yet it exerted a symbolic power. Napoleon and the Bourbons refused to return there. After the collapse of the second French Empire and the capture of Louis Napoleon, King Wilhelm I of Prussia was declared emperor of Germany in the Hall of Mirrors in the Palace of Versailles. This makes no sense apart from the German sense of humiliation throughout the seventeenth century and the Prussian revenge for that perceived servitude under the French domination.

Many of the conflicts about religion in particular in contemporary states

---

54 Miller, C. (1993) *Giambattista Vico: Imagination and Historical Knowledge*. Basingstoke: Macmillan, p. 22.

55 Verene, *Vico's Science of Imagination*.

can be traced back to ideas of the French Revolution and the establishment of secular state in France. The French Revolution inaugurated a persisting battle within our culture concerning the role of religion with public life. Europe is divided between those cultures that have retained the monarchy and an established form of Christianity like Great Britain, or the Netherlands, or Scandanavia (with the recent exception of Sweden) and secular states like France. Paradoxes abound here. The US, notwithstanding its strict division of Church and State is more evidently religious than "religious" states like Britain or Norway. This can lead to practical problems. In particular, the idea that only the secular state can guarantee rights and liberties. The question of the Muslim veils is a typical example. In an explicitly "secular" state, freedom is the freedom from religious tyranny and thus such public symbols are viewed as subversive. From another historical perspective, for example one like the US, where freedom was often perceived as precisely the freedom to practice one's religion, actions such as the ban on the scarf seem draconian.

Homo imaginans and the self imagined

Such reflections about the *universali fantastici* (imaginative universals) of Vico raises questions about the identity of self in relation to the imagination. Imagination enables the individual mind to relate to objects and thus investigate nature, whether in the limited sense of Hume or in the stronger transcendental sense of Kant. It also generates the space, as it were, of selfhood. The self can distinguish itself from other agents and thus to develop a domain of interiority through the employment of the "mind's eye." Self-consciousness relies upon imaginative powers, those that create a theater of consciousness. Dennett is scathing about this idea as the "Cartesian Theater," a temper of mind that he associates with residual dualism even for physicalist philosophers:

> Cartesian materialism is the view that there is a crucial finish line or boundary somewhere in the brain, marking a place where the order of arrival equals the order of "presentation" in experience because what happens there is what you are conscious of. [. . .] Many theorists would insist that they have explicitly rejected such an obviously bad idea. But [. . .] the persuasive imagery of the Cartesian Theater keeps coming back to haunt us — laypeople and scientists alike — even after its ghostly dualism has been denounced and exorcized.[56]

Dennett's argument is called into question by the empirical evidence of child development. Imagination plays a powerful role in childhood. This capacity seems to play an important role in the healthy psychological development of the child. The distinction between fantasy and reality, which is so important for the adult, requires the imaginative play of childhood. Autism seems to

---

56   Dennett, Daniel C. (1991) *Consciousness Explained*. London: Penguin, p. 107.

be grounded in a physiological infirmity of brain that produces instances of a failure to engage in imaginative play during childhood, a state that seriously inhibits the psychological capacity of agents to engage in the minds, intentions, and concerns of others. At the age of 2 years children are involved in make-believe activities, which can be distinguished from the straightforward sensory and motor actions of the earlier stage from birth. From 3 to 5 years this use of imaginative play develops with a narrative component, and in early school years the imaginative play of the child becomes increasingly internalized and helps to create and reinforce the sense of identity in the child. In this context the child can conform to the conventions and rules of the classroom while fantasizing about parallel universes.

This ability to be amphibious, to dwell in both the present and absent (through memories, imagined worlds, fantasies), is an important component in the development of the sense of an abiding self that can straddle different slices of time and space. But this presupposes the contrast between the finite solidness of the world of discrete physical objects and the infinite world of "personal inwardness." Dreaming is a philosophically intriguing instance of this interior world at work, but without the controlling force of reason. Dreaming is a very interesting instance of the imagination released from conscious control, and for just that reason is employed by psychologists as an indication of the contents and tendency of the subconscious mind. Fears and aggressions can be revealed through dreams, and for such reasons psychoanalysts in the wake of Freud have viewed dreams as a high road to the subconscious.

But philosophers from Plato to Descartes thought about these issues before the psychologists. Consider the famous dream of the ancient Chinese sage Chuang Tsu dreaming that he was a butterfly. Upon waking he did not know whether he was Chuang Tsu dreaming of a butterfly or a butterfly dreaming he was Chuang Tsu. This imaginative capacity has important ramifications for the view of the self. It means that one can avoid the absurdities involved either in strong materialism — that is, the view that awareness of self is just awareness of one's body — or the equally implausible view that the awareness of self as an item does not depend upon one's body. The first position does not seem to be able to provide any basis for rational persons as opposed to beasts or brutes. The second seems to disengage the person from the biological condition of conscious agency.

The ability to inhabit imaginatively other minds and other worlds also enable us to consider ourselves as essentially the same through and notwithstanding great physical changes. Bernard Williams, in his 1970 paper "The self and the future," offered a critique of thought experiments designed to show the plausibility of agents changing their bodies. To remain the same person one needs to hold on to certain skills. In the case of the gruff peasant placed (as it were) in the emperor's body[57] this does not seem at all obvious. Williams's point seems plausible in relation to the intersubjective domain.

---

57   Williams, B. A. O. (1973) "Personal identity and individuation," in *Problems of the Self: Philosophical Papers, 1956–1972*. Cambridge: Cambridge University Press, pp. 11–12.

How could one recognize the peasant in the Emperor or vice versa? Yet, diachronically, one can see that a parallel puzzle evaporates. Typically, the adolescent feels at odds with his or her body. Consider an adolescent after a strong growth spurt catching a reflection of his lanky form in the mirror or window and the gawky youth not recognizing himself. This need not be pathological but the awareness of a gap between body and spirit.

The small child and the great statesman have a continuous biological and conscious mental states (memories) history. But the child in short trousers and the politician share a common identity. The statesman can remember vividly images of his childhood; perhaps some of those experiences were not merely formative but inspirational for his adult vocation. In the Bhagavad Gita this sense of the core self is given drastic expression: Atman or soul is "Birthless, eternal, perpetual, primaeval."[58]

The person is more than the body in the simple sense that personal identity is shaped by memories, fantasies, and hypotheses. The child becomes aware of itself both as an item in space and time with certain properties and also as capable of imaginatively engaging in alien domains through the internal theater of consciousness, often as a process of escape. The identification with heroic or archetypal figures is significant, especially for boys. The young in particular explore certain traits that they see in archetypal or heroic types and integrate to varying degrees this imaginative work into their sense of identity.

One manner of conceiving these types is, in the wake of Vico, as imaginative universals, or poetic characters — that is, as poetic archetypes that lie somewhere between (both conceptually and historically) Plato's ideas and Jung's archetypes. Such *universali fantastici* are not abstractions: they are living forms that shape the here and now. Vico's central insight is his awareness that we are self-understanding creatures. But our self-awareness is not a stage in his meditations (as in Descartes) but the defining characteristic of philosophy. Reflective human beings are not the straightforward product of instincts and environment but are constituted by an inherited imaginary. Thus he can claim that "poetic truth is metaphysical truth." Imaginative universals are integral elements of this metaphysical truth:

> Take Godfrey of Bouillon as Torquato Tasso imagines him. He is the true military commander, and all commanders who do not entirely conform to this Godfrey are not true ones.[59]

Godfrey is not an invention of particular mind, one that can be traced to particular mind and psychology. Rather, the minds of individuals must be traced back to such archetypal figures. The archetype, like a Platonic form, is ontologically prior to any subjective awareness of assimilation to it.

The power of the imagination helps us to avoid two egregious philosophical errors. One is the model of the self as a transparent Cartesian ego, substantially distinct from the body. The other is the Humean conception

58   Bhagavad Gita, 2, §20, Winthrop Seargeant (trans.). Albany: SUNY (2009), p. 105.
59   Vico, *New Science*, p. 92.

of the self as a bundle of impressions. Both ideas are not without some insights of truth, but very inadequate ideas of the self.

Thoughts presuppose a thinker. Descartes was correct about that. But the thinking substance Descartes proposes with such confidence is genuinely elusive. There is a fragmented dimension of the human self as Hume recognizes, when he claims ignorance of an impression that could generate an idea of a self. But it cannot be accounted as the whole truth since agency and accountability evaporates. Kant seems to provide a via media through his "I" that accompanies our perceptions but that is not itself an object of possible experience. Kant's characteristically coy solution to the problem of the ego, however, looks like a sterile formal principle rather than an authentic bearer of conscious states and a rich domain of interior phenomenological and intentional states.

Imagination as the Shechinah in the heart

Imagination presupposes the mind's capacity for memory and retention. Philosophers have often discussed these problems in relation to association of ideas, which is discussed from Aristotle to Hobbes and Hume.[60] This is the attempt to expound a mechanism through which memory functions in terms of resemblance, contiguity, and succession. The model is atomistic and mechanical. In fact, David Hartley's eighteenth-century version of the theory was greeted as doing for the realm of the mental what Newton's theory of gravity had done for the physical world. He is paralleling the work of consciousness with the nervous system.

Coleridge, in his critique of Hartley and the empiricist tradition in his *Biographia Literaria*, is drawing upon the Kantian thought that the association of discrete experiences is an imperfect and, at best, limited model of knowledge, but it overlooks the vital synthetic role of the human mind. Although Coleridge shares this Kantian intuition, his real goal is Platonic. He wishes to expose the intolerable gap between particular sensory images and universal ideas that empiricism fails to explain. If ideas are derived from impressions and combinations of the kind Locke calls "complex ideas," then the mind's contents are derived causally. Aristotle and Thomas view the mind as a *tabula rasa* and knowledge as the product of experience. Universal ideas occur through the mind abstracting the essence of specific items. This depends upon the mind's capacity to remove the particular images of things and arrive at universal properties. The doctrine of the active intellect should explain this capacity to understand what transcends the senses.

The Platonist proposes imagination as grounded in an innate capacity of the soul. One might consider the image of the "storehouse" that St. Augustine's explorations about the nature of memory have an evident affinity with Plato's theory of memory, a doctrine linked to the Platonic

---

60 Coleridge, S. T. (1984) *Biographia Literaria; or, Biographical Sketches of My Literary Life and Opinions*, James Engell and Walter Jackson Bate (eds.). Princeton, NJ: Princeton University Press, pp. 106–15.

doctrine of the preexistence of the soul, and the theory expressed classically in the *Meno* that the soul could not derive its knowledge from sensory experience, but is remembering that which is derived from a previous existence. Augustine, in thinking about memory, observes that much of its contents could not have been derived from the senses but implanted by God.[61] On this Platonic-Augustinian account the human mind is no *tabula rasa*. This doctrine about memory as the source of genuine knowledge is the key to the Platonic theory of imagination. If the mind does not derive its contents exclusively from sense experience but from God in its creation or from the intelligible realm, one can expect the mind to possess a proleptic awareness or apprehension of realities that transcends its immediate empirical environment. This can be seen in Coleridge's famous definition of imagination: "As the prime agent of all human perception, and a repetition in the finite mind of the eternal act of creation in the infinite I Am."[62] Coleridge is assuming a consubstantiality of God and the human mind. Robert Barth helpfully drew an analogy between this doctrine and the medieval theory of the *concursus divinus*. God is imminent in all His creation. He is, however, immanent in a special manner in free agents. Human creativity is thus linked in a special way to Divine creativity.

The employment of imagination can "awaken the mind's attention from the lethargy of custom"; it can reveal "the loveliness and the wonders of the world before us."[63] Coleridge further claims that an "idea in the highest sense of that word cannot be conveyed but by a symbol.[64] The symbol is

> characterized . . . above all by a transcendence of the Eternal through and in the Temporal. It always partakes of the reality which it renders intelligible; and while it enunciates the whole, abides itself as a living part in that unity, of which it is the representative.[65]

Thus, in the symbolic imagination the transcendent and the finite overlap. Thus Coleridge, employing the terminology of the Jerusalem Temple, speaks of the Imagination in this exalted sense as the "Shechinah in the heart," as immanent Divine presence.[66]

61   Augustine, *Confessions*, 10. 8–28, R. S. Pine-Coffin (trans.). Harmondsworth: Penguin (1961), p. 207ff.
62   Coleridge. (1984) *Biographia Literaria; or, Biographical Sketches of My Literary Life and Opinions*, James Engell and Walter Jackson Bate (eds.). Princeton: Bollingen, 2, p. 156.
63   Coleridge, *Biographia Literaria*, 2, p. 80.
64   Coleridge, *Biographia Literaria*, 2, p. 156.
65   Coleridge. (1972) *The Statesman's Manual*. 1816. Lay Sermons. R. J. White. (ed.). London: Routledge & Kegan Paul, p. 28.
66   Coleridge, *Notebooks*. See also *Confessions of an Inquiring Spirit*.

Imagination and the *Concursus Divinus*

The empiricist has a greater need of imagination as an epistemological tool, as a means of constructing a world out of the "buzzing, blooming confusion" of sense data. The Platonist, however, sees the empirical world an enigmatic image of an intelligible transcendent reality. Ironically Plato and many Platonists have been critical of confusing the image with its transcendent archetype (a form of idolatry) and dangerous self-serving phantasies. Plato calls this *eikasia* in the cave simile of *The Republic*.

Within the empiricist tradition, imagination is seen as continuous with perception. Hobbes famously defines imagination as "nothing but decaying sense."[67] For another strand of thought, this limits unduly the nature of imagination. Here imagination is not so much a mode of (failed or illusory perception) but a primordial capacity to shape and organize the materials of sensation. Immanuel Kant is important for the development of the idea of imagination, particularly his distinction between the reproductive and productive (i.e. transcendental) imagination. The productive imagination is the spontaneous power that unifies sense and thought: a foundational power of the soul which furnishes *a priori* knowledge."[68]

Fichte takes up the idea of the productive imagination in Kant and it becomes central for German Romanticism, and in particular the philosophy of Schelling.[69] The fine correspondence of mind-independent objects to the confines of the human understanding is the result of this process. The productive imagination has imbued nature with its shapes and forms unconsciously. It then "discovers," as it were, an order that it has placed into the phenomena. Schelling writes:

> The splendid German word "imagination" (*Einbildungskraft*) actually means the power (Kraft) of mutual-forming into unity (*ineinsbildung*) upon which all creation is really based. It is the power whereby something ideal is simultaneously something real, the soul simultaneously the body, the power of individuation that is the creative power.[70]

In the terminology of imagination as the "forming into unity" we find a reference to the theological and Platonic background of Renaissance theories in which the universe is perceived as a Divine artwork. Its beauty is a counterimage of the beauty of God.[71] Philosophical knowledge, according to Schelling in his seminal *System of Transcendental Idealism* (1800), is ultimately aesthetic since Nature is striving towards consciousness (slumbering spirit) and imagination is "the primordial knowledge of which

67 Hobbes, T. and Pogson Smith, W. G. (1958) *Leviathan*. Oxford: Clarendon Press, p. 14.
68 Kant, Immanuel. (1982) *Critique of Pure Reason*, Norman Kemp Smith (trans.). London: Macmillan, pp. 145ff.
69 Engell, James (1981) *The Creative Imagination: Enlightenment to Romanticism*. Cambridge, MA: Harvard University Press.
70 Schelling, F. W. J. (1989) *The Philosophy of Art*, D. Stott (trans.). Minneapolis: University of Minnesota, p. 32.
71 Schelling. (1927) *Werke*. Munich: Beck, 4, p. 29.

the visible universe is the image."[72]

In Schelling, despite the elusive nature of his thought, protean phases and his polemic exchanges, we find an increasing tendency to become more explicit in his theology. He was a theologian by training and certain theological themes recur throughout his *oeuvre*. Through his elective affinities, Coleridge was particularly well placed to transmit some of Schelling's insights to the English-speaking peoples. Hence, for example, Emerson writes:

> Nature is the true idealist. When she serves us best, when, on rare days, she speaks to the imagination, we feel that the huger heaven and earth are but a web drawn around us, that the lights, skies and mountains are but the painted vicissitudes of the soul.[73]

To see nature properly is to employ imagination and to see the visible cosmos as the enigmatic reflection of the Divine mind.

The great occidental Platonists drew upon Islamic mystical sources.[74] Henri Corbin's spiritual hermeneutics of the Sufi mystical "visionary recital" draws upon Renaissance and Romantic ideas of the Imagination, a mirror of theophanies.[75] For Corbin, the imagination is conceived of as theophanic perception, a place where faith and knowledge, eternity, and history converge. This amounts to a metamorphosis of the knowing subject. Corbin's theory of imagination depends upon a Neoplatonic metaphysics hierarchy of being, which he identifies with the Cambridge Platonists just as he does with the "Persian Platonists." Within the emergence of matter from spirit, Corbin designates the intermediate realm of the *mundus imaginalis*, a place where spirit can be perceived through physical images. This requires an active employment of the imagination upon the part of the perceiver.[76] This active use of the imagination Corbin sees as both prophetic and philosophical.

The Temple has a unique role in the Christian imagination. Richard Hooker was Master of the Temple Church in London and the association of Church and Temple ran deep in the English Church. George Herbert called his collection of poems *The Temple* and this went through 13 editions from 1633 to 1679. For luminaries of the seventeenth century as diverse as Christopher Wren or Isaac Newton, the imagined structure of the Jerusalem Temple was pivotal for much of their work. In seventeenth-century English churches, one finds the tablet of the Law (Ten Commandments) above the altar — that is, within the "Holy of Holies." This means the presence of God among his people through the new covenant of Christ's blood, the blood

72 Schelling, F. W. J. (1966) *On University Studies*, E. S. Morgan and N. Guterman (trans.). Athens: Ohio University Press, p. 10.
73 Emerson, "Poetry and imagination," *Complete Works*, vol. 8, p. 13.
74 Flasch, Kurt. (2006) *Die Geburt der "Deutschen Mystik" aus dem Geist der Arabischen Philosophie*. Munich: Beck.
75 Corbin, Henri. (1998) *Alone with the Alone, Creative Imagination in the Sufism of Ibn Arabi*. Princeton, NJ: Bollingen, p. 179.
76 Corbin on the Romantic provenance of the Imagination, see *Alone with the Alone*, p. 179.

of the great High Priest, as the means of the restoration of paradise. Once we concentrate upon the symbolism of the Temple or the *Imago Templi*, as Corbin designates this tradition, we note the combination of the twin themes of sacrifice and the holy presence of God. Thus, the Temple is often used as an image of the prophetic vision of God, and for representing the theophanic imagination.

Prophecy and imagination

So much the rather thou celestial Light
Shine inward, and the mind through all her powers
Irradiate, there plant eyes, all mist from thence
Purge and disperse, that I may see and tell
Of things invisible to mortal sight.[77]

John Smith's seminal account of the theophanic imagination draws upon the "Agent Intellect" of the Arabic-Jewish tradition and the view of Prophecy in Philo and Justin as seeing the forms or the Divine ideas. I wish to relate this broader backdrop of Smith's Christian Neoplatonism to the powerful imagery of theater in his discussion of the problem of prophetic activity.

It is a commonplace that the Cambridge Platonists were most eclectic in their Neoplatonism of Maimonides and Muslim thinkers. One of the major legacies of the Islamic influence upon Western thought was the specifically Arabic development of the Agent Intellect. Aristotle, in *De Anima III 5*, speaks of two kinds reason, which are akin to the distinction between matter and form, one lower and the other higher. The lower dies with the body. The higher is "separate" and "impassible." This cryptic theory of the higher reason — the νοῦς ποιητικός — was developed by Alexander of Aphrodisias (second/third century AD), who identified the *nous poietikos* or *intellectus agens* as the working within the mind of a transcendent principle. It was the view of Alexander of Aphrodisias (combined with Neoplatonism) that influenced Al Farabi and particularly Avicenna, in which one finds a hierarchy of celestial intelligence that flows out to the agent intellect, which in turn illuminates the finite mind.[78] This distinctive Arabic development was treated with great caution or openly criticized in the West. Thomas Aquinas, who accepted the idea of an active intellect that guides the mind from potentiality to actuality, makes this an entirely immanent process of the finite soul.[79] The core idea that interests us in relation to Smith is that the mind of the prophet has access to an imaginative faculty, an angel, which makes possible the prophetic vision.

Within Islam, the doctrine of the agent intellect was an integral element

---

77   John Milton, *Paradise Lost*, book 3, pp. 51–55.
78   Davidson, H. A. (1992) *Alfarabi, Avicenna, and Averroes, on Intellect: Their Cosmologies, Theories of the Active Intellect, and Theories of Human Intellect*. New York; Oxford: Oxford University Press.
79   Aquinas, *Summa contra gentiles* 2.76–78; *Summa theologiae* 1.79.3–7.

of the distinctively Arabic theory of the prophet, and it is upon this rich tradition of speculation that Maimonides draws in his account of Prophecy in his *Guide of the Perplexed*.[80] Though scholars debate as to whether Al Farabi or Avicenna is the decisive influence lying behind Maimonides, they both employ a theory of prophecy as the result of an efflux or overflow of the agent intellect upon the individual potential and passive mind.[81] Prophecy depends upon a particular blend of intellect and imagination and requires intellectually and morally superior vessels for the reception of the agent intellect. Maimonides puts emphasis upon the psychological process of prophecy. Furthermore, the account of angels in terms of imaginative experience rather than literal historical descriptions of events prefigures some of the more adventurous exegesis of the Enlightenment, notably Spinoza.[82]

The theory of prophecy that Maimonides develops, though he refers to scripture, Aristotle, and other philosophers, is indebted to the Neoplatonizing Arabic Aristotelian tradition. In this tradition prophecy differs in degree, though not in kind, from true dreams.[83] Veridicial dreams are those furnished by a providential deity in which the human mind can see what is hidden or in the future. In prophecy the mind combines with the imaginative faculty. This imaginative faculty is, Maimonides, argues, represented as an angel. For Maimonides the "created forms" which the prophet "sees" are products of the imagination. Moses is distinguished from the other prophets by the fact that he does not require imagination and enjoys direct communion with the active intellect.

John Smith follows Maimonides on the points that prophecy requires an angel, which is construed as the agent intellect and he develops this in the specifically Maimonidean manner that the enactment of the prophetic works is primarily within the mind of the prophet. Aquinas argues that prophecy is a Divine gift and thus the requirements demanded by Maimonides are unnecessary. Aquinas claims that the gift of prophecy can be bequeathed on very unlikely candidates. Smith agrees with Maimonides that prophecy is the culmination of a continuum of enlightenment: from those who have "drowned all their sober Reason in the deepest Lethe of Sensuality" up to those who can attain the vision of God. However, Thomas Aquinas does not agree with Maimonides that the angels stand for the imagination — they are, rather, genuine mediators of Divine communication. In keeping with

80   This was also true for Hallevi, Ibn Daud, and possibly the Cabbala. See Davidson, *Alfarabi, Avicenna, and Averroes, on Intellect.*
81   Kaplan, L. (1977) "Maimonies on the miraculous element in prophecy," *Harvard Theological Review*, 70, 233–56; Davidson, H. A. (1979) "Maimonides' secret position on Creation," in Isadore Twersky (ed.), *Studies in Medieval Jewish History and Literature*, Cambridge, MA: Harvard University Press; Breslauer, D. (1980) "Philosophy and imagination: the politics of prophecy in the view of Moses Maimonides," *Jewish Quarterly Review*, 70, (3), 99–102; Wolfson, H. A. (1973) "Maimonides on the internal senses," in *Studies in the History of Philosophy and Religion*. Cambridge, MA: Harvard University Press, pp. 344–70..
82   Hutton, S. (1983) "The prophetic imagination: a comparative study of Spinoza and the Cambridge Platonist, John Smith," in C. de Deug (ed.), *Spinoza's Political and Theological Thought*. Amsterdam: North Holland Publishing, pp. 73–81.
83   Maimonides, M. (1963) *The Guide of the Perplexed*, Shlomo Pines (trans.), 2 vols. Chicago: University of Chicago Press, pp. 369ff.

the rest of his theology, Aquinas is concerned to keep the spheres of natural and revealed religion clearly distinguished. It is, we wish to suggest, quite logical that the Platonizing Smith should turn to the very Neoplatonic Arabic Aristotelians to counter the theory of Western Aristotelians.

Smith writes of the necessary accommodation of scripture to the finite mind:

> *Divine Truth* hath its *Humiliation* and *Exinanition*, as well as its Exaltation. *Divine Truth* becomes many times in scripture *incarnate*, debasing itself to assume our rude conceptions, so that it might converse more freely with us, and infuse its own Divinity into us . . . Truth is content, when it comes into the world, to wear our mantles, to learn our language, to conform itself to our dress and fashions . . . Which was well observed in that old Cabbalistical Axiome among the Jews, *Lumen Supernum nunquam descendit sine indumento.*[84]

This is a complex and rich passage: the word "exinanition" means the "process of emptying or exhausting, whether in a material or immaterial sense; emptied or exhausted condition."[85] It is used with particular refer-ence to St. Paul's Christological hymn of Phil. 2.8: "And being found in human form he humbled himself and became obedient unto death, even death on a cross." Smith's contemporary Jeremy Taylor speaks of how Christ was "to take upon him all the affronts, miseries and exinanitions of the most miserable."[86]

The idea of the "clothing" of revelation can, I believe, be found in the Zohar, and it is perfectly possible that this is the influence of the Lurianic tradition. Smith's interpretation of Maimonides is probably eclectic and fuses Maimonides with certain Cabbalistic concerns.[87]

Smith quotes Maimonides:

> *The true essence of Prophesie is nothing else but an Influence from the Deitie upon the Rational first,* and *afterwards the Imaginative Facultie, by the media-tion of the Active intellect.'* Which Definition belongs indeed to *Prophesie* as it is Technicallie so called, and distinguished by *Maimonides* both from that degree of Divine illumination which was above it, which the Masters attribute to *Moses,* and from that other degree inferior to it, which they call Spiritus Sanctus, that Holy Spirit that moved in the Souls of the *Hagiographi.*[88]

---

84 Smith, *Select Discourses*, p. 171–2.
85 I owe this reference to James Vigus.
86 See the *Oxford English Dictionary* for "Exanination" (Oxford: Oxford University Press, 1971) vol. 1, pp. 413–14.
87 Professor Philip Alexander of Manchester University has pointed out a passage from the Zohar Be-ha'olotka, 3. 152a, which speaks of the incarnation of the Heavenly Torah as clothed in "garments" appropriate to this world.
88 Smith, *Select Discourses*, p. 177–8.

Prophecy in Philo, Justin Martyr, and Clement
of Alexandria as "seeing" the forms

John Smith's model of prophecy is that of the seer grasping or intuiting the Divine ideas. For Philo, Moses contemplated the Divine ideas on Mount Sinai and for Justin Martyr, as well, the prophetic vision of the mind of God replaces the contemplation of the ideas in Plato.[89] Clement of Alexandria employs conscious analogies between the Greek mysteries and Christian contemplation on the grounds that Greek wisdom was indebted to the Mosaic revelation. Plato was an imitator of Moses and derived his vision of the good and the true from the revelation of true being as the I AM of Exod. 3.14. The philosophy of Moses, avers Clement, is fourfold: historical, ethical, physical, and metaphysical — the final metaphysical stage being the vision of God, a Divine science.

This is the contemplation of the God who calls himself I AM WHO I AM. The psalmist could be seen as reinforcing this Platonic deity: "Before the mountains were brought forth, or ever thou hadst formed the earth and the world, even from everlasting to everlasting, thou art God" (Ps. 90.2). When Christ asserts his equality with the Father, he uses the present tense of the Septuagint 3.14, "Before Abraham was, I am" (Jn 8.58).

Smith is well aware of Philo, Justin, and Clement, and he is drawing upon such sources when he speaks of the "Visa" that the prophet contemplates:

> It may be considered that God made not use of Idiots or Fools to reveal his Will by, but such whose Intellectuals were entire and perfect; and that he imprinted such a clear copy of his Truth upon them, as that it became their own Sense, being digested fully into their Understandings; so as they were able to deliver and represent it to others as truly as any can paint forth his Thoughts. If the Matter and Substance of things be once lively in the Mind, *verba non invita sequentur*: And according as that Matter operates upon the *Mind* and *Phantasie*, so will the *Phrase* and *Language* be in which it is express'd . . . And indeed it seems most agreeable to the nature of all these Prophetical *Visions* and *Dreams* we have discoursed of, wherein the nature of the Enthusiasme consisted in a Symbolical and shaping forth of Intelligible things in their imaginations and enlightening the Understanding of the Prophets to discern the scope and meaning of these *Visa* or *Phantasmata*; that these *Words* and phrases in which they were audibly express'd to Hearers afterwards or penned down, should be the Prophets own: For the Matter was not . . . represented alwaies by *Words* but by *Things*.[90]

The model of prophecy is that of a vision of God that is described in words. The words are those of the prophet, but these are descriptions of a visionary experience mediated through the imagination. Smith is quite firm in

---

89 Osborn, E. F. (2001) *Irenaeus of Lyons*. Cambridge: Cambridge University Press, p. 169.
90 Smith, *Select Discourses*, p. 273.

following Maimonides that God could not use "Idiots or Fools to reveal his Will by," but entire and perfect intellects. He does not wish to disparage the objectivity of prophecy, but Smith is using a less mechanical model of the prophetic function than that of verbal inspiration.

The imagery of the theater in Smith's writing: the problem of prophetic enactment

Smith also employs the image of the stage quite explicitly in his discussion of prophecy:

> The *Prophetical Scene or stage upon which all the apparitions were made to the Prophet*, was *his Imagination*; and that there all those things which God would have revealed unto him were acted over *Symbolicallie*, as in a *Masque*, in which divers persons are brought in, amongst which the Prophet himself himself bears a part: And therefore he, according to the exigencie of this Dramatical *apparatus*, must as the other Actors, perform his part.[91]

Shakespeare was able to give vivid expression to Renaissance Platonizing theories of art, which one can find in contemporaries like Sidney or Jonson. We are inclined to separate the Bard from the so-called "metaphysical poets" like John Donne. Yet Shakespeare's plays are suffused with metaphysics. A good example is the famous speech of Theseus in *A Midsummer Night's Dream*:

> The lunatic, the lover and the poet
> Are of imagination all compact.
> One sees more devils than vast hell can hold ;
> That is the madman. The lover, all as frantic,
> Sees Helen's beauty in a brow of Egypt.
> The poet's eye, in a fine frenzy rolling,
> Doth glance from heaven to earth, from earth to heaven.
> And as imagination bodies forth
> The forms of things unknown, the poet's pen
> Turns them to shapes, and gives to airy nothing
> A local habitation, and a name.[92]

Shakespeare's poet seems to be in a fine "frenzy" of Plato's *Phaedrus*: transported to the intelligible realm and returning to the sensible realm to body forth this vision into shapes and names.[93] Given the continuous significance of Shakespeare for the English mind, it seems very likely that Smith has in his mind the very words of Shakespeare's "imagination"

---

91 Smith, *Select Discourses*, p. 222.
92 Shakespeare, W. *A Midsummer Night's Dream*, 5.1.
93 See Hedley, Douglas. (2008) *Living Forms of the Imagination*. London: T&T Clark, pp. 173ff.

which "bodies forth the forms of things unknown," when he speaks of the
prophetic "shaping forth of intelligible things in their imaginations" in his
sermon on Prophecy as the Dean of Queens' College, Cambridge.[94]

At this point we might consider the concrete context of Smith's work.
The dining halls of Oxford and Cambridge had a very important part in
the development of drama in England, and many of the great playwrights
like Christopher Marlowe were "University Wits." Marlowe and many
others were an important part of a flourishing university dramatic culture
in which Queens' College played a very prominent role.

Smith writes of prophecy that:

> Great is the power of the *Prophets*, who while they looked down upon
> these Sensible and Conspicable things, were able to furnish out the
> notion of Intelligible and Inconspicable Beings thereby to the rude
> Senses of Illiterate people.[95]

There is a document in the Old Library of Queens' College that may give
us a clue as to why the theatrical images are so important for Smith. This
document dates from 1640 and includes the "Colledge stage." This is the
inventory of the pieces of wood and the instructions for their assembly for
the construction of a stage in the Dining Hall of the College. In a fascinating
article, I. R. Wright has argued that this 1640 inventory was that of a stage
that had been in use since the mid-sixteenth century, when Cambridge
was an important center of drama.[96] Queen Elizabeth came to watch plays
in Cambridge in 1564 and Charles I saw a play at Queens' in 1632. The
statutes of the College demanded the performance of plays by both scholars
and Fellows. Also, Queens' was a college with humanistic traditions, with
Erasmus himself as an alumnus, and Wright notes that the performance of
classical drama was part of humanistic doctrine. Smith was a Fellow just
after the Puritans had banned drama in 1642. However, it is tempting to
envisage the young man seeing Shakespeare while an undergraduate, and
certainly the abolition in 1642 (the discourse were composed as sermons in
the 1640s) must have been a source of debate about drama. D. F. McKenzie
observes that in this period "Trinity and Queens' seem to have been the
only colleges left in which plays were still performed with distinction."[97]

It is hard to avoid the conclusion that Shakespeare in his *A Midsummer
Night's Dream* was not aware of the Renaissance justification of the poet's art
as resting in the prophetic power of the poet's eye, which, in a fine frenzy
rolling, doth glance from heaven to earth, from earth to heaven. Is it not
appropriate that Smith should reappropriate this poetry for the definition
of the prophet in the turbulent age of the English Civil War, when drama
was banished but prophecy, some good, some ill, was abounding?

---

94   Smith, *Select Discourses*, p. 273.
95   Smith, *Select Discourses*, p. 173.
96   Wright, I. R. (1986) "An early stage at Queens'." *Magazine of the Cambridge Society*, 18,
     pp. 74–83.
97   McKenzie, D. F. (1970) "A Cambridge playhouse of 1638," in *Renaissance Drama*, 3,
     p. 270.

Enigmatic coincidence of Divine archetype and the visible image: the world as God's sacrifice

In Plato's *Theatetus*, Socrates is described as like a midwife. In the *Symposium*, Socrates describes the claim of Diotima that through producing physical offspring "the mortal nature is seeking as far as possible to be everlasting and immortal." Yet artistic creativity is a pregnancy of the soul that guarantees a far more desirable immortality. According to Diotima, "Who, when he thinks of Homer and Hesiod and other great poets would not rather have their children than ordinary ones?" Drawing upon this tradition, "conceiving" was ambivalent: both a physical and a mental propagation was possible.[98] In this way the ancients, medievals, or Renaissance thinkers could view finite creativity as resembling or even participating in Divine creativity. The medieval/Renaissance Platonist Nicholas of Cusa (1401–1464) developed explicitly the idea of creative participation in the Divine mind. Through his doctrine of the *docta ignorantia*, Nicholas attacks both the essentialism of contemporary Aristotelianism and the skepticism and voluntarism of the nominalists. Finite creativity is the unfolding (*explicare*) of that that is enfolded (*complicare*) within the Divine: the creativity of the artist in particular is a sharing in the Divine creative energy. Marsilio Ficino (1433–1499) develops the imaginative power (*vis imaginativa*) that is viewed as Divine presence within the human mind.[99] When Michelangelo speaks of "*l'immagine del cor*" or "*un concetto di bellezza*," he is referring to the inner vision that draws upon spiritual mysteries for its inspiration. And this thought comes to Shakespeare and the English Renaissance via Giordano Bruno and other émigrés from the Counter-Reformation.

Hermetic and magical sources in the Renaissance enhanced the sense of human creativity and imaginative power, especially the "god-making" dimension: so that even Cardinal Nicholas Cusa quotes the Hermetic *Asclepius* that man is the second god.[100]

> For just as God is the Creator of real beings and of natural forms, so man is the creator of conceptual beings and of artificial forms that are only likenesses of his intellect, even as God's creatures are likenesses of the Divine Intellect, with respect to creating. Hence he creates likeness of the likenesses of the Divine Intellect, even as [a thing's] extrinsic, artificial forms are likenesses of its intrinsic natural form.[101]

Nicholas seems to be saying that mankind's role is crucial because he is not merely a part, however significant, of the *scala naturae*, but a second God,

98 Plato, *Symposium*, 209D. Plato, Lysis, *Symposium*, Gorgias, W. R. M. Lamb (trans.). Cambridge, MA: Harvard University Press, pp. 200–1.
99 Walker, D. P. (2000) *Spiritual & Demonic Magic from Ficino to Campanella*, (new ed.). Stroud: Sutton, pp. 76–80.
100 Nicholas of Cusa. (1998) "De Beryllo," Jasper Hopkins (trans.). *Nicholas of Cusa: Metaphysical Speculations: Six Latin Texts*. Minneapolis, MN: A. J. Banning Press, p. 794.
101 Nicholas of Cusa, "De Beryllo," p. 794. I am grateful to Jacob Sherman for discussion of this.

a coworker in the cosmos. Here man's relation to the physical cosmos is a sacrificial rite, a "making sacred" if the hidden seed of the Divine is brought out of potentiality into actuality. Christology is the supreme instance of the congruence between human cognitive creativity and God's eternal act. Thus Nicholas can combine a surprising stress upon human autonomy as an instance of what Blumenberg famously refers to as "theonomic autonomy."[102] Though Cusa avoids the Hegelian thesis that creation depends upon human beings, he has a deep conviction in man as the unique organon through which God is unveiled and reconciled to the world.

By the seventeenth century, however, the analogy between finite creativity and the Divine *creatio continua* seemed increasingly remote in a Cartesian mechanistic universe. The Romantic extolling of Imagination was often the rearguard action of those who lamented the loss of a vital cosmos reflecting the Divine creative energy; the sigh of those who insisted upon viewing art as the perception of the infinite in the finite, or a Coleridge says so memorably, "a repetition in the finite mind of the eternal act of creation in the infinite I Am." In Marburg, in 1529 Landgraf Philipp von Hessen called a meeting of Luther and Zwingli: the debate was concerning the body of Christ as presence or sign in the Eucharist. Kamper thinks that this is the basic problem of aesthetics. In his book *Zur Geschichte der Einbildungskraft* (1981), he argues that the rift between Lutheranism and Calvinism expressed by the struggle at Marburg expressed a deep rift in the early modern period about the nature of reality. Is there an authentic experience of the presence of the Divine or is this a fiction?[103]

As we observed, the problem of sacrifice raises the broader question of the religious imagination, and in particular the nature of symbolic language. We should not, I suggest, think of the symbolic as merely figurative or literalistic. The language of sacrifice is important because is fuses different levels: the feast with the god(s), the killing, renunciation of self-interest. Our language preserves these layers of meaning: from the ritual to the ethical and the religious, culminating in the highest sense of the sacrifice of the will depicted in Dante's *Commedia*. *Pace* Kierkegaard, religion cannot be neatly distinguished from ethics. The archaic and cultic language of sacrifice, from the most primordial rites to the most sophisticated asceticism, continues to haunt the modern secular imaginary. In the dedication of the finite to the infinite, the Logos still speaks through mythos. Henry More observes that the whole world is *"ingens quoddam sacramentum*, a large sign of symbol of some spiritual truth that nearly concerns our soul."[104] The sacred, for theists, presupposes the existence of that which is entirely sacred: God. The world is a theophany. The scholastic distinction between the natural and the supernatural, the Renaissance and the Enlightenment have all reinforced a separation of the profane from the sacred. The Platonic sense of time as a

---

102   Blumenberg, H. (1985) *The Legitimacy of the Modern Age*, Robert M. Wallace (trans.). Cambridge, MA: MIT, p. 544.
103   Cf. Peuckert, Will-Erich. (1948) *Die Grosse Wende; Das Apokalyptische Saeculum Und Luther. Geistesgeschichte Und Volkskunde.* Hamburg: Claassen & Goverts.
104   More, Henry. (1660) *An Explanation of the Grand Mystery of Godliness; or a True and Faithful Representation of the Everlasting Gospel of our Lord and Saviour Jesus Christ*, p. 129.

"moving image of eternity" or the hermetic sense that below being a sign of, and enigmatically corresponding to, that which is above. The uncreated and the created realms are not strict opposites but are correlated: they form a dialectical unity in which the Divine is bodied forth in the finite realm. The world is a theophany in Schelling's sense of the world as the *Gegenbild* or counterimage: the icon of the Divine. In creating the world, God makes himself in another mode: the created order is a symbol of the Divine. Thus an image is not simply an index of Divine transcendence, but includes and reveals it. Thus the cosmos is the Divine sacrifice: the metamorphosis of God's identity in difference.

There are manifold mythic cosmogonies where creation is viewed as a sacrifice or self-immolation of the deity. In the Vedic tradition the primordial being creates the world through self-immolation *prajapi*.[105] Vedic sacrifice is the hub or navel of the world — it is the principle of continuous existence, the persistence of the Many in and through the One. Sacrifice is thus linked to cosmic order. (In the Taittiriya Upanishad) and in the *Bradhaaran Upanishad* the world is compared to horse sacrifice. In the *Chandogya Upanishad* we read that "man is sacrifice."[106] In the *Bhagavad Gita III 15* omniscient Brahman is established in sacrifice.

Is not the Christian theology of creation and redemption through the Logos crucified a mirroring of such cosmogonies? This may seem *prima facie* incompatible with the supreme cause whose goodness is a name of his unity: that characteristic of the principle that *must* be. Scripture provides a vision of God not as pure actuality but relishing the goodness of human beings. There has always been a drive away from the strict aseity of the Divine towards a theogony in which God is involved in the life of the universe and in which human beings play a role in the process of redemption. This should not be confused with crass Pelagianism, and can be qualified by Eckhart's bold assertion: "He strains for you a thousand times more forcefully than you for Him".[107]

We find parallels among the Islamic Neoplatonists. Ibn Arabi states "We have given Him to manifest Himself through us, whereas He has given us (to exist through him). Thus the role is shared between Him and us." Or, if he has given us life and existence by His Being, I also give Him life by knowing Him in my heart.[108] Ibn Arabi saw the forerunner of this in Abraham's offering a meal to the Angels. There is real reciprocity here. We must not, Corbin insists, cut off the *ens creatum* from the *ens increatum*. Creation is theophany in both Eckhart and Ibn Arabi.[109]

Mankind cannot make an object sacred. The sacred can only be derived from God. Man, however, can share in the "making sacred" and become a

105 Feuerstein, G. (1974) *Introduction to the Bhagavad Gita: Its Philosophy and Cultural Setting.* London: Rider, p. 65.
106 Heesterman, J. C. (1993) *The Broken World of Sacrifice.* Chicago, IL: University of Chicago.
107 Sermon on Lk. 2.42. Eckhart, Meister. (1955) *Deutsche Predigten und Traktate*, Quint, J. (ed. and trans.) Munich: C. Hanser, p. 456.
108 Corbin, *Alone with the Alone*, p. 247.
109 Corbin, *Alone with the Alone*, p. 247ff.

"living holocaust of Divine energy."[110] Yet this is only possible if our interior world is animated by God. Because the proper perception of the world as sacred requires the soul as well as the senses, the soul must be purified so that it can receive the light of Divine wisdom.

> [A]lthough our imagination is our soul's organ of perception and experience, it cannot perceive or experience the sacred dimension of things unless it also becomes God's organ of perception.[111]

It is the imagination reborn that can perceive the sacred: in Christian terms the rebirth of the soul through the Holy Spirit. Sacrifice reveals the Divine nature. The Cross is a symbol of the eternal and constant giving of the Godhead through the lamb slain from the foundation of the world. The Divine perfection is not a purely transcendent abstraction but that love and power which creates and redeems the world.[112] It is the dynamic interaction of the archetype and its image that begets the sacred. And since we are the priests of the Temple of the world, mankind has the task of "making sacred" a holy sacrifice by bring the world into consciousness:

> This status of man in relation to the physical world makes his participation in the process of "making sacred" — his participation in the sacrificial rite — as much a presupposition of its fulfilment as the activity of God. For although the physical world is so impregnated by Divine energies that everything bears within it its own creative logos or essence, its hidden seed of divinity, this divinity cannot come to fruition — cannot be brought from a state of potentiality to a state of actualization and revelation — without human cooperation. It is not that things — what we call material realities — are objects in the sense presupposed by modern science; but they remain in bondage, atrophied, stagnant, frustrated, unless they are animated by human sympathy and love. It is through man as the knowing subject that they are felt, imagined and sanctified. It is in and through us that the physical world is hallowed and that its intrinsic sacramental quality is revealed . . . man is the organ through which — or through whom — God unveils to this world its own mysteries.[113]

---

110   Sherrard, P. (1990) *The Sacred in Life and Art*. Ipswich: Golgonooza, p. 28.
111   Sherrard, *The Sacred*, p. 158.
112   Thus I can concur with the words of Findlay: "We have accepted the principle of Germanic theology, held by a long line of thinkers from the mediaeval mystics to Hegel, that a perfection that does not work itself out in creating and redeeming a world is a self-contradictory perfection, it is an empty and abstract thing and not a true perfection at all." Findlay, J. N. (1967) "The transcendence of the cave," in *Gifford Lectures Given at the University of St Andrews, December 1965 – January 1966*. London: Allen & Unwin, p. 183.
113   Sherrard, *The Sacred*, p. 12.

2

Costly Signaling or Hallowed Violence: Explaining Sacrifice?

The Carthaginians were a great civilised trading nation . . . Yet when Plato was speculating, this great people could so conceive the supreme powers of the Universe that they sacrificed their children to Molochas as an act of religious propitiation. The growth in generality of understanding makes such slavery impossible in corresponding civilizations today.

Human Sacrifice, Human Slavery are instance of great intuitions of religion and of civilized purposes expressing themselves by means of inherited brutalities of instinctual behaviour. Direct religious intuitions, even those of the purest origin, are in danger of allying themselves with lower practices and emotions which in fact pervade existing society.[1]

Sacrifice has been the subject of many anthropological attempts to explain the phenomenon of religion, especially in relation to the problem of violence in human society. Is sacrifice grounded in human nature or culture, aboriginal violence, or ingrained patterns of reciprocity? Since the Enlightenment, sacrifice has been a central element of secular theories of religion. We consider the theories of myth, imagination, and sacrifice as imagined by two counter-Enlightenment figures, Vico and Maistre, and conclude with a critical but positive appraisal of the visionary work of René Girard.

Sacrifice, exchange, and quid pro quo

Is the paradox outlined by Whitehead a genuine paradox? Should we be surprised that a society can be at the same time highly civilized while also exhibiting striking brutality? Freud sees civilization itself in primarily sacrificial terms:

If civilization imposes such great sacrifices not only on man's sexuality but on his aggressivity we can understand better why it is hard for him to be happy in that civilization.[2]

There is a view of sacrifice that sees it not as a religious practice or rooted in a man-God relationship of the kind envisaged by traditional theism.

---

1 Whitehead, A. N. (1967) *Adventures in Ideas.* New York: The Free Press, p. 25.
2 Freud, S. (1961) *Civilization and its Discontents.* New York: Norton, p. 62.

Sacrifice is understood instead as exchange. Here the idea is that sacrifice is really a mode of reciprocity.[3] The apparently "sacred" actions represent the reciprocal relations that allow human society to emerge and, indeed, has many affinities in the animal Kingdom, especially in higher primates such as bonobos. I give so that you give to me: (*do ut des* in the Latin tradition, *Dadami se, dehi me* in the Sanskrit tradition) can be seen as the core of sacrifice. This is the basic variant of searches for natural causes of sacrificial behavior (e.g. as a collaborative gesture signaling readiness to cooperate, or having cognitive features that lead to high transmissibility).

Such thinkers often announce their methodologically naturalist credentials, but having developed a putatively plausible-sounding hypothesis concerning "natural" causes of belief or behavior in an agent, they imply (or sometimes openly assert) that it is evident know that X is just natural (and this is often ahead of any real empirical support for the said hypotheses). Thus they can smuggle in metaphysical naturalism. It could equally be that their natural causes turn out to be empirically underdetermined even if theoretically plausible, or that natural and supernatural causes (spirit) are involved simultaneously.[4]

One way of understanding sacrifice is in evolutionary terms is that sacrifice is understood as essentially benign; for example, costly signaling theories. Sociality is important for protection and vital for hunting and warfare. But the group membership needs to be confirmed and reinforced. In fact, we have something of a paradox. If biologists have become interested in imitation or mimesis that Girard proposed in 1961, they have not dwelt upon the negative dimension so important for Girard.

Evolutionary accounts of sacrifice tend to depend upon a theory of reciprocal altruism. Girard is correct to emphasize the destructive and violent side. Game theory, for example, which considers problems of conflict divorced from the actual motives of real agents, is, I think, of little help. Motives are embedded in the imaginative narratives and interpretative schemes of agents of an organic and interrelated society within a particular history. Rather than a unique encounter that can readily be isolated from a web of antecedent relations, any given conflict situation belongs to a larger pattern of events and history. Thus no mathematical solution to a conflict between, say, Israelis and Palestinians or Republican or Loyalist Irishmen is feasible. The loyalties and fears, loves and hatreds must be part of those factors involved in attempts to resolve conflict. And, of course, one must be conscious of the dark and cruel dimension of those emotions.

The double perspective of Romanticism

Romanticism is a key juncture in Western thought because it brings together an interest in the cultural specificity of human life, the importance

3   Hogh-Oleson, Henrik. "The Sacrifice and the reciprocity-programme in religious rituals and in man's everyday interactions." *Journal of Cognition and Culture*, 6, 3–4: 499–519.
4   I am very grateful to David Leech for help and suggestions with these materials.

of tradition. Consider Maistre's famous lines:

> *La constitution de 1795, tout comme ses aînées, est faite pour l'homme. Or, il n'y point d'homme dans le monde. J'ai vu, dans ma vie des Français, des Italiens, des Russes, etc., je sais meme, grâce à Montesquieu, qu'on peut etre Persan: mais quant à l'homme, je déclare ne l'avoir rencontré de ma vie, s'il existe, c'est bien à mon insu.*[5]

Maistre reveals a deep aversion to abstractions. But he combines this interest in history, language, and culture with a strong sense of the transcendent. Maistre's great work on the French Revolution, his *Considérations sur la France*, begins with the supreme transcendent cause: God. And his attack upon the French Revolution is precisely an attack upon its Faustian ambitions. Maistre's view of the Revolution as satanic is based upon his critique of its failure to respect natural human limits.

The Romantic period was the age of a revival of Neoplatonism, first in England (e.g. Thomas Taylor), then in Germany (e.g. Friedrich Creuzer), and then in France (e.g. Victor Cousin). Maistre's own version of Neoplatonism is particularly derivative, based largely on Christian sources. The Neoplatonists generally have little interest in history or facts of culture. Plotinus, for example, shows little awareness of the fact that Plato and Aristotle inhabited very different intellectual worlds to third-century Alexandria or Rome. Nor does he seem to possess a sense of Plato struggling with problems in different phases of his writing. A writer like Maistre shares with Vico the combination of a strong sense of transcendence while stressing particularity, history, and contingency. Thus I think that Pranchère is quite wrong to say: "It is incontestable that Maistre absolutises the relative by affirming that the will of God is 'perfectly declared by the facts' and known above all by history."[6] This is to overlook the subtle dialectic of the eternal and the contingent in Maistre. Far from absolutizing the relative, Maistre combines the transcendent with the particular, the eternal with the historical. This characteristically Romantic combination, so evident in Maistre, is a very intriguing and important development in occidental thought. Both of the aspects of Romantic thought form the basis of an attack upon metaphysical naturalism.[7] This is the theory that all knowledge is derived from the natural sciences, especially physics. Maistre's attack on Bacon and Locke is motivated by their canonical role for the philosophes. Is culture (e.g. religion) the conventional shape of universal natural instincts? That is to say, is culture a level of life that rests neatly upon biological structures? If so, then a biological account of "religion" is feasible. However,

---

5   Maistre, Joseph de. (2007) "Considérations sur la France," in Pierre Glaudes (ed.), *Œuvres*. Paris: R. Laffont, p. 235.

6   Pranchère, Jean-Yves. (2001) "The persistence of Maistrian thought," in Richard Lebrun (ed.), *Joseph De Maistre's Life, Thought and Influence: Selected Studies*. Montreal: McGill-Queen's University Press, p. 314.

7   Here the contrast is with methodological naturalism — the position that experimental science proceeds by excluding any non-"natural" considerations while remaining agnostic about the ultimate constituents of the universe.

perhaps human culture is not the conventional shape of passions that are universal in human nature. This is the position of Hume or Voltaire. However, for Maistre the distinctively human passions are shaped by cultural traditions and history. This, I think, is a subtle and intriguing criticism of naturalism in ethics. Man is made by society, by institutions and rituals and, as such, human nature is irreducible to the stimulus-response model of the crude naturalists and barely explicable by the more sophisticated versions of naturalistic theory. Closely allied to this doctrine is Maistre's resolute innatism. We do not dwell in the same world as brute animals with an extra layer of culture or language added. The human world is radically different: through innate ideas mankind can interpret the visible world as the isthmus between the temporal and the Divine — and thus view the images of the Platonic "cave" as signs of a higher world.

There is a tradition in French thought that sees religion in primarily social terms. The *locus classicus* is Durkheim's *Les Formes élémentaires de la vie religieuse* (1912). But Durkheim's idea that religion is "society divinised" is the exact opposite of Maistre's view of society as the product of Providence — that is, Divine action. One is the theory of an agnostic who wishes to explain the nature of religion; the other is the doctrine of a stalwart theist who wants to see structures of society as embodying a sacred dimension.

Owen Bradley speaks of Maistre's "lay tone, the altogether worldly approach to ritual and to theodicy, from both of which alike the figure of the Christian deity virtually disappears."[8] Here, I think, Bradley is conflating two rather different elements. There is, of course, the tone of the salon. The structure and style of Maistre's pen is imbued with the wit and elegance of the drawing room rather than the scholastic asperities of the medieval university. We sense the urbanity and wit he shares with Hume and Voltaire. The count writes in a similar mode to the "moderns," but his philosophy is with the "ancients." I think that "worldly" is quite misleading. Metaphysical and theological is more appropriate.

Voltaire believed that the Christian God was morally inferior to the God of Deism. In his 1722 poem "*Epître à Uranie*," Voltaire notoriously claimed that God can only be offended by injustice and that humanity is judged by its virtues and not by sacrifices. Yet Voltaire did not entirely relinquish the idea of sacrifice. A celebrated writer since his youth and feted as an adult by the European literary elite, including the Francophile Frederick the Great of Prussia, Voltaire was eminently capable of self-dramatization. He eloquently presented his own life — indeed, with some justification — as a persecuted existence: in flight or exile or fearing jail for his thought. His lines in the *Dictionnaire philosophique* about the sacrificial role of intellectuals is telling:

Les gens de lettres qui ont rendu le plus de services au petit nombre d'êtres pensants répandus dans le monde, sont les lettrés isolés, les vrais savants renfermés dans leur cabinet, qui n'ont ni argumenté sur les bancs des universités, ni dit les choses à moitié dans les académies; et ceux-là ont presque tous été persécutés.

---

8   Bradley, O. (1999) *A Modern Maistre: The Social and Political Thought of Joseph De Maistre, European Horizons.* Lincoln; London: University of Nebraska Press, p. 190.

Notre misérable espèce est tellement faite, que ceux qui marchent dans le chemin battu jettent toujours des pierres à ceux qui enseignent un chemin nouveau. [. . .] Descartes est obligé de quitter sa patrie, Gassendi est calomnié, Arnauld traîne ses jours dans l'exil; tout philosophe est traité comme les prophètes chez les Juifs. Qui croirait que dans le XVIIIe siècle un philosophe [Hélvetius] ait été traîné devant les tribunaux séculiers, et traité d'impie par les tribunaux d'arguments, pour avoir dit que les hommes ne pourraient exercer les arts s'ils n'avaient pas de mains? Je ne désespère pas qu'on ne condamne bientôt aux galères le premier qui aura l'insolence de dire qu'un homme ne penserait pas s'il était sans tête: "Car, lui dira un bachelier, l'âme est un esprit pur, la tête n'est que la matière; Dieu peut placer l'âme dans le talon, aussi bien que dans le cerveau; partant je vous dénonce comme un impie". [. . .] Le plus grand malheur d'un homme de lettres n'est peut-être pas d'être l'objet de la jalousie de ses confrères, la victime de la cabale, le mépris des puissants du monde; c'est d'être jugé par des sots. Les sots vont loin quelquefois, surtout quand le fanatisme se joint à l'ineptie, et à l'ineptie l'esprit de vengeance. Le grand malheur encore d'un homme de lettres est ordinairement de ne tenir à rien. Un bourgeois achète un petit office, et le voilà soutenu par ses confrères. Si on lui fait une injustice, il trouve aussitôt des défenseurs. L'homme de lettres est sans secours; il ressemble aux poissons volants: s'il s'élève un peu, les oiseaux le dévorent; s'il plonge, les poissons le mangent. Tout homme public paye tribut à la malignité; mais il est payé en derniers et en honneurs.[9]

In *Les Soirées*, we find a remarkably trenchant rebuttal of Voltaire, a thinker that the learned count dismisses as a pernicious mountebank. In particular, Voltaire's presentation of the persecuted *hommes de lettres* and their noble sacrifices must have struck Maistre as an intolerable pretension. Imagine Voltaire in his grand house at Ferney, the most famous writer in Europe, receiving visitors and admirers, surrounded by servants and friends, he doubtless looked to Maistre as a strange candidate for the martyr's mantle. Especially for Maistre, who lived the sad life of an exile — a cruel separation from his family and home. The trenchant and paradoxical theological and metaphysical genius of Maistre is consciously pitted against the subtle and indefatigable talent of the consummate publicist, Voltaire. One can sense both Maistre's resentment of, and feeling of superiority towards, the literary icon of Enlightenment.

Sacrifice explained: Burkert and Girard

Burkert and Girard have produced two of the most influential modern theories of sacrifice. Both draw upon longer traditions: Burkert is the inheritor of the magnificent tradition of German Classical philology together with wider philological concerns (I am thinking especially of Nietzsche);

9 Voltaire (1838). "Lettres," in *Dictionairre Philosophique*. Par Voltaire. Paris: Cosse et Gaultier Laguionie, pp. 672–3. I owe this reference to Caspar Hirschi of Clare Hall, Cambridge.

Girard is clearly standing within a tradition of French speculation about sacrifice that goes back to the spirituality of Counter-Reformation. Both are proponents of grand and provocative theories of sacrifice. Burkert clearly thinks that Otto's influence upon theories of the sacred is baneful.[10]

Walter Burkert notes that even the great age of Aeschylus to Euripides possesses striking archaic elements within sacrificial contexts. If one thinks of the paradigmatic tragic cycle of the Oresteia, it is structured by a succession of failed sacrifices: from the sons of Thyestes through Iphigenia to Orestes's killing of his mother, Clytemnestra. The ubiquitous nature of sacrifice through Ancient Greek religion can be explored in various texts; however, Burkert pursues the ritual of sacrifice into the Palaeolithic age of our hunter-gatherer ancestors, and beyond. Burkert is inspired by the ethology of Konrad Lorenz, especially his *On Aggression* of 1963. Thus animal behavior is the paradigm for understanding human behavior. On the assumption that 90 percent of the evolutionary history of *homo sapiens* was in the hunter-gatherer state and must have at least vestigial influence in later civilization, Burkert pursues the roots of sacrifice in the hunting practices of our ancestors. His thesis is that the social and psychological phenomena of human pre-history can explain sacrifice and thereby religion: "Sacrificial killing is the basic experience of the sacred."[11]

Burkert's theory runs as follows: the emergence of the hunt through the development of groups of hunter-gatherer bands. The hunt, as now developed, required high levels of cooperation, sharing of the spoils, the development of tools, erect bearing, and even physical power among the hunting males: the slender, long thigh of the male emerges as part of this process of evolution. The remarkable distinction of task for male and female is also a product of the different roles that emerged through the role of the hunt in hominization.

Burkert lays particular emphasis upon the psychological dimension of the killing. The competitive and aggressive instinctual forces of the males must be directed towards the prey. The excitement and thrill of the hunt is also linked to remorse and guilt at the spilling of blood. Burkert thinks that this sense of guilt generates rites or actions that are supposed to atone for the bloodletting. As the practice of the hunt becomes ritualized it develops into sacrifice. Hence the similarities between the two forms: killing, sharing, and penitence. Thus sacrifice can be seen as the key to religion and the stories and ideas that develop in its wake. Religion is a ritual and symbolic performance of archaic hunting.

It is a moot point whether the Palaeolithic evidence is as convincing as Burkert avers. Perhaps there was more gathering than hunting, and more scavenging than heroic killing. That aside, my concern is that Burkert

10   See the useful discussion in Mack, Burton. (1987) "Introduction: religion and ritual," in Walter Burkert, René Girard, Jonathan Z. Smith, and Robert Hamerton-Kelly (eds.), *Violent Origins: Ritual Killing and Cultural Formation.* Stanford, CA: Stanford University Press, pp. 1–70.
11   Burkert, W. (1983) *Homo necans: The Anthropology of Ancient Greek Sacrificial Ritual and Myth*, Peter Bing (trans.). Berkeley: University of California Press, p. 3.

gives inadequate weight to the imaginative dimension of human culture. Is culture, in this case specially a cultural milieu with certain religious rites, merely the conventional shape of universal natural instincts? This seems to be Burkert's assumption. For example, Burkert's theory requires the generation of myth by ritual, which in turn is grounded in biosocial factors. The myths of gods and heroes are derived from rituals of sacrifice, which in turn are derived from ritualized hunting practices. If culture were a level of life that rests neatly upon biological structures, then a biological account of "religion," like Burkert's, would be feasible. But between biologically innate propensities of aggression to the complex rituals of sacrifice or war lies a huge gap. If we are correct about the foundational role of the injunction in human life, such an ingenious explanation for the widespread and disturbing practice of sacrificial animal slaughter is both speculative and reductive at once. As Vico, Burke, and Maistre insisted with profundity: art is man's nature.

Similar considerations apply to theories like that of Barbara Ehrenreich in her book *Blood Rites*.[12] Rather than seeing the experience of hunting as the key to human culture, Ehrenreich suggests that sacrificial rites emerged from the period of the shift from man's change from being an object of predation by more powerful carnivores to becoming a predator:

> Here, most likely, lies the source of our human habit of sacralising violence: in the terror inspired by the devouring beast and in the powerful emotions, associated with courage and altruism, that were required for group defense.[13]

Ehrenreich marshalls much cultural evidence of myth in which the enemy is a terrifying beast: Beowulf and Grendel or George and the Dragon are obvious examples. Herman Melville's *Moby Dick* is a reversal, whereby the hunter, the embittered Captain Ahab, becomes the hunted:

> Towards thee I roll, thou all destroying but unconquering whale; to the last I grapple with thee; from hell's heart I stab at thee; for hate's sake I spit my last breath at thee.[14]

Moby Dick concerns a whaling industry that is based upon killing. But Melville's Captain Ahab is presented as demonic in his relentless and malicious quest for the terrible eponymous whale. The whiteness of the beast is both sublime and eerie.[15] Melville, steeped in the transcendentalists and the Romantics, presents Ahab as a perverse version of Coleridge's Mariner. The Mariner is capable of love and can bless the snakes:

12   Ehrenreich, Barbara. (1997) *Blood Rites: The Origins and History of the Passions of War.* New York: Henry Holt.
13   Ehrenreich, *Blood Rites*, p. 47.
14   Melville, H. (1963) *Moby Dick*. London: Oxford University Press, p. 581.
15   Spinelli, Barbara. (2010) *Moby Dick o l'ossessione del male*. Brescia: Morcelliana, pp. 56ff.

He prayeth well, who loveth well/both man and bird and beast.[16]

But for Ahab, "all loveliness is anguish to me."[17] In Coleridge and Melville, the imagery of hunting and killing is tied to the imagining of harmony or division: salvation or life in death.

Vico and the sacrificial imagination

In the image of the crucified Christ, the values of the ancient warrior elite are inverted: The ruler of the universe assumes the posture of ultimate defeat.[18]

No theory of the sacrificial imagination can avoid the legacy of Giambattista Vico. Vico's thought has been shaped by two main strands: the Epicureanism of Pierre Bayle and the Augustinianism of the Port Royal. Bayle's *Pensées diverses sur la cométe* (1682) presents the Epicurean thesis of functioning atheism: that egoists, motivated by their passions rather than reason, could build a society without the aid of Providence. This was a real challenge for Vico. Vico's claim that there cannot be a functioning atheist society emerges out of these questions. He engages the atheists on their own terms and uses their concepts, but in order to refute them.[19] For Vico, not only does religion serve to break the tyranny of the appetites but also its function indicates an important fact about the relation of the passions or the appetites to culture. Human culture is not the conventional shape of passions that are universal in human nature, which is how Hume or Voltaire view the matter. Rather, the distinctively human passions are shaped by cultural traditions and history. Specifically human passions are the product of our emergence from the stage of the *bestioni*.[20] This, I think, is a subtle and intriguing critic of naturalism in ethics. Man is made by society, by institutions and ritual; as such, human nature is irreducible to the stimulus-response model of the crude naturalists and barely explicable by the more sophisticated versions of naturalistic theory. The idea of God is evinced in the history of the nations; morality and civilization presuppose religion.

The rambling and digressive style of Giambattista Vico's work makes him seem like an eccentric outsider for any philosophical canon. Many contemporary readings of Vico have been influenced by an interest upon the nonrational elements in man's mind and the inherent plurality of human cultures. Isaiah Berlin, in particular, viewed Vico as a fundamental breach with both the scientific tradition and Platonism, and thereby breaking with

---

16 Coleridge, *The Rime of the Ancient Mariner*, 649, pp. 613–14.
17 Melville, *Moby Dick*, p. 171.
18 Ehrenreich, *Blood Rites*, p. 165.
19 Robertson, John (2006) *The Case for Enlightenment: Scotland and Naples, 1680–1760.* Cambridge: Cambridge University Press. Robertson shows especially the importance of Bayle within Naples.
20 Mali, Joseph. (1992) *The Rehabilitation of Myth: Vico's "New Science."* Cambridge: Cambridge University Press.

the idea of enduring and eternal principles and values. Berlin's view of Vico as a pluralist is nevertheless hard to square with Neapolitan's insistence upon the *dizionario di voci mentale* that was common to all races and the *senso comune* that he saw as a bearer of these values. One can use the fact of translation to support Vico's point. The translation from one culture to another is weapon in the anti-skeptics arsenal: translation is necessarily an imperfect exercise — the perfect translation is unattainable — but that it is always possible to translate presupposes a common reality.

Vico has often appealed to thinkers who distrust Descartes's rationalism. He seems to offer a more holistic vision of human life and a view of mankind as historical and culturally conditioned. This, together with the widespread association of Vico with the "hermeneutical tradition," *verum-factum* hardly seems compatible with the high rationalism of the Platonic tradition. Indeed, insofar as it suggests relativism or constructivism, it might be construed as the opposite! It seems, perhaps, particularly perverse to associate the Neapolitan philosopher with Platonism. Plato bans the poets; Vico sees poetic wisdom as the foundation of thought. Plato is the advocate of timeless truths, Vico the herald of historicity and comparative cultural anthropology. Could the "Divine Plato" tolerate such a reversal?[21]

If we come from the heights of such generalizations and consider texts, one might offer a further observation. Platonists contemplating eternity often have no historical sense. Plotinus, perhaps the greatest philosopher after Plato with the Platonic tradition, seems to have no sense of different ages and cultures of the authors he discusses. The period between 1650 and the Enlightenment in Europe was an age of intense debate about history and culture. Vico was caught up in this controversy about the status of sacred history and the challenge of Hobbes and Spinoza.

However, such real differences between Vico and the "Platonists" obscure a deep affinity. I wish to argue that this affinity is linked to the question of the relationship between myth and logos and Vico's trenchant antinaturalism. Vico wants to show us how myths constitute a layer beneath the apparently rational, and how religion serves a providential role for the republic. He is also attacking a purely naturalistic account of society on the model of Hobbes.

Vico's interest in imagination came from Pico, while he was tutoring in Vatolla. That other eclectic Platonist, Giordano Bruno of Nola, was a native of the same region of Italy.[22] Vico names Plato as one of his four leading *autori*, alongside Tacitus, Grotius, and Bacon.[23] Notwithstanding Vico's appeal to modern relativists, he is concerned with a *storia ideale* eternal and this eternal ideal history is driven by Providence. It is true that he is committed to an organic view of human culture as part of an evolving process. Human institutions reflect three basic phases of human consciousness:

21   Vico, Giambattista. (1999) *New Science: Principles of the New Science Concerning the Common Nature of Nations* (3rd edn.), David Marsh (trans.) London: Penguin, §879.
22   Stone, H. S. (1997) *Vico's Cultural History: The Production and Transmission of Ideas in Naples, 1685–1750, Brill's Studies in Intellectual History.* Leiden: Brill.
23   Du Bois Marcus, Nancy. (2001) *Vico and Plato,* Emory Vico Studies. New York: P. Lang.

first, the Divine — an age of little reason and rampant imagination. This
period is followed by the age of heroes, a period that produces the sublime
poetry of a Homer or a Dante. Finally, history proceeds to the age of man,
the period of reason, reflection, and critical Enlightenment. The first epoch
is the purely mythopoetic: the age of the world animated by gods. The
second period is an age of heroes who are chastened by religion, its taboos
and limits. The third stage is an age of autonomous human laws. But this
is not a Whiggish story of inexorable progress. The third stage contains the
seed of its downfall. It is beset by the "barbarism of calculation" that is, the
rationalistic erosion of those bonds of religion that hold society together.

Vico is famous as a critic of Descartes, a Descartes who represents
the confidence in the new sciences and the deeply Platonic longing for
the refutation of skepticism and the attainment of certainty.[24] Descartes
had absorbed much Platonism: his rationalism and mind-body dualism
clearly has Platonic resonance.[25] While Vico's *capolavoro* has a Cartesian
title, *Principi di una scienza nuova*,[26] he turns the Cartesian project on its
head. In doing so, Vico seems to propagate an unmethodical relativism
and historicism. We can only know what we make: his celebrated *verum
factum* principle.

Yet let us not be hasty. Vico thinks that Descartes's cogito argument
commits the fallacy of failing to distinguish awareness or consciousness
(*conscientia*) from knowledge (*scientia*). The latter requires knowledge of
the causal ground; the former can be quite ignorant of it. Hence, Descartes
cannot answer the skeptical challenge because he is begging the skeptic's
question. The skeptic can concede self-knowledge as *conscientia* without
any worries: he merely needs to deny that *conscientia* amounts to *scientia*:
knowledge of the form or genus of any item.

Vico transforms our ignorance of physics into an argument for the
existence of God. He claims that only God can know the natural world
because he made it; we can know our culture, rituals, institutions, because
we made them. Let me bracket the debate concerning why the process of
facere implies the superior cognitive status of the epistemological subject.
Suffice it to say that Vico is operating with a Platonic-Aristotelian model of
causality. To understand a cause is more than the awareness of the necessary and sufficient conditions of an event A bringing about B. Not merely
efficient but material and formal causality is meant. If a skeptic admits that
the phenomenal world amounts to a collection of effects, then the *verum/
factum* principle demands a cause that can include the effects within its
form. As the doubt of the skeptic applies to all objects of experience, we
must rationally admit a cause that comprehends the forms of all effects.
Such a cause must be infinite and spiritual since it constitutes the source
of the finite, material cosmos: "Still, in the dense and dark night which

24   Robertson shows especially the importance of the interpretaton of Descartes within
     Naples. Thus, the hostility towards Descartes was part of a wider polemic against
     Epicureanism, especially via Bayle.
25   Menn, S. P. (1998) *Descartes and Augustine*. Cambridge: Cambridge University Press. ()
26   Vico. (1725) *The New Science (La Scienza Nuova)*. Revised 1729–1730, 1744.

envelops remotest antiquity, there shines an eternal and inextinguishable light."[27]

Vico held that philosophers like Descartes were so fixated by absolute certain knowledge, conceptual truths, that they could not supply any adequate account of freedom. Historians, on the other hand, lacked any systematic basis for their reflections and hence any claim to "science": they provide merely hypothetical contingent facts. Vico proposes to bridge the Rhodean gulf between truth and history. His science

> traces the *ideal eternal history* through which the history of every nation passes in time; and it follows each nation in its birth, growth, maturity, decline, and fall . . . Hence, I would venture to say that anyone who studies my Science will retrace this ideal eternal history for himself, recreating it by the criterion that it *had to, has to, and will have to* be so.[28]

A Platonic genealogy of imaginative universals: Vico and Christianity

Vico's relative silence about Christianity is perplexing. In the penultimate section of the *New Science*, Vico describes the vision of "an infinite and eternal good" as an essential difference between our true Christian religion and all other religions, which are false. Is this a Straussian moment in Vico, as it were? Is he mentioning Christianity merely to ward off the Inquisition?

It is also peculiar that Vico, given his great interest in poetry, has so little to say about Dante, the great Christian poet. It may well be that Vico was more interested in the collective spirit of the ancient Greeks than the brilliant individual mind of Dante.[29] Vico writes:

> Dante possessed this same barbarous nature which, being incapable of reflection, cannot feign, and is therefore naturally truthful, open, generous, faithful and magnanimous. For all his erudition and esoteric knowledge, Dante in his *Comedy* portrayed real persons and represented real events in the lives of the dead, And he titled his poem the *Comedy* because the Old Comedy of the Greeks portrayed real persons on the stage.[30]

It does seem odd that Vico should be so reticent about such a great exponent of the Christian imagination as Dante, his own countryman spiritually and literally as it were, and prefer to dwell on the pagan Homer. For some this might be a sign of Vico's own secret paganism. But I think that this is part

---

27 Vico, *La Scienza Nuova*, §331
28 Vico, *La Scienza Nuova*, §349.
29 Miller, Cecilia. (1993) *Giambattista Vico: Imagination and Historical Knowledge*. Basingstoke: Macmillan.
30 Vico, *La Scienza Nuova*, §17.

of Vico's concern to show that even without the Christian dispensation, human beings have access to the Divine: through myths and rituals — indeed, through an imagination that participates in the Divine.

Vico's poetic humanism, antinaturalism, and the role of Providence

Vico's view of history is dominated by the concept of the *ricorsi*, the cycles of history, the view of history that we tend to associate with (disreputable) historians like Spengler and Toynbee. Through the idea of *ricorsi*, we can see Vico interpreting historical events through poetic archetypes, and to see the facts of history as part of an intelligible structure.

> The poetic speech which our poetic logic has helped us to understand continued for a long time into the historical period, much as great and rapid rivers continue far into the sea keeping sweet the waters borne on by the force of their flow.[31]

Ancient and primordial images suffuse the modern mind.[32] Here we encounter what the Oxford philosopher-theologian Austin Farrer called "double agency": holding together the thought that human beings are free and responsible and yet vehicles of Providence.[33]

Vico's view of religion is a good example. Many thinkers have thought that human beings make gods, from Xenophanes to Feuerbach and Freud, but Vico thinks that in making gods man makes himself. Our essential humanity, overcoming the state of the *bestioni*, depends upon the providential working of religion. Vico notes that marriage and burial are particularly important rites in this respect. Sexuality is a domain where the beast in mankind is most transparent and linked to violence. Human societies do not generally admit copulation in public. Vico interprets this aversion as a part of a humanizing process. The religious ceremony of marriage sanctifies a private union that forms the basis of stable families and organized societies. In an account of Vico's Platonism, one might note the justified fear of those dimensions of life where the rational control is particularly weak. Alongside marriage, burial is important for Vico. In 129–30 of the *New Science* he writes:

> *Philosophy*, so as to *aid*[34] *the Human Kind*, must *uplift* and *sustain*[35] *fallen and weak man*, not rend his nature or abandon him in his own

---

31 Vico, *La Scienza Nuova*, §412.
32 See Mali, *The Rehabilitation of Myth*.
33 See Hedley, D. and Hebblethwaite, B. (2006) *The Human Person in God's World: Studies to Commemorate the Austin Farrer Centenary.* London: SCM Press.
34 The Italian reads, *giovare*, from the Latin, *iuvare*, akin to *ius*, or "right" (noted and translated by Marco Andreacchio).
35 These two acts are respectively *sollevare* (lit. "lifting to the sun") and *reggere* (from the Latin, *rex* or "king") or "sustaining" in the sense of "governing" (noted by Marco Andreacchio).

corruption.[36]

This 'Dignity' *distances*[37] from the School of this Science the *Stoics*, who want the *mortification of the senses*, and the *Epicureans*, who *make a rule out of them* — where both [parties] deny *Providence*: the former by making themselves be dragged by *Fate*; the latter, by abandoning themselves to *chance* (and the *second*, opining that *human souls die with bodies*); both of whom should be said *Monastic*, or *solitary Philosophers*[38]—while [this 'Dignity'] admits [in our Science] *Political Philosophers*, & principally the *Platonic*, who convene with all *Legislators* in these *three principal points*: that *Divine Providence* be 'given'; that *the human passions must be moderated to make human virtues of them*;[39] and that *human souls are immortal*; and consequently this 'Dignity' shall give the *three Principles of this Science.*

This passage is very instructive because it shows not merely Vico's identification with the Platonic as opposed to the Stoic or Epicurean schools but also his particular construal of the providential role of Platonism. Stoicism and Epicureanism are "monastic" (in modern jargon "elitist" perhaps!) because they cannot serve the body politic in the manner of Platonism. The fatalism of the one and the radical contingency of the other scheme means that neither can serve as a bulwark for a thriving society — and Vico is very much concerned with society. Not the flight of the one to the One for Vico! But it does place him in that tradition of Christian thinkers like Augustine who saw a providential role in Platonism: not so much *ancilla theologiae* as *praeparatio evangelica*.

Ethics, for Vico, develops out of the veneration of the Godhead, wedlock, and burial. Here we find a distinctive philosophical anthropology. But Vico's theory is not merely that human freedom is shaped by customs and

---

36   The Italian verb for "to rend" is *convellere*, identical in the Latin, and derived from *vello* — "to rip off" or to "overturn" (as in the English "convulsion," from the Latin *convulsum*); the action evokes a primitive identification of one's "nature" with one's own skin. The two alternatives given here by Vico — the rending and the abandoning — correspond respectively to tyranny and anarchy (noted by Marco Andreacchio).

37   The act (in the Italian denoted by *allontana*, or "to send far") is reminiscent of the provision made in Plato's *The Republic*, where Socrates provisionally sends poets out of the ideal city, only to bring them back at a later point. Vico's "distancing" is not as radical an act as expelling or exiling (noted by Marco Andreacchio).

38   Vico's monastic or solitary philosophy is a philosophy that is not civil-minded/spirited and thus does not know itself, for it does not know that man's true nature is social. Consequently, it does not seek the good as common, but as private: instead of seeking the true (i.e. the form of truth) as justice, it seeks wisdom aside from piety (cf. "Conclusion of the work," concluding paragraph) — as if man had access to a knowledge exonerating him from the need to give a public account of it. The morality of the monastic philosopher is juxtaposed to the civil morality of the political philosopher who recognizes the true horizon of morality, and therewith of religion, as public (compare "Idea of the work," paras. 1 and 5) (noted by Marco Andreacchio).

39   Here, as in the subsequent passages, the good is not so much "brought out of" passions as it is made *of* or *with* them. Rather than being something abstracted out of sense, civility coincides with passions formed by laws illuminated by "natural reason." As sense is formed, natural reason finds it easier to illuminate laws — that is, to discover natural form within their poetic or "made" civil form. Compare "Of elements," 47–49, 111–113, and "Conclusion of the work," para. 5 (noted by Marco Andreacchio).

traditions. It is also that through free acts Providence is evident. Human self-fashioning, for Vico, is not quite as autonomous as it appears to some of his secular interpreters. It is rather a dialectical process by which the construction of a human world evinces an overarching providential order:[40]

> But even *Providence*, through the *order of civil things* that in *these Books* has been reasoned,[41] makes itself openly sensed to us in those *three senses*, one of *marvel*, the other of *veneration* — which all of the *Learned*[42] until now have had of the unreachable *Wisdom of the Ancients* — and the third of ardent *desire*; whence [the *Learned*] were fervent in *seeking back* and in *attaining to* [the Wisdom of the Ancients];[43] for [these three senses] are factually *three illuminations of* [*Providence's*] *own Divinity*, which awakened for [the Learned] the aforementioned three most beautiful *righteous senses*—[senses] that later, from the *Learned's* own *conceit* united to the *conceit of the Nations* (which we proposed above as *first 'Dignities'* and that have been picked up again throughout all of *these Books*), *depraved themselves* — which are those whereby *all of the Learned admire, venerate,* and *desire to unify themselves with the Infinite Wisdom of God.*[44] In sum, from all that has been reasoned *in this Work*, it is to be finally concluded that *this Science* carried indivisibly with itself the *Study of Piety*; and that, without being *pious*, you cannot truly[45] be *Wise*.

Vico's philosophy of culture: the "tragic dimension" and Providence

Vico was also deeply aware of the danger that science and civilization creates: the "barbarism of calculation." This is the narrow rationalism that is cynical about past piety:

40　Croce is quite wrong on this. Cf. Croce, B. and Collingwood, R. G. (1913) *The Philosophy of Giambattista Vico*. London: H. Latimer, pp. 28ff. and 115ff.

41　Vico's reasoning is not merely a reasoning *about* but a rational articulation *qua* illumination of a subject of investigation, rooted in the subject's very nature, which in turn coincides with the subject's *civil birth*. See "Of the elements," 14–16 (noted by Marco Andreacchio).

42　Vico's *Dotti* (here, "Learned") are learned of doctrine, and so akin to the indoctrinated (*addottrinati*) (noted by Marco Andreacchio).

43　The Learned of Vico's times still marvel at and venerate Wisdom, but they apparently do not *desire* it. Ardent desire for the Wisdom of the Ancients belongs to the past. "Attaining" renders Vico's *conseguire* — here in the sense of retracing (noted by Marco Andreacchio).

44　Whereas all of the Learned desire the wisdom of God, only the Learned of the past identified Divine wisdom with the wisdom of antiquity, thereby retaining *pietas* in the Ciceronian or Virgilian sense. Those who abandon piety for a wisdom that is not *naturally* posited in the common birth of things (or at the heart of political things) certified by a tradition of doctrinal or legal learning, deprive themselves of the righteous senses *through which* we admire, venerate and desire to unite ourselves to truly Divine Providence (noted by Marco Andreacchio).

45　Vico, G. (2004) *La Scienza Nuova*. Milan: Rizzoli, 1111–12. Vico's *daddovvero* (here rendered as "truly") indicates *that* whence wisdom is true (noted and translated by Marco Andreacchio).

Like beasts, such people are accustomed to think of nothing but their own personal advantage and are prone to irritability, or rather pride, so that they are filled with bestial rage and resentment at the least provocation. Although their bodies are densely crowded together, their intentions and desires are widely separated. Like wild beasts, no two of them agree, because each pursues his own pleasure or caprice. Seeing all this, providence causes their obstinate factional strife and desperate civil wars to turn their cities into forests and their forests into human lairs.

In this way, long centuries of barbarism wear down the evil schemes of malicious minds. (This barbarism of calculation [*riflessione*] turns such people into beasts even more savage than did the primitive barbarism of the senses. For early peoples displayed a generous savagery, from which others could guard or defend themselves or flee. But decadent peoples practise an ignoble savagery, and use flattery and embraces to plot against the life and fortunes or their intimates and friends.[46]

The barbarism of calculation is closely linked to the arrogance that Vico identifies as the cardinal error of the great modern philosophers. The promethean view of men as *maîtres et possesseurs* is far removed from the proper attitude of piety and gratitude towards the Divine. Hence we sense Vico's stress upon the precarious nature of civilization: the subtleties of the Enlightenment wits produced beasts more savage through the barbarism of reflection (*riflessione*) than our distant ancestors: barbarians of sense. This barbarism is the product of reason combined with the rejection of the wisdom of traditional culture, tradition, and religious belief. We dismantle at our peril those institutions that have been vehicles of temperance and virtue.

Modern science and philosophy are presented by their most eloquent and sanguine proponents as harbingers of liberation. Bacon and Descartes envisage their philosophies as antidotes to skepticism: whether through rigorous experiment or clear and distinct ideas. The result of their philosophies was in fact to reinforce skepticism and to dismantle religion, tradition, rhetoric: philosophy was thus corroding and subverting the most useful bulwarks against the innate folly of man that the ancients possessed. The vaunted freedom of the moderns becomes a source of bondage. Unlimited freedom becomes terrible tyranny. While the moderns celebrated reason — though distorted by dogmatic falsehoods — Vico viewed mankind as fallen and feeble, a slave to irrational conatus. Thus, even certain errors deserve respect for their useful role in aiding mankind and should not be purged. Ultimately the order and authority of the Divine, not human reason, is the paradigm of Vico's philosophy: God draws fallen humanity back to himself though providential institutions.

In fact, as Mark Lilla has eloquently shown, Vico prefers Rome to Greece precisely because it shows how a society constructed upon law and religion is more durable than a culture of extreme brilliance but instability — fifth- and fourth-century BC Greek culture. Custom and authority are

46 Vico, *La Scienza Nuova*, §1106.

underestimated by intellectuals, but Rome can show how and why these forces can operate within Divine Providence.[47] Vico's tactic is to meet his opponents on their own territory. Hence he uses terms like "conatus," he admits the extent to which ignorance, custom, and irrational authority play in constructing society. Yet he makes these concessions in order to show how Divine *paideia* operates.

This age of Enlightenment, Vico is convinced, is also one of weakened imagination. Imagination is the requirement for human beings to become human through their mythopoetic activity. It is also required for the imaginative engagement with the relics of the past (i.e. texts or monuments or rituals). Thus rationalism, if it destroys imagination, corrodes those deep bonds and institutions that sustain human life. Vico was intrigued by the history of Rome and the chaos and misery that succeeded its glory and grandeur, and he was interested in the fate of Enlightened Europe.

Under the influence of Berlin, we are inclined to view Vico as a forerunner of Herder's nationalism. However, in his philosophy of culture, he might be usefully compared with English mythologists and philologists like Jacob Bryant, author of *A New System; or, An Analysis of Ancient Mythology* (1774), and, indeed, Sir William "Asiatick" Jones. These were figures who claimed that the belief in a transcendent deity, creator, preserver, and judge was furnished by even the most idolatrous of the nations. Hence, Vico is far from isolated in his tenet that Providence is work in mythology, even if he is far more articulate and original in his statement of it.

Providence, the civil world, and Vico's anti-contractualism

Vico attacks the leading Enlightenment theorists like Grotius, Pufendorf, and Selden, the theorists of a new natural law, a *ius gentium* fit for Europe after the 1648 Peace of Westphalia. If Christendom cannot provide a basis for the peaceful coexistence of nations, universal principles must be discovered. But Vico thinks that the heuristic displacement of religion is misguided. If religion evinces great cruelty, atheism is incapable of producing a nation.

Vico's critique of Grotius is linked to the fact that Grotius is essentially ahistorical. The basis for Vico's "philology" (in Vico's idiosyncratic use of that term) is an examination of the nations and it is based on history rather than anthropology.

Hobbes thinks that self-interest provides the motive for individuals submitting to the social contract. For Vico this reveals an absurdly sanguine view of human rationality. Human beings are simply not capable, according to Vico, of such rationality. Indeed, their incapacity for such rational cooperation is a powerful reason for seeing the rise of civilization as the work of Providence through religious institutions: "If people lose their

---

47   Lilla, Mark. (1993) *G. B. Vico: The Making of an Anti-Modern*. Cambridge, MA; London: Harvard University Press, pp. 108–17.

religion, nothing remains to keep them living in society."[48]

The Cartesian elimination of the great fruits of the Renaissance history and languages, poetry, and rhetoric as lacking the certainty of the natural sciences has produced a great impoverishment of vision. As a result, we are inclined to view our ancestors through an absurdly rationalistic prism. Human beings should be seen as spiritual beings and thus in terms of reasons rather than causes. However, the reasons are not to be reduced to merely instrumental or quasi-mechanical considerations, but a part of the warp and woof of ideas in religious institutions and rituals, of a history suffused by imagination. The history of humanity is the history of the human spirit. But we can only appreciate this history through intellectual and imaginative exertion.

Distinctive in Vico's project is the importance of virtue. Whereas philosophers like Hobbes saw virtue as an irrelevance (the proper functioning of the state is based upon fear), Vico sees virtue as key to the proper well-being of the commonwealth. Furthermore this virtue is not the product of rational Enlightenment but, rather, fear of God and, in the specifically Christian instance, grace: "In Christianity, Divine grace inspires virtuous works for the sake of an infinite and eternal good."[49]

Vico has been seen as a Hegelian or proto-Marxist, a good Catholic and Liberal. I cannot comment on these traditions of interpretation but it is clear that Vico is not a[50] slavish admirer of Plato. The poets, *pace* Plato, are not liars for Vico. And neither Vico's quasi-geometric mode nor his literary achievement would have impressed the Athenian. But we can, however, produce a case for seeing Vico as an erratic and eccentric Platonist. He is aware of his own work as being both a learned and an original account of the Divine source of human institutions. Whereas the ancient Platonists look to the harmonious workings of the cosmos for their theories of Providence, Vico argues that we should look, rather, at the economy of civil institutions as a meeting place of human freedom and Divine order.

Vico is an opponent of the skeptics and libertines of the Enlightenment, but his tactic is to concede a limited validity to the tenets of his opponents while denying their overarching theories. His is a new science. He places conatus at the center of his theory, like Hobbes or Spinoza, but he is implacably opposed to their theories. Not a mechanistic determinism or Stoic acceptance of the totality of pantheistic universe, but an awe for transcendent Deity — piety — is at the core of his metaphysics.

Vico holds together the sense of man's precarious social condition together with a sense of Providence. Religious terror can tame man in his savagery: "[I]f peoples lose their religion, nothing remains to keep them living in society."[51] One might sense prophecies of the Terrors and Purges and foreshadowing of Edmund Burke and Joseph de Maistre. It is certainly an implicit rebuke to the Enlightenment critics of religion, who saw priestcraft

---

48   Vico, *La Scienza Nuova*, §1109.
49   Vico, *La Scienza Nuova*, §1110.
50   For a lucid overview of the materials, see Lilla, *G. B. Vico*, pp. 237–49.
51   Vico, *La Scienza Nuova*, §1109.

as the root of savagery and suffering. Many of the Romantics came to employ Vician arguments when they observed the horrors of the Terror and the strange secular cults of the French Revolution. Vico's exploration of the religious institutions of the pagans is the tracing of the work of Providence. It is an original, indeed erratic, vision of man who does not clearly belong to a school. But it draws in a creative fashion upon core themes with the Christian Platonic tradition, and a polemic against atheism that goes back to Plato's *Laws*. This is Vico's response to the ancient injunction, "Know Thyself!"

Icons and iconoclasm

Contemporary theories of politics tend to cluster around debates about justice or legitimacy. Many liberal thinkers in the wake of Rawls see themselves as developing theories of justice. Critics of Rawls — for example, Raymond Geuss — see political philosophy as a sort of oxymoron. The real question of politics for many such commentators is one of legitimacy. Yet another way of looking at political theory is in terms of representation. What is it that enables a people to think of themselves as ruled and yet participating in that rule? Let us take an example from the English Civil War from 1642 to 1649.[52] It was a period of unparalleled violence on English soil and culminated in 1649 with the public execution of King Charles I. It was a war fought over power: the power of image. After his execution, the book *Eikon Basilike* was published. It is an apparent diary of the monarch in which he prays for his executioners and places his trust in God, and it is a defense of the absolute monarchy rejected by the English parliament. King Charles claims:

> I would rather choose to wear a crown of thorns with my Saviour, than to exchange that of gold, which is due to me, for one of lead, whose embased flexibleness shall be forced to bend and comply to the various and oft contrary dictates of any factions, when instead of reason and public concernments they obtrude nothing but what makes for the interest of parties, and flows from the partialities of private wills and passions. I know no resolutions more worthy a Christian king, than to prefer his conscience before his kingdoms.[53]

The poignant and overt comparison to Christ was very effective for the Royalists. It was an immensely popular and powerful work. Parliament was so worried by its popularity that commissioned John Milton to compose a reply. In the same year Milton published his *Eikonklastes*, in which he presents the identification of Charles with Christ as a blasphemous imposture:

---

52   I am very grateful to Russell Hillier for this suggestion.
53   Almack, Ed (ed.). (1904) *Eikon Basilike* or *The Kings Book*. London: De la More Press.

Many would be all one with our Saviour, whom our saviour will not know. They who govern ill those kingdoms which they had a right to, have to our Saviours Crown of Thornes no right at all.[54]

Milton was referring in exasperation to a monarch who infringed traditional English liberties as protected by common law, imprisoning without trial, confiscating land, and who raised taxes without parliament.

Furthermore:

[A]s his Charity can be no way comparable to that of Christ, so neither can his assurance that they whom he seems to pray for, in doing what they did against him, knew not what they did. It was but arrogance therefore, and not charity, to lay such ignorance to others in the sight of God, till he himself had bin infallible, like him whose peculiar words he overweeningly assumes.[55]

Charles became the sole saint formally canonized by the Church of England; though Queen Victoria had the official remembrance removed from the Book of Common Prayer. The famous debates between Locke and Filmer (1588–1653) *Patriarcha or; the Natural Power of Kings*, 1680 Knighted by Charles I and John Locke's *Two Treatises of Government* have their roots in these seventeenth-century disputes.

I am using this example of the identification of Charles I with the sacrifice of Christ because it highlights the close link between sovereignty and the language of the image in the early modern period. Many of the same issues were addressed with the overthrow and subsequent execution of Louis XVI (and, indeed, Czar Nicholas). One of the most important theorists of sacrifice, Joseph de Maistre, was the product of this turbulent period. Charles did not claim to represent as much as body forth the Divine on earth.

Medieval Christendom was never forced to express the Divine Right of Kings; it was largely assumed along with a sacramental universe. We might consider Charles Taylor's subtle "polemic against those 'subtraction stories'," that present the Enlightenment as the explanation how the agents of the secular modern world "liberated themselves from certain earlier confining horizons, illusions, or limitations of knowledge."[56] Taylor develops a narrative about a new set of "social imaginaries," which severed society from cosmos. The sacred order of intrinsic hierarchies was replaced with "the mutual respect and mutual service of the individuals who make up society."[57] Thus emerged a "public sphere [as] an association which is constituted by nothing outside of the common action we carry out in it: coming

---

54 Milton, John. (1970) "Eikonoklastes", in *Complete Works III*. Merritt Y. Hughes (ed.). New Haven: Yale, pp. 417–18
55 Milton, "Eikonoklastes", 657f.
56 Taylor, Charles. (2007) *A Secular Age*. Cambridge, MA: Belknap Press of Harvard University Press, p. 22.
57 Taylor, *A Secular Age*, p. 165.

to a common mind, where possible, through the exchange of ideas."[58] As a result, we have "social imaginary" of representative democracy, with its "crucial fiction of 'we, the people'."

Vico's thoughts about the role of the sacred in human society is a subtle challenge to any crude secularisation thesis. Vico thinks that if religion is lost among the peoples, they have nothing left to enable them to live in society. He presents the sacrifice of self as an integral part of the process of civilization. He writes:

> Because of their corrupt nature, people are tyrannized by self-love, and so pursue their own advantage above all else. Seeking everything that is useful for themselves and nothing for their companions, they cannot subject their passions to the conscious impulse that directs them to just ends. This leads us to establish the following principle. In his bestial state, a man loves only his own well being.[59]

But religion can help sublimate and liberate the savage from bestial self-aggrandising ego. Not least through institutions such as marriage and burial, laws and customs, language, and the arts. Vico writes of the sacred or holy as:

> that terrifying thought of a deity which imposed form and measure on the bestial passions of these lost men and made them human passions. Such a thought must have given rise to the *moral effort* or *conatus*, which is proper to the human will and which restrains the impulses that the body urges on the mind. By means of this effort, such impulses can be completely suppressed by the sage, and can be directed to better ends by the good citizen.[60]

One might observe that this is the opposite of Girard. Sacrifice is not part of mimetic savagery: this is contrary to Vico's sense of a providential dimension to human institutions and his sense of the corrosive impact of the "barbarism of reflection." It is critical reflection that lapses into irony and cynicism concerning those institutions that, notwithstanding their flaws and limits, have preserved and transformed humanity. Such cynicism and individualism in modernity radically underestimates the legitimate role of traditional loyalties and commitments fostered by religion.

Furthermore, any awareness of the limits and finitude of this contingent realm, the "fallenness" of the world in Christian tradition, will reinforce the insight that "offering up" is a necessity among scarce resources and an endangered environment. The Christian position lies situated between the extremes of the utopian and the cynical. There is a legitimate "sacrifice for the sake of." But its realization in this world is imperfect.

---

58   Taylor, *A Secular Age*, p. 192.
59   Vico, *The New Science*, §341.
60   Vico, *The New Science*, p. 340.

Making sacred

Joseph de Maistre's "On Sacrifices in General" is one of the most significant early treatises on sacrifice. Maistre shares many of Vico's interests and obsessions. Maistre was a Christian Platonist, but of a very original cast of mind. Maistre makes this thought explicit: mankind's proper relation to the physical cosmos is a sacrificial rite, a "making sacred." Through sacrifice, the hidden seed of the Divine is brought out of potentiality and into actuality. As such, the renunciation of the will, the sacrifice of self for an absolute good, must remain an integral element of human self-realization. Maistre, with Burke the most eloquent polemicist against Enlightenment, saw himself as the inheritor of the great philosophical inheritance of Europe and the relentless adversary of the trivialization and banalization of Western philosophy in so-called "philosophes" like Voltaire. Yet Maistre was no mere polemicist: he was an astute reader of Plato and the Platonic tradition, and his reflections upon the relevance of the concept of sacrifice reflect his deep immersion in the European philosophical canon.

Maistre starts by developing the idea of "substitution" as a common element in comparative ancient religion. Maistre had a very lively and informed interest in reports of ancient Aztec and Eastern religion. He was an admirer of the English mythologer Jacob Bryant and the foundational Orientalist Sir William Jones. Maistre sees substitution as an innate idea in mankind, which is often horribly perverted. Whereas many modern writers, whether for or against, assume the absurdity of the practice of sacrifice, the Savoy Count de Maistre does not. In almost oxymoronic *Eclaircissements sur les Sacrifices*, or *Enlightenment on Sacrifice*, he noted the oddity of the phenomenon that sacrifice is a universal and intractable element in human societies. He claims that the ritual of sacrifice furnishes institutions with both awe and terror: it makes them sacred. Maistre writes:

> Neither reason nor folly could have invented this idea, or even less got it generally adopted. It has its root in the very depth of human nature and history, on this point it does not present a single contrary example. The entire theory rests on the doctrine of substitution. It is believed (as it has always been believed and will always be believed) that the innocent pay for the guilty; from which it can be concluded that life being guilty, a less valuable life can be offered for another. So one offers the blood of animals; and this soul. Offered from another soul, the ancients called antipsychon, vicariam animam; as we say soul for soul or substitute soul.[61]

As a result of his foraging through the letters of antiquity, especially the Church Fathers, the descriptions of the Aztecs or the reports of the Asiatick Society, Maistre discovers this innate propensity of humanity.

In chapter 2 of the *Eclaircissements* , Maistre moves from nature to culture and he refers to Racine's account of the most famous and terrifying human sacrifice in Classical Antiquity: Iphigenia. Maistre rails against the impiety of

---

61   Maistre, *Sacrifices*, p. 359.

Lucretian claim that religion is rooted in fear. Feelings of terror and joy *coexist* inherently in religion. He stresses the extent to which the sacred is terrifying and ambivalent for the ancients. The gods are good and we owe to them the goods of life and yet there is anger of the gods and the need to propitiate them.

Thus he can argue that the consideration of the words of the ancients for sacrifice reveals this ambivalent nature of the sacred. The core meaning of the sacred is that which has been consecrated to the Divine. The sacrificial victim delivered for the Divine is the paradigmatic sacred object:

> We can see here why the word sacred (SACER was taken in the Latin language in both a good and bad sense) why this same word in the Greek language (HOSIOS) meant both what is holy and what is profane; why the gift worth anathema means at the same time what is offered to God as a gift and what is delivered to his vengeance; and finally, why in Greek as in Latin it is said that a man or thing has been desacralized (expiated) to express the idea that someone has been cleansed of a stain they contracted. The word desacralize (aspousioun, expiare) seems contrary to the analogy; the uninstructed ear would require resacralization or re-sanctification, but it is only an error in appearance, and the expression is very accurate. To sacralize in the language of antiquity, means that which is delivered to the Divinity, no matter what the reason, and that which is bound, so that punishment desacralizes, expiates or unbinds, just like the religious absolution.[62]

The pagan cults and myths contain truths, even if these truths are distorted or even perverted:

> How then can we fail to recognize that paganism could not be mistaken about an idea so universal and fundamental as that of sacrifices, that is to say redemption by blood?[63]

Maistre believed that he had discovered the basis of sacrifice in the ideas of substitution and reversibility. Rather than being a brute, irrational practice, it is based upon the mysterious law of the universe that "the innocent can pay for the guilty."[64]

Maistre notes that although the Jews were insistent upon separating themselves from pagan ceremonies, Moses went so far as to reinforce "the fundamental rite *of the nations*".[65] Furthermore, for Maistre, Christianity fulfils rather than denies the principle of sacrifice that forms the basis of the partial truth of heathen piety.[66] The pagans demand regularly repeated "communion in blood," while Christ sacrifices his Divinely innocent blood so that the heathen sacrifice, "redemption through blood," can find its *telos*.

---

62   Maistre, *Sacrifices*, p. 365.
63   Maistre, *Sacrifices*, p. 381.
64   Maistre, *Sacrifices*, p. 359.
65   Maistre, *Sacrifices*, p. 359.
66   Maistre, J. M. (1993) *St Petersburg Dialogues; or, Conversations on the Temporal Government of Providence*. Montreal: McGill-Queen's University Press.

Maistre's account is specifically aimed at the rationalism of the French revolution and the optimism of its theorists. Maistre thought that a failure to recognize human limits, frailty, and finitude would create terror.[67] Maistre's own vision is an apocalyptic view of the whole earth as a gigantic altar upon which there is a continual and terrible sacrifice of life until the final eradication of evil; the world is a vast altar on which each being must sacrificed until the final purification of evil; evil is not a refutation of Divine purpose and Providence but, rather, reveals the necessity for sacrificial expiation and redemptive substitution as part of a process of cosmic return to Divine Unity. This return is a Divine education of mankind realized through pain and sorrow.

There was a tradition that fed upon the vigorous rhetoric of Maistre through Donoso Cortés up to Carl Schmitt, and which used this apocalyptic vision to justify violence and war. The attempt of a thinker like Girard to distance Christianity from the very principle of sacrifice is doubtless both inspired by and in revolt against Maistre. Yet Maistre's own philosophy is better understood within a tradition of Christian theodicy than as some somber irrationalism of the kind diagnosed by critics like Isaiah Berlin.

First, his politics is conservative rather than radical. He quotes the critique of the sacrifice in Iphigenia but only notes that the abuse of sacrifice would "fade in comparison to the evils produced by absolute impiety,"[68] and that Epicurean dogmas would undermine religion and "the old Roman constitution in order to substitute for it an atrocious and endless tyranny."[69] Maistre thinks that religion is a necessary condition of social stability and the cultivation of virtue, and dwells upon the perversions of sacrifice than emerge through atheism. The horrors of the Terror during the French Revolution furnished the prime example for him.

Indeed, theologically Maistre is attached to the Greek Orthodox tradition of Origen and universalism. The ultimate interest of Maistre is in *Christus consummator* rather than violence, and his theodicy is an ingenious attempt to re-imagine sacrifice in a profane age. His is a brilliant reading of the relationship between literal and figurative sacrifice as one of continuity, not rupture.

Girard and the legacy of Vico and Maistre

René Girard, like Maistre whom he occasionally references, rejects naturalism and is scathing of the familiar critiques of religion emerging from the Enlightenment. Two figures that he considers with real vigor are Freud and Nietzsche, and I think it no accident that the key mythological figures discussed in *Violence and the Sacred* are the favored protagonists of Freud and Nietzsche respectively: Oedipus and Dionysus; in particular, Freud's book *Totem and Taboo* draws upon Frazer and Robertson Smith. Seeing

---

67　Bradley, *A Modern Maistre.*
68　Maistre, *Sacrifices*, p. 371.
69　Maistre, *Sacrifices*, p. 372.

Totemism as the earliest phase of religion, Freud sees it as ground in an original murderous act, where a primal horde, a group of brothers, execute their Oedipal desires by killing the father and appropriating his power. The horde then erect a totem in honor of and mourning for the father, which in turn helps to purge their sense of guilt. The Nietzsche who is important for Girard is the critic of the Christ crucified, who became the founder of the slave morality that is Christian ethics, a baneful product of the ressentiment of the priests. Girard regards Nietzsche as the great philosophical genius of the nineteenth century.[70] Not only is Nietzsche important as the mirror image of Girard's own Christian concerns but also Nietzsche's stress upon the murder of God as the end of the morality of the crucified, and his replacement through the new cult of Dionysus, has clearly exerted a profound influence upon Girard's thought.

Girard's inspiration is not biology but, rather, imaginative literature and he is rightly scathing of those who deny great literature the capacity to convey real truth. Furthermore, his theory of mimetic desire is consciously antinaturalistic. The imagining of the desires of others shapes desires. The object of human desires is thus molded by the imagination and imitation of the desires of others. Girard states: "The mimetic quality of childhood is universally recognized . . . [However, what is rarely acknowledged is that] adult desire is virtually identical, except that . . . the adult is generally ashamed to imitate other for far of revealing his lack of being."[71]

In Girard's theory, the social psychology of desire cannot be reduced to the push and pull of raw instincts, inclinations, and aversions.[72] Girard's theory of mimetic desire is derived from literature and quite incompatible with ethology.[73] Whereas Burkert's theory is naturalistic in the sense that sacrifice emerges out of the natural need to kill for food, Girard's theory is based on a monstrous act of murder. This arises from a mimetic desire that is inherently competitive and which generates an upsurge of violence with the community. Girard might agree with Ehrenreich:

> Culture . . . cannot be counted to be "on our side". Insofar as it allows humans to escape the imperatives of biology, it may do so only to entrap us in what are often crueller imperatives of its own.[74]

Girard uses the term "mimetic doubling" for this process by which rivalry for the mediated desires generates the monstrous double: the competitor locked into conflict over the desired objects, and the ensuing violence.

---

70   See Girard's most informative article: Girard, R. (1996) "Nietzsche versus the cruci-
      fied," in James Williams (ed.), *The Girard Reader*. New York: Crossroad Herder,
      pp. 243–61.
71   Girard, R. (2005) *Violence and the Sacred*. London: Continuum, p. 146
72   There is no truth not mediated by culture. See Girard and Gregory, *Violence and the
      Sacred*, p. 240.
73   Though Girard has become very interested in the evolutionary dimension of mimesis.
      See Girard, R., de Castro Rocha J. C., and Antonello, P. (2007) *Evolution and Conversion:
      Dialogues on the Origins of Culture*. London: Continuum.
74   Ehrenreich, *Blood Rites*, p. 235.

Rivalry is not the product of the fortuitous convergence of two agents desiring the same object. The one subject yearns for the object precisely because the rival wants it. Violence is not an unfortunate by-product of clashing desires, but the necessary upshot of mimesis: "the original act of violence is the matrix of all ritual and mythological significations."[75]

Mimetic doubling generates the mimetic crisis, in which swelling violence threatens social breakdown (Girard depicts as the erosion of hierarchy and distinction). The resolution of this mimetic lies in the redirection of the violence of the mob to a single victim. The society almost destroyed by conflict can unite itself by concentrating its ire upon a scapegoat. Hence the murder of a single victim both releases the violence of the mob and unites the many:

> The rivalrous and conflictual mimesis is spontaneously and automatically transformed into reconciliatory mimesis. For, if it is impossible for the rivals to find an agreement around the object which everyone wants, this very agreement is quickly found, on the contrary, against the victim whom everybody hates.[76]

Religion is a complex attempt to obscure the terrible truth of victimization at the root of human culture, sacrificial ritual the inadequate attempt to resolve the problem of violence at the root of all human relations, and myth is a language of concealment. The *Bacchae* of Euripides plays an important role for Girard since the relations among myth, ritual, and literary reflection are so porous. Girard's thesis rather oddly makes the surrogate victim, the scapegoat rather than God the sacred — or, indeed, as Girard writes: "the sacred is violence."[77]

There is on this point a great difference between Girard and Maistre. Maistre associates the sacred with predicates of the Divine, not with violence. Maistre writes:

> There is in man, despite his immense degradation, an element of love drawing him towards his fellowmen; compassion is as natural to him as breathing. By what inconceivable magic is he always ready, at the first beat of a drum, to cast off this sacred character and to be off without resistance, often even with a certain elation (which also has it peculiar characteristics), to blow to pieces on the battlefield a brother who has never offended him, and who on his side advances to do the same to him if he can?[78]

If Burkert, with his enthusiasm for ethology, fails to do justice to the crucial role of imagination in human culture, Girard sees mankind as almost

75 Girard, *Violence and the Sacred*, p. 117.
76 Girard, et al., *Evolution and Conversion*, p. 66.
77 Girard, R., Oughourlian, J-M., Lefort, G., Bann, S., and Metteer, M. (1987) *Things Hidden since the Foundation of the World*. Stanford, CA: Stanford University Press, p. 32.
78 Maistre, J. (2007) *St. Petersburg Dialogues; or, Conversations on the Temporal Government of Providence*. Montreal: McGill-Queen's University Press, p. 206.

universally condemned to a perversely overactive imagination: creating saviour figures out of ritual substitutes. Briefly, I think that Girard is wrong about myth as a process of concealment and his attempt to divorce Christianity from any mythic component. Christians become the Gnostic few who have grasped the secret curse of human culture.

Evolution and conversion

Maistre sees the ritual victim of sacrifices as an innocent debt payer for the guilty. Girard openly challenges this moral component to sacrifice. There is, he says, "no question of expiation.[79]". Indeed, Girard is intent on explaining both culture and religion in evolutionary terms.

For Girard, the religious is at the heart of human culture and it derives from the idea of sacrifice. More recently he has claimed that the mimetic thesis can be traced as far back as the animal. How did civilization emerge? Girard considers the problems of hominization. He claims:

> Therefore, in the final stage of the development of human culture, what was necessary was a mix of culture and Darwinian evolution which up to a certain point was incomprehensible. However, as regards the ethnological descriptions of two animals which attack each other, Konrad Lorenz says that animals who do not know each other inevitably attack in their uncertainty; they offer combat to the adversary. If the adversary responds in a non-combative manner, then both turn on a third target which, in my opinion, is already the origin of the mechanism of the phenomenon of the scapegoat. Thus, one could deduce that the increasingly complex and increasingly violent forms of this mechanism, became defuse during the final stages of the evolution of primates to homo sapiens sapiens [sic]. Therefore, human culture has its origins in the religious; the rite is the invention of human culture. We kill this victim regularly to avoid imminent crisis.[80]

Girard is presenting a genetic and secular account of human culture. Hominization, for Girard, emerges through the process of memtic rivalry and its attendant violence. As rivals bear semblence to each other, the violence grows until the selection of a scapegoat and its expulsion. Christianity, as revolution, is a *deus ex machina*.

Generally attempts by cultural evolutionists — social transmission, memes, and so forth look like grandiose and barely disguised apologies for an extravagant determinism and fatalism, deeply implausible theories about the absence of real human agency. Darwin himself was very coy in his ethical and metaphysical claims. He had a sense of human cognitive limits and that there are great "mysteries." He did not even think that selection

79   Girard, R. (2005) *Violence and The Sacred*. London: Continuum, p. 4.
80   Girard, (2002) *Journal of European Psychoanalysis*, number 14, Winter–Spring 2002, p. 14.
      See "Evolution and Conversion Dialogues on the Origins of Culture", 56ff.

was the only component of evolution.

In the *River Out of Eden*, the neo-Darwinist Richard Dawkins speaks of

> [u]niverse with no design, no purpose, no evil and no good, nothing but blind pitiless indifference . . . DNA neither cares nor knows. DNA just is. And we dance to its tune.[81]

Here, Dawkins sounds more like Schopenhauer than Darwin himself: "*Das Prinzip des Lebens ist Grundlos*"[82]: The basic principle of life is anarchic! There is a huge difference between claiming that the physical sciences cannot inform us about questions of value and thus cannot give us clues to the meaning of our lives, and the view of Dawkins that the physical sciences have proven that life has no meaning. This is a metaphysical or hermeneutical claim like that of Schopenhauer, for Girard. Thus:

> Dawkins' theory of imitation seems to me quite deficient overall. He proposes a theory for imitative transmission of culture which also never accounts for the negative effects of imitation.[83]

If I claim that Girard is essentially hermeneutical, then I think the same is true of Dawkins and others — even if they think they are being more rigorous. The endeavor to trace the origin of culture in nature is to grant too much to Neo-Darwinians. That is not to downplay the achievements in neuroscience and psychology, but merely to note that when we move into the realm of the emotions and the imagination, the domain of human culture, predictability, the index of hard science, becomes highly dubious. However illuminating Girard's theory as a hermeneutical account is, and I maintain that it is, I doubt that it provides a universal mechanism for the understanding of the move from hominids to humanity.

The problem of violence and the idea of order

The interest in violence in writers such as Girard or Burkert is telling. But what is violence? For the Platonic tradition, violence is violence against an order. Consider Dante. The structure of the *Commedia* reflects Dante's Platonic belief that the soul is shaped by the objects of its aspiration, and that the proper motor of the soul's ascent to God is love. The *Inferno* is the domain of disordered appetite: incontinence, physical violence (the inflicting of harm through force), and worst of all fraud (the spiritual violence of harming others through falsehood), culminating in the treason, especially that of Satan. *Purgatory* is the real of the disciplining of sinners into a proper vision of the Good. Here sinners have repented but they

81   Dawkins, Richard. (1995) *River out of Eden: A Darwinian View of Life*, New York: Basic, p. 133.
82   Schopenhauer, *The World as Will and Representation*, ss20, p. 106.
83   Girard, et al., *Evolution and Conversion*, p. 100.

still are maimed and frustrated by their sins and bad habits. Purgatory is a domain of the healing of the soul. Paradiso is the realm of the journey about the merely human, the domain where one can follow desires without sin.

Dante, no stranger to conflict and grim violence in real politics, employed the idea of sacrifice in a very prominent manner. Dante is a poet of exile. The biblical motif of Exodus pervades his *Commedia*. He is a poet who has been through the fiery furnace of the loss of his place of birth and his most intense worldly love. Canto 5 of the *Inferno* with Paolo and Francesca is a meditation on love, disordered love, and love lost. Canto 6 with his debate with Ciacca is the adumbration of the ground of his exile for the paradigmatic earthly city of the *Commedia*, Florence. Dante is the Florentine in exile. The brutal civil war in Florence ending in 1266 between the Guelphs and Ghibellines resulted in the victory of the Guelphs. And there was subsequently the later repetition of such battles between the White and Black Guelphs referred to by Ciacco: the period of the 1290s and the violence that erupted in 1300. One might consider also the meeting in *Inferno* 10 between Dante and Farinata, the great Ghibelline warlord. Suffering and salvation, exile and atonement are linked not just through happenstance but also integrally, on the model of crucifixion and resurrection. Dante in canto 11 in the *Purgatorio* highlights even the sacrifice of the will of the angels while praising God!

> As Thine angels make sacrifice to Thee of their will, singing
> hosannas, so let men make of theirs.
> *Come del suo voler li angeli tuoi*
> *fan sacrificio a te, contando osanna,*
> *cosi facciano li uomini de' suoi.*[84]

This is not an isolated passage in the *Commedia*. There is a striking parallel passage about the purgation of the soul in terms of a willing, even joyful, sacrifice of the will in the *Purgatorio* canto 23 with the words of Forese Donati:

> I say pain and ought to say solace,
> for that will leads us to the tree which lead Christ say gladly
> to say Eli, when with his own veins He freed us.
> *io dico pena, e dovria dir solazzo*
> *che quella voglia all'arbore ci mena*
> *che meno Cristo lieto a dire "Eli"*
> *quando ne libero con la sua vena.*[85]

Whereas the Inferno is the domain of incontinence, violence, and fraud, Purgatory for Dante (akin to the vision of Origen in *De Principiis*) is the

---

84 Dante, Alighieri. (1939) "Purgatorio," John D. Sinclair, (trans.). *The Divine Comedy of Dante Alighieri*. Oxford: Oxford University Press, p. 142.
85 Dante, "Purgatorio," p. 300.

place of the healing souls that have been damaged by sin, and the place where love is trained to be redirected towards the Good. Purgatory is for those sinners who have repented but still possess bad habits. It is an allegory of healing so that souls can ascend to paradise where they can follow desires without sin. Maistre's insistence upon suffering and sacrifice draws upon a deep Christian tradition as well as his provocative and idiosyncratic manner. Misery is viciousness and the vision of the Divine can only follow upon the purgation of the soul.

3

Failed Oblations and the Tragic Imagination

Sing the song of woe, the song of woe, but may the good prevail.[1]

Tragic Poetry is based upon the idea of sacrifice.[2]

Tragedie is to seyn a certeynstorie,
As olde bookes maken us memorie,
Of hym that stood in greet prosperitee,
And is yfallen out of heigh degree
Into myserie, and endeth wrecchedly.
And they ben versified communely,
Of six feet, which men clepen exametron.[3]

Upon such sacrifices/The Gods themselves throw incense.[4]

The concept of tragedy is puzzling and contentious. The idea of sacrifice is a helpful guide to the genre of tragedy and this also helps explain the real proximity of tragedy to theology. Why do we appreciate tragedy as art? It is perhaps puzzling why, notwithstanding the Enlightenment, so much art dwells upon guilt, violence, and redemption. Often, it is in works of imagination that we see what other dimensions of experience we ignore or repress. Often the artists have little reflective awareness of these questions as a problem of the intellect but they feel acutely. Classical, especially Attic, tragedy is based upon sacrifice imagined through mythic patterns and these myths contain perennial truths of the human condition, which the tragic poetic re-imagines. We reject theories of tragedy that revolve around the question of genre and attempt to consider the metaphysical and theological implications of tragedy. Tragedy is a form of *praeparatio evangelii*.

Sacrifice in Ancient Greek culture has been the subject of much learned research. This material concentrates upon the evidence we have for the sacrificial ritual practices of the ancient Hellenes.[5] Sacrifice plays an important

1 Aeschylus, *Agamemnon, Libation-Bearers, Eumenides, Fragments* with an English translation by Herbert Weir Smith. Cambridge, MA: Harvard, 2006.
2 Benjamin, W. (1978) *Ursprung des deutschen Trauerspiels*. Frankfurt: Surkamp, p. 87.
3 Chaucer. (1987) *The Monk's Prologue*, II, 1–102, *The Riverside Chaucer*. Oxford, Oxford University Press, p. 240.
4 Shakespeare, W. (1965) *King Lear*, 5.3, in *William Shakespeare, The Complete Works*, W. J. Craig (ed.). London: Oxford, p. 939.
5 Buxton, R. (2001) *Oxford Readings in Greek Religion*. Oxford: Clarendon.

role in a seminal form of Attic art: tragedy. Much of ancient Greek tragedy is an exercise in sacrifice imagined.[6] Goethe wrote of Catharsis:

> Within tragedy catharsis occurs through a form of human sacrifice, which may actually occur or through a benevolent deity be replaced by a surrogate, as in the case of Abraham or Agamemnon.[7]

Agamemnon is killed in a bathtub referred to in explicitly sacrificial terms as a λέβης, the sacrificial libation bowl.[8] This usage seems to be a *hapax legomenon*: the sacrificial allusions in Clytemnestra's murder of her husband could hardly be clearer. Girard and Burkert, in their different ways, tend to assimilate the discussion of Greek tragedy to the sacrificial ritual. The imaginative use of sacrificial myths in tragedy provides a rather distinct terrain for the playwright to explore. The beseeching Iphigenia of Aeschylus's *Agamemnon* is different from the heroine of Euripides's *Iphigenia in Aulis*. A playwright like Euripides can use the sacrificial myths to underline imaginatively the contrast between the martyr Iphigenia and the feckless Helen. The reliance of sacrifice in myth, rather than any focus upon the contemporary ritual practice, is key. Yet human sacrifice was still practiced until the decree of the emperor Hadrian (e.g. before the Battle of Salamis in 480 BC), and the avoidance of explicit violence on the tragic stage may well reflect persisting taboos and anxieties about human sacrifice in Greek society. The sense that a tragic hero could suffer and bear the burden of some terrible guilt has obvious sacrificial connotations. This seems to be Goethe's point when he notes that tragedy is a form of human sacrifice.[9]

Notwithstanding the imaginative potential of tragic drama for the exploration of human personality, the weirdness of the Attic genre of tragedy invites explanation. How did the risible "goat song" with satyrs, a part of the cult of Dionysus, perhaps originally some ancient Hellenic analogue to the drink-fueled abandon of the contemporary discotheque, become such a paradigm of artistic sublimity in Western culture? Some cultures do not possess this genre — the Muslim world, for example. But the tragic continues to exert a hold on contemporaries in a way that the epic, for example, does not. Why then does tragedy — such an odd genre and stuff of gloom — have such appeal to the occidental mind?

It cannot be beauty in any obvious sense. Even though the violence of Attic tragedy is offstage, it is hardly the stuff of beauty. But nor is the

---

6   Eagleton, Terry. (2003) *Sweet Violence: The Idea of the Tragic*. Oxford: Blackwell, pp. 274ff on radical critiques of tragedy as sacrifice for combining a "whiff of barbarism" with "self abnegation."

7   "In der Tragodie geschieht sie (die Katharsis) durch eine Art Menschenopfer, es mag nun wirklich vollbracht oder unter Einwirkung einer gunstigen Gottheit durch ein Surrogat geloest werden, wie im Falle Abrahams und Agamemnons." Goethe. (1827) "Nachlese zu Aristoteles Poetik," *Sammtliche Werke* (Weimarer Ausgabe), 41, 2, p. 248.

8   Foley, H. P. (1985) *Ritual Irony: Poetry and Sacrifice in Euripides*. Ithaca, NY: Cornell, p. 285ff.

9   See also Freud's remarks in *Totem and Taboo* Strachey (trans.). London: Routledge, 1961), p. 156.

satisfaction of tragedy to be found in some dark sadistic phantasies about killing or maiming. Or — perhaps less dramatically — the thrill of a horror film. The answer lies, as Schopenhauer argues, in the sublimity of tragedy.[10] In ancient tragedy this sublimity is often linked to the language of sacrifice. I wish to suggest that this link with sacrifice is important. Tragedy, through its use of the theme of sacrifice, holds together both the violence and the hope for resolution or salvation. In this I agree with Girard that sacrifice is a clue to the significance of tragedy, but I disagree with his own explanation. Nor do I find the view that tragedy appeals because the human mind requires sufficient distraction from homely comforts and the dullness of quotidian human life. The horror film suffices for that! Tragedy's special dignity in the Western canon may be explained by the fact that in tragedy we have a representation of the human mind or spirit in a form or genre that either consciously or unconsciously has its roots in sacrifice. It is a spectacle of sacred sacrifice sublimated in and through human agents in an agonistic world and divided society. By sacrifice I mean the ritual attempt to "make holy" through an offering to the deity.

Why all accounts of tragedy are speculative

Some distinguished philologists, most notably Wilamowitz but also more recent representatives, are scathing about speculative accounts of tragedy.[11] Yet in a sense, the speculative dimension is unavoidable. Tragedy, unlike philosophy, is an Athenian invention. Over 2,500 years ago, in 534 BC, Peisistratos inaugurated the first tragedy competition in Athens. It was exported to other cities, but we are dealing with an Athenian genre. We cannot be sure about the original performances, but at least from 510 BC onward each year three poets were offering either a trilogy or a tetralogy in competition for the prize within the parameters of the Great Dionysia. The initial form of tragedy as developed by Thespis consisted of music, dance, and a dialogue between a singing chorus and a speaking actor (*hypocrites*). The action or drama was generated through the interaction of chorus and actor. Gradually, Aeschylus and Sophocles added more actors. Since the festival was of Dionysus and one of the earliest mentioned titles of a tragedy was *Pentheus*, we can assume the strong influence of the cult of Dionysus upon the art form.[12]

The competition began in 534 BC and lasted until 404 BC. We only possess a tiny fraction of the plays presented, and we only possess one entire trilogy: the *Oresteia* of Aeschylus. Moreover, those that were preserved are the

10 Schopenhauer. (1969) *The World as Will and Representation*, E. F. J. Payne (trans.). New York: Dover, 1, pp. 203–4.
11 Gründer, Karlfried (ed.). *Der Streit um Nietzsches "Geburt der Tragödie"': Die Schriften von E. Rohde, R. Wagner, and U. von Wilamowitz-Möllendorff*. Hildesheim: Georg Olms.
12 Latacz, Joachim. (1994) "Fruchtbares Agernis: Nietzsches Geburt der Tragoedie und die graezistishce Trageoedienforschung," in J. Latacz (ed.), *Erschliessung der Antike: Kleine Schriften zur Literatur der Griechen und Romer.* Teubner: Stuttgart, pp. 469–98.

product of pedagogical considerations of which we are largely ignorant. Why were some plays of Aeschylus or Sophocles preserved? Moreover, the fact that we are almost entirely ignorant of the musical and choreographical dimensions of tragedy adds to the malaise.

The name is puzzling. τράγος is transparent to a Greek. It is not a name of alien provenance (*Iambos, Elegeia*) or just innocuous (like *epos*, word). Thus it is bizarre that the rather severe and stately grandeur of Aeschylus might be deemed *(τραγῳδικός) tragodikos* when tragedy. *(τραγῳδία) after all*, has the ridiculous connotations of the goat song.[13] Indeed, we know from grotesque phallic forms on vases that the cult of Dionysus was rather undignified — if not unsightly. This is one reason why Nietzsche's attempt to understand the Dionysiac in tragedy as more than an accidental genetic feature is compelling.

Hume and the problem of imaginative resistance

Consider one major unsolved problem in the literature since Plato's *The Republic*. Why should grisly tales of mythic figures still afford respectable pleasure? The gladiators doubtless provided pleasure in the Colosseum, but that is now shocking; perhaps as the Spaniard's delight in the bullfight is for the Englishman. The Anglo-Saxon debate about tragedy is often concerned with the question of "imaginative resistance." It was Hume who raised the problem of the limits of moral imaginings. Since tragedy is violent and often depicts wanton and terrifying cruelty, how can it afford aesthetic pleasure?

> Whatever speculative errors may be found in the polite writings of any age or country, they detract but little from the value of these compositions. There needs but a certain turn of thought or imagination to make us enter into all the opinions which then prevailed, and relish the sentiments or conclusions derived from them. But a very violent effort is requisite to change our judgement of manners, and excite sentiments of approbation or blame, love or hatred, different from those to which the mind, from long custom, has been familiarized. And where a man is confident of the rectitude of that moral standard by which he judges, he is justly jealous of it, and will not pervert the sentiments of his heart for a moment, in complaisance to any writer whatsoever.[14]

Hume is claiming that the moral imagination has definite limits. Whereas the reader of fiction may imagine most improbable states, it is much more difficult to entertain vastly different ideals of "morality and decency," and, indeed, it should be such. On this account, imagining immorality seems to

---

13 See Horace, *De Arte Poetica*, 220. See *Classical Literary Criticism*, D.A. Russell and M. Winterbottom (eds.). Oxford: Oxford University Press (1989), p. 103.
14 Hume, David. (1998) "On the standard of taste," in Stephen Copley and Andrew Edgar (eds.), *Selected Essays*. Oxford: Oxford University Press, p. 152.

be complicit with it. Hume had a very positive idea of humanity and little sense of the cruel depths of human agents. I suspect that in Hume's case we have a characteristically Enlightenment optimism about human nature. Kendall Walton has reinforced this line of thought:

> Can an author simply stipulate in the text of a story what moral prin-
> ciples apply in the fictional world, just as she specifies what actions
> characters perform? If the text includes the sentence, "in killing her baby,
> Giselda did the right thing; after all, it was a girl" or "The village elders
> did their duty before God by forcing the widow onto her husband's
> funeral pyre," are readers obliged to accept it as fictional that, in doing
> what they did, Giselda or the elders behaved in morally proper ways?
> Why shouldn't storytellers be allowed to experiment explicitly with
> worlds of morally different kinds, including ones they regard as morally
> obnoxious? There is science fiction; why not morality fiction?[15]

Walton, in fact, strenuously denies that we can enjoy "morality fiction." His argument relies upon the thought that moral properties supervene upon natural properties and thus it is impossible imaginatively to engage in some reprehensible morality. Walton is assuming the widespread distinction between facts and values and that moral values are dependent upon the preexisting facts, or, in the technical terminology, they relate to facts through supervenience. Such a theory assumes a moderate physicalism. There are no queer facts in ethics, but merely the emotions that we project onto the world.

Walton's underlying theory, as developed in *Mimesis as Make-Believe* in which he develops his theory of representational art, is based upon considerations about the extraordinary imaginative capacities of the young — especially the vivid make-believe strategies of small children.[16] Just as children can pretend that a tree stump is a bear with the parameters of a specific game of make-believe, a play in the theater is also a concerted effort and exercise in make-believe where spectators are encouraged to imagine a different world through the help of various props that aid the imaginative engagement. The thought is that although we possess this remarkable capacity to entertain sophisticated realms of counterfactual make-believe, we cannot so readily endorse widely differing moral schemes. Presumably this is because our attitudes that we spread onto the world have a limited range. New discoveries in physics or chemistry may reveal radical new worlds in front of our eyes, but we are unlikely to discover new values in our hearts.

One can almost imagine Hume using similar examples to Walton — drawn perhaps from the reports of the East India Company, since he is employing the same underlying model of ethics as spreading certain emotions of approbation and disapprobation onto the world of agents and

---

15   Walton, Kendall. (1994) "Morals in fiction and fictional morality I." *Proceedings of the
      Aristotelian Society*, Suppl. 68: 37.
16   Walton, Kendall. (1990) *Mimesis as Make-Believe: On the Foundations of the Representational
      Arts.* Cambridge, MA: Harvard University Press. See my remarks in *Living Forms of the
      Imagination*, pp. 176–8.

events. Walton seems to be assuming the liberal moral stance of the North American intellectual. Michael Tanner makes this point:

> Hume took it that there was a set of civilised values which everyone whom one could take seriously, not regarding them as barbarians or monkish, hare-brained fanatics, shares. And this set of values concerned not only the most basic matters . . . but also the overall way in which educated, rational, polite and elegant gentlemen would conduct themselves.[17]

Michael Tanner sees Walton as "living in a time warp,"[18] assuming a similar universalism to Hume. Tanner has Nietzschean reasons for objecting to Hume or Walton's ethicism.

Some philosophers criticize Walton for failing to distinguish between being unable and being unwilling to entertain morally repugnant worlds. Walton's examples are fairly uncontroversial: slavery and murder. Yet perhaps we are blind to the barbarism of our own age: the ecological disaster, the cruelty of modern warfare with encroachments upon civilians, the carnage on the roads. But the problem to me seems to reside in the failure to recognize the darker dimension of the human psyche. Hume asks:

> Would any man, who is walking along, tread as willingly on another's gouty toes, whom he has no quarrel with, as on the hard flint and pavement?[19]

Hume's example of the willful treading on the gouty toe seems a rather temperate and mild form of wickedness compared with the rank slaughterhouse of archetypal Attic drama and Hellenic mythology. Children's play, which Walton uses as the foundation of his aesthetic theory, often contains aggressive elements. Fairy tales notoriously contain grotesque violence and cruelty in the witches and monsters. Contrary to those philosophers obsessed with imaginative resistance, that tragedy shows the ease with which the audience can sympathize with the dark and irrational dimensions of human character: not merely aggression in a biological sense but also pointless and malevolent violence.

Schopenhauer's theory: art, metaphysics, and the ethics of renunciation

Philosophical natures even have a presentiment that hidden beneath the reality in which we live and have our being there also lie a second, quite

---

17 Tanner, M. (1994) *Morals in Fiction and Fictional Morality; Proceedings of the Aristotelian Society*, 68, pp. 51–66.
18 Tanner, M. *Morals in Fiction*, p 53.
19 Hume, D. (1979) *Enquiry Concerning Principle of Morals*. Oxford: Clarendon, p. 226.

different reality; in other words, this reality too is a semblance. Indeed Schopenhauer actually states that the mark of a person's capacity for philosophy is the gift for feeling occasionally as if people and all things were mere phantoms and dream images.[20]

Let us turn from an empiricist to a Neoplatonic theory of aesthetics. It is often remarked that the Neoplatonic idea of aesthetic beauty as an intimation of spiritual or intelligible beauty is simply incredible for the modern mind. Yet is rarely noted that one of the greatest periods of philosophical aesthetics in the modern period, the post-Kantians or German idealism, was in fact a period of the revival of just this idea. It is found not merely in Germany but also in Shelley's "Hymn to Intellectual Beauty": "The awful shadow of some unseen Power." That means that the poet can exclaim:

> Spirit of Beauty, that dost consecrate
> With thine own hues all thou dost shine upon.[21]

Tragedy was of great interest to the post-Kantian philosophers because it seems to express the tension between status of mind/subjectivity and the interpretation of world that pre-occupied the German idealists. Oedipus or Antigone become expressions of dreadful failures of mediation between self and world: issuing in the madness of the protagonists. Hegel views aesthetics as *"durchscheinen der Idee"* — that is, art points beyond itself to the intelligible and the sacred.[22] Hegel sees a theological dimension within the tragic in terms of the resolution of conflicts, which are essentially philosophical. Tragedy arises out of the conflict of equally valid claims. Famously he takes the *Antigone* of Sophocles as the paradigm of this conflict; the struggle between Creon and Antigone stands for those of the state and the family respectively. Unlike Aristotle and many critics in the Classical tradition, tragedy is not defined by formal criteria, but because of its disclosure of certain ontological facts. Schopenhauer and Nietzsche agree with Hegel that tragedy should be defined in terms of ontology, but, of course, disagree on how that should be construed.

Tragedy is a key point in his aesthetics. Schopenhauer, on the contrary, is an instance of ambitious metaphysical construction in which the tragic plays a very important role. Unlike the neoclassical approaches to tragedy, which tend to emphasize its morally edifying nature, Schopenhauer's view of art is robustly metaphysical. Like Plato and Kant, Schopenhauer distinguishes between the noumenal and phenomenal realms, but with a different estimation of the former.[23] The former is not, as it is explicitly for Plato and implicitly for Kant, a superior realm. What Schopenhauer,

20   Nietzsche. (2008) *Birth of Tragedy*, Raymond Geuss and Ronald Speiers (eds.). Cambridge: Cambridge University Press, p. 15.
21   Shelley (1988) *Poems*, Isabel Quigly (ed.). Harmondsworth: Penguin, p. 71.
22   Bungay, Stephen. (1984) *Beauty and Truth: A Study of Hegel's Aesthetics*. Oxford: Clarendon.
23   Magee, Brian. (1983) *The Philosophy of Schopenhauer*, Oxford: Oxford University Press, pp. 48–104.

perhaps infelicitously, designates "will" is in fact impersonal and utterly irrational. The Idea of Poetry is of "man in the connected series of his efforts and actions." Here the "Wille" is most transparent. Tragedy is "the summit of poetic art." In depicting "the terrible side of life . . . the unspeakable pain, the wretchedness and misery of mankind, the triumph of wickedness, the scornful mastery of chance, and the irretrievable fall of the just and the innocent, the "antagonism of will with itself,"[24] "chance and error" are the rulers of the world. For Schopenhauer the basis of ethics lies in the intuitive grasp of a common humanity and the renunciation of the relentless and rapacious will that drives and reinforces suffering and misery in the world. Schopenhauer's ethics, though based upon an utter rejection of the Christian metaphysic of Divine goodness and Providence, shares the Christian ethical interest in pity and sympathy. Hence the untranslatable words at the beginning of Wagner's *Tristan und Isolde*:

> *Wehe, wehe, du Wind! —*
> *Weh, ach wehe, mein Kind!*
> (Blow, oh thou the Wind!
> Woe, ah woe, my Child!)[25]

The value of tragedy for Schopenhauer is primarily cognitive. It gives us an insight into reality beyond the maya of mere representation. That becomes more potent in a world that is flooded by anodyne images. Why do we enjoy tragedy? Why does watching something sad give us pleasure? Because we are sadists? No! It provides insight, we might say, with Girard, into a violent world. I think Schopenhauer's thesis has some attractive features, even though I do not wish to uphold it in its entirety. It is a vehicle of insight into reality, even into what Schopenhauer calls the "crime of existence." If correct, this Neoplatonic view of art as an organon of truth, upheld by Schelling, Hegel, and Schopenhauer, must have application to an art form like tragedy. The insight yields satisfaction because we recognize its truth. Mothers kill children; sons and daughters kill fathers and mothers. It is a familiar truth that much violence and cruelty, rape, and abuse is perpetrated by family members, not by strangers. One reads of such violent and anarchic deeds in newspapers, and psychoanalysis has made the prevalence of violence fantasies towards family members rather familiar.

The sublime mood, suffering, and the sense of the sacred

With its elements of archaic ritual and grand poetry, tragedy communicates sublimity. Schopenhauer calls Kant's analysis of the sublime: "By far the most excellent thing in the Critique of Aesthetic Judgement [. . .] It is incomparably more successful than that of the beautiful."[26] Moreover, he states:

24 Schopenhauer, *World as Will and Representation*, 1, pp. 252–3.
25 *Tristan*, Act 1, Scene 2.
26 Schopenhauer, *World as Will*, 1.532.

[W]ith the sublime, that state of pure knowing is obtained first of all by a conscious and violent tearing away from the relations of the same object to the will which are recognized as unfavourable by a free exaltation, accompanied by consciousness, beyond the will and the knowledge related to it.[27]

On Schopenhauer's theory, there is a reduction of the empirical dimension of the self to a detached subjectivity. Through the sublime, an agent can have disinterested pleasure in the dreadful or the terrifying. Thus there is a double sense in the spectator of the sublime:

Simultaneously he feels himself as individual, as the feeble phenomenon of the will, which the slightest touch of these forces can annihilate, helpless against powerful nature, dependent, abandoned to chance, a vanishing nothing in face of stupendous forces; and he also feels himself as the eternal, serene subject of knowing, who as the condition of every object is the supporter of the whole world ... This is the full impression of the sublime. Here it is caused by the sight of a power beyond all comparison superior to the individual, and threatening him with annihilation.[28]

Here we see Schopenhauer's anthropology — the view of the subject wavering between knowledge and volition: whereas beauty offers concord and equanimity, the sublime reinforces the gulf between volition and contemplation. This is the key to why "our pleasure in the tragedy belongs not to the feeling of the beautiful, but to that of the sublime; it is in fact the highest degree of this feeling".[29] Tragedy is not beautiful to behold but sublime. Tragedy changes our mood (*uns so umstimmt*).

Yet what is unsatisfactory in Schopenhauer's account is why we might find the truths that he perceives as central to the tragic vision as sublime. Tragedy, on his account, merely confirms the ghastliness of existence. The centrality of sacrifice confirms an element within classical tragedy that is linked, however obscurely, to the making sacred of sacrifice. What is required is both a sense of the dark and violent dimension of human existence and the redemptive hope that sacrifice points to. It is this religious — sacrificial — dimension to tragedy that is highlighted by Schopenhauer's pupils: Wagner and Nietzsche.

Wagner's drama

Roger Scruton, in his *Death-Devoted Heart: Sex and the Sacred in Wagner's Tristan and Isolde*, develops a theory of Wagner's work that revolves around the sacrificial. Scruton concentrates upon the themes of erotic love and

27 Schopenhauer, *World as Will*, 1, p. 202.
28 Schopenhauer, *World as Will and Representation*, 2, pp. 204–5.
29 Schopenhauer, *World as Will and Representation*, 2, pp. 433.

redemption and presents a compelling case for the persisting relevance and power of Wagner's artistic vision, as the expression of the need for art to give expression to the sacred and the transcendent. In particular, Scruton sees the Kantian legacy as central for understanding Wagner's view of human beings as creatures who can be seen from two perspectives, an objective and a subjective — as items in the physical world subject to its laws and as free, rational agents. Scruton is correct to place Wagner within this broad post-Kantian context, even if he exaggerates the specifically Kantian element.

By the time of Wagner, the epic poem was obsolete and tragic drama, notwithstanding Goethe's much admired *Faust*, rarely attained the heights of the Attic or Elizabethan forms. In the Romantic age, the novel was considered, unfairly I think, in rather condescending terms as a vastly inferior genre to the great art forms such as epic poetry or tragic drama. The novel was presented as a rather domestic and feminine genre, a form of sublimated gossip as opposed to the virile and heroic dramas of epic and tragedy. Goethe made his name with a novel in his *Sturm und Drang* period, but his literary career culminated in the tragic drama of *Faust*. All the great English Romantics attempted a drama. It was seen as the appropriate vehicle for the more sublime themes of art. Perhaps it was not until later in the nineteenth century that the novel became a vehicle of really tragic status: George Eliot, Melville, or Hardy. In Melville, the themes of hubris and nemesis powerfully pervade his tale of Ahab's pursuit of the great white whale Moby Dick, however far the genre of his novel is from the festival of Dionysus in ancient Athens.

Wagner, especially in his operas from *Tristan und Isolde* onward, represents a remarkable attempt to revive the tragic genre for the contemporary world as *Gesamtkunst*. The world of gods, giants, and dwarfs is a consciously mythological universe. He conceived these as dramas rather than operas. The music serves the words and actions; the orchestra is seen as playing the role of the chorus (opera and drama); and his vision of a tetralogy at a *Festspielhaus* is modeled on the antique paradigms. His *Ring Cycle* is an instance of German Hellenism linked to German nationalism, but its Hellenism is genuine and fairly thorough. Wagner could read Greek and translated passages of Sophocles as a young man. Indeed, he even considered becoming a *Gräzist*! When he developed an enthusiasm for Aeschylus he looked at the original even if he worked primarily with a translation. Hellenism was important for his purposes since the Nordic myths, which Wagner had dug out of Grimm and Icelandic sources, were largely unfamiliar to his German audiences; whereas they would have been deeply familiar with the Greek gods. Hence the jealousy of Fricka to Wotan could be intelligible as akin to that of Hera's towards Zeus.

Wagner was deeply indebted to Schopenhauer, although his vision differs on certain central points. *Tristan und Isolde* could hardly have been composed by a man dedicated to Schopenhauer's doctrine of renunciation. For Wagner, salvation is to be achieved through love, even if erotic love is for Schopenhauer contaminated by its primordial link to *Wille*. Wagner is drawing upon a tradition of thought about the transforming power of love that has its roots in Plato's *Symposium* through Dante's *Vita Nuova*, the courtly love tradition, up to the Romantics. The vision of power without love wreaking destruction in the Ring Cycle is rather different from Schopenhauer's equally gloomy metaphysic, and closer to Christianity.

Scruton is right, I think, to view Wagner's own ambivalent and possibly incoherent attitude to Christianity as irrelevant. Wagner's oeuvre shows how powerfully certain mythic and Christian themes — the sacred, desacralizing, and making sacred or redemption — resound in the contemporary imagination.

Myth, fantasy, and imagination

The great instrument of the moral good is the imagination . . . poetry strengthens the faculty which is the organ of the moral nature of man.[30]

Hitherto we have looked at various metaphysical theories of tragedy. Armed with some of these ideas, let us now consider the metaphysical question, "what do we mean by the tragic?" Do we mean the kind of evil or disaster that can thwart human purposes that we see in Aeschylus, Racine, or Shakespeare? These are compatible with a Christian or Platonic affirmation of the ultimate goodness of the universe. Or do we mean ultimate, eternal, failure, and an absolutely unredeemable corruption of the good?[31] As Brian Hebblethwaite asks, are "these failures, tragedies and horrors ultimate, irredeemable facts . . .?"[32] Such a view is incompatible with Christianity, or, indeed, pagan Platonism. Of course, if tragedy is meant to reconcile us to the sufferings of others, then the outrage is justified. The theological interest in tragedy has its source in the proximity of the genre to theological questions. If I am correct to think that tragedy is essentially religious — as Wagner and Nietzsche observed — then theologians should reflect upon the persisting power of tragedy.

Wagner inherited the Romantic reappraisal of myth and his great operas use myth. Nietzsche argues in *The Birth of Tragedy* that "the demise of tragedy was at the same time the demise of myth"[33] — the thesis that Socratic rationalism was the death of tragedy. It is completely intelligible that tragedy emerged in a period of transition from tyranny to democracy. The Acropolis was the dwelling place of the tyrant, who was replaced by the gods. The age of Attic tragedy was a period of immense social and political transition culminating in the collapse of the Peloponnesian War. It is perhaps unsurprising that this period was one of reflection upon ancient

30 Shelley, *A Defense of Poetry*, ed. Cooke, p. 14.
31 Hebblethwaite, Brian. (1989) "Mackinnon and the problem of evil," in Kenneth Surin (ed.), *Christ, Ethics and Tragedy : Essays in Honour of Donald Mackinnon*. Cambridge: Cambridge University Press, p. 140.
32 Hebblethwaite, "Mackinnon and the problem of evil," p. 142.
33 Nietzsche. (1999) *The Birth of Tragedy and other Writings by Friedrich Nietzsche*, Raymond Geuss and Ronald Spiers (eds.). Cambridge: Cambridge University Press.

bonds and their erosion through reforms.

One of the reasons why sacrifice is so prevalent in ancient tragedy is because of the mythic-archaic material that the genre explores.[34] The eating of the children of Thyestes, the sacrifice of Iphigenia, the murder of Agamemnon, and Orestes's revenge are all presented as ritual killings. (It is probably an error to assume that the mythology precluded any innovation in storytelling — there were different versions of the same myths, the fate of Iphigenia being an obvious instance.) The gloom and foreboding of the tragedy are enhanced by the sense of this string of failed sacrifices. Rather than making sacred, these are sacrilegious acts, compounding violence and anarchy rather than redeeming it. Yet tragedy can be the revelation of paradise lost or obscured. It points to what could have been for Othello and Desdemona, or Brutus, and with that sense of what might have been, we can imagine how life ought to be structured and lived. The violence against a particular order, which is the common theme of many great tragedies, reinforces the very power of the ideal lost. Without the normative, tragic evil descends into meaningless chaos.

Here, I think, is the answer to the question of tragedy. Its nature is religious and this accounts for the prevalence of the imagery of sacrifice in Attic tragedy. Tragedy has its roots in sacral rites of the cult of Dionysus, but we know so little of the earliest phase that we can only conjecture about these roots. In its developed form in Aeschylus, Sophocles, and Euripides it explores the conflict between human instincts and desires and the non-chosen sacral bonds, obligations, or taboos (e.g. those of piety, kin, or death) and the costliness of the conflict with these bonds. Even if the ritual sacrificial roots have been obscured, the imagery of sacrifice remains in the transposition of the myth. Thus I think MacKinnon was correct to insist that tragedy poses a problem for naturalism. Any philosophy that attempts to explain human agency from a purely "natural" perspective — that is, solely from the viewpoint of the natural sciences — has problems with the unconditional and normative nature of the ethical. To take an extreme example, consider the following claim: "We are survival machines — robot vehicles blindly programmed to preserve the selfish molecules known as genes."[35] No philosophy based upon this account of human behavior can do justice to unconditional force of certain moral claims from "the inside." Unless Antigone feels the unconditional force of the normative demand to bury her brother, or Othello is aware that his punishment for the murder of Desdemona is hell, the respective tragedies do not function properly. Tragedy presents ethical decisions as inextricably linked to ideas of defilement and pollution. Orestes is chased by the hideous furies despite being commanded by Apollo to revenge his father. This is not just the problem of the double bind, a dilemma that cannot be satisfactorily resolved without choosing an option that will inflict pain and suffering — hence a dilemma for a Utilitarian. But the action invariably causes desecration. Matricide,

---

34 Through myth we are confronted with a narrative of violence. So far Girard is correct. But the violence is sometimes quite indiscriminate. It is not merely victim-directed.
35 Dawkins, Richard. (1976) *The Selfish Gene*. Oxford: Oxford University Press, p. x.

however justifiable in Orestes's position, pollutes him. Incest, however guiltless in the case of Oedipus, still defiles the perpetrator. Despite a tradition of the Christian rejection of the genre, we have instances of writers like Clement of Alexandria who was interested in the tragic; and in the Reformation period we have Jesuit and Lutheran tragedies. Perhaps it is particularly important for Christianity to envisage the tragic because of the narrative passion of Christ and the martyrs of the early Church, and subsequent theological accounts of suffering. If the religious — as opposed to the neoclassical — interpretation of tragedy is correct, then this explains the virulence of the theological critique of tragedy. Tragedy is a near neighbor of theology. MacKinnon thinks that a proper respect for the irreducibility of the tragic inhibits ambitious metaphysical construction.[36] He was wrong to speak of the ineradicability of the tragic, but quite correct to uphold its vital significance for Christian theology.

Let us return to one of our initial questions: why should we gain pleasure from it? Plato was very sensitive to the way in which tragedy draws upon the dark dimension of the human soul and saw this as a reason to ban it. Aristotle's theory that the emotions can be purged by tragedy is obviously an attempt, contra Plato, to explain why the polis can keep tragedy. Yet perhaps purging is the wrong model. Perhaps, following Jung, insight and integration are better. In the presentation of violence we are confronted, in a controlled, artificial manner, with the reality of existence. Tragedy can confront an audience with the shadow of the human psyche. The cruelty, gloom, and fear of tragedy do consist of alien external objects — for example, the fantastical terrors of the horror film — but also in the imaginative exploration of the dark dimension of the psyche in action, its turmoils and travails. If it is correct that much of the life of the psyche is submerged and internalized conflict, the view of the rational decision maker of much philosophical debate is necessarily only a partial description. The conscious ego is continually encountering projections and patterns, and unconsciously employing defense mechanisms that derive their structure from early childhood. Just as dreams can provide a release and expression of some of these submerged conflicts and internalized motives, so too drama can express the submerged dimensions of the psyche, especially those linked to sex and aggression.

Is tragedy dark fantasy or a sentimental and reality-denying consolation? Drama can ease inner conflicts by articulating them. It might be an instrument of projection, whereby vice becomes a merely external phenomenon, but powerful drama must relate to elements in the psyche that the audience can identify with. Agamemnon's unscrupulous ambition or Clytemnestra's desire for revenge can be readily understood as a part of our own makeup and we can imagine following their paths, and sufferings. In Orestes we can sense the ambivalence of many ethical decisions. He is called by Apollo to revenge his father and yet recognizes the horror of matricide. Thus drama can be a valuable mirror of inner problems and tensions. As Westcott observes, Aeschylus "looks beneath the manifold to the

36   Mackinnon, D. (1974) *The Problem of Metaphysics*. Cambridge: Cambridge University Press, p. 145.

one: he translates, unconsciously it may be, the symbol into the lesson."[37]

It is valid to use the distinction often misleadingly attributed to Coleridge — namely, the distinction between imagination and fantasy. (His was actually one of two forms of imagination: primary and secondary, and "fancy".) Fantasy, let us say, for example, the horror film or pornography, is the gratification of these deep instincts of violence and lust, and thus can reinforce the sterile preoccupations of the vulnerable and destructive ego. Imagination, by way of contrast, can be part of a healing and a reordering process. In that sense, imagination can be a means to attaining wholeness. Westcott again:

> The visible to the Christian eye is in every part a revelation of the invisible. The artist, like the poet sees the infinite in things, and under the conditions of his works, suggests it. He has, as it were to enter with the veil, and coming forth again to declare his heavenly visions to men. He is not a mirror but a prophet.[38]

For the theist, values are imperishable realities in the mind of God. Aristotle's account of catharsis as purging of emotion suggests a selfish benefit from the spectacle of tragedy, a transient relief from the tensions of living. Yet perhaps it is the representation of a law of being; temporal goods can perish or be transformed into another state. It represents not only many of the fearful aspects of violence, cruelty, pain, and loss, but also the purging and transforming potential of the spirit. Aeschylus or Shakespeare, for all their severity and grandeur, are more uplifting than the witty and elegant ennui of a Noel Coward farce. The chorus of Aeschylus, "Sing the song of woe, the song of woe, but may the good prevail," expresses the baffling conflict between eternal values and very earthly forces. It is true that Aeschylus is far from any romantization of suffering. His is not the testing of Job; nor do we find the suffering of Goethe's young Werther. The suffering is the brutal punishment inflicted by the gods upon those who disregard *dike* and *sophronsune*. This is not a providential order in the Christian sense, but equally it is far from either the utilitarian claim that experience will teach the fool (*eventus magister stultorum*) or the quasi-existential view that the human agent as subject can only appreciate certain facts through suffering. The claim of Aeschylus is that the highest power will instruct humans through suffering "*dass eine höchste Macht den Menschen durch Leiden etwas lehren will.*"[39]

Aristotle, hardly the most poetic of philosophers, argued that poetry and philosophy possess a deep kinship. This is because, according to Aristotle, great poetry deals with great human challenges and dilemmas. Thus, it

37 Westcott, B. F. (1891) *Essays in the History of Religious Thought in the West*. London; New York: Macmillan, p. 66.
38 Westcott, *Essays in the History of Religious Thought in the West*, p. 334.
39 Dörrie, Henrich. (1956) "That a highest power wishes to teach mankind through suffering." *Leid und Erfahrung: Die Wort und Sinn-Verbindung.* Παφεῖν μαφεῖν. *im griechischen Denken, Akademie der Wissenschaften unter der Literatur, Abhandlung der Geistes und Sozialwissenschaftlichen Klasse*, 5: 1–41, 36.

is within the ancient Greek tradition that the plots of comedy, relatively trivial matters, or topics of import ironized, can be created by the invention of the dramatist. However, the subject matter of tragedy, always a topic of deep significance, is provided by familiar myths. The poet gives such familiar universal topics and themes particularity. In a related, though more consciously Neoplatonic, mode (as discussed extensively in Chapter One), the great bard says that the

> lunatic, the lover and the poet are of imagination all compact . . . the poet's eye, in fine frenzy rolling, doth glance from heaven to earth, from earth to heaven; and as imagination bodies forth the forms of things unknown, the poet's pen turns them to shapes, and gives to airy nothing a local habitation and a name.[40]

Here is a theory of poetry as providing knowledge.[41] Certain the power of the greatest poems, such as *The Divine Comedy* and *Paradise Lost* or *The Prelude*, rests upon a substrate of philosophical ideas.

One of the perplexing questions in contemporary culture consists in the nature of art. As a result of Romanticism in the West, art has gained a rank and status that is remarkable, particularly "beaux arts" or "die schöne Künste." But with the increased status of the artist it has become increasingly mysterious what his/her proper task should be. The artist is a mirror of society. As self-conscious and expressive animals (self-understanding creatures in Charles Taylor's fine phrase) the great task of art is communication. This is not to claim that the artist is necessarily a great philosopher. But the artist is capable of an attunement and imaginative engagement with the environment. This may be merely descriptive: the artist may, like T. S. Eliot in *The Waste Land*, give expression to widely held mood of decay or anxiety. But the great artist is also capable of a prescriptive element, a vision by which the artist can comment upon the world observed. The great artist perceives the infinite in the finite. On the basis of the theophanic imagination, I would want to hold to some version of ethicism, albeit not in the version upheld by Walton. Great art does inspire and transform, whereas amusement, trivial or vicious, merely distracts — or worse, depletes and corrupts the soul.

Girard versus Nietzsche

Nietzsche is important. His thought is the narrative through which Darwin becomes transformed into a moral and spiritual ideology.[42] For Nietzsche sacrifice is about violence. And it is wasteful. Girard is quite correct to place Nietzsche closer to fascists than to his left-wing adherents in postwar France. In *The Will to Power*, Nietzsche writes:

40 Shakespeare, *A Midsummer Night's Dream*, 5.1.7–17.
41 See Hedley, Douglas. (2008) *Living Forms of the Imagination*. London: T&T Clark, p. 162ff.
42 Moore, Greg. (2002) *Nietzsche, Biology and Metaphor*. Cambridge: Cambridge University Press.

> Dionysos versus the "Crucified One:" there you have the opposition. It's not a distinction regarding their martyrdom — just that this martyrdom has different meaning. Life itself, its eternal fruitfulness and recurrence, conditions of torment, destruction, the will to annihilation . . . in the other case suffering, "the Crucified as the innocent," counts as an objection to this life, a formula to condemn it.[43]

One divines that the problem here is that of the meaning of suffering: whether a Christian meaning or a tragic meaning. In the former case it's held to be the path to a blissful existence; in the latter, existence is held to be blissful enough to justify even monstrous suffering: he is strong, full.

> The Christian says No even to the happiest earthly lot: he is weak, poor, disinherited enough to suffer from life in whatever form . . . "the God on the cross" is a curse on life, a hint to deliver oneself from it. Dionysos cut to pieces is a *promise* to life: it will eternally be reborn and come home out of destruction.[44]

The point that Nietzsche is making is that in both cases, the Dionysiac and the Crucified One, we have martyrdom or violent sacrifice. What is different is how they should be interpreted.

For Girard the phenomenon of tragedy is grounded in sacrificial ritual. And here I think he reveals a Romantic obsession — most of the English Romantics tried to write a tragedy. The Augustan age saw tragedy in moralizing quasi-Stoic terms. It was Romanticism that saw tragedy as an essentially religious affair: a shift that leads to Wagner's *Gesammtkunstwerk*. Nietzsche's work on tragedy, dedicated to Wagner, is part of this Romantic context.

Classical philology in the great German tradition saw itself as rooted in Wolf's emancipation of the subject from theology in Halle in 1787. The precocious parson's son, who held a chair before obtaining his doctorate, insisted upon the religious roots of tragedy. His *bête noire* (his Girardian double!) Wilamowitz, notwithstanding the evident jealousy and rivalry born from shared schoolboy days at Pforta, was assuming the role of status of philology as *Wissenschaft*.

Nietzsche's *Birth of Tragedy* is a remarkable document of intuitive genius. Nietzsche was clearly ambivalent about his profession as a philologist and suffered violent attacks from philologists for his intuitive and idiosyncratic understanding of tragedy as arising out of a fusion of the Apollonian and Dionysian dimensions of Attic culture. Wilamowitz poured scorn upon the Apollo-Dionysus contrast as an inane abstraction like Schiller's naïve and sentimental poetry. There is much justice to some of the criticisms of Nietzsche. Most strikingly, Dionysus is not god of music. Yet Nietzche's interest is metaphysical rather than philological-historical:

43 Nietzsche, Friedrich. (2003) *Writings from the Late Notebooks*, Rüdiger Bittner (ed.), Kate Sturge (trans.). *Cambridge Texts in the History of Philosophy*. Cambridge: Cambridge University Press, pp. 249–50 (=KGW 8.3:14[§89]).
44 Nietzsche. (2003) *Writings from the Late Notebooks*, pp. 249–50.

This is the first effect of Dionysiac tragedy: state and society, indeed all divisions between one human being and another, give way to an overwhelming feeling of unity which leads men back to the heart of unity. The metaphysical solace which, I suggest, we derive from every true tragedy, the solace that in the ground of things, and despite all changing appearance, life is indestructibly mighty and pleasurable, this solace appears with palpable clarity in the chorus of the satyrs, a chorus of natural beings whose life goes on ineradicably behind and beyond all civilization, as it were, and who remain eternally the same despite all the changes of generations and in the history of nations.[45]

In *Ecce Homo*, while considering, retrospectively, the distinction he introduced in the earlier text, Nietzsche claims that the discovery of the "amazing phenomenon of the Dionysian" was due to his "own innermost experience." This type expresses an affirmation of life, unlike both the narrow rationalism of the Socratic mind and the Christ type. Nietzsche promulgates the starkest contrast between these two types: the ascetic desire to flee from this world and the affirmation of life, the superman who affirms "a becoming which is actively grasped, subjectively experienced, as a raging voluptuousness of the creative man who also knows the wrath of the destroyer."[46]

Nietzsche writes:

Through Christianity, the individual was made so important, so absolute that he could no longer be sacrificed: but the species endures only through human sacrifice . . . Genuine charity demands sacrifice for the good of the species — it is hard, it is full of self overcoming, because it needs human sacrifice. And this pseudo-humaneness called Christianity wants it established that no one should be sacrificed.[47]

Girard has a deep respect for Nietzsche, first because of his intuition of religion and violence at the heart of culture and that violence illuminating ritual and myth. And his view of the similarity of the deaths of Dionysus and Christ.

Girard views Nietzsche as an antidote to the Jungians who turn myth into the Bible. He shows rather, for Girard, the opposition of Christianity and mythology. If Nietzsche was ambivalent about Christianity at the time of *The Birth of Tragedy*, he was certainly not as hostile as his later retractions suggest. He refers to Luther and the Reformation as an instance of the Dionysiac spirit in Europe. The source of the interest in Dionysus and Christ springs out of Romanticism — in particular the controversial work of neoplatonic mythologisiers: Creuzer and Schelling.

Girard presents an anti-Rousseauistic vision of fallen humanity, like Joseph de Maistre. He presents a vision of the symbolic dimension of

45   Nietzsche, *Birth of Tragedy*, p. 39.
46   Nietzsche, *Writings from the Late Notebooks*, p. 81.
47   Nietzsche, *The Will to Power*, Walter Kaufmann (ed.). New York: Vintage Books, 542–43.

man and society, which means that it cannot be reduced to naturalistic factors favored by the Enlightenment. This is his power. My experience of reading of Girard is that the world looks different after being exposed to his "visionary gleam." Just as the Romantics were terrified by the French revolutionary Terror and the scale and rapacity of Napoleon's ambition and ruthlessness, Girard grew up in Europe ravaged by the General Will to Power that Joseph de Maistre prophesied would emerge out of the Satanic dimension of the French Revolution.

The key to sacrifice is not the scapegoat but, rather, renunciation. The making holy of sacrifice is expressed in the hymn of *Philippians* 2:7 and the kenotic theology therein. Christ is, as *Hebrews* 9.14 puts it, both priest and victim. The point is not that Christianity perceives reality for the first time from the perspective of the victim but that Christians have in Christ not merely a substitute (not I but Christ in me) but also a pattern. This pattern of self-sacrificial love is neither reciprocal altruism nor scapegoating. Not the scapegoat but renunciation is the true sacrifice. It is, incidentally, a dimension of Christian view of life admired by Schopenhauer and Wagner and detested by Nietzsche.

4

Thraldom, License, and Liberty: Sacrificial Renunciation

To do *amiss*, is not *Power* but *Deficiency* and *Deformity*: and infinite power includes not in it a Possibility of Evil.[1]

If ethics is conceived axiologically, sacrifice of immediate interests or goods for the *summum bonum* is a part of the moral life. Any adequate account of morality must be grounded in an anthropology. In this chapter we argue for Origen's/Cudworth's position, *ceteris paribus*, of the hegemonic self as the key to distinctively ethical, as opposed to merely prudential, agency. This has roots in a Platonic conception of ethics as renunciation and a Platonic interiorisation of the tragic. What in tragedy is presented imaginatively and outwardly as the sacrifice of the individual will is paralleled by the philosophers in the abnegation and devotion of the self to the absolute Good. We pursue how Kant, Hegel, and Kierkegaard reflect upon the topic of self-sacrifice as renunciation *and* self-realization.

A. N. Whitehead argued eloquently for the decisive combination of the Platonic concept of the Good and the priority of the soul amidst the flux of existence and the Christian ethics of love as providing a decisive inspiration for European civilization. "In this way," he writes, "Plato is justified in his saying, The creation of the world — that is to say, the world of civilized order — is the victory of persuasion over force."[2] Whitehead sees the great reforming achievements of Western civilization as links to this vision of the lure of the Good over against sub-ethical views of the Divine as a cosmic despot. The great secular reformers of the eighteenth and nineteenth century Bentham and Comte did not seem aware that the benevolence underlying their reforming principles was just as vulnerable to rational attack as any of scholastic theological and metaphysical principles they assumed to be exploded errors. Hume's critique of the soul, and the publication Darwin's *Origin of the Species*, appearing in 1859, seem to dismantle the metaphysical basis of such a project. If nature is pitiless, whence the rational springs of human benevolence? After all, many human societies past and present have no concept of "rights." Do not somber Malthusian doctrines of population fit much better with the biology? The Platonic doctrine of the infinite value of the human soul and the rational status of free agency, as fused with Christian theology, had indeed influenced the great social and political reformers like Wilberforce and Shaftesbury. However,

---

1 Whichcote, B. (1930) *Dr Whichcote's Aphorisms* §13. London: Elkin Mathews & Marrot, p. 2.
2 Whitehead, A. N. (1961) *Adventures of Ideas*. New York: Collier-Macmillan, p. 25.

much a despotic image of the Divine may have persisted throughout the centuries, the dominant model was that the inherited view of the soul as a seat of agency. The Humean Darwinian challenge to the Platonic Christian vision is momentous.

The Christian and the secular ethicist share many common values. This is no accident. Kant's view of the ethical as defined by treating other agents as members of a kingdom of ends is an instance of the transposition of Christian values into a secular framework. Henry More's indefatigable defense of freedom of conscience is another. The genetic origin of many "secular" values in Christian/Hellenic thought is undeniable. Some Christian apologists make the mistake of confusing the genesis of certain beliefs, such as "human rights" and their status. The philosophical question concerns the status of beliefs: why are we entitled to certain values? Christians and agnostics may agree about human "rights" but the Christian can offer a justification for this idea — that is, that mankind is made in the image of God. Both may talk of life as a "gift," but that must be a very weak metaphor for an atheist; whereas for the theist this is a literal truth. What reasons can one give for a rational interest in the moral? Let us bracket the arguments in the social sciences (especially psychology, evolutionary biology, and economics) concerning cost-benefit analysis of action towards others and expense to the agent. The typical arguments about reputational altruism, reciprocal altruism or the hedonistic account of altruism reduce morality to some form of egoism. In this chapter, I wish to suggest that Cudworth's concept of the hegemonical power is still of immense value. On this basis, we can explain altruistic behavior without trying to collapse it into egoism or resorting to theological positivism.

Ralph Cudworth is one of the most significant English philosophers of the seventeenth century. His writings possess less charm than those of Smith and are less speculative than those of More, a group of which John Tulloch wrote:

> In the case of the "Cambridge Platonists," it is eminently true that, with all their faults, philosophy in England never reached a more ideal height — a summit of pure intellectual contemplation than it did with them.[3]

And the Platonists still possess enormous relevance today. They address broader issues about normativity, that domain that the evolutionary-biological and/or neurological social sciences cannot address. Normative issues are linked to subjectivity: they pertain to the first person perspective and the process of giving *reasons* as opposed to causes. Normative questions are irreducibly first person. They concern that what ought to be said, believed, or done cannot be evaded. The world is "fraught with ought," as Sellars famously said. Here, Plato's images of the ship and the charioteer are helpful. The agent is not a passenger on a ship, pushed and shoved by forces of attraction and repulsion. The agent-soul *has* to maneuver the

---

3 Tulloch, John. (1872) *Rational Theology and Christian Philosophy in England in the 17th century*, vol. 1, p. viii.

chariot. Even Freud's famous utterance, *"wo Es war, soll Ich werden"* (what was It (or Id) should become I (or Ego))" suggests that for psychoanalysis the cultivation of a normative subjectivity is prized. The unavoidability of these normative questions leading a life is often associated with ancient philosophy by Pierre Hadot.

Reason and passions

A modern adherent of the Enlightenment tradition, Simon Blackburn, in his book *Ruling Passions*, attacks the rationalist tradition from Plato to Kant. I wish to argue that Maistre's Platonism represents an even more radical version of Blackburn's rationalist target than Kant. My aim is to argue that, far from being an irrationalist, Maistre resembles an extreme instance of rationalism. This, I further claim, can be traced to Maistre's particular devotion to the thought of the great Alexandrian Divine Origen.

Blackburn thinks the problem with the rationalist model of agency lies precisely in placing desires, impulses, and appetites into an asymmetrical relationship with reason. In particular, he concentrates on Kant's idea of the noumenal self by using an analogy of a ship. The image is taken from Plato:

> Conceive this sort of thing happening either on many ships or on one: Picture a shipmaster in height and strength surpassing all others on the ship, but who is slightly deaf and of similarly impaired vision, and whose knowledge of navigation is on a par with his sight and hearing. Conceive the sailors to be wrangling with one another for control of the helm, each claiming that it is his right to steer though he has never learned the art and cannot point to his teacher or any time when he studies it [. . .] they take command of the ship, consume its stores and, drinking and feasting, make such a voyage of it as it expected from such.[4]

Simon Blackburn is a contemporary philosopher who rightly sees ethics as presupposing a particular ideal of human nature and agency. In particular, Blackburn attacks the view implicit in Plato and Kant and radicalized in Maistre, that morality is at war with our passions. Blackburn rather wishes to see morality as the upshot of our passions. Blackburn deploys the Platonic image of the self as a ship from *The Republic* (488a-c). He employs his image to attack a Platonic-Kantian version of the core self as the controlling rational part. This, the "spurious figure of the Kantian captain" according to Blackburn, is a patriarchal authoritarian phantasy. To which he opposes a variant of Hume's bundle — the self as a network of forces, of which reason is only a part. On this model, the crew members correspond to distinct forces within the self, and these forces will come into conflict:

> After one voice has prevailed, various things may happen to the losers: they may be thrown overboard and lost altogether, or more likely they

---

4   Plato. (1987) *The Republic*. 488a–c., D. Lee (trans.). Harmondsworth: Penguin, p. 282.

may remain silenced just for the occasion, or they may remain sullen and mutinous, or they may continue to have at least some affect on the ship's course.[5]

For Blackburn, the image of the ship represents the image of mutual cooperation. Reason is only a part of a web of or network of impulses, desires and values. Its function, for Blackburn, is that of selection of input. Reason is like the lookout situation in the crow's nest that can view and examine the world and then relay the information to the rest of the crew. But reason cannot, nor should, exercise pure hegemony. The input selected by reason is shaped by preexisting appetites and inclinations. Thus the relation between reason and the passions is one of mutual determination. In terms of the metaphor, the "ship" of the agent will only function properly through cooperation of the sundry members of the crew.

The mistake of the Kantian model of the self is placing the passions in an asymmetrical relationship with reason. The captain of the "Kantian" ship does not engage with a fractious crew but determines them as a principle of rational hegemony. Unlike the Humean model, where the person is represented by the totality of the crew, for Kant the true self is the captain of the ship as pure practical reason and pure freedom. The agent is heteronomous when determined by the passions — that is, within the imagery of the ship, individual members of the crew.

Blackburn's imaginative employment of the ship metaphor neatly captures the opposition between the retrieval of the passions characteristic of many Enlightenment philosophers like Hume or Adam Smith and the Platonic-Kantian principle that reason should exert authority over other (inferior) aspects of the self; the position Blackburn attacks as the bogus captain of the rationalists. Maistre radicalizes precisely this rationalist model through the vision of humanity as a "monstrous centaur." The rhetorical gloominess of this language should not deflect from the "rationalistic" stamp of Maistre's mind. Rather than being constituted by web of mutually reinforcing parts (Hume or Blackburn), the agent is determined by the agonistic asymmetry of reason and the passions.

Blackburn's cardinal objection to the rationalist model is that it erroneously divides the subordinate elements of the self from the ruling principle. He writes:

Making desires the *object* of deliberation, rather than features of the person determining the selection and weighing of external features, inevitably leads to postulating an inner deliberator. This is a noumenal, transcendental, self whose relationship to desires is uncannily like my relationship to the world, yet mysteriously unlike it in not itself needing second-order desires to drive it.[6]

5   Blackburn, S. (1998) *Ruling Passions: A Theory of Practical Reasoning*. Oxford: Clarendon Press, p. 245.
6   Blackburn, *Ruling Passions*, p. 255.

Blackburn, of course, wants to view desires as, at the very least, just as an essential part of the self as reason. Yet in dividing the passions from the rational self, Blackburn accuses Kant of estranging a good part of the self. Maistre would counter that the self *is* divided and alienated from itself. This is the testimony of scripture and the greatest ancient philosophers and we see it in the cruelty and brutality of history and politics. On Maistre's view the self is alienated from its own core. Duplicity is an unavoidable dimension of the human condition, a state known to the ancient pagans:

> Plato tells us that in contemplating himself, he does not know if he sees a monster more duplicitous and more evil than Typhon, or rather a moral, gentle, and benevolent being who partakes in the nature of divinity. He adds that man, so torn in opposite directions, cannot act well or live happily without reducing to servitude that power of the soul in which evil resides, and without setting free that which is the home and the agent of virtue. This is precisely the Christian doctrine, and one could not confess more clearly the doctrine of original sin.[7]

The violence and suffering of the world must be understood from the perspective of the divided self: man is "the monstrous centaur," part steeped in violence and terrible crimes, and yet capable of love and compassion. How can we explain the inward conflict between conscience and appetite? We will consider two bad responses to this question. The first, that of Hobbes, denies the distinction between will and appetite. Will is just the decisive appetite. The second poor answer is that the conflict between desire and ought arises from the distinction between the distinct faculties.

Cudworth and the ruling principle or "hegemonikon"

At this point we shall turn to Cudworth and especially his striking employment of the Origenian idea of the *hegemonikon* or the ruling principle of the soul as the principle of freedom. Cudworth has a distinctly Platonic view of the self as a hierarchical composite within which there can be considerable discord, and the *nous* furnishing a means of settling conflict by perceiving the Good. Within this framework, Cudworth looks for a view of the intelligent will as self-determining agency. In *A Treatise of Freewill* (1848) he does not present the will as a faculty of the soul, distinct from reason. The will is rather the capacity of the soul capable of driving the soul towards the good. The will is quite properly inspired by the Good and this process, the "ever bubbling fountain in the center of the soul, an elater or spring of action."[8] This is linked also to the thesis of Plotinus 6.8 that contemplation is the source of action. Insofar as the finite will is conformed to, contemplates and

7 Maistre, Joseph de. (1993) *St Petersburg Dialogues; or, Conversations on the Temporal Government of Providence*. Montreal: McGill-Queen's University Press, p. 38.
8 Cudworth, R. (1996) "A treatise of freewill," in S. Hutton (ed.), *A Treatise Concerning Eternal and Immutable Morality*. Cambridge: Cambridge University Press, p. 173.

participates in, its transcendent source, boniform, as it were, right actions follows. The goal is not the coordination of the separate faculties of will and intelligence as the integration of will and intellect it as "that which is properly we ourselves."[9] Cudworth uses the term "hegemonikon" (τὸ ἡγεμονικόν) to mark his distinctly Christian philosophy. The ruling self is not oblivious to the suffering, misery, and misfortune of the humble and the unlettered like the great Stoic or Platonic sages. Following Origen, Cudworth thinks that love fulfils the Platonic ideal of Goodness.[10]

Origen or Hobbes and Spinoza?

Hobbes, that "Modern Atheistick Pretender to Wit" in Cudworth's terms,[11] is the source of a particular paradigm in Anglo-Saxon thought in which desire is the causal force and action is considered in a morally neutral manner as the relation between desire and intellect.[12] For Hobbes, will is "appetite" and necessitated. Men are best considered as mechanical structures and the actions of men as the result of *external* forces. The scientific understanding of human nature shows that there is no specifically or irreducibly ethical component. Many contemporary critics of Hobbes, like Bramhall, viewed the intellect as informing the will (as the motivational power) and enabling the will to choose one or another option. Understanding or intellect is without power, will is without insight. Cudworth's critique rejects such an appeal to faculty psychology:

> [A]ll this while it is really the man or the soul that understands, and the man or the soul that wills, as it is the man that walks and the man that speaks or talks, and the musician that plays a lesson or the lute. So it is one and the same subsistent thing, one and the same soul that both understandeth and willeth, and the same agent only that acteth diversely. And thus may it well be conceived that one and the same responsible soul in us both will understandingly, or knowingly of what it wills; and understand or think of this or that object willingly.[13]

In its positive construction, he is offering a profound appeal to the irreducible nature of human agency, of what he calls "a power over oneself." These considerations furnish Cudworth's reflections with a highly contemporary flavor. Rather than the erratic descendants of Erasmus, as they

---

9   Cudworth, "A treatise of freewill," p. 178.
10 See Taliaferro, C. C. and Teply, A. J. (2004) *Cambridge Platonist Spirituality*. Mahwah, NJ: Paulist Press.
11 Cudworth. (1845) *True Intellectual System of the Universe*, J Harrison (ed.). London: Tegg, vol III, p. 418.
12 Foot, Philippa. (1990) "Locke, Hume, and modern moral theory: a legacy of seventeenth and eighteenth century philosophies of mind," in G. S. Rousseau (ed.), *The Languages of Psyche: Mind and Body in Enlightenment Thought*. Berkeley: University of California Press, pp. 81–104. Cudworth on Hobbes, see Cudworth, "A treatise of freewill," p. xxix.
13 Cudworth, "A treatise of freewill," p. 171.

are portrayed in Cassirer's well-intentioned but misleading account of the Cambridge School, these are thinkers who, as Stephen Darwall has stressed, realized the significance of the "internal ought" as true autonomy. Freedom is defined by Cudworth axiologically. Ultimately, it is moral control of one's self. Yet this is grounded in the law of a rational being: as Cudworth insists we are properly "a law unto ourselves." The decisive fact about ethical obligation is its intrinsic nature. To act ethically is to be true to ourselves and to be properly autonomous. Cudworth is proposing a very significant idea about agency. He claims that be a properly human agent, one cannot ignore the ethical dimension.

The ability to "do otherwise" is the necessary but not *sufficient* condition of freedom for Cudworth. He is concerned with a *gradus libertatis*. Higher than spontaneous action is the deliberate choice of one act rather than another:

> There can be no just blame or dispraise, but only where the objects, being in themselves really unequal, the one better, the other worse, a man refuseth the better and chooseth the worse.[14]

Cudworth thinks that this is revealed in our reactive attitudes, our intuitive feelings of praise or resentment towards other human beings, which we do not have towards animals or machines. Whereas the determinist Hobbes saw punishment as grounded in deterrence, Cudworth sees its proper basis in the intuition that we are responsible for faults and deserve punishment. Praise and blame reward and punishment presuppose axiological freedom.

Consider also the other great philosopher of the age who, alongside Hobbes, inspired the anxiety of Cudworth: Spinoza. It has often been noted that Spinoza is very close to Hobbes in his ethical concerns. Humans are mechanistically driven by the conatus for self-preservation and thus self-interest. Hobbes provided a view of goodness is subjective and based upon convention and even apparently altruistic acts like pity or charity are in fact self-regarding. Spinoza is more wide-ranging and proposes an ethics that is a liberation from ephemeral interests and the enjoyment of eternal felicity. Yet, notwithstanding the deeper spiritual dimension of Spinoza, the parallels with Hobbes remain deep. For example, consider self-sacrificing altruism in Spinoza. Individual agents, he claims, necessarily endeavor to maintain or preserve life (conatus) to their own individual advantage. Resources are often restricted and interests may be incompatible. What of an agent who, instead of gaining advantage at the cost of others, decides to help others at his or her own cost? Spinoza would say that since the sacrifice is not good for the individual it must be the result of domination by passion.[15] This is linked to his rejection of Christian virtues such as humility, pity, or repentance. These are versions of sadness and deficient power. But there is a puzzling dimension to all such versions of psychological

---

14 Cudworth, R. (1996) *A Treatise*. Cambridge: Cambridge University Press, p. 166.
15 See Garrett, Don. (1997) "Spinoza's ethical theory," in *Cambridge Companion to Spinoza*. Cambridge: Cambridge University Press, pp. 267–314, p. 304.

hedonism. Whitehead uses the example of heroic Roman general Marcus Atilius Regulus (307–250 BC):

> Consider the patriotism of the Roman farmers, in the full vigour of the Republic. Certainly Reguus did not return to Carthage, with the certainty of torture and death, cherishing any mystical notions of another life — either a Christian heaven or a Buddhist Nirvana. He was a practical man, and his ideal aim was the Roman Republic flourishing in this world. But this aim transcended his individual personality; for this aim he entirely sacrificed every gratification bounded by such limits. For him there was something else in the world which could not yet be expressed as sheer personal gratification — and yet in sacrificing himself, his personal existence rose to its full height.[16]

One might note that it is not absolutely clear that Regulus would have had no sense of an afterlife. Latin epic poetry seems to suggest that some notion of an afterlife was current among the Romans, as among the ancient Greeks. But basically Whitehead's point still stands. What should we make of such acts of heroism or altruism? Cudworth, in rejecting the Hobbesian paradigm, draws on ancient roots. The will is conceived of in Origenistic tripartite terms as the ascetic struggle by which the hegemonic core self tries to orient itself to the good: the ruling part of the self is caught trying to steer in precarious middle state, between the brutish and the Divine likeness. Yet the problem is not the breaking in of brute passions. Rather, the true issue is that of the ultimate authority by which reason can exercise its authority. In the process of the development of godlikeness, there is no absolute but only limited self-determination. The cultivation of certain dispositions is an important part of becoming god-like (Christlike). The question of ethics and freedom becomes one of metaphysics: what are we?

The Plotinian answer lies in his striking but austere doctrine of the true or core self that exists beyond the flux of becoming. Such an ideal of interiority and tranquility is a genuine goal of philosophy within the Platonic tradition. In the *Symposium* (175ab) Socrates is depicted as falling in an absentminded trance, while the servant is calling Socrates to come in. Agathon tells the servant to exert some pressure on Socrates but Aristodemus says, "let him alone. It's a way he has. He goes apart sometimes and stands still wherever he happens to be."[17] Festugière sees this passage, for both philosophical and philological reasons, as the font of a tradition of concentration of the soul and separation from the body in the *Phaedo*, and the Neoplatonists:

> There can be no doubt that this living example of Socrates influenced the doctrine attributed to him by his disciple in the *Phaedo* concerning concentration (67c 7, 83A 6). Purification consists in separating as much as possible the soul from the body; the soul must learn to isolate itself, to

---

16   Whitehead, *Adventures of Ideas*, p. 290.
17   Plato. (1988) *Symposium*, W. Hamilton (trans.). Harmondsworth: Penguin, p. 37.

draw itself together as a mollusk retracts and detaches at all points from its shell . . . and thus retire from all sense impressions.[18]

Festugière views this passage as the source within the Imperial age of the imperative to concentrate and retire into oneself. The goal is clearly the tranquil soul. Retreating from society is not enough: in order to attain tranquility the soul must be purified. One might consider the following text from Plotinus:

> Shut your eyes, and change to and wake another way of seeing, which everyone has but few use.
> And what does this inner sight see? When it is just awakened it is not able to look at the brilliance before it. So that the soul must be trained, first to look at beautiful ways of life: then at beautiful works, not those which the arts produce, but the works of men who have a name for goodness: then look at the souls of the people who produce the beautiful works. How then can you see the sort of beauty a good soul has? Go back into yourself and look; and if you do yet see yourself beautiful, then just as someone making a statue which has to be beautiful cuts away here and polishes there and makes one part smooth and clears another till he has given his statue a beautiful face, so you too must cut away excess and straighten the crooked and make it bright, stop working on your statue! till the Divine glory of virtue shines out on you, till you see "self-mastery enthroned upon its holy seat" . . . For one must come to the sight with a seeing power made akin and like to what is seen. No eye ever saw the sun without becoming sun-like.[19]

The image Plotinus is employing is that of the sculptor cutting away at the stone. The true self has to strip away all inessential accretions: not least those that pertain to the body. For Plotinus, ethics is rather becoming what one already is, but which is obscured by the body and society, sensuality and convention. Plotinus has taken this notion of the search for the true self beneath the accretions from *The Republic* 611 and the image of the embodied soul as Glaucus the sea god covered in sea weed. It is a model of salvation by purification of the self by which the particular facts about the contingent individual are stripped away.

Origen is preferable for Cudworth because in the term "hegemonikon" he can insist upon both what is right *and* wrong with the Plotinian view. Within Christianity Christ is the true "self." One of Origen's favorite biblical texts is John 1.26, about the dwelling of Christ among the people. In a piece of exegesis as brilliant as counterintuitive, Origen reads the "in the midst" announced by John the Baptist to mean in the interior man. For

---

18 Festugière. (1954) *Personal Religion among the Greeks.* Berkeley: University of California Press, p. 59.
19 Plotinus, *Ennead* 1.6(9). Cf. the chariot in Plato's *Phaedrus*. Cambridge, MA: Harvard, 1966), p. 229.

Origen, this is Christ as the hegemonikon of the soul: the ruling principle.[20]
The Cambridge Platonist George Rust, a great admirer and propagator of
Origen's thought, writes:

> [W]hatever happen'd to Christ the Captain of our Salvation, to whose
> image we are in all things to be conform'd, the same is mystically to
> be wrought in us: so that as he was crucified and died, so that which
> is mortal in us, the body of death and sin, was to be crucified and die
> likewise; and as he was raised from the dead by the glory of the Father,
> so we should walk in newness of life.[21]

Rust's identification of the true man with the indwelling Christ explains different view of humility and sympathy, and the greater emphasis upon the
gratuitous (though not arbitrary) nature of salvation. Cudworth wishes to
avoid the strong version of the soul is Divine "in essence" thesis. However,
without some version of the true self doctrine one has the self as a merely
functional composite.[22] Cudworth states:

> In these place it is plain that the soul of man hath a reciprocal energy
> upon itself, or of acting upon itself — so that it is not merely passive to
> that which it receives from god- a power of being a (co-worker) with
> God, a power of improving itself further and further, and of keeping and
> conserving itself in good, all of which cannot be without a non-necessity
> or contingency.[23]

The principles of God and the Soul are closely related. Just as behind
the continent flux of appearances lies the necessary and ultimate being
of Divine principle, so too the self is that underlying unity that persists
beyond the flux of phenomenal sensation and the vicissitudes of the body.
The parallel with the teaching of the *Gita* is again striking. Radhakrishnan
observes:

> Yoga is getting to God, relating oneself to the power that rules the uni-
> verse, touching the absolute. It is yoking not merely this or that power of
> the soul, but all the forces of heart, mind and will to God. It is the effort
> of man to unite himself to the deeper principle. We have to change the
> whole poise of the soul into something absolute and uncompromising
> and develop the strength to resist power and pleasure. Yoga thus means
> the discipline by which we can train ourselves to bear the shocks of the

20 Hengstermann, C. (2010) "The 'dignity of God's image': Origen's metaphysics of man,"
    in *Natur und Normativitaet*. Muenster: Lit Verlag, pp. 45–62, p. 53.
21 Rust, *A Letter of Resolution Concerning Origen and the Chief of his Opinions*. London, 1661,
    p. 122.
22 Consider the fascinating parallels with the doctrine of the ruling-imperishable self in
    the famous second chapter of the Bhagavad Gita, Winthrop Sargeant (trans.). New York:
    SUNY, 2009. See Fuerstein, G. A. (1974) *Introduction to the Bhagavad Gita Its Philosophy
    and Cultural Setting*. London: Rider.
23 Cudworth, *A Treatise*, p. 184.

world with the central being of our soul untouched . . . We can discipline the emotions and realise the supreme by a soul surrender to God.[24]

The surrender of which Radhakrishnan speaks is described in the Bhagavad Gita through the language of "sacrifice." Krisna exhorts Arjuna in the chariot in the Bhagavad Gita that he must fight with detachment. This means that the "warrior yogi" Arjuna should "perform action for the sake of sacrifice" and links this to the very nature of creation of Prajapati, Sacrifice becomes the key image of renunciation — or at least detachment.[25]

Purpose, suffering and imagination

The sense of personal identity presupposes a primordial but inchoate sense of unique identity, a thrown-ness into the world, an idea that is expressed in myths by the idea of the preexistence of the soul. But the attainment of a mature and rational self is closely linked to the awareness of the dictates of conscience and the experience of suffering. This is why, we have argued, the notion of tragedy is so important in our culture. Consider the following speech from Shakespeare's Hamlet to Horatio prior to the "play within the play" in which a murder of the king is enacted:

> Since my dear soul was mistress of her choice,
> And could of men distinguish, her election
> Hath seal'd thee for herself: for thou hast been
> As one, in suffering all, that suffers nothing;
> A man that fortune's buffets and rewards
> Hast ta'en with equal thanks: and blest are those
> Whose blood and judgement are so well commingled,
> That they are not a pipe for fortune's finger
> To sound what stop she please. Give me that man
> That is not passion's slave, and I will wear him
> In my heart's core, ay, in my heart of heart,
> As I do thee.[26]

Shakespeare is expressing the Renaissance view of the Christian gentleman. From this perspective, it is the realization of purpose (i.e. the will) that is the task of imagination. Purpose is the index of personality, and the healthy personality is oriented to the future rather than the past, and "is not passion's slave." Imagination is the vinculum or bond among "subjectivity" (that is, the irreducible "my-ness" of the experience), teleology (those purposes and goals that form a coherent identity of self), and the capacity

24 Radhakrishnan, S. (1929) *Indian Philosophy* (revised edn.). London: George Allen, p. 532.
25 For example, Gita, 3, §§9ff; 4, §32–3. See Eliade, M. (2009). *Yoga, Immortality and Freedom.* Princeton, NJ: Princeton University Press, p. 157ff.
26 Shakespeare, *Hamlet.* 3.2.

for freedom as the domain of the forging of a self, notwithstanding and sometimes through adverse and painful experiences: "As one, in suffering all, that suffers nothing." In extreme cases, suffering can eclipse and destroy the sense of self and thereby the will to live. But these extreme cases — for example, concentration camps or very severe illness — need not be taken as paradigmatic. On the contrary, they may be the exceptions that prove the rule. The self needs to overcome suffering and disappointment to forge a coherent sense of self, but that same personal identity may be destroyed by sore adversity.

The distinction between fantasy and imagination is also connected to the metaphysics of the self. Fear grounded upon superstition is the product of those fantasies that pander to the self. Selfishness is reinforced through fantasies and can become extremely disturbing and destructive. The imagination proper is a challenge to the immediate and comfortable ego, and it should inspire the soul to the expansion of its interests and concerns.

Hobbes and Spinoza think that self-preservation is the primary and ruling motivation of an agent. But human beings clearly have the ability to jeopardize their security and safety for ideals of self or society. In fact, the sacrifice of the selfish ego and the emergence of a more substantial self requires an imaginative discipline of desire and concentration upon higher values. Polonius says:

> This above all, — to thine own self be true;
> And it must follow, as the night the day,
> Thou canst not then be false to any man.[27]

It is typical of Shakespeare's dramatic irony that some of his most deeply felt and serious lines are uttered by whimsical characters or in comic contexts. An ideal conception of self — requiring imaginative engagement — is only coherent if the Hobbesian view of the self as a raw given or datum is false. In religion and art we find various ideal conceptions of self.

Narrative and self

Linked to the element of imagination in selfhood is that of narrative: Alasdair MacIntyre has powerfully argued that any adequate account of agent as opposed to event causality requires explanation in terms of narrative. If we are looking for reasons as opposed to causes of events, a narrative element is unavoidable. Caesar crossed the Rubicon or Constantine became Christian for reasons best explained in terms of intentions, purposes, and psychological and social history rather than efficient causality and covering laws.[28] The kind of transparency of motives or interests that might explain a self-conscious agent's behavior often requires considerations about that agent's

---

27 Shakespeare. *Hamlet*, 1.3.
28 MacIntyre, A. (1981) *After Virtue*. MacIntyre, Alasdair. *After Virtue* (2nd edn.). Notre Dame: University of Notre Dame Press, pp. 205–11.

character, projects, and history, which in turn narrative considerations. Thus agency, *sensu proprio*, is not just a sequence of one brute fact after another, but a coherent and meaningful pattern. The historian may try to explain Caesar or Constantine in terms of the former's ambition or the latter's piety since these are patterns required in any plausible explanation of agency.[29]

Charles Taylor presents an account of identity and freedom that looks surprisingly close to that of Cudworth: as agents we have the capacity to judge our desires as possessing value or not. But he adds a narrative component to this:

> Since we cannot do with an orientation to the good, and since we cannot be indifferent to our place relative to this good, and since this place is something that must always change and become, the issue of the direction of our lives must arise for us. [In] order to have a sense of who we are, we have to have a notion of how we have become and of where we are going.[30]

Narrative is used not just in the psychological sense that people do in fact understand themselves in the mode of story or narrative, but the normative sense that narrative is important: a life unified in terms of overarching values is a better life than one that is disoriented and incoherent: the "ne'er do well" or the indolent searching for distraction from boredom or anxiety or amusement. Taylor is consciously drawing upon the *Bildung* tradition of German philosophy, but one could also place it in relation to the ancient tradition of the spiritual exercises.[31] This can diffuse the objection that the appeal to narrative is narcissistic and egoistical. Traditions of formation of the self in antiquity or the modern period have often employed the language of sacrifice.

Amour pur and sacrifice

Clement of Alexandria states:

> Now the sacrifice which is acceptable to God is unswerving abstraction from the body and its passions. This is really true piety. And is not, on this account, philosophy rightly called by Socrates the practice of death.[32]

The Christians had a special interest in the concept of death because of Christ's words "he that findeth his life shall lose it; and he that loseth his life

---

29 On the question of explanation generally, see Knowles, Dudley (ed.). (1990) *Explanation and its Limits*. Cambridge: Cambridge University Press.

30 Taylor, Charles. (1989) *Sources of the Self: The Making of Modern Identity*. Cambridge: Cambridge University Press, p. 47.

31 Hedley, Douglas. (2008) *Living Forms of the Imagination*. London: T&T Clark, p. 157ff.

32 Clement, *Stromata*, 5.11. Clemens Alexandrinus, Stromata 1-VI. Berlin: Akademie-Verlag (1985), p. 370.

for my sake shall find it" (Mt. 10.39) and St. Paul's conception of entering into the death of Christ in Philippians 3 and 2 Corinthians. Christianity is the world religion grounded upon the death of its founder. The use of the Platonic definition of philosophy as the practice of death (μελέτη θανάτου) has a particular resonance in a religion like Christianity with the Pauline conviction in the participation by believers in the death and resurrection of its founder. Pierre Hadot notes that there is a striking resemblance to the passage in Porphyry's *Sentences* in the work of Evagrius the monk. This Desert Father says:

> To separate the body from the soul is the privilege only of Him who has joined them together. But to separate the soul form the body lies as well in the power of the person who pursues virtue. For our fathers gave to the training for death and to the flight from the body a special name (i.e. the monastic life).[33]

By "our fathers" he probably means Clement of Alexandria, who says that the acceptable sacrifice for God consists in separation without return from the body and its passions. Such is the truth, the real piety towards God. And perhaps this is why Clement pertinently calls philosophy "practice."

E. R. Dodds provides an illuminating (albeit critical and skeptical) account of the mood and practice of asceticism in his seminal work *Pagans and Christians in an Age of Anxiety*. But this was not just a feature of the age of anxiety — that is to say, late Antiquity. The idea of a dying life as opposed to a living death was a central tenet of Christian spirituality. In the seventh century, Maximus the Confessor employs this language of practicing death: "In accordance with the philosophy of Christ, let us make our life a practice of death by letting our free will overtake nature, and before death comes, by cutting the soul off from the concerns for bodily things." But the interest in the *spiritual dying to live* was not limited to the East, where the tradition remained continuous. Even in the West, the influence of Macrobius in particular meant that much of the school discussion of the topic of spiritual death was powerfully felt, and in particular the concept of the double death. The Christian mystical tradition was deeply indebted to the idea of the practice of death. This can be seen in the use of the idea of the birth of the soul in Eckhart, which follows the pattern for the purification of the soul laid down by Fathers and pagan Platonists; it is detachment from the appetites and intellectual autonomy — the liberation from the partial, libidinous, and avaricious ego and the attainment of a clearer vision of reality. Eckhart's *Abgeschiedenheit* (detachment) is the direct descendant of the *practice* of Porphyry and Evagrius. That distant descendant of Eckhart in seventeenth-century England, the Cambridge Platonist John Smith, writes:

> Though by the Platonists' leave, such a life and knowledge as this is, peculiarly belongs to the true and sober Christian, who lives in Him who

---

33   Hadot, P. (1995) *Philosophy as a Way of Life* Oxford: Blackwell, p. 138.

is life itself . . . and an infant-Christ . . . formed in his soul.[34]

Here, John Smith is consciously aligning Plato's *Phaedo* with Paul's notion of the mystical death in Christ. Smith avers that 'we should 'endeavour to preserve that Heavenly fire of Divine Love and Goodness...alwaies (sic) alive and burning in the Temple of our Souls, and to sacrifice our Selves back to him'.[35] Smith's use of "meditation" of death is an imagining or thinking about one's own mortality. The main point of the "practice of death" is the element of continual training. Perhaps Smith is influenced by the "De Meditatione Mortis" of Thomas à Kempis. A. E. Taylor notes that

> μελέτη means the repeated practice by which we prepare ourselves for a performance . . . the thought is that "death" is like a play for which the philosopher's life has been a daily rehearsal.[36]

Taylor reminds us of the fact that for Attic Greeks μελέταν means training. The idea is that there is a highest good for human beings which is essentially otherworldly. The best life for the soul is continually to attempt to imitate this eternal good in time. This good life is thus well thought of as a dying to the habitual appetites and lusts of the unreflective creature and becoming a new creature, and a continual training for postmortem communion with the Deity. This is a tenet that Smith interprets as Pauline:

> [B]y *Self-denial* I mean, the Soul's quitting all its own interest in it self, and an entire Resignation of itself to him (sc. God) . . . The Soul in which Religion rules, saies as *S.Paul* did, *I live ; and yet not I, but Christ liveth in me* . . . As a good man lives *above himself* in a way of *Self-denial*, so he lives also above himself as he lives in *the Enjoyment of God*: and this is the very Soul and Essence of true Religion, to unite the Soul in the nearest intimacy and conjunction with God, who is . . . as Plotinus speaks.[37]

Nygren famously proposed an opposition between *eros* and *agape*. *Agape* is the true Christian love whereas *eros* is incompatible with love of the Divine. The familiar objection to this is the recognition of sublimated love in Plato, especially the *Symposium*, and the influence of this idea upon the Church Fathers. Jacques Le Brun discusses a complexity within the idea of love as *eros* as inherited from the Greeks.[38] Perhaps — with characteristic Gallic deference to psychoanalysis — we might see a deep link between love and death, as Freud suggested in the wake of the horrors of the Great War.

Consider the examples of Achilles and Patroclus or Alcestis and Admetus. Is such a devoted or self-sacrificial ultimately egoistic or altruistic? Is the dreadful grief and fury of Achilles or the devotion of Alcestis to

34 Smith, J. (1660) *Select Discourses*. Cambridge. Reprint New York and London: Garland (1978), p. 21.
35 Smith, *Select Discourses*, p. 157.
36 Taylor, A. E. (1929) *Plato: The Man and His Works*. London: Methuen, p. 179.
37 Smith, *Select Discourses*, p. 389.
38 Le Brun, Jacques. (2002) *Le pur àmour de Platon à Lacan*. Paris: Seuil.

Admetus an instance of giving or taking? In Plato's *Symposium*, Phaedrus claims love is the most ancient and powerful deity, that the bond of love makes a man prepared to die (180b). Apollos offers Admetus life if he can find a substitute and his wife Alcestis does this (179b).[39] The gods are so impressed that they release her from the underworld. Orpheus, by contrast, tried to find Eurydice but without making any sacrifice. Phaedrus contrasts Achilles and Orpheus. The first sacrificed his own life for his lover. The second was a coward who tried to go to Hades rather than death.

The great French mystic Fénelon (1651–1715) meditated upon the meaning of Christ's words, "He that findeth his life shall lose it. He that loseth his life for me shall find it."[40] According to Fénelon, to lose oneself in this sense is highest in man. He thought that the instance of Dido in the *Aeneid* proved that the pagans understood disinterested love. Fénelon used the example of Alcestis and Admetus. As Scruton observes,

> [t]he tragic hero is both self sacrificed and a sacrificial victim; and the awe that we feel at his death is in someway redemptive, a proof that his life was worthwhile. Love and affection between people is real only to the extent that it prepares the way for sacrifice — whether the *petits soins* that bind Marcel to Saint Loup, or the proof offered by Alcestis, who dies for her husband. Sacrifice is the core of virtue, the origin of meaning and the true theme of high art.[41]

The *Thaetetus* (176a) states that evil "patrols this earthly realm" and

> [o]ne should try to escape as quickly as possible from here to there. The escape-route is assimilation to God, in so far as this is possible, and this assimilation is the combination of wisdom with moral respect for God and man.[42]

For the Neoplatonists, the reverse side of this idea of ethics as "becoming like God" was the idea of "practicing death." The conception of the flight is logically linked to the idea in *The Republic* of the bestial nature of the passions — the "savage part of the soul," which does not "stop short of any madness or shamelessness" (*The Republic* 571d).[43] As long as we keep to the body and the soul is contaminated with this imperfection, there is no chance of our ever attaining satisfactorily to our object, which we assert to be truth (*Phaedo* 66b). Death is referred to as release from the fetters of the body (67d), a purification (67a-c) and wisdom as a cleansing (69d). It is why Gregory of Nazianzus refers to Plato's talk of practicing death and separating as far as possible, the soul from the body, or from the tomb, to speak like him, if you practice this philosophy.

---

39 Plato. (1987) *The Symposium*, trs. W. Hamilton (trans.). Harmondsworth: Penguin, pp. 44ff.

40 Mt. 10.39.

41 Scruton, Roger. (2009) *Beauty*. Oxford: Oxford University Press, p. 193.

42 Plato. (1987) *Thaetetus*, Robin Waterfield (trans.). Harmondsworth: Penguin, 176b.

43 Plato. (1987) *The Republic*, Desmond Lee (trans.). Harmondsworth: Penguin, p. 392.

The Platonists were, of course, not the only school in Antiquity, which placed great emphasis upon the philosophical significance of death. For Epicurus the awareness of one's finitude furnishes an infinite value to the *laetus in praesens*. For the Stoic, meditation upon death helps to lead man to the acceptance of fate.[44] But it was Platonists who defined Philosophy itself as dying: a fact which can be seen from Plato's *Phaedo* to the Neoplatonic *Prolegomena Philosophiae* a thousand years later.[45] John Smith can refer to Plotinus as "the Greek Philosopher." Quoting the famous passage in Porphyry's *Life of Plotinus* where Porphyry reports that Plotinus was ashamed to be in the body, Smith proceeds to state:

> It is only True Religion that teaches and enables men to dye to this world and to all Earthly things, and to rise above the vaporous Sphere of Sensual and Earthly pleasures, which darken the Mind and hinder it from enjoying it from enjoying the brightness of Divine light; the proper motion of Religion is still upwards towards to its first original.[46]

John Smith is, of course, referring to Plato's famous definition of Philosophy as "practicing death" (*Phaedo* 67d; 67e; 80e; 81a). Hence Smith can plead for, "as they are wont to call them, several steps and ascents out of this miry cave of mortality, before they could set any sure footing with their intellectual part in the land of Light and Immortal being": the ascent out of the cave and up the divided line. The reference to this "miry" cave of mortality is surely a reference to the *Phaedo*'s depiction of embodied mankind as wallowing in a mire of ignorance (82e). In this text, Socrates suggests that the worldly think of philosophers as morbid, but although they are correct about this, they are so for the wrong reasons. They cannot appreciate that "death" for the philosopher has primarily a spiritual sense.

Socrates gives three examples. First, the Philosopher will not be driven by physical lusts and appetites or by vanity and fine garments. Second, the Philosopher will be acutely aware of the inadequacy of the senses to furnish knowledge rather than illusion, and the body often interferes in and distracts the business of contemplation. Smith observes:

> Plotinus hath well concluded concerning the body, "should a man make use of his body in his speculations," it should entangle his mind with so many contradictions, that it would be impossible to attain to any true knowledge of things.[47]

Third, the proper objects of science are nonsensual. The less the knower is dependent upon sensual apparatus the better. Hence Socrates presents knowledge as a gradual purging of the bodily and progressive spiritualization. It would thus be absurd for the philosopher who has been actively

---

44 Hadot, *Philosophy as a Way of Life*, p. 68; pp. 93ff; 217–37.
45 (1990) *Prolegomenes a la philosophie de Platon*. Paris: Les Belles Lettres.
46 Smith, *Select Discourses*, p. 396.
47 Smith, *Select Discourses*, p. 82.

pursuing this purgation or continual death to the body, to bring this process to fruition in death — that is, complete separation in which reality can be contemplated in its fullness. Furthermore, those wars and political upheavals that do most to distract and disturb contemplation are directly linked to the follies of the body and its passions.[48]

The definition of philosophy as a form of dying is a part of an exhortation to the disinterested love of truth.

Foucault and his conception of ancient philosophy as a "l'art d'existence" or "culture du soi"

The Platonic conception of the spiritual exercises and sacrifice of self as renunciation has been the subject of much explicit criticism in modern philosophy. Michel Foucault stridently reversed Plato's idea of body as the prison of the soul with his infamous "L'ame, prison du corps."[49] Bentham, as a militant hedonist, was severely critical of asceticism, while Spinoza famously declared that philosophy should be meditation upon life, not death (*ejus sapientia non mortis, sed vitae meditatio est*).[50] The most strident critic of the tradition of philosophy as the practice of death is perhaps Nietzsche: he interprets Socrates as a decadent who opposed life and instinct with his rationalism, universalism, and view of living as an illness to be cured by death.[51]

In this late work, in which he was clearly influenced by Pierre Hadot, Foucault presents the ethics of the ancient world as an ethic of pleasure which he finds the inspiration and model for contemporary philosophy as an *"esthétique de l'existence."*[52] Christianity initiated for Foucault a shift in the conception of morality from the model of ethics as an art of existence to the view of morality as a code of laws or rules, or obedience to Divine will. Foucault was interested in the relevance of a morality of a personal ethics as opposed to a code of rules for a society that has lost confidence in the idea of morality as submission to a set of rules. At the center of such an "aesthetics of existence" is the concept of pleasure. The ascetic element in ancient philosophy was not in order to deny but to control pleasure: "In the place of violent, uncertain and temporary pleasures, access to the self enables the substitution of a form of pleasure which one can grasp for oneself in serenity and perpetually."[53]

Pierre Hadot, in a vigorous and characteristically limpid essay, chastises Foucault for his blithely hedonistic appropriation of Stoic ethics in his essay '*Réflexions sur la notion de culture de soi*'.[54] Hadot attacks Foucault on two

---

48　Plato, *Phaedo*, 65b–67b.
49　Foucault, M. (1975) *Surveiller et Punir*. Paris: Gallimard, p. 34.
50　Spinoza, *Ethics*, 4.67.
51　See Nehemas, A. (1998) *The Art of Living: Socratic Reflections from Plato to Foucault* Berkeley: University of California, pp. 128–56.
52　Foucault, M. (1984) *Histoire de la sexualité: Le souci de soi*. Paris: Gallimard, p. 83.
53　Foucault, *Histoire de la sexualité*, pp. 83–4.
54　Foucault, M. (1989) *Philosophe, Rencontre internationale*. Paris 9.10.11. Janvier 1988. Jean

points: pleasure and self. He argues that it is quite misleading to conflate
joy (*gaudium*) with pleasure (*voluptas*) because the Stoics carefully wish to
distinguish the two. Furthermore, it is quite misleading to say that the Stoic
is finding this pleasure in the self "dans son 'moi'". The Stoic is interested
in the best part of the self, which is part of a universal reason. This second
point about the nature of the ego is one Hadot presses very hard against
Foucault. The Stoics or Platonists are not so much seeking "techniques
de soi" as liberation from individuality in order to become more universal.
Hadot writes:

> That which Foucault calls the "practices of the self according the Stoics,
> but also according to the Platonists, that is true, corresponds to a
> movement of conversion towards the self: one liberates oneself from
> exteriority, the passionate attachment to exterior objects, and the plea-
> sures which they can procure, one observes oneself, to see if one has
> progressed in this oneself and to find happiness in liberty and interior
> independence. I agree with all these points. But I think that the move-
> ment of interiorisation is inextricably linked to another movement
> whereby one raises oneself to a higher psychic level in which one discov-
> ers another type of exteriorisation, another relation to the exterior, a new
> manner of being to the world, and which consists in becoming aware of
> oneself as a part of nature, as part of universal reason. There is a radical
> transformation of perspectives, a dimension radically universalist and
> cosmic which Mr Foucault has not sufficiently insisted — or so it seems
> to me: interiorisation is the transcending of self and universalisation.[55]

We have seen in our analysis of the practice of death is the opening the
limits of the selfish ego to the universal. Hadot sees this point as the weakness of Foucault:

> Mr Foucault proposes a culture of self which is too purely pure aesthetic,
> that is to say, I fear, a new form of dandyism, a version for the end of
> the 20th century.[56]

In our culture, which is saturated with the rhetoric of autonomy and self
sufficiency, the ancient vision of true philosophy as a form of sacrifice may
seem morbid and obscure. How can a discipline dedicated to 'super aude'
(dare to be wise) succumb to such monkish mortification. Yet the theme of
sacrifice still pervades much ethical theory in the modern age.

Claude Milner, Paul Veyne, Francois Veyne, Francois Wahl (eds.). Paris: Seuil, pp. 261–8.
55 Hadot, *Philosophy as a Way of Life*, p. 267.
56 Foucault, *Philosophe, rencontre Internationale*, p. 267: "M Foucault propose une culture
   du soi trop purement esthetique, c'est-a-dire, je le crains, une nouvelle forme de
   dandyisme, version fin du XXe siècle."

Religion and sacrifice

Joseph de Maistre develops the theme of renunciation within Platonism and Christian spirituality as part of his own counter revolutionary historiography. In Maistre's political and social reflections, the Age of Enlightenment is depicted as an age of violent crisis. The seventeenth century represents, by contrast, a period of relative tranquility — the age of stability based upon a culture of willing Christian self-sacrifice. That stable epoch is ravaged and destroyed by the eighteenth century — an age of abstraction, of individualistic, critical reason, corroding the traditions of past centuries without replacing them. Within the framework of Maistre's thought the recent age of secular destruction, with the unleashing of the passions under the violent impulses of the selfish part of the soul, was the age when "the holy laws of humanity were struck down, innocent blood covering the scaffolds that covered France; men frying and powdering bloody heads, and even the mouths of women stained with human blood."[57] Far from glorifying violence, Maistre is producing an unflinching protocol of its baneful presence in the world. According to Maistre, it is not religion that is the cause of conflict but, rather, mankind's fallen nature, and sacrifice is the attempt to stem it. Suffering is purgative as well as punitive. Humanity's fallen nature can be expiated only by sacrifice, which is *vicaria anima*, a substitute soul. Maistre sees instances of this practice throughout the heathen world. Ancient pagans did not sacrifice wild or useless animals. But

> the most precious for their utility were chosen, the most gentle, the most innocent, the ones closest to man by their instincts and habits [. . .] the most human victims, if one may express oneself in this way. Before Christ a sacrificial victim was anthropomorphic. After Christ, the paradigmatically human is the willing self-sacrifice. Christianity is distinctive because for it sacrifice is ethical, as self-renunciation. The Christian aims to be Christlike in self-abnegation: under the empire of this Divine law, the just man (who never believes himself to be such) nevertheless tries to come up to his model through suffering. He examines himself, he purifies himself, he works on himself with efforts that seem to surpass humanity to obtain finally the grace of being able to return what has not be stolen.[58]

One might fruitfully consider Glaucon's claim in Plato's *The Republic* that the righteous man will be humiliated and tortured, bound, blinded, and crucified:

> They will say that the just man, as we have pictured him, will be scourged, tortured, and imprisoned, his eyes will be put out, and after enduring every humiliation he will be crucified, and learn at last that

---

57   Maistre, *St Petersburg Dialogues*, p. 371.
58   Maistre, *St Petersburg Dialogues*, pp. 381–2.

one should want not to be, but to seem just.[59]

Evidently these lines were composed after and in the light of the death of the suffering and execution of Socrates. Socrates had been publically humiliated by Aristophanes, the most popular writer of comic plays in Athens. Yet he had to endure not merely the mockery and humiliation through the wit of the poet but also vicious attack on his piety and the accusation of corrupting the youth in court. The actual death of Socrates was not as described — it was, in fact, the serene death of a free citizen. The actual description of the suffering of the just is closer to the violence and humiliation of Golgotha. The King of the Jews, descendant of King David, executed through a slave's death.[60]

In his *Religion within the Boundaries of Mere Reason*, Kant discusses the crucifixion of Christ as the sacrifice "Holy One" of the Gospel, especially in the section concerning the evil principle's rightful claim to dominion over the human being, and the struggle of the two principles with one another".[61] Kant is here drawing upon his theory of "radical Böse" in humanity as expressing the innate disposition to evil. Kant, like Plato, emphasizes the manner in which the righteousness of Christ provoked the "prince of this world" to humiliate and kill him:

> He finally pursued him to the most ignominious death, without achiev-ing anything in the least against him by this onslaught by unworthy people upon his steadfastness and honesty in teaching, and example for the sake of the good.[62]

Christ's death serves to manifest goodness. It reveals the capacity of the free agent to exhibit autonomy and the power of the moral law over inclination: the contrast between the freedom of the children of heaven and the bondage of a mere son of earth[63]. It is a paradigm of the capacity of the virtuous agent to prevail over the most difficult of circumstances. Moreover, within Kant's rational theology Christ's death can convey a powerful awareness of mankind's moral vocation, the potential for liberation from bondage to inclination, and as the perfect representation of holiness: the utter cor-respondence of disposition to the moral law.

It means that sacrifice is unavoidable: those in the world who adhere to the good principle should always be prepared for physical sufferings, sacrifices and mortifications of self-love.[64]

This suggests a difference of emphasis at least between the *Groundwork* and Kant's *Religion*. The motivational rigorism of the *Groundwork*, of the

59 Plato and Lee, H. D. P. (1987) *The Republic* (2nd edn.). Harmondsworth: Penguin, p. 362.
60 Benz, E. (1950) "*Der gekreuzigte Gerechte bei Pato, im Neuen Testament und in der alten Kirche,*" *Akademie der Wissenschaften und Literatur in Mainz*, 12: 1–46.
61 Kant, I. (1998) *Religion within the Boundaries of Mere Reason*. Allen Wood and George di Giovanni (eds.). Cambridge: Cambridge University Press, p. 96.
62 Kant, *Religion* 6.81.
63 Kant, *Religion*, 6.82.
64 Kant, *Religion*, 6.83.

thesis that actions are only morally good if prompted by duty rather than inclination. On this thesis the special value of ethical sacrifice is that it can be an index of the sovereignty of the moral law. Kant shares this perception of suffering:

[T]he sublimity and inner worth of the command is the more manifest in a duty, the fewer are the subjective causes for obeying it and the more there are against.[65]

Thus virtue "reveals itself most splendidly in suffering."[66] In the *Religion*, Kant is explicit:

The emergence from the corrupted disposition into the good is in itself already sacrifice (as "the death of the old man," "the crucifying of the flesh") and the entrance into a long train of life's ills which the new human being undertakes in the disposition of the Son of God.[67]

Kant quotes St. Paul's notion of being crucified with Christ. If we bracket the complex and opaque idea of grace in Kant as a surplus imputed via Christ's death, the dominant idea is the symbolic crucifixion of the inclinations and sharing in the sufferings of the just man *par excellence*: an idea that is strikingly akin to Plato's vision of the innocent suffering of the righteous man in *The Republic*. Here we have the language of "sacrifice" is, of course, often employed when considering the core metaethical problem of moral worth. One of the most striking instances of the Christian model is Hegel.

Hegel

Sacrifice has a fundamental role in Hegel's metaphysics.[68] This should not be surprising. John Findlay acutely observes:

For the Christianity of Germany, as witnessed by countless, infinitely affecting altar pieces, has always been one that could best distil beauty from agony, and which could see what was most Divine in the lifting of the ordinary griefs, frustrations, and pathetic needs of men into a region that transcends the human. The Christian God is essentially redemptive, of a self alienation that returns to self in victory. If Hegel was nothing better, he was at least a great Christian theologian.[69]

65 Kant, I. (1981) *The Moral Law; or, Kant's Groundwork of the Metaphysic of Morals*, H. J. Paton (trans.). London: Hutchinson, p. 88.
66 Kant, I. (2004) *Critique of Practical Reason*, Mary J. Gregor (ed.). Cambridge: Cambridge University Press, 5.156.
67 Kant, *Religion*, 6.74.
68 There are 57 occurences of *Aufopferung* (sacrifice) in Hegel's *Phenomenology of Spirit*.
69 Findlay, J. N. (1977), foreword to G. W. F. Hegel. *Phenomenology of Spirit*, A.V. Miller (trans.). Oxford: Oxford University Press, p. xxvii.

Edward Caird, in his useful little introduction to Hegel, identified the "die to live" as the core of Hegel's thought.[70] First, our animal being is sacrifices to the force of understanding. In this way we become, for Hegel, self-conscious agents. His emphasis is clearly upon self-sacrifice: it is his use of the term *Aufopferung* or self-sacrifice that is common rather than the word *Opfer* (sacrifice).

The *Phenomenology* is

> the path of the natural consciousness which presses forth to true knowl-
> edge; or as the way of the Soul which journeys through the series of its
> own configurations as though they were the stations appointed for it by
> its won nature, so that it may purify itself for the life of the Spirit, and
> achieve finally, through a completed experience of itself, the awareness
> of what it really is in itself.[71]

Note the imagery of the stations of the cross that Hegel employs. Sacrifice is linked through the *Phenomenology* with Hegel's theory of determinate negation (*bestimmte Negation*). At various levels of the journey of conscious-ness, it posits another in the face of which consciousness itself suffers some form of loss or negation. Out of this initial negation of consciousness, some form of renunciation or surrender of self, a new level of subjectivity can emerge. The protean subjectivity that is Hegel's *Geist* depends upon various phases of sacrifice. Hegel claims that virtue has to subordinate individual-ity, "requiring nothing less than the sacrifice of the entire personality as proof that individual peculiarities are in fact no longer insisted upon."[72] Furthermore, Hegel employs the language of self-sacrifice in relation to the state. Self-sacrifice is the renouncing of "possessions and enjoyment and acts" for the benefit of the community.[73] Such elements of sacrifice are acts of conscious negation.

I want to consider here Hegel's critique of egotism as a defense of a theory of sacrifice. Hegel is providing a basis for a theory of altruism (contra Popper and others) in reminding us of the dialectical nature of the personal. Subjectivity is constituted by relations with other subjects. Indeed, the constitutive body of relations to others is at least as significant as the striving for goods or the fulfillment of proximate desires. Nor can the former be reduced to the latter. As F. H. Bradley later observed, the self "is penetrated, infected, characterised by the existence of others, its content implies in every fibre relations of community."[74] Hegel presents two important arguments. First, self-awareness of a subject requires corroboration or affirmation from other agents. This is the basis of his important theory of recognition and its psychological truth can be readily appreciated. Agents who, within family or society, have failed to obtain proper recognition are particularly prone to

70 Caird, E. (1909) *Hegel*, Edinburgh: William Blackwood & Son, p. 163.
71 Hegel, *Phenomenology*, §77, p. 49.
72 Hegel, *Phenomenology*, §381, p. 228.
73 Hegel, *Phenomenology*, §504, p. 306.
74 Bradley. (1876) "My station and its duties," *Ethical Studies*, Oxford: Oxford University Press, p. 172, cf pp. 251–312.

psychological breakdown. Second, Hegel emphasizes the requirement of the expression of subjectivity through work, especially insofar as this work is tangible and visible. Both in recognition and in work the agent finds a mirror of selfhood but also, importantly, resistance. It is in the overcoming of this initial resistance to self — whether in the opposition claims and interests of another subject or the toil of labor — that richer form of subjectivity emergences. In this way sacrifice can represent the resistance of the other to the self, and the process of self-realization in the overcoming of this resistance. This is the key to the master-slave dialectic: self-consciousness is constituted by its relation to the other. There is no authentic recognition of another self without sacrificing one's own absoluteness self-conscious being is thus not limited by the other as material objects are because the spiritual life is a perpetual dying to self and rising again. In making that which seems, *prima facie*, a limit a very part of itself, spirit or self-reflection has no absolute limit. It knows its own limit, can integrate and thus transcends it. I am not convinced that the master-slave is an instance of failed recognition. Rather, it is a myth that reveals the paradox of self-consciousness: we find ourselves in losing ourselves. The slave according to the French Enlightenment or Hume is a lesser being than the Lord: he cannot fulfill his natural desires and is in bondage to arbitrary tyranny. Hegel's reversal is meant to show how shallow the materialistic/naturalistic position is. Sacrifice and self-realization are two aspects of the same selfhood and concrete freedom. Self-conscious life is properly a continual dying to live. Thus for Hegel the problem of human identity eludes biological or sociological analysis because the real self of a human being is not an observable, empirical item at all but, rather, is constituted by the sublimation of the immediate ego through a process of transformation. Selfhood is a goal rather than a presupposition, a process rather than an item open to inspection or even introspection. Self-conscious spirit is the continual sacrifice and restoration of identity through resistance and recognition.

Hegel's theory of sacrifice is an instance of his famous theory of double negation. Hegel presents the imposition of form and order as the "sacrifice" of the Spirit: hence the famous line from the end of the *Phenomenology*, *"Seine Grenze wissen, heisst sich aufzuopfern wissen"*[75] ("To know its limits is to know how to sacrifice itself.") For Spirit that is conscious of itself as spirit, the path to self-realization is through the *sacrifice* of the natural and immediate life of the self whereby it is in opposition to the not-self. Self-conscious or spiritual life is not the development and then cessation of energy but a continual shattering of the immediate self and renewal and realization of that self in and through the not-self. That is to say, without *resistance* to the natural inclinations and desires of the ego, there is no real selfhood: pleasure dissolves like Helen in the arms of Faust.

Terry Pinkard, a leading exponent of the revisionary, quasi-analytic Hegel takes Spirit to be a fact about human recognition or *Anerkennung*. On this account, human subjects are constituted by their mutual recognition. Whereas Kant sees identification of an external world as presupposing subjectivity in the transcendental unity of apperception, Hegel is claiming that self-consciousness

---

75   Hegel, *Phenomenology*, 763, p. 9.

presupposes the recognition of other foci of self-consciousness.

> "Spirit" . . . denotes for Hegel not a metaphysical entity but a fundamental relation among persons that mediates their self consciousness, a way in which people reflect on what they have come to take as authoritative for themselves.[76]

On the contrary, I think that Hegel's work is an *itinerarium mentis in Deum*. Hegel's metaphysics is best understood as the attempt to fuse the *Geistesmetaphysik* of Plato and Aristotle with the post-Cartesian and Kantian philosophy of subjectivity. But Pinkard's interpretation cannot do justice to the religious language that Hegel in fact employs. If Spirit is sacrificing itself in encountering and overcoming its limits, this is both a *kenosis* or empting and an externalizing or revelation of Spirit. The explicit language of *kenosis* makes no sense if there is no Divine Spirit to be emptied! That is, if talk of spirit is merely another way of expounding the facts of intersubjectivity and not the self-surrender and sublimation of the absolute spirit qua *absolutum*. Schopenhauer's and Nietzsche's trenchant strictures on this crypto "theology" of the absolute are rather more convincing than Pinkard's attempt to secularize Hegel.[77]

Hegel's seemingly ambivalent attitude to religion emerges out of a critique of two extremes: the Enlightenment incomprehension of religion and the futility of reactionary fideism. Sacrifice as crude ritual offering or as pointless renunciation were rightly targeted by Enlightenment critics, but they in turn failed to see the metaphysical truth contained within the imaginative language of sacrifice. Hegel's dialectical integration of sacrifice is the attempt to outline the core of truth contained with the language of sacrifice while discarding the irrational husk.

Whatever doubts we may have about Hegel's theory of the Spirit, one can find very similar thoughts in severe critics of Hegel's absolute system like William James. James is playing on the very same paradox of the spirit observed in the master-slave dialectic when he writes:

> It is, indeed, a remarkable fact that sufferings and hardships do not, as a rule, abate the love of life; they seem on the contrary to give it a keener zest. The sovereign source of melancholy is repletion. Need and struggle are what excite and inspire us; our hour of triumph is what brings the void.[78]

Yet in knowing its limits, spirit transcends them. If Hegel's "metaphysical prejudice" is for the "eternal and the necessary over the temporary and the contingent," it is also the case that *only* through the sacrifice in the finite and contingent realm — the cup of history in Schiller's poetic imagery — that

76 Pinkard, T. (1996) *Hegel's Phenomenology: The Sociality of Reason*. Cambridge: Cambridge University Press.

77 Schopenhauer. (1959) *The World as Will and Representation,* Payne (trans.). London: Dover, 1.521, 2.43, 82. See Ryan, Chris. (2010) *Schopenhauer's Philosophy of Religion: The Death of God and the Oriental Renaissance*. Leuven: Peeters.

78 James, W. (1956) *The Will to Believe*. New York: Longmans, Green, & Co., p. 47.

the infinity of Spirit foams forth, in Hegel's quotation from Schiller at the
end of the *Phenomenology*

> [F]rom the chalice of this realm of spirits
> foams forth for Him his own infinitude.
> (Aus dem Kelche dieses Geisterreiches
> schäumt ihm seine Unendlichkeit.)[79]

There is, however, a deeply troubling dimension of Hegel's legacy. This is
the view of all history as a grim inexorable altar upon which individuals,
societies, peoples are immolated:

> Freedom is itself its own object of attainment and the sole purpose of
> Spirit. It is the ultimate purpose to which all world history has continu-
> ally aimed. To this end all sacrifices have been offered on the vast altar
> of the earth throughout the long lapse of ages.[80]

The terrifying implications are clear: history is the altar in the sense of
the slaughter-bench of the development of the Spirit. The sacrifice of the
absoluteness of individuals is justified as the necessary subordination of
the particular to the Universal. Here we can see the danger of the excessive
stress upon immanence in Hegel's theology: too close a link between the
Divine unfolding and the events of history.

Kierkegaard's critique

For Hegel the eternal idea is not a refuge from, but is to be grasped
within, the real conflicts and limitations of actual history. The vehemence
of Kierkegaard's critique of Hegel is not appreciated by those who fail
to recognize Hegel's deep and elective affinity to the Christian mystical
tradition and his deep admiration for the "love feast" of Greek sacrifice.
Henry Harris notes that the religious ceremony enhances the sense that

> we are not simply maintaining ourselves until death comes in the
> ordinary course of nature, but we are maintaining the immortal life of
> which "the course of nature" is only an abstract image.[81]

Kierkegaard's worry is that the real individual is swallowed up by the
process of Hegelian sacrifice. He wishes to deny the Hegelian thought that
self-sacrifice is the path to self-realization. This amounts for Kierkegaard
to a domestication of the real scandal of Christianity.

---

79   Phenomenology of Spirit, Harris (trans.), p. 493.
80   Hegel, G. W. F. (1953) *Reason in History*, R. S. Hartmann (trans). New York: Liberal Arts
      Press, p. 25.
81   Harris, H. S. (1972) *Hegel's Development: Towards the Sunlight (1770–1801)*. Oxford:
      Oxford University Press, p. 396.

Kierkegaard's contrast between Agamemnon's sacrifice of Iphigenia and Abraham's sacrifice of Isaac is a subtle critique of what Kierkegaard views as the essentially pagan nature of Hegel's philosophy. Agamemnon renounces himself in sacrificing his daughter, but he has the recognition of his men, waiting to sail for Troy. But there is no way of mediating Abraham's desires and his duty. His challenge is to commit a murder as a holy act. Silentio expresses his admiration for Abraham's great love of god, faith, and his terrible suffering. Some distinguished commentators, especially Merold Westphal, have observed that the real point of the story of *Fear and Trembling* is not sacrifice but, rather, faith. But if Kierkegaard was deeply aware of the sacrificial language in Hegel's philosophy, it is fitting critique that he should dwell upon the problems raised by the Abraham and Isaac story. Silentio claims:

> [T]he ethical expression for what Abraham did is that he meant to murder Isaac; the religious expression is that he meant to sacrifice Isaac.[82]

Here Kierkegaard is pitting the image of sacrifice against Hegel's idea of *Sittlichkeit*. Kierkegaard's account of the suffering, sacrifice, and renunciation as essential to the genuinely religious life, that of the knight of faith, is powerful and moving. But in so doing he seems to breach the idea of the univocal goodness of God.

There are two reasons why Kierkegaard's description of the near sacrifice of Isaac cannot amount to a Divine command theory. First, Abraham as the "knight of faith" is distinguished from the "knight of infinite resignation." The latter is like a man who loves a princess and yet has resigned his possession of her. In resigning his possession, he also resigns his care. Were he to achieve a relationship with the princess, he would not feel genuine joy. Her presence is not a necessary component of his love. In the case of Abraham, however, the Knight of Faith has resigned infinitely; but through the absurd, he has received Isaac with real joy. However mysteriously, Abraham trusts in Divine benevolence and his faith is indeed rewarded. Thus it is not the case that faith simply trumps ethics. Rather, the two are related mysteriously. Moreover, the wording of the *teleological* suspension of the ethical makes it clear that faith does not simply override the ethical *tout court*. However, while not explicitly espousing a Divine Command theory of ethics, Kierkegaard's stress upon the absurd or paradoxical nature of the demand made upon Abraham raises the knotty problem of evil and the goodness of God. Here we might look for a midway between Hegel's total resolution of negativity into the necessary process of reality and Kierkegaard's retreat into paradox.

Notwithstanding his remarkable literary gifts and innovative genius, Kierkegaard marks a return to the theology of the inscrutable Divine will in his *Fear and Trembling*, With all his esprit and irony, it amounts to the theology of Divine Command that was promulgated by the Nominalists

---

82   Kierkegaard. (1974) *Fear and Trembling*, W. Lowrie (trans.). New Jersey: Princeton University Press, p. 74. See David Palin (1981)'Abraham and Isaac' in Perkins, R. L. *Kierkegaard's Fear and Trembling: Critical Appraisals*, pp. 10–42.

in the Middle Ages and by early Modern Calvinists. The axiological theory of ethics that we have been proposing in this chapter, essentially that of Cudworth, presupposes the univocal nature of ethical statements about God. Whatever else may be proposed of God by analogy, the ethical may not. The appeal to a distinctly theological view of goodness is not a genuine option. But, of course, if we hold fast to the univocal theory of Divine Goodness, we must face the problem of theodicy.

5

Evil, Sacrifice, and the
Bloodstained Logos

Now John does not [present] the Word of God mounted on a horse naked. He is clothed with garment sprinkled with blood, since the Word who became flesh, and died because he became flesh, is invested with traces of that passion, since his blood also was poured forth on the earth when the soldier pierced his side. For, perhaps, even if in some way we attain the most sublime and holy contemplation of the Word and of the truth, we shall not forget completely that we were introduced to him by his coming in our body.[1]

Evil is a fact of human experience. Does this disprove the existence of a good and omnipotent God? Or does the fact of evil itself reveal to the imagination the vision of life as a sacrificial drama of redemption? In this chapter I will consider an attempt to argue for God's existence and Divine goodness by a reversal strategy. The fact of evil and its presence in human nature and actions becomes the basis for a reflection upon reality. I shall draw upon Maistre's employment of Origens's view of life as the drama of the return of the soul to God. Within this teleological drama, suffering becomes a pedagogic instrument for human reorientation to the Good. God's omnipotence on this model is limited not just by logic but also by goodness. Whitehead observed that Christianity fulfilled the Platonic ideal of goodness through its image of God operated through persuasion rather than force. In this sense the image of God crucified is an image of persuasion through love and goodness rather than by force. Maistre may seem an odd paradigm since he dwells so vividly (some might say gratuitously) upon suffering and punishment and his view of life as an arena of punishment. Yet it should be remembered that, as in the case of his great theological mentor Origen, Maistre is placing the suffering of souls within a soteriological context. The quotation from Origen that follows shortly should reveal Origen's view of the Logos as clad in bloodstained clothes. He is not interested in suffering or punishment *per se*, but their role within a Divine pedagogy of which the suffering Messiah is the focal point. This is the theodicy associated with John Hick's account of the vale of "soul making" and the various versions of the free-will defense that can be traced in recent philosophy back to debates between Mackie and Plantinga. We do not wish to rehearse the arguments for this theodicy but, rather, explore how the imagery of sacrifice operates within the parameters

---

1 Origen. (1989) *Commentary on John*, Robert E. Heine (trans.). Washington: CUA Press, books 1 and 2, p. 110.

of an overarching theodicy.

In his magnificent burlesque novel *The Master and Margarita*, Bulgakov depicts the arrival of Satan and his entourage to Soviet Moscow. Like Thomas Mann's *Dr Faustus*, it is remarkable as a depiction of the presence of the Devil in secular, officially "atheistic" twentieth-century Europe. There are three entangled plots: the Devil arriving in Moscow during the horrors of the purges; the trial of Jesus at the hands of Pilate, and a third story about a writer called the Master who is writing about Jesus and his lover, Margarita. It was written amidst the horrors of the purges and the height of cruel repression of Stalin's regime. The comedy starts with a debate between the Devil and a party official about the existence of Jesus Christ; the Devil tries to persuade the unfortunate party official of the reality of the supernatural and then murders him. The novel concludes with "educated and cultivated people" (the naturalists) holding to the official state philosophy, denying the experiences of the supernatural in the form of the Devil. These explanations are, in fact, evidently improbable phenomena such as mass hypnotism or ventriloquism. Bulgakov, learned in theology, presents the five ways of Thomas and Kant's moral argument for the existence of God. But he adds a seventh argument for the existence of God: the existence of the Devil. As shadow proves the existence of substances, so too evil can prove the existence of a Good God.[2] The core thought is that the supernatural and the natural are interwoven. Any world, like that of Stalin's Russia, with its dogmatic denial of supernatural reality cannot "save the appearances," not least the fact of evil.

Consider again Maistre's vision of the world as an "immense altar" that is "steeped in blood." His brilliant rhetoric can suggest a man obsessed with violence. Yet it reflects a highly sensitive and inquisitive mind perplexed by the anomalies of human existence.[3]

Maistre's theology is a lamb in wolf's clothing. For all his somber pronouncements, Maistre, like the seventeenth-century Cambridge Platonist and Bishop of Dromore, George Rust, or his own venerated Origen, is robustly universalist in his *Letter Concerning Resolution Concerning Origen and the Chief of his Opinions of 1661*. George Rust was a great admirer of Origen because the Alexandrinian seemed to present an alternative to Logic of Terror in St. Augustine's dreadful doctrine of the *massa damnata*. His own thesis that since God is love (1 Jn 4.16) then God must (contra Augustine) wish the salvation of all of his creatures. Such universalism has a strangely Kantian flavor:

> God hath the greater advantage to magnific his love in our Recovery, and Man will have the transcendent Pleasure, to have escaped out of so great Dangers and Miseries [. . .] hereby is an occasion given us of exercising those perfection, which otherwise there could not have been

2   Ericson, E. E. (1991) *The Apocalyptic Vision of Mikhail Bulgakov's The Master and Margarita*. Lewiston, Australia: Mellon, esp. pp. 9–24.
3   Maistre, Joseph Marie. (1993) *St Petersburg Dialogues; or, Conversations on the Temporal Government of Providence*. Montreal: McGill-Queen's University Press, p. 217.

opportunity for, as Patience, Self denial [. . .] Compassion [. . .] and faith in him (i.e. God).[4]

Owen Bradley, in his learned work *A Modern Maistre: the Social and Political Thought of Joseph de Maistre,* refers to the heterodox character of Maistre's Catholic Neoplatonism.[5] Joseph de Maistre is writing prior to *Aeterni patris* of 1879. With this document, Thomas Aquinas became the official philosopher of Roman Catholicism, and a rather narrow interpretation of the angelic doctor came to prevail. Maistre cites Aquinas enthusiastically, yet he is not a Thomist but a Christian Platonist. Indeed, Aeterni patris was motivated not just by the fear of atheism but by the Romantic Neoplatonism that formed the backbone of much nineteenth-century Catholic theology. By the standard of mid-twentieth-century textbook Thomism, Maistre is heterodox, but so are Nicholas of Cusa and Malebranche — that is to say, the Platonic strand. I think we should be cautious about placing too much emphasis upon the "heterodox" Maistre, if only for fear of crass anachronism. Maistre, like Rust, departs from the mainstream of Western theology in the wake of Augustine's doctrine of grace and its influence in those grim theories of double predestination that emanated from the African doctor. We shall see that Maistre develops distinctly Origenistic themes of punishment and education as the process of redemption. The suffering of the world is a punishment for fallen souls but it is not based upon a brutal and cruel theology of Divine retribution but rather the punishment is part of a Divine therapy and pedagogy. God is both the shepherd and the doctor of his children. Another admirer of Origen, B. F. Wescott, wrote:

> In Augustine history is a mere succession of external events; the Divine teaching through heathendom lies in the utterances of the Sibyls and not in the course of Empires. For Origen, in spite of his idealism, life has a moral significance of incalculable value: for Augustine, in spite of his realism, life is a mere show, in which actors fulfil the parts irrevocably assigned to them. The Alexandrine cannot rest without looking forward to a final unity which still he confesses more than once that he is unable to grasp: the African acquiesces without a difficulty in an abiding dualism in the future, which must seem to other minds not less oppressive to the moral sense that the absolute dualism of the Mani.[6]

Bradley notes that the Savoyard Count's critique of Enlightenment highlights a remarkable awareness of the fundamental ambivalence of human action. Thus Maistre can be retrieved in the postmodern milieu as an improbable precursor to Freud or Foucault. Bradley seeks "to make of Maistre the ambiguous, equivocal, undecidable figure I believe he ought to

---

4   Rust. (1661) *Letter of Resolution Concerning Origen*. London: n.p., 61.
5   Bradley, O. (1999) *A Modern Maistre: The Social and Political Thought of Joseph De Maistre,* *European Horizons*. Lincoln; London: University of Nebraska Press, p. 172.
6   Westcott, B. F. *Essays in the History of Religious Thought in the West*. London; New York: Macmillan, p. 248.

be for modern thought rather than a monster plain and simple."[7] Rather than revealing a morbid obsession with violence, Maistre presents ritual sacrifice as a spiritualizing process that reduces the violence required to sustain social order.

As Bradley has argued most eloquently, Maistre's thought depends upon the *mot clé* "sacrifice." Judicial punishment and war are domains where ritualized violence upholds the social order through representing the legitimate power of the sovereign. Notwithstanding the interpretation of Berlin, Bradley claims that Maistre "was among (. . .) the first to thematise how power is based not merely on coercion but also, and even more fundamentally, on the symbolic, on custom, representation, and belief."[8] The real issue is order and disorder within a larger logic of history. How can we understand justice, wickedness, mercy, and forgiveness as part of a providential and law-governed process of expiation and redemption?

This is a brilliant restatement of Maistre's prodigious intellectual legacy as a critic of the Enlightenment. Indeed, Maistre is warning of the danger of underestimating man's potential for violence. But I am unsure that this makes the Savoyard Count into a modern. One might just as readily compare Maistre with Euripides. Euripides in his *Bacchae*, writing in the Peloponnesian war, reveals the violent and destructive dimension of their world to the Athenians of the Athenian Enlightenment; the Savoyard Count can show how the French Enlightenment is equally blind to its own destructive potential. I think that Bradley's is a brilliant and illuminating reading of Joseph de Maistre; but it does not go quite far enough.

I wish to emphasize not so much the modern as the Romantic Maistre. He is very much a philosopher of tradition, opposed to the Cartesian doubt or the principle of individual judgment. Like Vico, Maistre is a trenchant critic of the paradoxical barbarism of Enlightenment and the hidden Providence of tradition. Maistre sees decadence as the fruit of Baconian science, skepticism and the erosion of the religious foundations of society.

The main issue addressed by Maistre is that of *le bonheur des méchants* and *le malheur des justes*. Bradley claims:

> The justification to man of the ways of the world was one of Maistre's central preoccupations, motivated I would argue not so much by a mystical fascination with Providence for its own sake as by the attempt to refute what he understood as a revival of the Gnostic depiction of man's world as radically unjust and unjustifiable, in need of total renovation.[9]

Terms like "mystical" are potentially misleading. First Maistre, like Milton, wishes to "justify the ways of God to men," emphatically not the ways of the world! And his sources are often explicitly "mystical": from Origen to the Cambridge Platonists St. Martin and Fénelon. The great Ultramontane defender of Catholic authority is happy to appeal to heretical and Protestant

7 Bradley, *A Modern Maistre*, p. xviii.
8 Bradley, *A Modern Maistre*, pp. 90–1.
9 Bradley, *A Modern Maistre*, p. 167.

thinkers that share in a common mystical tradition in which salvation consists in "likeness to God."

Further, I think we should be cautious about Bradley's claim that Maistre's idea of Providence was barely traditional: "While like every providentialist he does insist that the world obeys final causes that tend toward the good, neither God nor his personal intentions appear anywhere in Maistre argument."[10] Yet in *Les Soirées* we have an explicit reference to the incarnation: *L'Homme-Dieu* (Man-God), the Godman called us to be his friends. This, I think, is explicitly Christian. A philosophy deeply sympathetic to Christianity, Kant's, speaks of the "Holy One of the Gospel," but even he shrinks before the explicitly Calcedonian "Godman." A deist or atheist, quite apart from a Jew or a Muslim would not have written thus. "Whatever topic one treats one always speaks of her" says Maistre; but not because it is a bland topic. I think that Bradley is failing to stress the full force of the theological dimension in Maistre's work, especially *Les Soirées*.

Bradley becomes rather sidetracked by a debate about Gnosticism. "Gnosticism" has been much discussed in figures like Jonas and Voegelin. However, I don't really think that Maistre sees the philosophy of the Enlightenment as tainted by Gnosticism. For him it is empiricism and naturalism that constitute the problem. And philosophy is, as Maistre tells us in a wonderful and characteristically pungent passage, like counterfeit money. A few rogues produce it, and then it passes through the hands of many honest men: *"Mais les fausses opinions ressemblent à la fausse monnaie qui est frappée d'abord par de grands coupables, et dépensée ensuite par d'honnêtes gens, qui perpétuent le crime sans savoir ce qu'ils font."*[11] Among the false tenets circulated by the philosophes is an unwarranted and dangerous optimism about human nature. Maistre avers:

> There is nothing but violence in the universe; but we are spoiled by a modern philosophy that tells us *all is good*, whereas evil has tainted everything, and in a very real sense, *all is evil*, since nothing is in its place. The keynote of the system of our creation has been lowered, and following the rules of harmony, all the others have been lowered proportionately. *All creation groans*, and tends with pain and effort towards another order of things.[12]

One solution to the problem of evil was to deny the existence of a providential Deity and to seek remedy for ills in cultural reform: the abolition of Church, monarch, and aristocracy. Maistre saw the shallowness of this approach as typified by Voltaire. In contrast to the jejune optimism of the French Enlightenment, the Savoyard diplomat presents a view of the world as the training ground of the soul and as a domain of painful and often grim

10 Bradley, *A Modern Maistre*, p. 170.
11 Maistre, Joseph de. (2007) "Les Soirées de Saint-Pétersbourg," in Pierre Glaudes (ed.), *Œuvres*. Paris: R. Laffont, p. 464.
12 Maistre, Joseph de. (2007) "Considérations sur la France," in Pierre Glaudes (ed.), *Œuvres*. Paris: R. Laffont, p. 218; Maistre, "Les Soirées de Saint-Pétersbourg," p. 709.

anomalies which point to the Fallen state of humanity. The violence and suffering of this world are both a clear repudiation of the perfectionism of the Enlightenment and the foundation for Maistre's view of suffering and violence as fuel for the transformation of the soul: a tending towards 'another order of things'. If this were 'the best of all possible worlds' the natural longing for transcendent reconciliation and peace would be unmotivated. But this, we shall argue, is far from glorifying or expressing any perverse delight in the savagery or horror of violence. Maistre is a man traumatised by violence, not its advocate. And his theology provides the proper context within which one should evaluate his reflections on the human condition.

But Maistre is fascinated by the ethical ambivalence of warfare and its relation to society. Doubtless the Count would have regarded many of the wars of the twentieth century as an instance of a brutality unrestrained by "traditional" decency. Perhaps the primary shock of Maistre's meditations upon war is the product of our contemporary anesthetic civilization. Maistre is scandalous to the contemporary mind because of the remarkable capacity of a highly developed technological society not merely to prevent pain for its own members but also to hide suffering. One does not have to be an adherent of Foucault to see the craving for comfort and security as part of an attempt to administrate life and eradicate the unsightly and troubling: avoiding confrontation with the old and the sick. For democratic politicians understandably worried about votes, the dead and the wounded of wars are rendered, as far as possible, invisible.

Consider the paradoxical claim that "war is Divine." It is typical of his penchant for misleading rhetoric. In fact, Maistre refers again to the "horrible enigma" that is the anomalous status of war: *"Rien n'est plus contraire à sa nature, et rien ne lui répugne moins: il fait avec enthousiasme ce qu'il a en horreur."*[13] Yet in Maistre's account of war much is quite true. Post-Napoleonic warfare had become more brutal than warfare under the *ancien régime*. The political order of the early modern period prior to the French Revolution was largely dynastic-sacred rather than national-secular. The Ottomans were not "Turks"; the Prussian court spoke French during the age of Goethe; the emperor of the Germans sat in Vienna or Prague. The Holy Roman Empire, neither Holy nor Roman perhaps, nevertheless expresses the residual feudal ideals of the old European order. It was doubtless an imperfect order, but order it was.

The wars of religion in the seventeenth century created devastation in Europe. Writers like Grotius tried to develop an influential secular justification of the political order, one that moved from transcendental or sacerdotal reasons to issues of human need and justice. The Enlightenment in Europe was distinguished by this shift from religious to secular legitimization. Grotius was a Christian, but he was motivated by the brutality and disruption of the European wars of religion.

One of the great ironies of the twentieth century was that prominent "secular" national totalitarian states were crueler than the empires of the *ancien régime*.

---

13   Maistre, "Les Soirées de Saint-Pétersbourg," p. 660.

The divine spirit, which has particularly blessed Europe, has even mitigated the scourge of eternal justice, and *European war* will always have a special place in annals of the world. Undoubtedly Europeans killed, burned, ravaged, and even, if you wish, committed thousands of useless crimes; but nevertheless they began war in the month of May and ended it in the month of December; they slept under canvas; soldiers fought only soldiers. Whole nations were never at war, and all that was weak was sacred amidst the dreary scenes of this devastating plague.[14]

Note first that Maistre is not glamorizing warfare. He speaks clearly of war as "this devastating plague" and the functions of the soldier are terrible. His point is rather that war too reflects a "great law of the spiritual world." Progress can only be through suffering and renunciation. Just as the war chariot of Arjuna becomes a seat of meditation for thoughts about the Absolute Brahman in the Gita, thoughts that culminate in a vision of the creator. Maistre uses war as an object of meditation on God and his relation to the world.[15] In one of the most important works on Indian epic, Alf Hiltebeitel uses ritual, especially sacrificial ritual, in his reading of the *Mahabharata*. It would not be lost on Maistre that the foundational epics of the East and West, the *Iliad* and the *Mahabharata*, are stories of war as sacrificial.[16]

Carolina Armenteros notes that the modern period is seen by Maistre as veering between the relative calm of the seventeenth century and the turbulence of the eighteenth century.[17] The violence of the eighteenth century can be seen to correspond to the loosening of bonds that reduced and controlled the violent dimension of human nature:

In the blink of an eye, the customs of the Iroquois and the Algonquin; the holy laws of humanity trod under foot; innocent blood covering the scaffolds that covered France; men curling and powdering bloody heads, and the very mouths of women stained with human blood.

Here is the *natural* man! It is not that he does not bear within him the indestructible seeds of truth and virtue: his birthrights are imprescriptible; but without divine fertilization, these seeds will never germinate or they will produce only dubious or unhealthy fruit.[18]

The critics of Christianity were correct to note that the Church colluded in great injustice, absurd privilege, and authoritarianism, but at least it provided an ethical structure and culture for Western civilization that,

---

14   Maistre, "Les Soirées de Saint-Pétersbourg," p. 658.
15   Bhagavad Gita, 11.15–31. Winthrop Seargant (trans.)., Christopher Key Chapple (ed.), foreword by Huston Smith (2009). Albany, NY: State University of New York Press.
16   Hiltebeitel, A. (1976) *The Ritual of Battle: Krishna in the Mahabharata*. Ithaca, NY: Cornell.
17   Armenteros, Carolina. (2008) "Revolutionary violence and the end of history: the divided self in Francophone thought, 1762–1914," in Carolina Armenteros, Tim Blanning, Isabel DiVanna, and Dawn Dodds (eds.), *Historicising the French Revolution*. Newcastle: Cambridge Scholars, p. 19.
18   Maistre, Joseph de. (2007) "Eclaircissement sur les sacrifices," in Pierre Glaudes (ed.), *Œuvres*. Paris: R. Laffont, p. 824.

contra Machiavelli and Hobbes, was at odds with any politics based on arbitrary power. Maistre predicted that modern utopias would generate terrible tyranny. Burke and Maistre appealed to the Terror of the French Revolution as a harbinger of future horrors and as a vindication of their conservatism. But Burke was not a theologian. Maistre was more sensitive to any arbitrary dimension in Christian theology, especially in its ultra Augustinian forms. Augustine's doctrines of double predestination and the damnation of unbaptized infants would have been hard to accommodate in a thinker like Maistre, a thinker so committed to the idea of Christianity as a guardian against the arbitrary violence of the state. Thus I suspect that the attraction of Origen resided in the latter's resolute attachment to the goodness of God. The espousal of a God of inscrutable will, the Augustine so important for Luther and Calvin as well as Jansenism, is problematic for a thinker like Maistre. Origen is the Church Father who is dedicated to freedom.[19] Yet significantly, for Origen the Christian view of the world is that of a place of warfare as well as a festival and celebration of the Divine.[20] Only in the midst of conflict and violence can virtue, as man's true nature, emerge. The world and history is thus the arena of human freedom within the parameters of Divine Providence.[21]

Voltaire and the ambivalence of violence

Maistre is deeply opposed to Voltaire's claim that "Whoever can make you accept absurdity, can make you commit injustice." Voltaire presented Christianity as not just false but also immoral. Through his *Candide*, Voltaire is the thinker most associated with the critique of theodicy. His *Traité sur la Tolérance à l'occasion de la mort de Jean Calas* of 1763 is a critique of iniquity perpetrated in the name of religion, inspired by the persecution and execution of the French Protestant Jean Calas by the Toulouse magistrature, the last man to be executed on the wheel in France on the trumped-up charge of murdering his son (in all likelihood it was a suicide). Voltaire's moving and scathing critique of the cruelty inflicted upon Calas became celebrated throughout Europe and 39 of Voltaire's works were placed upon the Index. One gains a sense of the more intransigent and polemical side of Maistre's nature in his remarks about the doubtful innocence of Calas. Yet it is perhaps helpful to view his metaphysics of punishment in the context of the controversy raised by Voltaire.

Maistre's interest in punishment is philosophical, not pathological. Generally a philosophical justification of punishment is either retributive (e.g. Kant or Hegel) or consequentialist (e.g. Hobbes or Rousseau): either punishment redresses an intrinsic wrong or produces favorable results for

---

19 Kobusch, T. (1980) "Die Philosophische Bedeutung Des Kirchenvaters Origenes," *Theologische Quartalschrift*, 165 (1985): 9–31.
20 Schockenhoff, Eberhard. (1990) *Zum Fest Der Freiheit: Theologie Des Christlichen Handelns Bei Origenes.* Mainz: Grünewald, pp. 258ff.
21 I would therefore reject as mistaken the view that Maistre is "deistic," except possibly from the perspective of a very extreme Augustinianism.

society at large (e.g. protection from violence, theft, or dishonesty). Many of Maistre's Enlightenment "opponents" maintain that the "just desert" of retributive punishment is either atavistic (i.e. revenge) or illusory (because it is metaphysically impossible). Some, like Foucault, may claim that punishment merely reflects the desire to exert power over others.[22] Both the ultraliberal and the Foucault positions rest upon the anti-Platonic view that there are no objective values. For both the liberals and Foucault, punishment is just a human institution — not a natural fact — and it could theoretically be dispensed with. For Maistre, punishment is not an arbitrary fact about human society, but reflects a spiritual law of punishment. Warfare and punishment are indexes of mankind's duality: man is, for Maistre, "the monstrous centaur."[23]

I think that this Platonic dimension of Maistre's thought can be seen in his emphasis upon the mirroring of eternal justice upon earth, however obliquely. The executioner represents order amidst disorder. For all the horror of his acts, they are not — *pace* Foucault — the expression of brute power. Let us consider the notorious executioner passage. It is remarkable in its imaginative engagement with the person of the executioner, as well as his ambivalent status in society:

> In outward appearance he is made like us; he is born like us. But he is an extraordinary being, and for him to be brought into existence as a member of the human family a particular decree was required, a FIAT of creative power.[24]

What does Maistre imply with the allusion to the "Fiat Lux" of the Vulgate? In the creation story of Genesis, God creates heaven and earth and light and darkness, and the light is good. Maistre suggests that the executioner is an organ of Divine justice:

> There is then in the temporal sphere a Divine and visible law for the punishment of crime. This law, as stable as the society it upholds, has been executed invariably since the beginning of time. Evil exists on the earth and acts constantly, and by a necessary consequence it must constantly be repressed by punishment.[25]

Rather than akin to the *bellum omnium contra omnes* of Hobbes, Maistre's perspective is quite the opposite: resolutely providentialist. For Hobbes, sovereignty is grounded in the pressing need to combat the chaotic violence of man's natural state. For Maistre, the existence of society at all presupposes the victory of justice, however imperfectly realized, over sheer power. The institution of capital punishment is a shadow of the eternal

---

22 Foucault, Michel. (1977) *Discipline and Punish: The Birth of the Prison*. London: Allen Lane, p. 23.
23 Maistre, *St Petersburg Dialogues*, p. 38.
24 Maistre, *St Petersburg Dialogues*, p. 19.
25 Maistre, *St Petersburg Dialogues*, p. 20.

and immutable Divine law that lies at the basis of human association and society. Whereas the God of Hobbes is at best a *Deus absconditus*, for the Platonic Maistre God is the transcendent source of earthly and temporal justice and order. In the words of Dante:

> *La gloria di colui che tutto move*
> *per l'universo penetra e risplende*
> *in una parte più e meno altrove.*[26]

Maistre avers that we must turn our eyes to the invisible world as the explanation of the visible, *"tenons nos yeux fixés sur ce monde invisible qui expliquera tout."*[27] Even when considering the person of the executioner, Maistre sees him as part of a broader providential scheme, notwithstanding the horror of his work:

> Consider how he is viewed by public opinion, and try to conceive, if you can, how he could ignore this opinion or confront it! Scarcely have the authorities assigned his dwelling, scarcely has he taken possession of it, when other men move their houses elsewhere so they no longer have to see his. In the midst of this seclusion and in this kind of vacuum formed around him, he lives alone with his female and his offspring, who acquaint him with the human voice. Without them he would hear nothing but groans . . .
>
> Is this a man? Yes. God receives him in his shrines and allows him to pray. He is not a criminal, and yet no tongue would consent to say, for example that he is virtuous, that he is an honest man, that he is admirable, etc. No moral praise seems appropriate for him, since this supposes relationships with human beings, and he has none.
>
> And yet all greatness, all power, all subordination rests on the executioner.[28]

Maistre is speculating about the anomalous status of the executioner. He stands without relation to other creatures. Moral categories seem subverted. While necessary for the well-being of the state, the executioner is regarded with a mixture of anxiety and awe by his fellows. Yet this uncanny figure is presented psychologically from a very human perspective. Maistre depicts the literally dreadful loneliness of the executioner's role. The executioner is an organ of justice and yet isolated from human contact: only his own family "acquaint him with the human voice." In this short passage, sometimes cited by critics as evidence for Maistre's sadism, we find a remarkable empathy for the human being performing this grim task.

26   "The glory of Him who moves all things penetrates the universe and shines in one part more and in another less." Dante, Alighieri. (1939) "Paradiso," in John D. Sinclair (trans.), *The Divine Comedy of Dante Alighieri*. Oxford: Oxford University Press, p. 19.
27   Maistre, *St Petersburg Dialogues*, p. 661.
28   Maistre, *St Petersburg Dialogues*, p. 19.

Just war?

Rene Girard sees war as the redirection of aggressive instincts that of danger with the community to external powers. Thus he can claim stridently that war is "merely another form of sacrificial violence."[29] A Christian writer such as Maistre can draw upon a long tradition of speculation about war and its justification. The idea has often been "baptized" as it were, by Christians. On this view sacrifice is good because it is modeled upon Christ, and the suffering and death of warriors is Christlike. Here biblical passages like Jn 15.13 and Rom. 5.6-8 are often cited.

Yet warriors are not merely the victims of violence; they perpetrate it.[30] Can Christians tolerate such violence? Bainton sees essentially three paradigms: pacifism, just war, and the crusade. These have dominated the early Church, the Fathers, and the medieval Church respectively. Most Christians will find either extreme unpalatable. Pacifism can reinforce violence, and crusades, of course, can produce terrible atrocities.

Augustine is clear on this:

[T]he wise man, they say, will wage just wars. Surely, however, if he remembers that he is a human being, he will be much readier to deplore the fact that he is under the necessity of waging even just wars . . . Let everyone, therefore, who reflects with pain on such evils, upon such horror and cruelty, acknowledge that this is misery. And if anyone either endures them without anguish of soul, his condition is still more miserable; for he thinks himself happy only because he has lost all human feeling.[31]

But the view of war as a necessary evil does not accord well with the heroic code of the Western martial culture. From the "lifelong glory" of King Aethelstan, the 'lord of heroes' at the Battle of Brunanburh or Dr Johnson's thought that "every man thinks meanly of himself for not having been a soldier," relish of violence and pride of prowess seems the dominant tone. Maistre makes this point when he uses the thought-experiment of an extra-terrestrial visiting the world presented with the two kinds of men allowed to kill: the soldier and the executioner. Given that the former kills honest and good men and the latter kills criminals, the visitor will doubtless be surprised to discover the esteem exhibited for the warrior and the ignominy of the executioner.[32] Voltaire observes that it is forbidden to kill; therefore all murderers are punished unless they kill in large numbers and to the sound of trumpets. (*Il est défendu de tuer; tout meurtrier est puni, à moins qu'il n'ait tué en grande compagnie, et au son des trompettes.*[33]) Maistre uses the example of war to attack materialistic theories of human behavior such as "God is always on the side of the big battalions." On the contrary,

29   Girard, R. and Gregory, P. (2005) *Violence and the Sacred*. London: Continuum, p. 251.
30   Bainton, R. (1979) *Christian Attitudes to Peace and War: A Historical Survey and Critical Re-evaluation*. Nashville, TN: Abingdon Press.
31   Augustine, *On the City of God*, 19.7. Harmondsworth: Penguin, (1984), pp. 861–2.
32   Maistre, *St Petersburg Dialogues*, p. 206–7.
33   Voltaire. (1771) *Dictionnaire Philosophique*, Section 1, Droit: Droit des Gens, Droit Naturel, p. 2.

here laws of physical force are often quite impotent: "*C'est l'imagination qui gagne et qui perd les batailles.*" (It is imagination that wins or loses battles.)[34] In such passages Maistre is attacking the crude mechanical anthropology employed by prominent philosophes like La Mettrie or d'Alembert. The violence of warfare is grounded in man's (ambivalent) spiritual nature and resists mechanical explanation. Nor is war, as for Clausewitz, merely politics by other means. Its horrors can only be explained theologically — as punishment and sacrifice. Moreover, notwithstanding its real horrors, war generates much that is positive for human life: it is a dreadful "scourge" and yet "the real fruits of human nature — arts, sciences, great enterprises, noble ideas, manly virtues — are due especially to the art of war."[35]

Much of Maistre's polemic is directed at crude materialistic or anthropological theories of war. The Chevalier uses a theory of brute force; he says: "kings order you, and you must march."[36] The Count dismisses this idea peremptorily. Nor is glory or prestige sufficient to explain the fact of war. The only explanation is theological: "an occult and terrible law demanding human blood."[37]

Closely linked to this doctrine is his resolute innatism or "original notions common to all men, without which they would not be men." Through these innate ideas men can interpret the visible world as the symbolic juncture between the temporal and the Divine. I was lately told a tale of a small terrier in rural England, one that was uncommonly fond of a cat in the same household. When the cat died, the tiny dog went into the garden, dug up the corpse of the cat, dragged it through the cat flap and licked it clean for the owner, who found his cat thus "resurrected' when he arose the next morning. The dog's devotion to his feline companion is startling and touching, but one is reminded of Vico's thoughts about the uniqueness of burials for human beings.[38] Maistre makes a rather similar point when he describes an execution with his dog and he describes the very different world of the dog. He and the dog have the same phenomenal experiences but dwell in different worlds. The dog can sense the crowd or the action of the guillotine but has no conceptual or symbolic awareness of the cessation of a human life or the execution of justice; these are ideas and symbols beyond his ken.[39] The dog and his master have different perceptions of the world, different inputs. Bradley claims that Maistre "was among the first to thematize how power is based not merely on coercion but also, and even more fundamentally, on the symbolic, on custom, representation, and belief." This emphasis upon the figurative is essential for Maistre: the physical world is a set of signs or Divine language: all things are suffused by the Divine and the whole cosmos points back to its creator. God is not a superfluous addition to the world, but the transcendent and sustaining

34 Maistre, *St Petersburg Dialogues*, p. 665.
35 Maistre. (1994) *Considerations on France*, Richard Lebrun (trans.). Cambridge: Cambridge University Press, p. 29.
36 Maistre, *Conversations*, p. 205.
37 Maistre, *Conversations*, p. 211.
38 Vico, Giambattista. (1999) *New Science: Principles of the New Science Concerning the Common Nature of Nations* (3rd edn.), David Marsh (trans.) London: Penguin, p. 130.
39 Maistre, *St Petersburg Dialogues*, p. 131.

source of its meaning. Thus even the horrors of war or execution are not strictly "natural." The distinctly human sense of cruelty and disorder in warfare and the terror of violent punishment presuppose a realm of transcendent meaning utterly removed from the sensorium of the brute. War and punishment fill the heart with dreadful awe and terror — yet not because mankind is thereby unveiled a wolf unto to itself (*"homo homini lupus est"* in Hobbes's invocation of the adage of Plautus in his *De cive* of 1651) but precisely, as Seneca said, because man is a thing sacred to man (*homo sacra res homini*).[40]

Suffering and substitution

Maistre stands between Kant and Hegel. The former proposed the abolition of war, the latter saw war as necessary and, sometimes, civilizing. Maistre views war as a part of the broader problem of evil.

The motor of Maistre's theology of evil is his theistic metaphysics. If "mystical" is shorthand for "irrational," I would claim that there is nothing mystical about the problem of theodicy. It has interested serious philosophers since Plato. Indeed, if the fact of evil disproves the theistic idea of God, that is momentous.

> Every right-thinking mind is convinced by intuition that evil cannot come from an all-powerful being. It was this infallible feeling that formerly taught Roman good sense to unite as if by a necessary bond the two august titles of MOST GOOD and MOST POWERFUL. This magnificent expression, though born under the sign of paganism, appeared so just that it has passed into your religious language, so delicate and so exclusive. I will even tell you in passing that is has occured to me more than once to think that the antique inscription, IOVI OPTIMO MAXIMO, could be put in full on the pediments of your Latin temples, for what is IOV-I if not IOV-AH?[41]

How can a God who is good and all-powerful allow evil, or, if God exists, why do we experience evil? Let us extend the classic problem as formulated by the Senator to include knowledge. How can evil exist if God is good, omnipotent, and omniscient? Consider the following argument:

1. God is good, omnipotent, and omniscient.
2. If God is omniscient, he knows about all evil.
3. If God is omnipotent, God can remove all evil.
4. If God is good, he will desire the removal of evil.
5. Evil exists.
6. If evil exists, God does not know about it, cannot remove it or does not wish to.
7. Therefore God does not exist.

40   Seneca, L. A. (1961) *Ad Lucilium Epistulae Morales*, Richard M. Gummere, (trans.). Loeb Classical Library, 3 vols. London: William Heinemann, 95.33.
41   Maistre, "Les Soirées de Saint-Pétersbourg," p. 466.

So expressed, this argument is valid but not necessarily sound. Are all the premises correct? Any deductive argument is valid when, given true premises, the truth of the conclusion is guaranteed. A deductive argument, however, can only be deemed sound if and only if its structure is valid, and its premises are indeed correct.

Maistre starts by turning the traditional problem around. He uses evil as an argument for Divine existence. Maistre's position may be summarized thus:

1. Evil exists.
2. Without an intuition of goodness, we could have no sense of evil: cosmic disorder presupposes order.
3. We have a sense of our own interior discord as a source of evil — indeed, as the primary source of evil in the world.
4. The existence of evil illuminates both God's existence and nature. If the world consisted wholly and uniquely of goodness and righteousness there would be no need for God since the world itself would be Divine. God exists because evil exists and this means in particular that through freedom mankind is thrust back to the reality of God.
5. God cannot force men to love Him. But he can provide a world in which the love of God (subjective and objective genitive!) can be realized through prayer and sacrifice. In particular, innocent suffering represents the expiation of the guilt of sinners by the just.

In *Les Soirées*, Maistre avoids two unattractive solutions to the problem of theodicy. One is the overarching harmony model. On such an account, it is argued that the quantity of goods in the world outweighs the number of evils. Dostoevsky seems to bite here: "I reject that higher harmony. It's not worth one little tear from one single little tortured child."[42] The difficulty resides in any quantitative justification of the existence of evil. Such theories seem to minimize the reality of suffering in the world and, indeed, can even be seen to provide a *ratio essendi* for suffering. No one could accuse Maistre of minimizing the extent and intensity of suffering in the world. It becomes integrated into the drama of redemption.

Another response to the problem of evil is the opposite extreme: the praxis model. This maneuver consists in dismissing the theoretical question and attempting to overcome evil through a Christlike life. The Christian should take up the cross and ignore theoretical justification. Yet such a position depends upon a Christocentric positivism, in which Christ is the unique revelation of the suffering of God. Such an approach to theodicy just begs the question. If the God of theism is problematic on account of the problem of evil, the status of a Christian God in a world of egregious ills seems at least as unsettling for any notion of Providence. Moreover, any practice must depend upon a satisfactory theory and the radical irrationality of the world does *prima facie* support the atheist case.

One of the most powerful challenges to theodicy comes from David

---

42 Dostoevsky, F. (1991) *Crime and Punishment*, David McDuff (trans.). Harmondsworth: Penguin Books, p. 307.

Hume's brilliant *Dialogues Concerning Natural Religion* of 1779.[43] Hume either argues that the theologian claims too much for the argument from design and then we cannot avoid the problem of evil or he claims ignorance of Divine purpose and avoids the problem of evil — but with the unfortunate consequence of conceding to the agnostic the futility of philosophical theology. If God is posited radically beyond human comprehension, he cannot be worshiped. There must be some link between the transcendent and human experience. Indeed, Maistre brilliantly avoids Hume's theological fork. Maistre is anti-apophatic: he argues against an undue stress upon the unknowability of the Divine. He writes that philosophy warns us that God is not like us, but that it is religion which makes us like unto God. The God-man called us to be his friends.

We must distinguish between the conviction in the incomprehensible Divine mystery and the idea of God as unknowable. The first principle is essential for any serious theology. The second means the impossibility of natural theology. If we can know the divine at all – apart from those appeals to revelation which can hardly be employed by philosophers – then it must be on the principle of imaginative analogy and a belief in the scale of Being. The transcendent God of Maistre's philosophy is veiled and we are placed at an epistemic distance from his Being. Made in the Divine image, we are commanded to pursue the Divine likeness.

Indeed, the principle of correspondence between the material and the spiritual worlds is a recurring theme of Maistre's metaphysics:

> *Nous sommes tous attachés au trône de l'Etre suprême par une chaîne souple, qui nous retient sans nous asservir.*
>
> *Ce qu'il y a de plus admirable dans l'ordre universel des choses, c'est l'action des êtres libres sous la main Divine. Librement esclaves, ils opèrent tout à la fois volontairement et nécessairement: ils font réellement ce qu'ils veulent, mais sans pouvoir déranger les plans généraux. Chacun de ces êtres occupe le centre d'une sphère d'activité, dont le diamètre varie au gré de l'éternel géomètre, qui sait étendre, restreindre, arrêter ou diriger la volonté, sans altérer sa nature.*[44]

The image of the *aurea catena homeri* (see *Iliad* 8.18) and that of the Divine geometer are typically Neoplatonic motifs and both are integral to Maistre's tenet of correspondences between the spiritual and material levels of existence.[45] "Correspondences" exist on manifold levels. Life properly ordered means that reason controls the passions, just as a king ruled his subjects, the parent ruled the child, and the sun governed the planets. However, chaos present in one realm is mirrored in other realms. Shakespeare's *King Lear*, for example, reveals the horror of chaos pervading family, state, and mind: the madness of Lear mirrors the terrors of nature (the raging storm). Lear

---

43 Hume. (1993) *Dialogues and Natural History*, J. C. A. Gaskin (ed.). Oxford: Oxford University Press.
44 Maistre, "Considérations sur la France," p. 199.
45 Lovejoy, A. (1964. First published 1936). *The Great Chain of Being: A Study of the History of an Idea*. Cambridge, MA: Harvard University Press.

compares his insanity to "a tempest in my mind."[46]

Maistre's apologetic tactic starts from the human side: the experience of evil. Rather than produce a theodicy in the sense of a reason for God or a defense in the sense of Leibniz, Maistre endeavors to turn the argument of the skeptic on its head. Evil becomes an integral aspect of his theological vision. Hence he expends much effort attacking materialism, especially Locke.[47] (Locke was not, in fact, a materialist, but he was perceived in such terms by the French Enlightenment.)

> Divine justice can be contemplated and studies in ours more than we usually believe. Do we not know that we have been created *in the image of God*, and have we not been ordered to work to *make ourselves perfect like him?* I understand very well that these words are not meant to be taken literally, but they always show us what we are since the least resemblance to the sovereign being is a title of glory that no one can imagine. Resemblance having nothing in common with equality, we are only using our rights in glorifying ourselves with this resemblance. He himself has declared himself our father and the *friend of our souls*. The God-Man called us his *friends*, his *children*, and even his *brothers*; and his apostles never ceased repeating to us the precept *to be like unto him*. So there is not the least doubt on this august resemblance. Man deceives himself twice with respect to God: sometimes he makes him similar to man by lending him our passions; sometimes, on the contrary, he is deceived in a way more humiliating for his own nature by refusing to recognize there the divince characteristics of his model. If man knew how to discover and contemplate these characteristics, he would not mistakenly judge God after his cherished creation. It is sufficient to judge him according to all our virtues, that is to say, according to all the perfections that are contrary to our passions, perfections of which every man feels himself susceptible, and which we are forced to admire in the depths of our heart, even when they are foreign to us.[48]

Let us first distinguish among three kinds of evil.

1. Natural evil (Malum physicum): that is, earthquakes, famines, droughts — events that are usually not due to direct human agency.
2. Moral evil (Malum morale): here one might think of serial killers, genocide.
3. Metaphysical evil (Malum metaphysicum): this is the most moot sense of evil. It is mythologically expressed in various forms. In the Christian scriptures, it is personified by or embodied in Satan.

At the heart of Christianity is a deep ambivalence about the source of evil. Ultimately it is grounded in free will, and yet it is the product of a Fall beyond the moral orbit of a particular agent. Maistre reflects this Christian ambivalence in seeing moral evil as the root of natural evil: "*S'il n'y avait*

---

46   Shakespeare, *King Lear*, 3.4.
47   Yolton, J. W. (1991) *Locke and French Materialism*. Oxford: Clarendon Press.
48   Maistre, "Les Soirées de Saint-Pétersbourg," pp. 552–3.

point de mal moral sur la terre, il n'y aurait point de mal physique."[49] Yet this moral evil is not an accidental disposition to wrongdoing but a deeply entrenched structural inclination to evil ground in the division or dividedness of the human soul. The cosmos is the arena for a painful return to God through submission of the will on the model of Christ's suffering love. War and disease are part of the *via purgativa* to be endured by a sinful humanity. But this does not mean that Maistre has a crude understanding of pain and suffering as due deserts for man's sinfulness. That would be inconsistent with the poignant and tender description of the pious girl suffering from cancer at the end of the third Soirée. Maistre's vision is gloomy rather than cruel.

The idea of sacrifice is inalienable in Christian thought because of the idea of the Fall: the special sense of the imperfection of the world. Redemption in Christian terms, unlike both Judaism and Islam, requires much more than a renegotiation of the relation between God and man, but a radical liberation from the fallen state. John Henry Newman observes that those "who know nothing of the wounds of the soul" will not seek deliverance.[50]

Sacrifice is important for Christian ethics because it discloses a level of reality otherwise obscured in quotidian human society. Sin is a state of dispersion, of being torn asunder like Isis or Pentheus. And the violence of man's fallen state reflects this dispersion. The visible world is a portion of that transcendent spiritual domain from whence the former is derived. As human beings, our vocation is a harmonious communion with this intelligible universe that is the mind of God. Prayer and sacrifice are forms of communion with God. Christian Platonism starts from the soul, the unique individuality ignored by materialism, an individual who must experience life in apocalyptic terms as the struggle between good and evil.[51] Sacrifice is the expiation of the vicious duality in the human being:

> [L'homme] gravite [. . .] vers les régions de la lumière. Nul castor, nulle hirondelle, nulle abeille n'en veulent savoir plus que leurs devanciers. Tous les êtres sont tranquilles à la place qu'ils occupent. Tous sont dégradés, mais ils l'ignorent; l'homme seul en a le sentiment, et ce sentiment est tout à la fois la preuve de sa grandeur et de sa misère, de ses droits sublimes et de son incroyable dégradation. Dans l'état où il est réduit, il n'a pas même le triste bonheur de s'ignorer: il faut qu'il se contemple sans cesse, et il ne peut se contempler sans rougir; sa grandeur même l'humilie, puisque les lumières qui l'élèvent jusqu'à l'ange ne servent qu'à lui montrer dans lui des penchants abominables qui le dégradent jusqu'à la brute. Il cherche dans le fond de son être quelque partie saine sans pouvoir la trouver: le mal a tout souillé, et l'homme entier n'est qu'une maladie. Assemblage inconcevable de deux puissances différentes et incompatibles, centaure monstrueux, il sent qu'il est le résultat de quelque forfait inconnu, de quelque mélange détestable qui a vicié l'homme jusque dans

---

49   Maistre, "Les Soirées de Saint-Pétersbourg," p. 473.
50   Newman, J. H. (1985) *An Essay in Aid of a Grammar of Assent*, I. T. Ker (ed.). Oxford: Clarendon Press, p. 321.
51   See Armenteros, "Revolutionary violence and the end of history."

son essence la plus intime.[52]

Maistre is insistent that, however this tenet may seem to the philosophes, the doctrine of an original sin has its counterpart in the pagans. He refers explicitly to Plato's dialogue, the *Phaedrus*:

> Plato tells us *that is contemplating himself, he does not know if he sees a monster more duplicitous and more evil than Typhon, or rather a moral, gentle, and benevolent being who partakes in the nature of the divinity.* He adds that man, so torn in opposite directions, cannot act well or live happily *without reducing to servitude that power of the soul in which evil resides, and without setting free* that which is the home and *the agent of virtue.* This is precisely the Christian doctrine, and one could not confess more clearly the doctrine of original sin.[53]

There is a long tradition of identifying redemption with Isis picking up the dismembered parts of Osiris.[54] Plutarch, the Middle Platonist and one of Maistre's favorite authors, writes in the following manner:

> Therefore the effort to arrive at the Truth, and especially the Truth about the gods, is a longing for the Divine. For the search for truth requires for its study and investigation the consideration of sacred subjects, and it is a work more hallowed than any form of holy living or temple service; and not least of all, it is well-pleasing to that goddess whom you worship, a goddess exceptionally wise and a lover of wisdom, to whom, as her name at least seems to indicate, knowledge and understanding are in the highest degree appropriate. For Isis is a Greek word, and so also is Typhon, her enemy, who is conceited, as his name implies, because of his ignorance and self-deception. He tears to pieces and scatters to the winds the sacred writings, which the goddess collects and puts together and gives into the keeping of those that are initiated into the holy rites, since this consecration, by a strict regimen and by abstinence from many kinds of food and from the lusts of the flesh, curtails licentiousness and the love of pleasure, and induces a habit of patient submission to the stern and rigorous services in shrines, an end and aim of which is the knowledge of Him who is the First, the Lord of All, the Ideal One. Him does the goddess urge us to seek, since He is near her and with her in close communion. The name of her shrine also clearly promises knowledge and comprehension of reality; for it is named Iselon, to indicate that we shall comprehend reality if in a reasonable and devout frame of mind we pass within the portals of her shrines.[55]

52   Maistre, "Les Soirées de Saint-Pétersbourg," p. 487.
53   Maistre, "Les Soirées de Saint-Pétersbourg," p. 489.
54   Lieb, Michael. (1994) *Milton and the Culture of Violence.* Ithaca, NY; London: Cornell University Press.
55   Plutarch. (1959) "Isis and Osiris," in Frank Cole Babbitt (trans.), *Moralia,* vol. 5. London: W. Heinemann, pp. 8–11.

The imagery reinforces the Neoplatonic metaphysics of the Fall from primal unity and the return of all being to its transcendent source. The (Platonic) metaphysics of unity plays a central role in Maistre's theory of sacrifice and reversibility. It is because of the arcane kinship of mankind that the fragmentary state of the current world can be transformed through Providence into the ultimate point of reconciliation where God will become all in all.

> Truth indeed came once into the world with her Divine Master, and was a perfect shape most glorious to look on: but when he ascended, and his Apostles after him were laid asleep, then straight arose a wicked race of deceivers, who, as that story goes of the Ægyptian Typhon with his conspirators, how they dealt with the good Osiris, took the virgin Truth, hewd her lovely form into a thousand peeces, and scatter'd them to the four winds. From that time ever since, the sad friends of Truth, such as durst appear, imitating the careful search that Isis made for the mangl'd body of Osiris, went up and down gathering up limb by limb, still as they could find them. We have not yet found them all, Lords and Commons, nor ever shall doe, till her Master's second comming; he shall bring together every joynt and member, and shall mould them into an immortall feature of loveliness and perfection. Suffer not these licensing prohibitions to stand at every place of opportunity forbidding and disturbing them that continue seeking, that continue to do our obsequies to the torn body of our martyr'd Saint.[56]

Maistre's vision of the disordered soul is deeply Origenistic. And when Maistre says that disorder presupposes order — "*Ils parlent de désordre dans l'univers; mais qu'est-ce que le désordre*"[57] — he is producing a similar argument. I suggest Maistre gets the right balance between the theoretical and the hermeneutical or existential dimension of the problem. His is a vision of the return of the cosmos to God. God is drawing the universe towards him.[58] Hence Joseph de Maistre is starting from the human side, from the experience of evil. Rather than produce a theodicy in the sense of a reason for God or a rationalistic defense in the manner of Leibniz.

Notwithstanding the macabre note of "*régénération dans le sang,*" the key concepts of Maistre are those of the restitution of creation and theosis. He presents a theodicy in his account of the world as a process of purification and communion in which prayer and sacrifice play a central role: "*La terre entière, continuellement imbibée de sang, n'est qu'un autel immense où tout ce qui vit doit être immolé sans fin, sans mesure, sans relâche, jusqu'à la consommation des choses, jusqu'à la mort de la mort.*"[59] Here we find the Pauline sense of how the "whole creation groans and travails in pain."[60] The world seems to present a spectacle of infinite conflict, waste, and ravaged atrophy. This

---

56 Milton, John. (1644) *Areopagitica: A Speech for the Liberty of Unlicenc'd Printing*. London: Little Humanist Classics, p. 29.
57 Maistre, "Les Soirées de Saint-Pétersbourg," p. 698.
58 Rather like the omega point of Teilhard de Chardin.
59 Maistre, "Les Soirées de Saint-Pétersbourg," p. 661.
60 Romans 8.22.

is indeed incompatible with the naked perfection of the world. But does it mean that the world is just a seesaw of brute and cruel force in the sense of Schopenhauer's *Wille*? Clearly not. *"Y a-t-il quelque chose de plus certain que cette proposition: tout a été fait par et pour l'intelligence,"* Maistre exclaims.[61] The proposition that everything has been made by and for intelligence is rationalist, not irrationalist. Schopenhauer's metaphysical pessimism would represent a kind of position that all Platonists from Origen to Maistre would identify as disappointed hedonism parading as a bogus realism. The fundamental question goes back to Plato's *The Republic*. Is the Good, or goal of ethics, pleasure or a principle of goodness that radically transcends human inclinations and immediate interests?

From Maistre's Christian perspective, in which the supremacy of love (*la loi d'amour*) is the core tenet, we can see — albeit dimly — that the apparent wasteland is part of a larger process of love, a process of struggle in which love is revealed as self-sacrifice.[62] Here we have the note of *Christus consummator*, the one who is the omega point of the cosmos (in Teilhard's terms). There is a correspondence among physical, moral, and spiritual. Evil is not a hindrance to Divine design and purpose but makes it clearer: it shows the necessity of expiation and substitution. The most profound evil is the obscuring of the Divine presence.

Let us not forget that Christianity views evil as overcome through transformation rather than separation. The cross is an image of the man-God suffering and transforming evil and violence into peace and harmony. The key to evil is thus not separation but, rather, absorption and change. There are doubtless enormous problems in the attempt to articulate an adequate theoretical framework: both with the highly problematic Anselmian move that God needs a sacrificial object or victim to appease his wrath and the position that God is the subject of the sacrifice — he is sacrificing himself in the quasi-Cabbalistic sense of a self-contraction or limitation, for example in German Idealism where God is the infinite who sacrifices himself for the finite and finite beings must sacrifice themselves to reveal the infinite. No one can seriously deny problems for Christian theology arising from discontent since the Enlightenment with the doctrine of penal substitution. But these difficulties should not obscure the philosophical basis for seeing the idea of sacrifice as an immensely important part of an adequate anthropology, and the basis for a critique of a narrow reductionism.

Origen Redivivus

Adolf von Harnack called Origen the great theologian of sacrifice: *der grosse Opfertheologe*.[63] Maistre's theory of sacrifice — *Régénération dans le sang* — presupposes a traditional dichotomy of the rational self and its passions and the objectivity of morality. Commentators sometimes refer

61 Maistre, "Les Soirées de Saint-Pétersbourg," p. 836.
62 Maistre, "Les Soirées de Saint-Pétersbourg," p. 823.
63 Harnack, A. (1990) *Lehrbuch der Dogmengeschichte*, I. Tubingen: Mohr Siebeck, p. 478.

to his Augustinianism, but Maistre is strangely reticent about the African doctor and enthusiastic about the Alexandrian Divine: Origen (AD 185–254), the doctor of universal salvation, whose speculations about the cosmic process through which all things descended from an initial unity in God and the process that produces a final return to unity. This is Origen's treatise "On Principles," which develops the idea of restitution of all to the Divine source ἀποκατάστασις πάντων (*apokatastasis panton*), *restitutio universalis*. This universalistic doctrine is the opposite of double predestination and Augustine's grim doctrine of the *massa damnata*. Let us reflect again upon the famous lines about the earth as an altar:

> The entire earth, perpetually steeped in blood, is nothing but an immense altar on which every living thing must be immolated without end, without restraint, without respite, until the consummation of the world, until the extinction of evil, until the death of death.[64]

The reference to the "consummation of the world, until the extinction of evil, until the death of death" is an allusion to the *apokatastasis panton*. Like Descartes, Maistre was trained by the Jesuits and developed a loathing for the Augustinian Jansenists, whom he saw a proto-Protestants or philosophes. Maistre presents an Origenist vision of a fallen mankind:

> [E]very man as man is subject to all the misfortunes of humanity: the law is general, so it is not unjust. To claim a man's rank or virtues should exempt him from the actions of an iniquitous . . . tribunal is precisely the same as wanting such honours to exempt him from apoplexy, for example, or even death.[65]

It is original sin, viewed as cosmic fall, that determines the existence of suffering, death, and evil. But all mankind is suffering and will be redeemed through Christ: "the blood that was shed on the Calvary was not only useful to men, but to the angels, to the stars, and all other created beings."[66]

Maistre sees empiricism — that is, a sensualistic epistemology — as the core error of the French Enlightenment. For Maistre this means an unacceptable rejection of the classic Platonic-Aristotelian-Christian identification of the rational self or soul as the Divine component of a composite human being and its replacement with a naturalistic theory of human cognition and action. "Know Thyself" for Plato, Aristotle, or the Christian humanists like Justin, Clement, or Origen, meant "Know thy Divine self." The "odious Hume," as Maistre calls him[67], and the celebrated authors of the radical French Enlightenment, were engaged in the attempt to dismantle this tenet. It should be noted that this construal of the Delphic Oracle is not triumphalistic in Maistre. It has its epistemic dimension: he

---

64 Maistre, *St Petersburg Dialogues*, p. 217.
65 Maistre, *St Petersburg Dialogues*, p. 16.
66 Maistre, *St Petersburg Dialogues*, p. 382.
67 Maistre, *St Petersburg Dialogues*, p. 373.

admired and supported the innatism of the Cambridge Platonists against
Locke. But it is the basis of terrible tension in human nature that requires
expiation through sacrifice:

> [Man] gravitates [. . .] toward the regions of light. No beaver, no swallow,
> no bee wants to know more than its predecessors. All beings are calm in
> the place they occupy. All are degraded, but they do not know it; man
> alone has the feeling of it, and that feeling is at once the proof of his
> grandeur and of his misery, of his sublime rights and of his incredible
> degradation. In the state to which he is reduced, he does not even have
> the sad happiness of ignoring himself: he must contemplate himself
> without cease, and he cannot contemplate himself without blushing; his
> very greatness humiliates him, since the lights that elevate him toward
> the angels serve only to show him the abominable tendencies within
> him that degrade him toward the beast. He looks in the depths of his
> being for some healthy part without being able to find it: evil has soiled
> everything, and man entire is nothing but a malady.[68]

But Maistre avoids the Manichaean tendency of Augustine. Thus Origen
rejects not only the literal narrative of the Fall of Adam and Eve in the
garden but also the Augustinian idea of a collective fall in Adam. Grace
must not impede freedom and God cannot be confused with any arbitrary
power. Quoting Origen, Maistre states:

> Those who have adopted it, do not think the words of the apostle the flesh
> lusts against the spirit (Galatians 5:17) should be taken to mean the flesh
> properly speaking, but to this soul, which is really the soul of the flesh: for,
> they say, we have two souls, the one good and heavenly, the other inferior
> and terrestrial: it is of the latter that it has been said that its works are
> manifest, and we believe that this soul of the flesh resides in the blood.[69]

Maistre insists that evil is tied to human free will but it is also through free
will that mankind returns to God. Mankind is like a "tree that an invisible
hand is pruning, often to its benefit."[70] The cosmic and historic process of
return to primeval unity is really a Divine education of mankind. Faced with
the question, why is human life marked by so much inequality and suffering,
Maistre wishes to claim, like Origen, that God is not to blame for evils and
injustice by appeal to a fall of each soul into the world: "it is man who is
charged with slaughtering man."[71] The apparently pathological interest in
violence and suffering in Maistre is linked to his Origenistic desire to avoid a
tyrannical deity who has preordained misery in his inscrutable will. The suffering of humanity is the price to be paid for preserving an arena of genuine
freedom: such is the *la loi d'amour* ("law of love") that entails the making

---

68 Maistre, *St Petersburg Dialogues*, p. 43.
69 Maistre, *St Petersburg Dialogues*, p. 355.
70 Maistre, *Considerations on France*, p. 28.
71 Maistre, *St Petersburg Dialogues*, p. 217.

inward of sacrifice, the ethical submission to goodness and spirit.[72] Here is the liberal humanist theologian in Maistre, so indebted to Origen. Ironically, the Maistre who was identified by Isaiah Berlin as the political theorist at the origins of modern irrationalism, emphasizes the dark and cruel dimension of human experience in order to avoid an irrationalist and voluntarist theology that rests upon the twin doctrines of human depravity and inscrutable and arbitrary Divine will. Therapeutic dimension of punishment:

> That such is the infinite Goodness and infinite Wisdom of God, as he knows how to bring good out of evil, and is acquainted with all the Circumstances of Beings [. . .] that there are infinite degrees of Beings within with the sphere of omnipotency, and it is suitable to Divine goodness in its productions to reach the utmost limits of Possibility.[73]

Maistre from Dante to Dostoevsky

Maistre, I suggest, should not be viewed as a specifically modern figure, but as a Christian thinker in the great tradition of Christian metaphysics.

Yet Maistre also exerted considerable influence upon the nineteenth century. He stayed in Russia for 14 years and had considerable personal influence amidst the court. He was esteemed by the Slavophiles. Franz von Baader (1765–1841), who saw Russia and the Orthodox religion as a bulwark against Western rationalism and materialism, was a great admirer of Maistre. He wrote one of the first essays on Maistre's thought and was appreciative. His close friend, Dostoevsky, one of the greatest literary figures to emerge out of the Slavophile world, was referred to as a Russian Joseph de Maistre.[74]

> The blood that's on everyone's hands . . . that flows and has always flowed through the world like a waterfall, that is poured like champagne and for the sake of which men are crowned in the Capitol and then called the benefactors of mankind. It is, in fact, worth noting that the majority of those benefactors and guiding spirits of mankind were particularly fearsome bloodletters.[75]

The Maistrian element in Dostoevsky extends beyond the rhetoric of blood. The whole of *Crime and Punishment* (1866), for example, is about the freedom that consists in self-renunciation and the salvation that emerges from the recognition of guilt and evil. The physical crime of Raskolnikov corresponds to the spiritual crime that is grounded in his self-assertion, and

---

72 Maistre, *St Petersburg Dialogues*, p. 371.
73 Rust, *An Account of Origen*. (1933) A letter of resolution concerning Origen and the chief of his opinions reproduced from the edition of 1661, with a bibliographical note by Marjorie Hope Nicolson. New York: Columbia University Press.
74 Miltchyna, Vera. (2001) "Joseph de Maistre in Russia," in Richard Lebrun (ed.), *Joseph de Maistre's Life, Thought and Influence: Selected Studies*. Montreal: McGill-Queen's University Press, p. 263.
75 Dostoevsky, Fyodor. (1991) *Crime and Punishment*. Harmondsworth: Penguin, p. 312.

his banishment to Siberia mirrors the profounder fact of his exile from God. It is the figure of Sonya who says: "You must accept suffering and redeem yourself by it."[76] The novel revolves around this law of the spirit — that positivistic science cannot, *per definitionem*, grasp. The law is the principle of atonement and redemption. Here we should recall both the joy and the Light. Light is a very important image for the Platonic tradition: one need only think of the Cave in Plato's *The Republic* or of enlightenment in the seventh letter. The philosophy of Plotinus has often been described as a metaphysics of light.

One might consider the beautiful surroundings of the introduction to the first *Soirée*, which starts with the light of the splendid northern European summer:

> Nothing is rarer, nothing is more enchanting than a beautiful summer evening in St Petersburg. Whether the length of the winter and the rarity of these nights, which gives them a particular charm, renders them more desirable, or whether they really are so, as I believe, they are softer and calmer than evenings in more pleasant climates.[77]

Maistre says in his typically tender manner:

> If heaven in its goodness reserved for me one of those moments so rare in life where the heart is flooded with joy by some extraordinary and unexpected happiness, if a wife, children, and brothers separated from me for a long time without hope of reunion were suddenly to tumble into my arms, I would want it to happen here. Yes, I would want it to be on one of these beautiful nights on the banks of the Neva among these hospitable Russians.[78]

It is a soirée. Maistre refers explicitly to the Platonic *Symposium* with its association with wine and conviviality.[79] Remember that for Maistre mankind "gravitates . . . to regions of light." But then we are plunged into the abyss of the Fallen world. The vision is akin to that of Dante or Dostoevsky. The complacency of worldly hopes and ambitions must be broken. Here philosophy and theology converge. It was Plato who defined philosophy as the practice of death, and through his formative experience of the *Pénitents noirs*, Maistre knew the dimension of the *memento mori* of Platonic philosophy and Christian theology. I would also like to note the special role of the Psalms. These have always appealed to Christian mystics, and they play a core role in *Les Soirées*, especially the notorious seventh dialogue.

Sacrifice is ambivalent in the sense that it represents both a nonreducible cultural and a transcendent dimension to human experience. As such, it provides a double bulwark against the naturalist. For the naturalist can neither provide a satisfactory reduction of the irreducible hermeneutical dimension of sacrifice, its role in our stories about ourselves, nor do justice to the sense of the transcendent in the making sacred of sacrifice.

76   Dostoevsky, *Crime and Punishment*, p. 489.
77   Maistre, "Les Soirées de Saint-Pétersbourg," p. 455.
78   Maistre, "Les Soirées de Saint-Pétersbourg," p. 457.
79   Bradley, *A Modern Maistre*, p. 6.

6

Responsibility, Atonement, and Sacrifice Transformed

The Cross of Christ is the Jacob's ladder by which we ascend into the highest heavens . . . That cross is a tree set on fire with invisible flame, that illumineth all the world.[1]

Traditional Christian theology depends upon a theology of sacrificial atonement. Yet this distinctive doctrine of Christianity, marking it off drastically from Islam and Judaism, seems morally bizarre. How can any person's moral failings be atoned by the cruel death of a Galilean rabbi in a first-century Roman province? In this chapter we critically consider the sacrificial theory of atonement of the contemporary philosopher of religion, Richard Swinburne. Both the Temple context of New Testament theology and, specifically, philosophical considerations mean that no theory of atonement can avoid the problem of sacrifice.

In the quoted passage, Thomas Traherne presents the cross as an organ of ascent to the Divine mind. One might think of Bernard of Clairvaux who remarked that the cross of Christ is a burden like the wings of birds: one that lifts up. One might note also the reference to the tree suggests a parallelism between the tree of paradise and the cross. Christ is recapitulating and transforming human life as inherited from Adam. We could consider the tenet that the cross is a source of illumination. These three ideas – the ascent to God through the cross, Christ's recapitulation and transformation of Adam and the illuminating dimension of Christ's death – constitute important features of the defense of a sacrificial theory of atonement, which I present in this chapter. I wish to focus upon the theory of Richard Swinburne. I think he is correct to concentrate upon the model of sacrifice, but that he does so for the wrong reasons. As a symbol, sacrifice cannot be properly construed in narrowly rationalistic and forensic terms as a necessary and sufficient means of reconciliation between man and God. This is to obscure the imaginative and emotional power of the symbol, its polyvalence, the capacity of the archetypal symbol to speak to the soul of the believer and to express the transforming power of participation in the life of transcendent Logos made flesh.

---

1 Traherne, Thomas. (1927) *Centuries of Meditations*. London: Dobell, I, §60, p. 41.

Salvation and sacrifice

The word "salvation" is open to many meanings. Consider the etymological connotations of well-being or security, health or help in the Latin *salus*. This lends itself to a broad range of interpretations. Contrast Horace's *Salus populi suprema lex esto*: Let the welfare of the people be the highest law, and Cyprian's *nulla salus extra ecclesiam*: without the Church there is no salvation. The first has the sense of the common weal or health. Think of *salut* in French (consider the English word "hale" in "hale and hearty"). Compare this with the second and much more specific theological sense requiring an idea of a postmortem existence. Nor is the choice exclusively between on the one hand, the Christian theological and, on the other, the popular/vulgar versions of salvation as well-being. Ancient Greek philosophy has its σωτηία and Sanskrit thought (Brahmin and Buddhist) has its *moksa*. One might think here of the eschatological end of Plato's *The Republic* or the *Gita*.

The word "sacrifice," however, has unavoidable associations with an outdated and possibly barbaric practice. This is, of course a subject of some scholarly debate as to whether sacrifice must be "violent."[2] However, generally speaking, the desire for salvation is widespread and intelligible in different idioms, whereas sacrifice seems an outmoded means of salvation: a rebarbative relic of a more barbaric age. The topic of sacrifice rests uneasily between the crass and cruel dimension of religion from the Aztecs to contemporary Muslim "martyrs" on the one hand and the utter demythologizing and psychologizing of religion on the other in ultra-liberal Christianity, whereby evil and wickedness become just the wounds and anxieties of the psyche. One of the most forceful critiques of the traditional sacrificial models of salvation is ethical. How can a good God demand sacrifice?

There is a deeply held conviction that the doctrine of atonement distorts the relationship between God and mankind. Indeed, the violent sacrificial theories of atonement clash with the basic teaching of Christ: the paternal love of God. Christ's stress upon ethical and spiritual purity is contradicted by the grisly theology of sacrificial propitiation of Divine wrath. Christ's teaching assumes human goodness; Christian theology seems to assume evil that requires punishment. Jesus's teaching of love was replaced by a Christian theology of judgment.

> The term "sacrifice" has been used to speak of the playing out of Jesus' (voluntary) vulnerability. But this metaphor undermines the idea of solidarity between God and Jesus by picturing God as requiring, and Jesus as performing, a tragically necessary self-immolation. Sacrificial theology tears apart the solidarity between God and Jesus. Sacrifice rein-scribes the ancient suspicion of God as chaotic, capricious and cruel. The notion that God required a human sacrifice is fatal to all tender values.[3]

2   McClymond, Kathryn. (2008) *Beyond Sacred Violence: A Comparative Study of Sacrifice.* Baltimore, MD: John Hopkins University Press.
3   Finlan, M. (2007) *Options on Atonement in Christian thought.* Collegeville, MN: Liturgical Press, p. 50.

Modern theology has been decisively affected by Socinian objections based upon rationalistic atomistic individualism and the perceived violence of sacrifice (moral seriousness) characteristic of modernity. For Socinianism, the Racovian Catechism (§5, ch. 8) states that satisfaction for sin is incompatible with forgiveness.[4] Hence the exemplarist theory of atonement that is usually associated with Abelard was much reinforced by Socinian objections to apparent cruelty of penal satisfaction.

In this chapter, I consider an attempt within the analytic tradition to address this question, Richard Swinburne's *Responsibility and Atonement*. In his book, he develops a theory of atonement that draws primarily upon the idea of sacrifice. It is the most important and extensive treatment of the topic of salvation by a major analytic philosopher.

Despite its centrality, the doctrine of atonement has not been subjected to the thorough definitional scrutiny applied to, say, the Trinity or the Incarnation. Anselm's *Cur Deus Homo* is the first systemic account of atonement, even though the Church Father produced theories. What we have in the Fathers is a baffling array of competing and sometimes mutually exclusive theories of salvation. Christ's death is presented as a victory over evil forces in the universe or as a ransom paid to the Devil. Penal substitution is the theory that retribution for sin must be paid and that Christ is the substitute for the sin of mankind. The traditional substitutionary theory of atonement seems too crassly forensic, and a mere exemplification theory of the cross too insipid. But to attain the just balance between the subjective and the objective dimensions of sacrifice is difficult. On a subjective theory, Christ becomes little more than an inspiring model like the Buddha or the "great-souled" Gandhi. (After all, some Buddhists have developed the doctrine of the "Buddha nature" that a practitioner can assume.) The objective theory is needed but almost always seems sub-ethical or bizarrely anthropomorphic. Richard Swinburne's work here is far from being an abstruse reflection on ancient established and widely accepted doctrines. It is, rather, a forceful contribution to a contemporary understanding of the key and most distinctive Christian doctrine. Judaism and Islam have doctrines of the sufficiency of the law (of Moses and Mohammed, respectively). Christianity stands or falls with its account of salvation as an atoning process through the death and resurrection of Jesus of Nazareth.

The moral demand and the need to be redeemed

We might first distinguish between theories of propitiation (with its etymological roots in *propitiare* — to appease or conciliate) and expiation as making amends or cleansing. Propitiating an angry, wrathful deity

---

4   Rees, Thomas. (1818) *The Racovian catechism, with notes and illustrations; translated from the Latin. To which is prefixed a sketch of the history of of the history of Unitarianism in Poland and the adjacent countries*. London: Printed for Longman, Hurst, Rees, Orme, and Brown, pp. 304ff.
        See also Adams Brown, W."Expiation and atonement," Hastings, *James Encyclopedia of Religion and Ethics*, vol. 5, pp. 635–71, p. 646.

looks very dubious as the basis for a theory of atonement (cf. the cynical Lucretian thesis that religion is based upon fear). But the longing for expiation is a deep and legitimate need and may quite properly be the sign of a sophisticated and refined moral sensibility. A key difference here is that the object of propitiation is God whereas the object of expiation is sin. Any serious theory of atonement needs to combine an account of God's justice and God's love. Sin needs to be redeemed for the sake of justice. However, God's nature as love is evinced by the help that he offers for this. This is compatible with a theory of expiation but not with a theory of propitiation.

The moral gap, and here I am employing John Hare's useful terms, refers to the desideratum of the moral life for the theist. Let us assume that we should "love God with all our heart, mind and strength and our neighbours as ourselves"[5] and that we consistently fail. How can we fulfill the demands of morality if we are imperfect? And how can God as the transcendent source of Being help us? This is also Richard Swinburne's starting point. He begins by offering a theory of moral goodness and responsibility and then explores the theological implications of his account. His theory is that Christ's sacrifice is a substitute for our reparation and punishment. What is sin? Original Sin is the doctrine that mankind is at least structurally if not inherently alienated from God. Swinburne rejects the Augustinian theory of biologically transmitted guilt and talks of a "genetically inherited proneness to sin."[6] He explicitly refers to the Alexandrian theologians of the early Church. Swinburne defines it as "failure in a duty to God,"[7] but sin also includes the deeper sense of a radical estrangement from God in which wrong-doing is a by-product. Indeed, Swinburne distinguishes between objective and subjective sin, whereby objective refers to a broader alienated domain within which human actions occur (i.e. collective frailty and imperfection in which all are involved) and subjective refers to conscious wrong-doing.

Swinburne's theory

Richard Swinburne rejects the "ransom," "victory," and "penal substitution" theories of atonement as irrational. "On the Penal model, God also acts as a punishing judge. There is no parallel for that in the sacrifice model and that is much to its credit."[8] Sacrifice, on Swinburne's account, is to be preferred to the models of ransom, victory, and penal substitution.

Swinburne's theory of the structure of salvation might be summarized in the following manner:

5   Lk. 10.27; Matthew 22.37.
6   Swinburne, Richard. (1989) *Responsibility and Atonement*. Oxford: Clarendon Press, p. 143.
7   Swinburne, *Responsibility and Atonement*, p. 124.
8   Swinburne, *Responsibility and Atonement*, p. 155.

1. Guilt is an obstacle to salvation.
2. Reconciliation between two human beings demands repentance, apology, and reparation where achievable and penance.
3. God is personal and the same principle applies to him.
4. Culpability towards other humans is also a transgression towards God.
5. Human agents can provide repentance and apology but not atonement.
6. Christ offers a perfect life and his death is a sacrifice mankind can offer to God as atonement for sins.
7. Salvation means divesting ourselves of guilt by explicitly appealing to the death of Christ as atonement.

The core thought is that repentance and apology are insufficient and that reparation and penance can only be offered by man to God through Christ. John Hick has challenged this vigorously:

> It rests upon a category mistake by which God is treated as another individual within the same moral community as ourselves. For a moral relationship with another person presupposes the possibility of actions that can benefit or injure that other person; but we cannot benefit or injure our creator over and above our actions in benefitting and injuring our fellow creatures.[9]

The force of this critique, I suggest, is more rhetorical than real. (Perhaps we can reply to Hick by distinguishing clearly between a voluntaristic and an essentialist model of the Divine nature.) The language of God being harmed by sin sounds rather like a headmaster reluctantly administering punishments to wayward young boys. Swinburne's view of God as a benefactor deserving gratitude could be thus construed. But ethical realism and theism could uphold:

1. if certain values like justice and goodness are constitutive parts of the fabric of the universe
2. if these values are grounded in the Divine mind.

It follows that falling short of these values disrupts or disturbs the order of the universe. In the language of the Greek Fathers, our freedom rests in possessing the image but not the likeness of God. Our wrongdoings poison our fellows and our environment, both literally and metaphorically. And yet, remarkable souls are able to redeem this damage through self-sacrificial love and forgiveness. Christ as the perfect expression of our humanity is the most egregious instance of this mysterious capacity to transform evil into good.

If there is some analogy between human and Divine life rather than merely a relationship of metaphor, then the issues of punishment and forgiveness point to a need for real atonement as a genuine readjustment and

---

9   Hick, J. (1994) "Is the doctrine of atonement a mistake?" in A. G. Padgett (ed.), *Reason and the Christian Religion: Essays in Honour of Richard Swinburne*. Oxford: Clarendon, pp. 247–65.

repair of damage done. On Hick's own (neo-Kantian) view, such analogies are impossible to sustain, on the grounds that since God or the Real radically transcends our conceptual apparatus that such analogical language employed by the theist must be radically inadequate. Thus, Hick's critique will only work if we accept Hick's own background assumptions and theories. Let us assume for present purposes that some version of analogy is philosophically acceptable.

Forgiveness

John Hick argues that Divine forgiveness cannot be rationally thought to depend upon a propitiatory or expiatory sacrifice. Hick also notes that this seems incompatible with Jesus's own teaching about forgiveness, especially the parable of the prodigal son. Is Hick correct about forgiveness? Let us consider one of Richard Swinburne's most illustrious predecessors at Oriel College, Oxford: Joseph Butler. For Butler's classic analysis of forgiveness, resentment, revenge, and the notion of shared humanity are the pivotal ideas. Butler's thesis is that resentment is the precondition of forgiveness. He sees forgiveness as the "foreswearing of revenge,"[10] but thinks that this presupposes a genuine resentment towards the agent who has inflicted the injury. The motive for forgiveness is the recognition of a common humanity. Butler dwells upon the command of Jesus to "love thy enemy."[11] Rather akin to the spirit of Kant's distinction between practical and pathological love, Butler thinks that though an affection cannot be commanded, rather one is required to view one's enemy as another human being and thus to recognize their frailty and imperfections.

Butler differentiates between anger and resentment. The former is "hasty and sudden" anger[12], whereas the latter is deliberate and sustained over time by one agent towards another. Anger, so understood, has its classic expression in Homer's reference to the "gall of anger that swarms like smoke inside a man's heart and becomes sweeter than the dripping of honey."[13] Butler further notes that resentment normally implies a moral estimation, one based on a sense of unfairness. Charles Griswold, in his impressive book *Forgiveness: A Philosophical Exploration*, notes that the etymology of resentment (in French *re-sentir*) supports Butler's distinction between the instantaneous emotion of anger and the sustained sentiment of resentment. The victim has not merely been harmed, through some physical or mental damage, but also wronged. Butler thinks that a further condition of forgiveness is the resentment felt by the victim towards the wrongdoer. This is a natural and proper feeling. However, it can, if excessive, lead to revenge. Resentment is not inconsistent with goodwill; we often see both together in very high degree, not only in parents towards

10   Griswold, *Forgiveness*, p. 38.
11   Mt. 5.44.
12   Butler, *Fifteen Sermons*, p. 103.
13   Homer. (1961) *Iliad*. 18.107–110. R. Lattimore (trans.). Chicago: University of Chicago Press.

their children but also in cases of friendship and dependence, where there is no natural relation. These contrary passions, though they may lessen, do not necessarily destroy each other. We may therefore love our enemy and yet have resentment against him for his injurious behavior towards us. But when this resentment entirely destroys our natural benevolence towards him, it is excessive and becomes malice or revenge.[14] Thus the victim of an injury may still harbor resentment towards an offender but these sentiments remain in proportion to the offence.

As Pope remarked, "To err is Humane, to Forgive; Divine."[15] However, forgiveness should not be confused with becoming supine.[16] Does not arbitrary forgiveness undermine morality? This claim is made by Celsus against Origen.[17] Forgiveness can seem close to condoning or forgetting a wrong. A recent philosopher, Brudholm, has argued forcefully that forgiveness is often irrationally preferred over resentment:

> [T]he preservation of outrage or resentment and the refusal to forgive and reconcile can be the reflex expression of a moral protest and ambition that might be permissible and admirable as the posture of forgiveness rather than the first stage in the process of forgiveness.[18]

There are prudential reasons for forgiveness, which, ethically, does not seem very compelling. However important it may be for one's psychic health to "let go" of resentment towards someone by whom one has been injured, this does not seem to have much of a basis in morality in the strict sense. Hick's critique of Swinburne depends upon a view of forgiveness that omits some of the complexity surrounding the concept. Ironically, Hick's God becomes a rather arbitrary being. Forgiveness cannot consist in the disregard for justice.

Punishment and Divine goodness

The concept of forgiveness also shows the metaphysical inadequacy of naturalism in dealing with ethical questions and the theological frontiers of ethics. Could animals forgive? The answer is clearly no. The capacity to forgive presupposes a uniquely human (or Divine) responsibility and rationality. In the wake of so many theories of both "religion" and "altruism"

14 Butler, J. (1726) *Sermons Preached at the Rolls Chapel*. Sermon 7, J. H. Bernard, (ed.). London: Macmillan (1913).
15 Pope, Alexander. *A Essay on Criticism*. (2nd edn.). London: Lewis (1713) p. 26.
16 As Kant observed, if you make yourself a worm, people will step on you. Kant, I. (1996) *The Metaphysics of Morals*, Mary Gregor (ed.). Cambridge: Cambridge University Press, 6: 436–7; pp. 187–8.
17 Origen. (1953) *Contra Celsum*, 3.59ff, Chadwick (trans.). Cambridge: Cambridge University Press, pp. 168ff. Griswold emphasizes the extent to which ancient ethicists use *syngnome* to refer to those instances of ignorance, force, or emotions affecting negatively the behavior of an ethical agent.
18 Brudholm, Thomas. (2008) *Resentment's Virtue: Jean Améry and the Refusal to Forgive, Politics, History, and Social Change*. Philadelphia, PA: Temple University Press, p. 4.

that are grounded in evolutionary biology or cognitive science, forgiveness is an instance of a distinctly human space of reasons that are hard to reduce to considerations of adaptation and survival. Thus, a full-blooded metaphysical account of forgiveness can be a welcome antidote to implausibly reductive accounts of interpersonal relations. Perhaps our general tendency to generate ill and wrongs is not a set of bizarre projections onto a bare and meaningless moral landscape but, rather, the infringement of an objective moral order.

If the rationale for punishment is not just utilitarian principles like deterrence or prevention of crime, questions of justice and freedom, forgiveness or mercy cannot be arbitrary. It is the conscious and free act of the offender that makes punishment necessary. The closely related concepts of mercy and forgiveness need to be distinguished. Forgiveness is a mental state whereas mercy is an act.[19] The former is a revision of one's attitudes or dispositions, whereas the latter is the mitigation of an otherwise merited punishment. To treat a person with mercy may involve giving them less than their just deserts. However, if the virtuous agent embodies justice and mercy, there must be some consistency. Mercy, Jeffrie Murphy claims, can be "morally dangerous sentimentality."[20] Mercy requires a theory of retribution since utilitarianism, or deterrence theories of punishment. As Swinburne claims, "mercy can only be meritorious if retribution is right. Mercy goes beyond justice."[21]

This could be construed as a conceptual requirement. Without a prior sense of just deserts, the very concept of mercy collapses.

What can be redeemed in the language of sacrifice?

The distinguished Oxford philosopher J. R. Lucas raises a more specific objection to Swinburne's use of the sacrifice model. He writes:

> The same questions obtrude as with the ransom and penal theories. To whom was the sacrifice made? Why should the death of Jesus make up for alleged wrong doing on our part? What real difference should it make to the situation of Plato, who lived a long time before, or us, who live a long time after?[22]

Sacrifice describes, but does not explain, Christ's death.[23] In order to answer Lucas's critique we need a robust contrast between the symbolic and the metaphorical. Sacrifice is more deeply entrenched within the Christian imaginary because of the scriptural language concerning the Temple and also because of ontological issues. If we accept a hierarchy of values of a

---

19 Swinburne speaks of punishment as a performative act, but I am not sure that this is adequate.
20 See Murphy, Jeffrie. (2003) *Getting Even*. Oxford: Oxford University Press, p. 17ff.
21 Swinburne, *Responsibility and Atonement*, p. 99.
22 Lucas, J. R. (1994) "Reflections on the atonement," in A. G. Padgett (ed.), *Reason and the Christian Religion: Essays in Honour of Richard Swinburne*. Oxford: Clarendon, pp. 265–75.
23 Lucas, "Reflections on the atonement," p. 269.

broadly Platonic kind, devotion to the higher domain becomes an ethical requirement, and such devotion will often incur a "cost."

Lucas's definition of sacrifice as "description" as opposed to "explanation" is, I think, inadequate. The context of New Testament language is that of the Temple and Christ's double nature as both priest and sacrificial victim. Lucas's remark seems to assume that sacrifice is one metaphor alongside other metaphors like ransom or the bait. Is Lucas correct to say that there is a vicious parallel between sacrifice and the ransom/penal theories of atonement? I think not, for two reasons. First, we have a theological reason. The Jerusalem Temple is a crucial part of the *Sitz im Leben* of the New Testament. The scholarship of Margaret Barker in particular has revealed the extent to which the Temple is clearly a central motif in the documents that make up the New Testament and presumably in the teaching of Christ himself. Some of this imagery is polemical: it is the language of the rejection of the Jerusalem Temple of Christ's contemporaries. The true Lamb of God is offered in the stead of the countless lambs offered in the physical Temple. The slain Lamb is a central focus of the Apocalypse.

Second, sacrifice has a symbolic dimension that is very important. Not only can it hold together the idea of a discharge of duty required by a believer towards a good God but also it can tell us something about that God. The poet Traherne writes:

> It is a well of life beneath in which we may see the face of heaven above: and the only mirror, wherein all things appear in their proper colours: that is, sprinkled in the blood of our Lord and saviour.[24]

I suggest that sacrifice is a symbol in the sense of having an analogical dimension and that, as Swinburne says, the historical Jesus viewed his own death as "an offering to God to make expiation in some way for the sins of men."[25] I think he is correct to emphasize this sacrificial dimension of Christ's ministry. Martin Hengel's book *The Atonement* powerfully refutes the ultra-liberal thought that the doctrine of Atonement was an addition of St. Paul and the early Church. Hengel demonstrates clearly that Paul must have presupposed some doctrine of Christ's atoning death. In Hebrews, Christ is both the victim and the priest. Christians are thought to participate in this sacrifice. They are exhorted in ch. 13 of Hebrews to offer a "sacrifice of praise." Furthermore, "doing good" and sharing of possessions are seen as sacrifices pleasing to God. St. Paul in Romans 12 speaks of the need to present your bodies as a "living sacrifice." The psalmist in Psalm 51 speaks movingly of the "broken and contrite heart." The awareness of both guilt and remorse and the redeeming activity of God constitute a central element of the Psalms (which have played a very important part of the Anglican choral tradition, since Cranmer and beyond). There is the common sense of "atonement" as reparation: renewing or restoring through making amends. Of course, the Christian tradition draws not merely upon the Psalms.

---

24 Traherne, *Meditations*, §59.40–1.
25 Swinburne, *Responsibility and Atonement*, p. 122.

Deutero-Isaiah (of chs. 40–55 of the book of Isaiah) describes a "Suffering Servant" — a figure who "has borne our grief's and carried our sorrows . . . he was wounded for our transgressions, he was bruised for our iniquities; upon him was the chastisement that made us whole, and with his stripes we are made whole" (Isa. 53.4-5).[26] Thus we can see sources of the Christian doctrine of sacrificial Atonement in some of the most ancient writings of the Israelites. *Nolens volens*, the language of sacrifice is too deeply entrenched in Christianity to be jettisoned without distortion or loss.

The second reason is philosophical. We can demythologize the language of sacrifice or turn it into a merely figurative language or a contingent feature of the ancient context of Christ's life. But, I wish to argue, it tells us something substantial about God's nature and the moral properly conceived. Images of the "bait'" or "ransom" or even the "scapegoat" are metaphors that can generate insight into the effects of atonement but they are more peripheral for any understanding of Christian Gospel. The idea of "Sacrifice" as a symbol "throws together" the ritual origins of the concept in an offering up to God with the sublimated sense of renunciation. The sacrificial item is precious — unlike the scapegoat. It is a precious creature like a lamb. The imagery of sacrifice thus leads naturally into the ethics of renunciation and has an ontological dimension because it pertains to the values of justice, mercy, and forgiveness in the following way. We are the products of an evolutionary process in which strife and conflict plays a central role. Loss, suffering, and painful toil constitute the stuff and substance of conscious human existence. However, when this "giving up" is inspired by the Divine, it becomes sacrifice in the true sense of a "making holy" or *sacra facere.*

Swinburne's model of sacrifice still bears the stamp of the older sacrifices offered up to God by man. Swinburne says:

> If redemption works by Christ providing a sacrifice which we can offer to God, then in the light of that model we can understand how Christ's life and death is a victory and, in a less literal sense, redeems us. It is a victory over evil because as a result of it we are no longer inevitably guilty; we have only to use it to throw off our guilt.[27]

Note here the emphasis upon the life of Christ. Swinburne does not think that the death of Christ is necessary and, indeed, his contingent history was part of the perfect life of Christ.

I think I agree with that, as long as we insist that the offering of the Sacrifice through the doctrine of incarnation is an utter transformation (of those ubiquitous gifts to the Divine, not those offered in the hope of appeasing a wrathful deity). The Christian model of sacrifice is a complete transformation of the pagan paradigm. Since Christ is both victim and priest, we, in a sense, plead Christ's death, but in a manner completely

26 North, Christopher. (1950) *The Suffering Servant in Deutero-Isaiah: An Historical and Critical Survey.* London: Oxford University Press.
27 Swinburne, *Responsibility and Atonement*, p. 162.

unlike the offering of lambs in the Temple. Simone Weil observes, "the false God changes suffering into violence, the true God changes violence into suffering".[28] In Christianity, the sacrifice, after all, is top-down: it is from God to man rather than from man to God. It unveils the Divine essence. Further, it reveals a fact about the constitution of the world. If sacrifice is so construed, it points to facts about the Godhead and the world, which cannot be adequately expressed through forensic or martial metaphors. If the Lamb has been slain from the foundation of the world, one can infer that self-sacrifice is properly the foundation of society. One has an ontological foundation for the redemptive power of self-sacrificial love.

Perhaps one can extend Swinburne's model by employing a slightly different paradigm. Whereas Swinburne's reflections are based upon the benefactor (God) and the beneficiary (man) and the reparation required to restore the proper relationship between God and man, we might add a modified paradigm of the restoration of the relation between God and man — that of the vicarious significance of the suffering of the innocent. Christ, on this model, is the supreme and unique exemplification of vicarious suffering, which one can observe in manifold human relations. We can assume some mysterious principle of unity and transferability or substitution of guilt among human beings, where the sufferings of the innocent atone for the deeds of sinners. One might think of the role of the martyrs in the early Church, or the saints.

This idea fits well with the Sermon on the Mount. The Evangelist presents Christ as the new Moses, a Moses who radicalizes the Law.[29] His followers are commanded not merely to employ the golden rule and treat others as they would themselves. The meekness enjoined in the third beatitude, coming after the beatitude for the suffering, inspired Tolstoy, Gandhi, and Martin Luther King, Jr. to try to transform the world through nonviolence.[30] The crucifixion coheres with this teaching: violence and evil must be embraced, transformed, and overcome. Retaliation or revenge is the natural reaction to violence, cruelty, and wickedness and that has an obvious role to play in any persuasive story about our evolutionary development. John Mackie, for instance, sees the roots of the idea of retribution in evolutionary terms. Survival depends upon the capacity to avoid exploitation by others competing for goods and advantages. Yet contemporary society has been transformed by visionaries like Christ, Wilberforce, or Gandhi who challenged the cruelty and violence in ethical conventions and many entrenched social and economic structures. In the twentieth century, those who preached the victory of the warlike or the proper economic structure (whether "the will to power" or "collective ownership of the means of production") were frequently frustrated by the events. The very fact of the Roman Empire converting to the religion of the "pale Galilean" is a very puzzling phenomenon, one that has perplexed

28 Weil, S. (1995) *Gravity and Grace*. London: Routledge, p. 65.
29 Mackie, J. L. (1991) "Retributivism: a test case for ethical objectivity" in Joel Feinberg and Hyman Gross (eds.). *Philosophy of Law* (4th edn.). New York: Wadsworth, pp. 677–84.
30 I am very grateful to Jan Rohls for this point.

historians from Gibbon to Lane Fox.

This principle of vicarious suffering can be used in quite a practical manner. Consider the case of euthanasia or suicide. On utilitarian principles sufferings are simply meaningless and faced with unavoidable suffering, one can see how the utilitarian can readily justify euthanasia or suicide. But a Christian can argue that such sufferings are not devoid of significance, and hence can offer a different response to such situations. Psychic or physical suffering can be understood as participating in the sufferings of Christ: "I admire to see thy Cross in every understanding, Thy Passion in every Memory, Thy crown of Thorns in every Eye, and thy bleeding, naked wounded body in very soul."[31]

It is, of course, important to distinguish this from any pathological or sadomasochistic tendencies. Nietzsche famously developed a lacerating attack on what he perceived as the debilitating effect of Christian teaching about suffering. His critique depends upon the view expressed in the title of *Beyond Good and Evil*.

In John's Gospel this is expressed by the iconographic dimension of the cross. The very form of Christ's death points to the reconciliation of heaven and earth. In his body he suffers humiliation, scorn, and violence unjustly. These punishments are cruelly inflicted upon the *Rex Judaeorum*. Just as his kingship and rule is genuine and not ephemeral like the monarchs and tyrants of the visible world, so too his death is a victory — an overcoming of evil. Thus, the physical pose of the crucified body with its outstretched arms symbolizes the embrace of a sinful and fallen world by God. His forgiveness of his malefactors further expresses this victory over and sublimation of evil. Westcott writes eloquently:

> There is a terrible contrast between man's power and man's achievements; there is a terrible contrast between that which (as we are made) we feel must be the purpose of creation and the facts by which we are encountered. Viewed in themselves, the phenomena which would suggest a design of love in the order of the world issue in deeper sorrow . . . But the record of the life of Christ, the thought of the presence of Christ changes all. Christ, as He lived and lives, justifies our highest hope. He opens the depth of vision just below the surface of things. He transforms suffering: He shews us the highest aspirations of our being satisfied through a way of sorrow. He redresses the superficial inequalities of life by revealing its eternal glory. He enables us to understand how, being what we are, every grief and every strain of sensibility can be made in Him contributory to the working out of our destiny.[32]

This is "Christus consummator." Some other form of execution — for example, beheading or hanging — would not have served this symbolic purpose. What is unveiled in Christ is neither the arbitrary anthropomorphic deity

31 Traherne, *Meditations*, §86.62.
32 Westcott, B. F. (1891) *Essays in the History of Religious Thought in the West*. London; New York: Macmillan, p. 349

of much superstitious and subrational folk religion of all ages nor, significantly, the impersonal God of Aristotle or Spinoza. The cross becomes in the words of Traherne: "The cross is the abyss of wonders, the centre of desires, the school of virtues, the house of wisdom, the throne of love, the theater of joys and the place of sorrows; It is the root of happiness, and the gate of heaven."[33] For Traherne, the suffering and sacrifice of the innocent have redemptive power. Traherne defines meekness as the "most supernatural" transcendent or Divine virtue for the following reason:

> To do good to an innocent person is humane, but to be kind and bountiful to man after he hurts you is Divine.[34]

Meekness is the capacity to further peace "in despite of all the Corruptions and Violences in the World"; "the Master Point of Art/In Christian Religion,/Which my saviour taught on the Cross," is an "immortal, sovereign, Divine, invincible" love of one's enemies.[35]

Thus the imagery of sacrifice bears an analogical and not merely metaphorical relation to reality. It is reality symbolized whereas ransom and forensic substitution are mere metaphors that convey the effect of Christ's death upon the believer. But though the images of the kidnap, the law-court, or the battlefield are heuristic. They are illustrations but that do not refer literally to the economy of salvation. For example, the struggle of an agent to master passions or inclinations that he or she recognizes as destructive or harmful might mean that the imagery of a war could be compelling psychologically. Or, to take another example, guilt is often portrayed as a debt. If X injures Y in some way, there is no borrowing or loan involved. The same applies to punishment. The language of sacrifice, however, points to a wider life in broader ethical commitments and the vicarious power of innocent suffering. Sin, by contrast, is selfishness and self-assertion.[36] But also through its imagery, grounded in cultic roots, sacrifice expresses vividly the violence and suffering of human experience. Many contemporary minds find this dimension of the language of sacrifice disturbing, but I think it is an advantage of Christianity that it encompasses these facts of our existence.

Hence, another virtue of Sacrifice not available to the penal and ransom models is the link with sanctification. In the Gospel of St. Paul the Christian is exhorted to become a living sacrifice. St. Paul's parallelism of Adam and Christ suggests as much. In Paul the true substitution is that through which the Christian becomes a new creation in Christ — through identification with him. Hence the inadequacy of a merely forensic reestablishment of the relation between man and God of the kind presented by Swinburne,

---

33   Traherne, *Meditations* 1, §58.39.
34   Traherne, T. (1968) *Thomas Traherne, Christian Ethics* Carol L. Marks and George R. Guffey (eds.). Ithaca, NY: Cornell University Press, p. 393. I am grateful to Elizabeth Dodd for this reference.
35   Traherne, *Thanksgivings*, pp. 396–70.
36   Westcott, B. F. (1888) "The power of sacrifice," in *The Victory of the Cross*. London: Macmillan, p. 23.

and the importance of the idea of renewal or *paideia*. The righteousness of Christ is not just an external gift but also a source of transformation. It has been argued that substitution or *admirabile commercium* is inextricably linked to propitiating a wrathful deity or penal substitution. But it can mean replacement or substitution of a fallen with a renewed life.

The imagery of both baptism and the Eucharist are important. Baptism is the death rite of Christianity (dying to an old life and rising to a new identity, deepened and more intense in the communion with the faithful), which becomes the Feast or the Banquet of the Lord's Supper. In the sacrifice of the Eucharist, Christians offer something acceptable through Christ's indwelling. Through him sinners can genuinely offer a holy life. But this is not a forensic transaction; it is an imaginative engagement.

How does this identification occur? We can offer some limited analogy from aesthetics. Reading a novel or watching a play furnishes the possibility of imaginative identification with a protagonist. Similarly, the Christian liturgy provides a forum that furnishes the possibility of imaginative engagement with this life provided by Christ. And the Church provides a community within which this can be realized, however imperfectly. But if it remains at this aesthetic level, then this is very unsatisfactory. To rise to the level of the ethical and/or religious, some offering up of oneself, of one's selfish and petty interests and desires, is needed, to become a living sacrifice. Sanctification requires sacrifice.

7

Madness, Metamorphosis, and the Pathetic God: Dionysus and the Crucified

It is as if Christ, as the infinite that has entered finitude and sacrificed it to God in his own human form. Constituted the conclusion of antiquity. He is merely there to draw the boundary- the last god . . . (Christ) was the apex and the end of the world of the gods of antiquity.[1]

(Es ist, als ob Christus als das in die Endlichkeit gekommene und sie in seiner menschlichen Gestalt Gott opfernde Unendlichkeit den Schluss der alten Zeit machet; er ist bloss da, um die Grenze zu machen- der letzte Gott . . . zugleich der Gipfel und das Ende der alten Götterwelt.[2])

Anthropologists who fancy . . . that every dying god must be a representative of the seedling corn or the dying year, have things the wrong way round. That the seed must "die" in order in order to come alive again need not be the first thought of religious metaphysicians: it may represent a deeper truth, that the creator must "die" in order to create.[3]

Suffering has the core meaning of undergoing or experiencing passively rather than the feeling of pain. In this chapter we consider sacrifice in terms of the identification with and transformation through the strange divinity of Christ/Dionysus. We explore Clement of Alexandria's idea of Christ as the true Bacchic. It was the Romantic revival of this idea that lead to the prominence of Dionysus in the Romantic age and, paradoxically, Nietzsche's employment of the image of Dionysus as an anti-Christian topos.

Evolution and culture: continuity and rupture

For me, all insight into human origins must be anthropological.[4]

In a sense, sacrifice is a deeply Romantic topic: it fits in with the Romantic preoccupation with myths, rituals, and symbols. Wagner's *Tristan und*

---

1 Schelling. (1989) The Philosophy of Art. Minneapolis: Minnesota, p. 64.
2 Schelling, *Philosophie der Kunst*, 1/5.432.
3 Clark, S. R. L. (1986) *The Mysteries of Religion: An Introduction to Philosophy through Religion*, Philosophical Introductions. Oxford: Blackwell, p. 164.
4 Girard, R., de Castro Rocha, J. C., and Antonello, P. (2007) *Evolution and Conversion: Dialogues on the Origins of Culture*. London: Continuum, p. 124

Isolde is the culmination of a Romantic fascination with sacrifice from Vico
to Maistre and Schopenhauer. The title of Roger Scruton's excellent *Death
Devoted Heart* is taken from the libretto. Isolde sings of the *Todgeweihtes Herz:*
it could translated as the Death Consecrated Heart. The primary sense of
the German verb *weihen* is to consecrate or dedicate — that is, when a priest
is consecrated or *zum Priester weihen*. Thus Wagner was clearly employing
these resonances of the "con-secrated" heart in the "Todgeweites" Herz.[5]

Réne Girard is famous for his critique of Romanticism, more specifically the "Romantic lie" and the truth of the novel. The sweep of Girard's
theory of sacrifice is reminiscent of idealist-Romantic descriptions. In fact,
many of his detractors ridicule him as a Mr Casaubon figure out of Eliot's
Middlemarch, searching for the key to all mythology. Girard is an intellectual
hedgehog.[6] His thought is a search for origins in his analysis of a genetic
mechanism at the origins of human culture and he is resistant to Derridean
theories of deconstruction.[7]

The truth of the novel, according to Girard, is that of mimetic desire. This
amounts to the difference between the Romantic stress upon human autonomy and those works (especially his favorites, Proust and Dostoevsky),
who recognize this vaunted autonomy as a treacherous chimera. If human
desire is essentially mediated through mimesis, freedom and autonomy
in the Romantic sense must be denied. Drives are binary but desires are
triadic. In this sense we are *inter*dividuals rather than individuals:

> Don Quixote has surrended to Amadis the individual's fundamental
> prerogative: he no longer chooses the objects of his own desire —
> Amadis must choose for him. The disciple pursues objects which are
> determined for him, or at least seem to be determined for him, by the
> model of all chivalry. We shall call the model the mediator of desire.
> Chivalric existence is the imitation of Amadis in the same sense that the
> Christian's is the imitation of Christ.[8]

This is an internal mediation. There is no dangerous rivalry here. But

> [v]iolent opposition, then is the signifier of ultimate desire, of Divine
> self sufficiency, of that "beautiful totality" whose beauty depends on
> its being inaccessible and impenetrable. The victim of this violence
> both adores and detests it . . . Desire clings to violence and stalks it like
> a shadow because violence is the signifier of the cherished being, the
> signifier of divinity.

5   Although devoted has etymological roots in sacrifice: *vovere*, to consecrate.
6   In the sense made popular by Isaiah Berlin in *The Hedgehog and the Fox: An Essay on
    Tolstoy's View of History* (London: Weidenfeld & Nicolson, 1953).
7   McKenna, *Violence and Difference: Girard, Derrida and Deconstruction*. Illinois: University
    of Illinois Press.
8   Girard. (1966) *Deceit, Desire and the Novel: Self and Other in Literary Structure*, Baltimore:
    Johns Hopkins University Press, pp. 1–2. The French original is aptly titled *Mensonge
    romantique et vérité romanesque*.

Girard, I suggest, is a Romantic figure, despite himself. Now it would seem that Girard's reaction to Romanticism has been modified: "*"J' entre dans Clausewitz par Chopin.*[9] The fifth chapter of *Battling to the End* (*Achever Clausewitz*) is called "Hölderlin's Sorrow" (*"Tristesse de Hölderlin"*).[10]

For Machiavelli or Hobbes, sacrifice — whether ritual or sublimated — is incompatible with the social contract. Girard has produced an odd mirror and reversal of contractual theory in which sacrifice provides the basis of society. Contra Grotius, Locke, or Rousseau it is not rational consent but primordial violence that is the basis of the body politic. Ritual sacrifice reenacts a founding murder. Thus Girard can tell the cultured despisers of "religion" that religion is the basis of culture. In fact he sees the rationalist and Enlightenment blindness to the dimension of religion a great hindrance for and limitation in anthropology. Whereas our ancestors knew that human society was nurtured through religion, our culture has lost or ignores this insight. This seems to me a deeply Romantic element of Girard. He, like Schleiermacher, Coleridge, and Maistre, is addressing the cultured despisers of religion.

Another element where Girard is an inheritor of Romanticism is his emphasis upon "symbolicity." Scientists have the tendency to overlook the emergence of symbolicity as the force behind the discontinuity between animals and humans. Girard is very concerned to emphasize the leap — or even break — between the human and the animal "triggered by the emergence of the symbolic sphere." Girard thinks that "in order to have symbolical power you must have an origin of it, and to me that is the scapegoat mechanism."[11]

A certain brain size is a necessary but not sufficient condition of symbolicity — you need a center of signification, argues Girard, and this is provided by the scapegoated victim. The capacity to imitate led to development of what Girard calls "acquisitive mimesis," which, in turn, led to an escalation of violence — the mimetic crisis. During one of these conflicts a hominin or proto-human killed a competitor. The repetition of this leads to the realization that the killing is effective. Thus a mechanism develops that anticipates the mimetic crisis. A victim is taken to preempt violence. Thus the feast dimension — the celebration that represents ritually the mimetic crisis and the sacrifice that resolves it. Thus the scapegoat mechanism or surrogate victim deflection forms a basic buffer against intraspecific violence.

Could we not even say that mimesis is a component of the human social imaginary? The incremental and contagious dynamic of mimetic desire is a collective imagination. It is not the objects of desire *per se* but how we imagine their desirability. This assumes a radical difference between the human and the animal. It is not surprising, I think, that Girard developed this

9   Girard. (2009) *Battling to the End*, Mary Baker (trans.). East Lansing, Michigan State University Press, p. 193.
10 Girard, *Battling to the End*, p. 109ff.
11 Girard. (2007) *Achever Clausewitz (Entretiens avec Benoît Chantre)*, Carnets Nord (ed.). Paris, p. 104.

insight out of the novels of Proust, Dostoevsky, or the plays of Shakespeare.

Of course there is a deep difference. The sacred for Girard is deeply ambivalent whereas for the Romantics it is much more positive. For those Romantics the sacred is linked to the idea of God; for Girard it is linked to the scapegoat. Girard also takes over the Romantic view of myth as an oblique or obscured truth. The Neoplatonist claims that myths are things that never happened but always are: spiritual truths. Myths for Girard, by contrast, camouflage certain terrifying facts about our origins.

The two elements that Wagner highlights are myth and renunciation.[12] Girard's view of myth as too negative and identification of the sacred with the scapegoat produces problems. In the Romantic age, we find a much more positive account of myth. Not only is myth subordinated to ritual but also myth is essentially an exercise in concealment. Myth represents obliquely the original mimetic crisis and the scapegoat murder. It has an element of truth, but it radically conceals and distorts.

Christianity is a myth but it is a true myth. Of course the dying and rising God of Christianity cannot be divorced from those myths that suffused the ancient world. The prevalence of those myths no more disprove the facts of Christianity than the paradigmatic power of Achilles can erase the facts of Alexander the Great. Girard sees myth in decisively negative terms. It is a form of concealing violence:

> Myths incorporate the point of view of the community that has been reconciled to itself by the collective murder and is unanimously convinced that the event was a legitimate and sacred action, desired by God himself, which could not conceivably be repudiated, criticized or analysed.[13]

By contrast the Christian scripture has the effect of desacralizing violence.[14] Maistre, I think, has a much more plausible vision of the links between pagan and Christian thought, when he exclaims: "What truth cannot be found in paganism?"[15]

Girard's negative view of both sacrifice as the killing of victim or expulsion and myth are closely linked. There are historical reasons for this. Totalitarian states the sacrifice of the self for the group from Robespierre to Himmler. Sacrifice is part of an instrumentalization of violence and of a course historically. Girard is, in a sense, for all his evident admiration for Durkheim, a thinker who rejects a liberal individualist account of society and the priestcraft critique of religion coming from the Enlightenment. Yet one might object to Girard's view of religion as an exaggeration of a classic Enlightenment view of religion as the root of all evil and an opposing

12 Scruton, Roger. (2004) *Death Devoted Heart: Sex and the Sacred in Wagner's Tristan und Isolde.* Oxford: Oxford University Press.
13 Girard, R., Oughourlian, J-M., Lefort, G., Bann, S. and Metteer, M. (1987) *Things Hidden since the Foundation of the World.* Stanford, CA: Stanford University Press, p. 148.
14 Girard, *Things Hidden*, p. 153
15 Maistre, Joseph de. (2007) "Eclaircissement sur les sacrifices," in Pierre Glaudes (ed.), *Œuvres.* Paris: R. Laffont, p. 379.

vision of Christianity as divorced from any "natural" religion: a revelation in absolute purity. But this would open Girard to the objection of double standards. If the myths of pagan cults should be treated with suspicion as disguising the sacrificial mechanism, on what basis is Christianity utterly exempt from such suspicion?

Girard shares with Maistre a fear of the violence that erupts through the erosion of "degree." Both agree with Shakespeare's Ulysses:

> Take but degree away, untune that string,
> And hark! What discord follows . . .
> Then everything includes itself in power,
> Power into will, will into appetite:
> And appetite, a universal wolf,
> So doubly seconded with will and power,
> Must perforce a universal prey,
> And last eat up itself.[16]

Girard sees the corrosion of difference as fueling terrible violence, just as Maistre saw the same egalitarianism of the French Revolution generating innocent blood covering "the scaffolds that covered France" during the Revolution. His emphasis upon the scapegoat also has the effect of generating rather *mechanical* view of human relations being dictated by the structure of mimetic desire, mimetic doubling, mimetic crisis, and the single-victim mechanism and an ultimate solution to culture's malaise in the Christian revelation that reveals the true nature of the mechanisms. Christianity seems to function as a *deus ex machina*. There is no account of human spirituality nor of possible parallels between the longing of the Divine in pagan or Christian traditions, nor between Christianity and other faiths.

The genius of Girard lies not in the details of his theory, his anthropology, or his readings of the great works of Greek tragedy, but in his bleak vision of human society. Like many of the Romantics it is a vision of a deeply alienated society, a culture that is fallen. Girard's is one of the most remarkable accounts of how we might envisage a sinful or fallen society, in which violence is not the exception but its motor and secret core.

Love and sacrifice

A much older Frenchman, the medieval Christian humanist William of Conches, provides a striking contrast to Girard. William described the dismemberment of Bacchus as akin to the breaking of the bread in communion. Peter Dronke observes that the link between the "hieros logos" of the sparagmos or dismemberment of Bacchus and the sacred tale of the Last Supper would have been clear to William's medieval audience: "the dismemberment of Bacchus is a sacred tale because it contains a truth about the soul and the body, and how the soul is purified of its bodily cravings,

---

16   Shakespeare, *Troilus and Cressida*, 1.3. 101ff.

how it must die in order to be reborn."[17]

In Euripides's final enigmatic masterpiece, *The Bacchae*, maenads and Pentheus seem like animals. The maenads are like hounds of frenzy. Argave proclaims that she has risen by hunting beasts with her hand while grasping the head of her own dismembered son. On various occasions during the *Bacchae*, Pentheus is compared to Actaeon (337, 1290). In Bruno's *Eroici Furori*[18], the intrepid Nolan employs the Myth of the Hunt of Actaeon, paradigmatically expounded in Ovid's *Metamorphoses* (III 138–250). Actaeon, son of King Cadmus, is the unfortunate young hunter who accidentally sees Diana/Artemis, virgin goddess of the hunt and wild places, bathing. In Ovid's version she fears that he will boast of his vision and turns him into a stag and sets his own hunting dogs upon him. He is torn to pieces by his hounds and so was the "wrath of the quiver-bearing goddess appeased" (*ira pharetratae fertur satiata Dianae*).[19] This horrible tale of the *ira satiata* of Diana probably suggests the terror of female beauty, a variant on the theme of Helen of Troy. In Bruno's account, however, inspired by Plato (especially *Phaedo* 66c2), Actaeon is identified with the speculative Intellect. The nakedness of Diana symbolizes the *nuda veritas*. The unapproachable Godhead is made manifest in the beauty of Diana.[20]

Bruno deliberately refers to Plato's *Symposium* and *Phaedrus*, to Dante's *Convivio* and to Ficino's *De amore*. In this tradition of the "Poetic fury," Bruno explores the idea of the love of intellectual beauty fused with the great Platonic tradition of the mystical *ars moriendi* that goes back to Plato's *Phaedo* 67e. All truth is constituted by the sacrifice of love where the soul is stripped of all. This is the meaning of the myth of Actaeon for Bruno; it becomes an image of the transforming power of transcendence and the ecstatic renewal of the self. Whosoever aims at the realm of the ideas, Bruno avers, has to employ a heroic effort to rise above the senses and to be united with intelligible truth. It is the homesick nature of the soul that inspires this heroic ascent and it cannot shun suffering. Indeed, it seeks out the "Gethsemane of the soul," which issues in the harmony of all things. Bruno is making the sound point, derived from Plato and shared by Aquinas, that love constitutes a principle of motion — *impeto razionale*. Indeed, rather than making blind, love illuminates the *scala naturae*.[21]

The myth becomes an allegory of the transformation of the soul through its confrontation with the intelligible realm. Bruno uses the image of death to express the abstraction (*morte di bacio*) and the *sparagmos* of Actaeon is the

17   Dronke, P. (1974) *Fabula: Explorations into the Uses of Myth in Medieval Platonism*. Leiden: Brill, p. 23.
18   Bruno, G. (2004) *Eroici furori*. Roma-Bari: Caterza, esp. 53ff.
19   Ovid. (1977) *Metamorphoses* (3rd edn.), Frank Justus Miller and G. P. Goold (eds.). Loeb Classical Library. London: W. Heinemann, 3.252.
20   A very useful account of the hermeneutical considerations is Alfons Reckermann's superb interpretation of the Carracci frescoes in the French Embassy in Rome, the Farnese Gallery: *Amor Mutuus: Annibale Carraccis Galleria-Farnese-Fresken und das Bild-Denken der Renaissance* (Cologne, Vienna: Böhlau, 1991), pp. 61–87.
21   Bremer, Dieter. (1993) "Don Juan and Faust: *Mythische Figurationen Neuzeitlichen Bewusstseins*." *Arcadia*, 28, (1): 12–13.

liberation from the prison of the flesh (*libero dal carnal carcere della materia*). Whatever Bruno's attitude to pantheism in other works, here his concern is with the Divine as a transcendent unity (*unità superessenziale*). Here access to God is not cosmological primarily, through the starry heavens, but through the mind, "*ma procedendo al profondo della mente.*" Bruno, in Augustinian fashion, speaks of the Kingdom of God in us "*regno de Dio in noi*" as an infinite center (*centro infinito*). The philosophical hunter of Bruno's great allegory has the Deity already contracted within (*già avendola contratta in sé*).[22]

Myth, Dionysus, and the mysteries

"Myth in the nineteenth century" is a thoroughly researched academic topos. However, these discussions are often pursued from the perspective of "Germanistik," or as a chapter in the history of German idealism or Romanticism, or fueled by a political narrative such as the relation of "myth" to imperialism, Orientalism, or National Socialism. I wish to explore this theme with a different aim: to envisage the recovery of myth in the Modern Age — especially through Romanticism — as a period of rediscovering the sacred in the apparently desecrated or profane-secular world. It is also an example of how the Christian Platonic theory of the imago or *Bild* from Eckhart to Schelling has exerted an enormous and often underrated influence in occidental culture. Sometimes narratives of secularization can distort or disguise the persisting and pervasive strain of Christian metaphysics in our contemporary inheritance.

Giordano Bruno was a focal figure for the German idealists. His work was used polemically by F. H. Jacobi as a precursor of Spinozistic pantheism and Schelling published a deeply Neoplatonic dialogue entitled *Bruno* in 1802. Gerhard von Graevenitz in particular has highlighted the pivotal role of Bruno for German Romanticism. Graevenitz shows the continuity and power of the Platonic Image theory — the *imago Dei* in a dialectic of likeness and un-likeness from Bruno and Vico to the Romantics.[23] And in Britain, Coleridge was a great admirer of Bruno and expressed his debt explicitly in the *Biographia Literaria*:[24]

Here, I shall concentrate upon Creuzer and Schelling's revival of Dionysus as a suffering-redeemer god, one who providentially pre-figures the incarnation of Jesus Christ. This forms the context of Holderlin's famous parallels between Dionysus and Christ in the poems "*Brot und Wein*" and "*Patmos.*" The work of Creuzer and Schelling constitutes an instance of the *Bildtheologie* evident in Bruno, and it is combined with the idea of the Divine origin of all great human institutions, the theory known as the *prisca theologia*.[25]

---

22   See Beierwalter, W. (1985) "Actacon: Zu einem Mythologischen Symbol Giordano Brunos," in *Denken des Einen: Studien zur neuplatonischen Philosophie und ihrer Wirkungsgeschichte.* Frankfurt: Klostermann, pp. 424–35.
23   Graevenitz, Gerhart von. (1987) *Mythos: Zur Geschichte Einer Denkgewohnheit.* Stuttgart: Metzler.
24   Coleridge, *Biographia Literaria*, 1.144–5.
25   Walker, D. P. (1972) *The Ancient Theology: Studies in Christian Platonism from the Fifteenth*

The philosophical exploration of myth runs from the Romantics, Friedrich Schlegel, Creuzer, and Schelling to Max Mueller, Wagner, and Nietzsche.[26] Myth is seen as a force for the renewal of society, conceived of as a religious and ethical unity. The programmatic text is the *Oldest System Programme of German Idealism* (*Älteste System Programme des deutschen Idealismus*). This is written in Hegel's handwriting and is now generally thought to be his work. Schelling and Hölderlin were both fascinated by the question of myth and especially the idea that myth could become the vehicle of the reanimation of the moribund German public life and the reenchantment of nature. Some have seen the author of this document as Schelling, some as Hölderlin. But it clearly expresses the interests and obsessions of the genial Tübingen "*Dreigestirn*." This was the age of Schiller's *Götter Griechenlands*, a period when Hellenism, reforming politics, and a mythopoetic aesthetics went "hand in hand." Hölderlin's poetry is shaped by a vision of the people as a community celebrating the presence of the gods through poetry, a conscious revival of the holy festivals and mysteries of the Hellenes.

The most extensive and profound exegetical work of this period on myth is Friedrich Creuzer's *Symbolik und Mythologie der alten Völker* (1810–1812).[27] Creuzer was, apart from a brief spell in Leiden, Professor of Classics at Heidelberg. Though an expert philologist, he harbored great philosophical and theological ideas and saw his philological labors as part of a great spiritual program of comparative theology.[28]

The emphasis of his work is on the Asian and "irrational" roots of Greek religion, a vision quite unlike Winckelmann. The *Symbolik* is an important term for Creuzer. In *Living Forms of the Imagination,* I discussed the theory of the symbol that lies at the heart of Creuzer's theory.[29] But the *Symbolik* refers not only to the theory of the individual symbol as the primary locus of religious experience but also to a web of symbols that form a decisive narrative: the esoteric mystery religion of salvation and renewal that is, for Creuzer, the enigmatic center of Greek religion.[30] This symbolism of redemption is based upon an interpretation of the Eleusinian mysteries. The God whom Homer treats rather fleetingly or contemptuously, Dionysus, becomes the key to Creuzer's *Symbolik*. This god Dionysus forms the focus of a single oriental theology, which was derived from India. The emphasis of Creuzer upon Dionysus (especially as the *suffering* god), rather than the conventional Olympians, also enabled Creuzer to view the essence of Greek religion as a forerunner of Christianity.

Creuzer presents a version of the ancient theology or *prisca theologia*

   to the Eighteenth Century. London: Duckworth.
26 Hedley, Douglas. (2008) *Living Forms of the Imagination.* London: T&T Clark, pp. 173ff.
27 Creuzer. (1836) *Symbolik und Mythologie der alten Voelker besonders der Griechen.* Leipzig and Darmstadt: Carl Wilhelm Leske, 6 vols.
28 Münch, M. M. (1981) *Joseph-Daniel Guigniaut Et Sa Traduction De La Symbolique De Creuzer,* Interférences. Rennes: L'Institut de Littérature Générale et Comparée de L'U.E.R. Litterature, Université de Haute Bretagne.
29 Hedley, *Living Forms,* p. 133.
30 Feldman, B. and Richardson, R. D. (1975) *The Rise of Modern Mythology, 1680–1860.* Bloomington, IN: Indiana University Press.

(Hermes Tristmegistos or Orpheus). Only in Creuzer's version, the roots of these Hellenic mysteries lie in the mediations of the Brahmins. Here Creuzer is drawing upon the work of Herodotus and an exponent of the *prisca theologia*, Sir William Jones, founder of the Asiatic Society.[31] In 1786, in *The Sanscrit Language*, Jones posited the kinship of Sanskrit with Latin and Greek as well as its superiority to both, and its affinity with "gothic" and "celtic" tongues. But the "Asiatick" Jones, one of the greatest of those many unjustly maligned "Orientalists," was inspired by theology as much as by philology. He was deeply influenced by scripture and the esoteric writings of Newton and mythologist Jacob Bryant (1715–1804) and the philosophical and theological reflections of Cudworth in *The True Intellectual System of the Universe* (1678). Jones saw the religion of the Brahmins as an essentially monotheistic faith that could be traced back to Noah:

> A version of the Jōg Bashest [Yoga-Vāsiṣṭha] was brought to me the other day, in which I discovered much of the Platonick metaphysicks and morality; nor can I help believing, that Plato drew many of his notions (through Egypt, where he resided for some time) from the sages of Hindustan.[32]

Jones notes that within Brahmanic theology:

> The doctrine is that of Parmenides and Plato, whom our Berkley [sic] follows, and I am strongly inclined to consider their philosophy as the only means of removing the difficulties which attend the common opinions concerning the Material world.[33]

Creuzer, similarly, is motivated by theology and produces his own version of a *prisca theologia*. He is also drawing upon Herodotus's belief in the dependence of the Greeks upon the Egyptians. The Cabiri theology came from Egypt via Samothrace and became the core of the mysteries at Eleusis, the site of rites for Demeter and Persephone, whereby the seasons reflect the misery of Demeter during Persephone's absence in hell with Hades. These mysteries were for Creuzer the continuation of the deities of Samothrace: Axieros (qua Demeter), Axiokersa (qua Persephone) Axiokersos (qua Hades). The final Cabric deity was Kasmilos who appears as Iakchos-Dionysus, the child of the virgin Persephone. Iakchos-Dionysus is essentially a reintegrating deity.

Dionysus is not just the wine god and the presiding deity of tragedy and drama. He is also a demiurgic figure and in association with Zagreus is the

31   Cannon, G. H. (1990) *The Life and Mind of Oriental Jones: Sir William Jones, the Father of Modern Linguistics.* Cambridge: Cambridge University Press.
32   Cannon, G. H. (1970) *The Letters of Sir William Jones.* Oxford: Clarendon, vol. 2.646. Quoted in Urs App, (2009) *William Jones's Ancient Theology.* Philadelphia: University of Pennsylvania, p. 16.
33   Sir William Jones, *Letters: The Letters of Sir William Jones.* Cannon, Garland H. (ed.). Oxford: Clarendon Press, 1970) pp. 669–70. Quoted in App, op. cit. p. 18.

suffering god, torn to pieces by the Titans: the deity of the sparagmos.[34] Dionysus, for Creuzer, is the principle of multiplicity; Apollo, that of unity.[35] This arcane pagan mystery theology rather than the epic tales of Achilles in Troy or the travels of Ulysses constitutes the genius of Greek culture. Homer is demoted from the front rank of Greek culture.

Creuzer provoked a massive and heated controversy.[36] He was a professor of Classical philology and perceived by many of his colleagues as betraying the Enlightenment ideals of the new subject. The mystical musings of his *Symbolik* threatened various dearly held tenets of many German humanists, who were still sensitive to the recent emancipation of Classical philology from theology in the wake of Wolff. Creuzer's *Symbolik*, with its clear links with the older *prisca theologia* of the Renaissance or Cambridge Platonists, seemed like a retrograde and reactionary exercise in obfuscation. His emphasis upon the mysteries as the key of the Hellenic *Symbolik* served to play down precisely the defining features of the ancient Hellenes, their "noble simplicity and serene greatness" in words of Winckelmann's great paean; the beauty and elegance of Greek art, and their virile epic poetry. Even worse, Creuzer's reconstructed ancient theology threatened the principle of Hellenic uniqueness. The Greeks, for Creuzer in the footsteps of Herodotus, were the recipients of alien cults, which would culminate in Christianity. It is precisely the universal dimension of the mysteries that constitute their interest for Creuzer. The implicit principle of the superiority of Classical to Christian civilization, which Gibbon expressed neatly in the title of his magnum opus as the "Triumph of Barbarism" denied resoundingly.

Finally Creuzer's emphasis upon the priests and the rituals of the *Symbolik* seemed to provide a covert justification of Catholicism, in the lands divided by the Treaty of Westphalia, where *cuius regio, eius religio*. Creuzer seemed to many of his contemporaries, especially the pugnacious polemicist Voss, to be a crypto-Catholic. His stress upon religion practice and ritual in the mysteries seemed to fit a Catholic sense of the world as a cultic arena better than a strict biblical Protestantism. The world is for Creuzer, as for Schelling, the arena of Divine action and, even more radically, theogony.[37]

From Nietzsche to Schelling

Nietzsche's famous deployment of the figures of Dionysus and Apollo has deep, if rarely acknowledged, roots in the Romantic movement. Max Baeumer, in particular, has shown that Nietszche was drawing on a century-long-established tradition of Dionysian-Apolline contrast.[38] The

34 Lieb, Michael. (1994) *Milton and the Culture of Violence*. Ithaca, NY; London: Cornell University Press.
35 Williamson, G. S. (2004) *The Longing for Myth in Germany: Religion and Aesthetic Culture from Romanticism to Nietzsche*. Chicago, IL; London: University of Chicago Press.
36 Williamson, *The Longing for Myth in Germany*.
37 See Peetz, Siegbert. (1988) *Die Wiederkehr im Unterschied: Ernst von Lasaulx*. Freiburg: Alber.
38 Baeumer, M. L. (1976) "Nietzsche and the tradition of the Dionysian," in James O.

relation between Nietzsche and Schelling's thought in particular has been expertly analyzed by J. E. Wilson.[39] The obvious affinities may be briefly mentioned: Schelling's view that art is a key mode of engaging in reality in his *System of Transcendental Idealism* of 1800 and his emphasis upon "nature" and "will" (the pre-conceptual). Certainly, Schelling is the paradigm of a highly positive and Christological view of Dionysus that will feed into the early Nietzsche. But the interest in Dionysus is explicitly the product of Schelling's later phase of philosophy, a phase when he becomes much closer to Christian theology and espouses a form of theistic metaphysics.[40] From 1804 onward and certainly from 1809, Schelling becomes less political and more theological. The world is envisaged in terms of a Fall and the Absolute is referred to as God. In the wake of his intense vision of the world as a dynamic fallen arena of salvation, Schelling picks up Creuzer's *Symbolik* as source book for his new (and never completed) philosophy of mythology.

Schelling viewed Creuzer's work on Dionysus as the most important contribution. But he disagreed with Creuzer's tenet that Dionysus was from India. Nietzsche's *The Birth of Tragedy* was obviously influenced by Jena Romanticism and idealism.[41] The problem is that Dionysus is a topic of the later Schelling and there is very little evidence that Nietzsche read any later Schelling. The crucial work is that of Manfred Frank in his book *Der kommende Gott*, in which he developed parallels between the mysteries in the philosophy of mythology.[42] Frank uses the idea of *Trunken-Nüchtern* (compare the Patristic idea of *ebria sobrietas*): "*Das Geheimnis der wahren Poesie* "in demselben Augenblick trunken und nüchtern zu sein."[43]

The symbiotic relationship between Creuzer and Schelling, both brilliant philologists and with elective affinity for Neoplatonism, explains the shift in Schelling's relationship with Christianity and Christian theology during his Munich period. In Tübingen and Jena, Schelling had shared a widespread belief in the culpability of Christianity for the malaise of the Modern Age, especially in comparison with the great Age of the Greeks. In Munich, he came to take up a much more positive view of Christianity and his developing interest in the link between Christianity and the mystery religion is coextensive with Creuzer's formidable researches. We have the basic scheme in Schelling of the following development:

Flahery and Timothy F. Sellner (eds.), *Studies in Nietzsche and the Classical Tradition*. Chapel Hill: University of North Carolina.

39   Wilson, J. E. (1996) *Schelling und Nietzsche: Zur Auslegung Der Frühen Werke Friedrich Nietzsches*, Monographien Und Texte Zur Nietzsche-Forschung. Berlin: Walter de Gruyter.

40   See Clayton, Philip. (2000) *The Problem of God in Modern Thought*. Grand Rapids, MI; Cambridge: Eerdmans, pp. 208–29.

41   Behler, Ernst. (1988) "Nietzsche, Marx und die Deutsche Romantik," in *Studien Zur Romantik Und Zur Idealistischen Philosophie*. Paderborn: Schoening.

42   Frank, Manfred. (1982) *Der Kommende Gott: Vorlesungen Über Die Neue Mythologie*. Frankfurt am Main: Suhrkamp, pp. 245ff.

43   See Daniélou, Jean. (1953) *Platonisme Et Théologie Mystique: Essai Sur La Doctrine Spirituelle De Saint Grégoire De Nysse* (new edn.). Paris; Aubier: Éditions Montaigne, p. 292.

1. A primordial phase in which gods represent Natural powers.
2. The development of more spiritual and ethical deities in Greek literature like Hercules.
3. The development of the gods as expressions of poetical ideals.
4. The recognition in the Greek mysteries that the Olympians are fantasies
   that will disappear. In this epoch Dionysus becomes metamorphosized
   into Christ.
5. The gods are allegorized by the Neoplatonists.

Dionysus is thus, as for Creuzer, the pivotal figure in Greek religion, which
is seen in its esoteric rather than its exoteric aspect. Creuzer stresses the
mysteries of Eleusis rather than the public festivals of the ancient Greek
polis. Dionysus has three modes: Zagreus, Bacchus, and Iacchos. Zagreus is
the wild nature and underworld god; Bacchus is the public form in which
Dionysus is worshiped, and Iacchos is the Dionysus of the mysteries. In
this form Dionysus is the god of the future. This tertiary development
of Dionysus parallels the evolution of Christianity — as understood by
Schelling — from the Petrine (that is, the Roman Catholic stage) to the
Pauline (the Protestant) into the third and spiritual phase of Christianity: the
Johannine. This is the awareness of the theogony. Stephen Clark remarks:

> So long as God does not "surrender" real power to His creation there *is*
> no genuine creation, for the imagined creatures exist only as fantasies,
> that make no real demands and impose no real burdens. If creation is
> to be genuine, the essentially unlimited Creator must limit himself,
> must become as-it-were a finite being, even if it is with a view to a re-
> integration of the fragmented deity, or a taming of the rebellious creation.
>
> Any Divine creator must therefore be considered as a self immolating,
> sacrificed god.[44]

Christ is not, like the ram of Abraham, a mere representation or notional
substitute but an image of innocence and perfection of the highest principle.
If that highest principle is love, then Divine love is revealed both in the self
contraction that was creation and in the death of His "only begotten Son."
When Eckhart or Tauler speak of the God's own need (*Not*) to seek out
humanity for reconciliation, they represent a vision of God as essentially
love, and that love expressing itself in self-sacrifice.

The idea that the world is produced by sacrifice is also to be found in the
Vedic tradition.[45] Not only is the world generated by sacrifice, but sacrifice
in the finite sphere allows the infinite, the Divine, to emerge. One finds a
spiritualized version of this view of sacrifice as the "navel of the world" in
the discovery of true Atman in the *Bhagarad Gita*.[46]

44　Clark, S. R. L. (1986) *The Mysteries of Religion: An Introduction to Philosophy through
　　Religion, Philosophical Introductions.* Oxford: Blackwell, p. 164.
45　Heesterman, J. C. (1993) *The Broken World of Sacrifice: An Essay in Ancient Indian Ritual.*
　　Chicago: University of Chicago Press.
46　Radhakrishnan S. (1929) *Indian Philosophy* (revised edn.). London: George Allen, vol.
　　1, 519ff.

Dionysus, suffering, and value: sacrifice revisited

In his important article, "Loss of self, suffering, violence: the modern view of Dionysus from Nietzsche to Girard," Albert Henrichs traces the fortune of Dionysus from the ancient deity of wine to the Nietzsche-inspired God of death and violence, from the cozy medieval Bacchus to the grotesque violence of Girard's Dionysus in *Violence and the Sacred*.[47] Henrichs starts by contrasting Kerényi's Jungian *Dionysos: Archetypal Image of Indestructible Life* and Detienne's structuralist *Dionysos mis a mort*. The first associates Dionysus with wine through the symbolism of wine and the phallus. The second concentrates upon Dionysiac sacrifice and especially the horrible maenadic sacrifice with its consumption of raw meat.

Dionysus has also been very important to Girard's thought. Alongside *Oedipus*, *The Bacchae* of Euripides is of immense significance for Girard, and is linked to his view of sacrifice as key to an understanding of the tragic.[48] Girard emphasizes concealment and the danger of spying on the mysteries; he considers Euripides as a skeptic towards the cults and presents the sympathy of the poet as with Pentheus. Girard's reading of the figure of Dionysus is extremely negative:

> Throughout the play the god wanders from place to place, engendering violence and crime with the artfulness of a satanic seducer. Only the quixotic masochism of our own age, the result of long immunity to the violence that threatens primitive societies, allows us to see anything attractive in the Dionysus of the Bacchae . . . the god has no proper being outside the realm of violence. All his attributes are linked to violence."[49]

Girard's reading of Dionysus as the god of violence is itself quixotic! Dionysus is the strange, foreign member of the Olympian Pantheon, associated with the East, Thrace, and India, and — of course — with wine.[50] There are a number of parallels with the figure of Christ: he descends into the underworld and is murdered by the Titans. He is also known as the liberator (*Eleutherios*) from the habitual self, and can thus be fused with the mystical Christ of St. Paul or St. John. Dionysus is akin to the alien and disturbing dimension of Christ, who can say that "the Son of man has no place to lay his head."[51]

Martin Hengel further argues that there are considerable parallels between Dionysian religion and Christianity.[52] The Marriage of Cana could be interpreted in the light of Dionysian cults. Also, the scene where

47   Henrichs, A. (1984) "Loss of self, suffering, violence: the modern view of Dionysus from Nietzsche to Girard." *Harvard Studies in Classical Philology*, 88: 205–40.
48   Girard, R. and Gregory, P. (2005) *Violence and the Sacred*. London: Continuum, pp. 134–51.
49   Girard, *Violence and the Sacred*, p. 141.
50   Kerényi, Karl (1976) *Dionysos: Archetypal Image of Indestructible Life*, Ralph Manheim (ed.). London: Routledge & Kegan Paul.
51   Mt. 8.20.
52   Hengel. (1974; 2005), *Judaism and Hellenism* (2 vols.). London: SCM.

Dionysus is charged of arrogating Divinity in the *Bacchae* is compared to the trial scene in St. John's Gospel. Both Christ and Dionysus fused wine with blood and overcame death with the promise of salvation for their followers. Dionysus combines violence with redemption. In some sources Dionysus was referred to as λύσιος, "the liberator or unbinder."

Jane Harrison used William Robertson Smith's theory of sacrifice in her thinking about the Dionysus-Zagreus myth, and thus, like Frazer in *The Golden Bough*, interpreted the dreadful meal of the maenads as a sacrament, and cognate with the Christian Eucharistic meal.[53] However odd J. G. Frazer or Jane Harrison's speculations about the proximity between Christian and pagan sacrament, we might consider the thought of Clement of Alexandria and the ensuing tradition of Christianizing pagan mysteries.[54]

Nietzsche famously rejected Christianity as Platonism for the people. The great Church Father Clement of Alexandria (AD 150–215) uses not only the Dialogues of Plato but also Euripides's *The Bacchae,* with particular emphasis in his strategic employment of pagan sources for his theology. It is not surprising that those Church Fathers who emerged out of Middle Platonism and Neoplatonism employed terminology for baptism or the Eucharist that was derived from the mysteries.[55] They could appeal to St. Paul as a precedent and even Plato. Plato says the philosopher is the true Bacchant.[56]

Clement is unrelenting in his critique of the crudity and immorality of the mystery cults. Notwithstanding his ferocious polemic against and scorn for pagan rites, he can also see them in a providential light. Clement attacks human sacrifice in the third chapter of the *Protrepticus*. Though perhaps drawing on Herodotus, Clement uses details from the plays of Euripides, especially *Iphigenia in Tauris*.[57] He exploits the negative depiction of Heracles in *Alcestis and Heracles*. Clement also uses the language of the mirror of Dionysus. Here the Bacchants were supposed to view themselves in the sacred mirror. Clement is following a typology established by Justin Martyr:

> [W]hen they say that Dionysus is born of Zeus's union with Semele, and narrate that he was the discoverer of the vine, and that, after that, after he was torn to pieces and died, he arose again and ascended to heaven.[58]

53   Harrison, Jane. (1972) *Themis, A Study of the Social Origins of Greek Religion.* Cambridge: Cambridge University Press, p. 136ff. See also her *Prolegomena to the study of Greek Religion,* Princeton University Press, 1991.
54   See Reckermann, *Amor Mutuus*, 172ff.
55   Rahner (1963) *Greek Myths and Christian Mystery.* London: Burns & Oates.
56   *Phaedo* 69cd, see also Plato's *Phaedrus* 250c. Walter Hamilton (trans.) Harmondsworth: Penguin (1973), and Plutarch's *Progress in Virtue* (De *Profectu in Virtute*). F. C. Babbitt (trans.). Babbitt, *Plutarch's Moralia.* Cambridge , MA: Loeb, 1927.
57   Rogers, S. R. (1991) "Christian adaptations of Euripidean themes in Clement of Alexandria's Protrepticus and Stromata," (doctoral disseration). Catholic University of America, p. 19.
58   Justin. (2003) *Dialogue with Trypho,* 69.2. T. B. Falls (trans.). Washington, DC: Catholic

In Clement, as in his forerunner Justin, the man-god Dionysus is contrasted with the true God-man Christ who will bring light and salvation. Rather in offering the substitute in Christ, Clement appeals to the pagan Hellenic imagination, especially Euripides, "the philosopher of the drama." In this way Clement can show how the Greeks sought redemption with drama, music, and the mysteries, even if paganism ushered in a cruel god who destroyed. The Bacchae, in particular, is the instrument of a "providential propaedeutic."[59] The mad violence that results in the death of Pentheus is contrasted with the love, compassion, and mercy of the Christian God. The pagan form leads to tragedy and human sacrifice; the Christian sacrifice forms a path to redemption and renewal. The wild and dissolute throng on Mount Cithaeron is contrasted with the unified group of the righteous on Mount Zion:

> Come, Thou frenzy stricken one, not resting on thy wand, not wreathed with ivy. Cast off thy headdress, cast off thy fawn-skin, return to sober-ness. I will show thee the Word, and the Word's mysteries, describing them according to thine own semblance of them. This is the mountain beloved of God: not a subject of tragedies, like Cithaeron, but one devoted to the dramas of truth, a wineless mountain of Sobriety, shaded by hallowed groves.[60]

This mountain is not the domain of maenads sharing out the flesh of the spar-agmos, the maddened women of Thebes, but those sober maidens who are devoted to the true Logos. However, Clement then changes to refer to Christ as the one who supersedes Dionysus. Christ offers the true bacchic rites. Rather than present Bacchus as the heathen opposition to Christ, Dionysus is an odd prefiguration of Christ. It is the new and superior Dionysus:

> O truly sacred mysteries! O pure light! In the blaze of these torches I have a vision of heaven and of God. I become holy by initiation.[61]

Then Clement considers the "bacchic rites" of the true Christian mysteries that culminate in the vision of God. Clement even uses the language of the dance: "If thou wilt, be thyself initiated and thou shalt dance with the angels around the unbegotten and imperishable and only true God."[62]

Clement is adamant that the true sacrifice is the conquest of the passions and assimilation of the soul to God. Where the pagans practice assimilation to man, the Christian practices assimilation to God. The true sacrifice is the self-sacrificial assimilation to God through adoption by Christ and philan-thropy. "Wherefore also Plato says, in the second book of *The Republic*, 'It is those that sacrifice not a sow but some great and difficult sacrifice,' who ought to inquire respecting God."[63]

University of America, p. 107.

59   Clement. (1919) *Exhortation to the Greeks*. London: Loeb, pp. 163–73.
60   Clement, *Exhortation to the Greeks*, p. 255.
61   Clement, *Exhortation to the Greeks*, p. 257.
62   Clement, *Exhortation to the Greeks*, p. 257.
63   Clement, *Stomata*, 5.10, p. 460.

Thus Clement can assert that the Christian life both completes and transcends the initiations and sacrifices of the mysteries:

And his whole life is a holy festival. His sacrifices are prayers, and praises, and readings in the Scriptures before meals, and psalms and hymns during meals and before bed, and prayers also again during night. By these he unites himself to the divine choir, from continual recollection, engaged in contemplation which has everlasting remembrance.[64]

We might contrast Clement with those theologians who, in the wake of Frazer's *The Golden Bough*, assault the historical foundations of Christianity and who turn Incarnation and Atonement into subhistorical cults of the dying and rising God. One might think of the endeavors of figures like Drewermann or assorted feminist theologians, whose hermeneutical concerns effectively preempt any transformative potential of revelation. However, a virgin-giving-birth or the God-man-sacrificed-rising-from-the-dead appear like clear instances of the mythic imagination. We cannot remove the historical claims from Christian theology. But perhaps there remain common ground between the pagan imagination and the Gospel.

"God makes creatures make themselves." That is, self-fashioning is through images and myths. These images provide the stuff of revelation, the very materials of Providence. But our age is characterized, as Vico puts it, by the "barbarism of reflection" because scientific tools cannot explain human nature. We have a natural need to recover our identity through the engagement of imagination. But this does not necessarily mean either irrationalism or crass reduction to the merely figurative. I do not see the revaluation of myth as necessarily implying the rejection of Christian eschatology.[65] Consider, for instance, the momentous Hellenic apocalypse of Plato's myths. Consider Westcott's remarks on Plato's celebrated vision of the journey of the soul chariot in the *Phaedrus*:

There is no grander passage in Greek literature than that in which Plato describes how the contemplation of absolute justice, temperance and knowledge is the sustenance of the Divine nature. There are times of high festival, he says, in the world above, when the gods in solemn procession mount to the topmost vault of heaven, and, taking their place upon its dome, gaze over the infinite depths of perfect truth. This spectacle supports the fullness of their being. Nor are they, he continues, alone in the enjoyment of the magnificent vision: all the souls that can and will follow in their train. Such of these as are able to gain the fair prospect and keep it before their eyes, while the spheres revolve, remain in the possession of supreme joy. The rest baffled, wearied, maimed, sink down to earth and are embodied as men. Henceforth, he adds, their condition

---

64 Clement, *Stromata* 7.7, p. 537.
65 Dalferth, *Jenseits von Mythos und Logos: Die christologische Transformation der Theologie.* Freiburg: Herder (1993), p. 104.

in this lower life depends upon their past apprehension of the Truth. Their human existence is a striving toward the glory which they have once seen. They live still, so far as they really live, by the recollection of that which has filled them with noble passions. The life of man is thus according to the highest thought of Greek Philosophy remembered truth. Such an intuition of noble souls found its confirmation and fulfilment in the word of the Lord: *This is,* he says, *the life eternal.*[66]

For the Christian Fathers, like Clement, Christ became the great charioteer, and in the Vatican catacombs Christ is represented on a solar chariot.[67] For Westcott, Christ is the full truth intimated by the pagans in philosophy as he was prophesied by the Prophets. In St. John's Gospel, the God of the Greeks, the God who creates the world as an image of himself because he is without envy (and this is the language of mimesis and generosity of Plato's *Timaeus*), becomes the God who offers one perfect and sufficient sacrifice. The genius of St. John, like that of St. Paul, is not to reject the pagan mind but to deepen its insight through their own forceful minds and what we Christians can only think of as inspiration more Divine than poetical, providential rather than philosophical. Christianity has a much higher estimate of sympathy than its Stoic or Platonic rivals. It accepts the fact of suffering rather than pleading for detachment. In so doing, it conveys through its Christology and Trinitarian theology an image of the Divine nature that, however enigmatically, integrates sorrow, sympathy, and love in the Godhead. Westcott was convinced that "the Word for which Plato longed, as a sure support, has been given to us in Him Whom St John has made known."[68]

The Greek Fathers exploited the doctrine of Christ as the principle of the world and the ἀνακεφαλαίωσις or recapitulation of all. All things are gathered up in Christ says St. Paul in Ephesians 1. Here is a sense of Christ as the culmination of humanity while making the invisible God visible. Christ is not a *deus ex machina* nor a historical accident but he is a way of seeing the invisible "where the spiritual eye grows dim, the thought of Christ in which we are removes the mists."[69] Westcott speaks of the "open vision of God in Christ."[70] He is the "witness to the essential unity of earth and heaven." Westcott argues that this Christus recapitulans lived the humble life to show us that all life is potentially Divine. Here we have "the promise of unity which lies in the true view of his person."[71] From this perspective, the death and resurrection of Christ makes intelligible the spiritual life of humanity.

66   Westcott, B. F. and Christ Jesus. (1886) *Christus Consummator: Some Aspects of the Work and Person of Christ in Relation to Modern Thought (Sermons).* London: Macmillan.
67   Daniélou. (1977) *Gospel Message and Hellenistic Culture.* Philadelphia: Westminster, p. 81.
68   Westcott, B. F. (1891) *Essays in the History of Religious Thought in the West.* London; New York: Macmillan, p. vi.
69   Westcott, *The Christian Life,* London: Macmillan, p. 34.
70   Westcott, *Essays in the History of Religious Thought,* p. 37.
71   Westcott, *Christus Consummator,* p. 103.

The split: the protecting and the release of the self

We may at this point try to explicate the issue psychologically. Hugo Rahner writes, "with all due caution, we are entitled to say that the mystery cult was entirely a religion of feeling. 'The mystai are not intended to learn anything, but to suffer something and thus be made worthy'" runs a fragment from Aristotle. The aim of initiation is οὐ μαθεῖν ἀλλὰ παθεῖν "not to learn but to suffer."[72]

Through feeling we exercise the capacity to value. An agent whose sensibility has been disturbed or poisoned by traumas or poor education will find it difficult to latch on to and appreciate objects of genuine value. This is the clearly the case with television and the sensory overload of much contemporary culture — for example, iPods, the internet. Sometimes an agent who has been "well-bred," as it were, lacks the proper discernment of value. In such cases, suffering can be a teacher. The figure of Dionysus can express mythically or symbolically the link between suffering and value. Consider an analogy from Jungian psychology: the idea of a psychic split.[73] The psyche is naturally inclined to protect itself from threatening experiences and in the face of traumatic experiences develops a defense mechanism that will protect — for example, the child from an overcritical or abusive parent or the anxiety incurred by a divorce of the parents. The psyche splits. Part of the psyche, the vulnerable self, is concealed or submerged, while another part develops, precociously and constructs a defense system. However, this protection structure can come to persecute the very self that it developed to protect. This self-sufficient protective structure becomes a kind of prison of the psyche. It has also repressed the spark of the Divine in the soul. On the Jungian model, sacrifice is seen in much more positive terms than Freud. Sacrifice becomes in Jung a model of the process of the ego experiencing the deeper reality of the personality or self, a process Jung terms individuation.[74]

In myths there are repeated accounts of encounters with real suffering inducing a revelation of the Divine. The shock of bereavement or illness can awaken the soul to a sense of the invisible beyond the veil of appearances. Simone Weil observes: "The extreme greatness of Christianity lies in the fact that it does not seek a supernatural remedy for suffering but a supernatural use for it."[75] As we have argued throughout this book, the rediscovery of the Divine in the midst of suffering is core theme of both tragedy and mystical spirituality: mystical union or deification and the apotheosis of the tragic hero express symbolically and imaginatively a cognate truth and intimations of the atonement of man and God in Christ. We turn now to Titian's image of this.

72   Rahner, Hugo. (1990) "The Christian mystery and the Pagan mysteries," in Joseph Campbell (ed.), *The Mysteries*. Princeton, NJ: Bollingen, p. 351.
73   See Kalsched, Donald. (1996) *The Inner World of Trauma: Archetypal Defenses of the Personal Spirit*. London: Routledge.
74   *The Collected Works of C.G. Jung* (London: Routledge, 1970), 5, pp. 394ff. See Cottingham, J. (2005) *The Spiritual Dimension*. Cambridge: Cambridge University Press, pp. 145ff
75   Weil, Simone, *Gravity and Grace*. London: Routledge, p. 73.

The painting by Titian of *The Flaying of Marsyas* (c.1570–1576) has provoked much debate. The painting was not, it seems, commissioned and appears to have been chosen by Titian himself.[76] It is the product of his extreme old age, possibly his nineties.

According to the myth as recounted by Ovid, Marsyas discovers Athena's flute, learns to play it, and becomes expert with it. Apollo, himself a player of the lyre, is jealous and challenges Marsyas to a musical competition: the spoils of victor will be the skin of the vanquished. The contest is judged to be a draw but Apollo craftily proposes that the match should continue with instruments upside down: easy with the lyre but impossible with Athena's flute. Marysas is vanquished and Apollo wreaks terrible vengeance. The unfortunate Silene is tied to a tree and skinned alive. Marysas's blood turns into a river. Ovid writes:

> The skin was torn off the whole surface of his body: it was all one raw wound. Blood flowed everywhere, his nerves were exposed, unprotected, his veins pulsed with no skin to cover them. It was possible to count his throbbing organs, and the chambers of the lungs, clearly visible within his breast. Then the woodland gods, the fauns who haunt the countryside, mourned for him; his brother satyrs too . . . The fertile earth grew wet with tears, and when it was sodden, received the falling drops into itself, and drank them into its deepest veins. Then from these tears, it created a spring which it sent gushing forth into the open air . . . It is the clearest river in Phrygia, and bears the name of Marsyas[77].

The story of Marsyas lends itself to symbolic polyvalence.[78] Marsyas is part of the company of Dionysus, and his destruction has links with Dionysus/Zagreus. The myth also invites ideas about sacrifice and salvation, destruction and creation, nature and culture, appearance and reality.

Titian's depiction of this terrible theme has provoked much learned debate. It seemed typical of the darker dimension of Titian's later work, and many have thought that the fierce and striking nature of these works reflected the misery and anger of the man himself.[79] But it has been argued that Titian's work reflects the discussion of tragedy in Renaissance Italy. Though Titian was not a scholar or philosopher, he was very familiar with the debates, interests and obsessions of the humanists. It has also been suggested that the decisive shift in Titian's art occurred in Rome through his encounter with the *terribilità* of Michelangelo — especially the awe-inspiring depiction of suffering and the sublime grandeur of Michelangelo's work. The techniques that Titian employed in his later work, including the dark paint and rough strokes, were often linked to themes of pain and redemption. It is possible that this did not merely reflect

---

76   Wyss, Edith. (1996) *The Myth of Apollo and Marsyas in the Art of the Italian Renaissance: An Inquiry into the Meaning of Images.* Newark, NJ: University of Delaware Press, p. 134.

77   Ovid, 6:388–401

78   See Cottingham, John, *The Spiritual Dimension*, p. 95ff

79   Puttfarken, Thomas. (2005) *Titian & Tragic Painting: Aristotle's "Poetics" and the Rise of the Modern Artist.* New Haven, CT; London: Yale University Press, p. 97ff.

a personal shift in Titian, but the thematic and intellectual challenge that Michelangelo provided.[80]

Iris Murdoch took this painting to represent the necessity of pain for art, believing that artistic insight only comes through suffering. There is a precedent in the Renaissance Neoplatonists; Wind noted in his classic work: "To obtain the 'beloved laurel' of Apollos, the poet must pass through the agony of Marsyas."[81] Wind also refers to Pico's claim that "inspiration by Apollo always requires in us the dismemberment of Osirus."[82] In the syncretistic humanism of the Florentines, Osiris is linked to Dionysus and thus with Marsyus the Silene. One might add, however, David Brown's position that the painting is concerned with the transformation of suffering and evil into good.[83] David Brown, however, thinks that it was about transformation of evil into good. Water implies purification. Furthermore, the painting suggests the experience of the Divine through and amidst suffering. The painting itself is both terrifying and yet tranquil.

Art historians tend to concentrate upon whether or not a painting should be interpreted as Neoplatonic or Aristotelian (e.g.Wind or Panofsky); or in more mundane or practical terms related to the interests or designs of the patron (e.g. Hope). Yet the Neoplatonic content is sometimes misconstrued — not least when it is identified with a blithe humanistic optimism. The (Christian) Neoplatonic tradition that has its core in Ficino's Florence, and shaped the young Michelangelo, was deeply conscious of human sacrifice and suffering. One might only think of the east side of the Sistine Chapel and its depiction of the damned, or the famous "unfinished" slaves in the Accademia bursting out of the shackles of matter.

This theme of suffering and sacrifice — so central for Michelangelo's entire oeuvre — is taken up in Giordano Bruno's highly Neoplatonic *Gli Eroici Furori* (1585), which was dedicated to Sir Philip Sidney. Giordano Bruno is a key figure in the transmission of ideas of the Italian Renaissance into England, not just to courtly figures like Sidney but also beyond to the greatest English dramatist of the age, William Shakespeare. In his poem, the myth of Actaeon is interpreted in a positive manner to denote the transformation of self through suffering.[84] The idea of the hunt is possibly derived from Nicholas of Cusa's *venatio sapientiae*. The "*furore eroico*" or "*entusiasmo*" is not supposed to be irrational. God cannot be comprehended directly, but may apprehended through an indirect progression from the shadows to the Absolute, a movement that requires both reason and emotion.

In *The Flaying of Marsyas*, the figure of Midas is probably a self-portrait

80 Puttfarken, *Titian & Tragic Painting*, p. 109ff.
81 Wind, Edgar. (1980) *Pagan Mysteries in the Renaissance* (2nd edn.), Oxford Paperbacks. Oxford: Oxford University Press, p. 144.
82 Wind, *Pagan Mysteries in the Renaissance*, p. 144.
83 Brown, David. (2007) *God and Grace of Body: Sacrament in Ordinary*. Oxford: Oxford University Press, pp. 211ff.
84 Bruno. (1964) *Heroic Frenzies*, Pualo Eugene Memmo Jr. (trans.). Chapel Hill: University of North Carolina.

of Titian.[85] The figure of Midas-Titian is strangely separated from the action of the flaying. While the others are tending to help Apollo in the grim task and gazing at the tortured body, Midas-Titian is contemplating the face of Marsyas. This structure seems to remove Midas-Titian from the collective punishment, and emphasis the particular perspective of Midas as the co-viewer. Also, the cutting is taking place on the side of Marysas away from Midas. The Pan figure (with his water pail) and the dog seem to block off Midas-Titian physically from the actions of the others. Midas is presenting gazing at the horrific scene. The horror is accentuated by the line of pink-red colors from Midas-Titian to the blood near the puppy, the red boots of Apollos, and the pink of the musician.[86]

In this depiction of the victory of Apollo over the Silene one might consider the famous adage of Benjamin: "there is no document of civilization which is not at the same time a document of barbarism."[87] Yet there may also be a historical event that inspired the theme. In 1571, the Venetian captain Marcantonio Bragadin was taken by the Ottomans in Famagusta on Cyprus and was tortured and flayed alive and publically. This horrific execution was a great shock for the Venetians.[88]

But I think that Titian wants to say more. The painting is not merely a reflection upon the violence of human culture (the Ottomans and Venetians were both great "cultures"), but also a meditation upon redemption, upon sacrifice and salvation. It is easy within historic "Christendom," given the familiarity and ubiquity of the sign of the cross, to forget the horrific nature of the crucifixion. The cross is a representation of terrible violence and cruelty. It has often been noted that the flaying of Marsyas is like a heathen martyrdom — especially insofar as it resembles the inverted crucifixion of St. Peter. In Plato's *Symposium*, Alcibiades talks of Socrates by analogy with Marsysas before and after flaying. This idea of Socrates as the Silene Marsyas would have been well known, quite apart from and beyond the sphere of influence of the Florentine Platonists. Erasmus popularized it through his *Adages*:

> About what appears ridiculous from outside and at first glance . . . but admirable when contemplated from inside. For sileni were those little images that were so fashioned that they could be opened. Closed they had a ridiculous and deformed look, but opened they displayed a god. To these Alcibiades compared Socrates in Plato's Banquet, because he was much different inside than he appeared from outside.[89]

Erasmus uses the image of outer ugliness and inner beauty to emphasize

85 Wyss, Edith. (1996) *The Myth of Apollo and Marsyas in the Art of the Italian Renaissance: An Inquiry into the Meaning of Images*. Newark, New Jersey: University of Delaware Press, p. 136.
86 Hart, Melanie. (2007) *British Journal of Psychotherapy*, 23, 2 (Jan.): 267–80.
87 Benjamin, *Theses on the History of Philosophy*, 7 (1940).
88 Wyss, *The Myth of Apollo and Marsyas in the Art of the Italian Renaissance*, p. 134.
89 Erasmus, *Collected Works*, vol. 34. R. Mynors (ed.). Toronto: University of Toronto Press, p. 262ff.

the Platonic/Christian thought that a man's worth does not depend upon outward attributes but moral and spiritual qualities. The theme of "*intus non extra*" is very powerful in a Christian humanist like Shakespeare, who is writing very much in this Erasmian Christian tradition when Falstaff instructs Shallow about the requisite qualities of the warrior:

> Will you tell me, Master Shallow, how to choose a man?
> Care I for the limb, the thews, the stature, bulk and big
> Assemblage of a man? Give me the spirit . . .[90]

Or with the animadversions of Gloucester with the Prince of Wales:

> No more can you distinguish of a man,
> Than of his outward show, which, God he knows,
> Seldom or never jumpeth with the heart.[91]

Wyss notes that in the Basel 1515 edition of the *Adages*, the image was extended to saints and even Christ himself as a "wondrous silene."[92] He documents how widely known this idea of the Silene suggests that the upside-down execution (not only in Titian representation) may reinforce the sense of inside out.[93]

The musician in the top left of the painting suggests the ultimacy of the eternal harmonies of the spheres, the laws of the universe.[94]

> How sweet the moonlight sleeps upon this bank!
> Here will we sit, and let the sounds of music
> Creep in our ears: soft stillness and the night
> Become the touches of sweet harmony.
> Look, how the floor of heaven
> Is thick inlaid with patines of bright gold:
> There's not the smallest orb that thou behold'st
> But in his motion like an angel sings
> Still quiring to the young-eyed cherubins;
> Such harmony is in immortal souls;
> But, whilst this muddy vesture of decay
> Doth grossly close it in, we cannot hear it.
> Come, ho! and wake Diana with a hymn:
> With sweetest touches pierce your mistress' ear,
> And draw her home with music.[95]

One might add that Apollo is not a triumphant deity in the picture. But he is one who can reveal obscure truths.

---

90   II *Henry IV*, 3.2.257–60.
91   *Richard III* 3.1.9–11
92   Wyss, *The Myth of Apollo and Marsyas in the Art of the Italian Renaissance*, pp. 130–1.
93   Screech, M. A. (1980) *Ecstacy and the Praise of Folly.* London: Duckworth, pp. 29ff.
94   See Wyss, *The Myth of Apollo and Marsyas in the Art of the Italian Renaissance*, pp. 138–9.
95   Shakespeare, *Merchant of Venice*, 5.1.

In Bruno we find the Neoplatonic idea of the *divino furore* as the motor of the confrontation of the profane with sacred. Dante, no stranger to conflict and grim violence in real politics, employed the idea of sacrifice of self in relation to the creativity of artist. At the beginning of *Paradiso* the poet calls on Apollo for Divine inspiration:

> *Entra nel petto mio, e spira tue*
> *sì come quando Marsïa traesti*
> *della vagina delle membra sue*

> Enter into my breast and breathe there
> As when you drew Marsyas
> From the sheath of his limbs.[96]

The brutal image of Apollo's flaying of Marsyas is invoked at the crucial first canto of the *Commedia*. The indwelling of the spirit and the renewal of self (e.g. *Paradiso* 1.1.70: *trasumanar significar per verba non si poria*: the passing beyond humanity (that) cannot be put into words, or Dante's *Vita Nuova*) are key concepts in Dante's oeuvre. This vision of human transformation and renewal through sacrifice is at the heart of Dante's thought. At the beginning of the *Paradiso*, in a passage about vows, we read:

> The greatest gift that God in His bounty made in creation, the most conformable to His goodness and the one He accounts the most precious, was the freedom of the will, with which these creatures with intelligence, all and only these, were and are endowed . . . if it be such that God consents when thou consentest; for in the establishing of the compact between God and man this treasure, being such as I have said, becomes the sacrifice, and that by its own act.

> *Lo maggior don che Dio per sua larghezza*
> *fesse creando ed alla sua bontate*
> *più conformato e quel ch'e' più apprezza,*
> *fu della voluntà la libertate;*
> > *di che le creature intelligenti,*
> *e tutti e sole, fuoro e son dotate.*
> *. . . s'è sì faato*
> *che Dio consenta quando tu consenti;*
> *chè, nel fermar tra Dío e l'uomo il patto,*
> *vittima fassi di questo tesoro*
> *tal quale io dico; e fassi col suo atto.*[97]

In this canto Dante criticizes Jephthah's and Agamemnon's faithful

---

96 Dante, Alighieri. (1939) *Paradiso*, John D. Sinclair (trans.) *The Divine Comedy of Dante Alighieri*. Oxford: Oxford University Press, 1.19–21.

97 Dante, *The Divine Comedy: 3 Paradiso*, 5. 19–30.

execution of their dreadful vows. One can only guess how Dante would
have interpreted Abraham and Isaac!

The Dionysian dimension as integrated within Christian theology can
stand for the process of renewal through a giving up of the protective
structure of the psyche and an experience of Christ as the archetypal
energy of the soul, in the language of the medieval mystics, the Divine
spark. Together with "I live, yet not I but Christ liveth in me" (Gal. 2.20).
The Dionysiac can represent the suffering as a mode of release, but it can
also refer to the exhilarating dimension of this release. Nietzsche's use of
an antagonism between the serene Apollo and wild Dionysus is essentially
Romantic-Schopenhauerian. Apollo is the God of *Vorstellung* — plastic
form, preeminently sculpture, form, and law, the *principium individuationis*.
He represents the serenity of Greeks so admired by Winckelmann or by
Goethe. Yet the *Wille* of Dionysus existed behind the Apolline mask of
Hellenic culture and while Apollo constituted the mask, Dionysus is the
irrational, primordial energy of life; Attic tragedy constituting a brief
period of harmony between these two principles. Nietzsche writes of this
primordial experience of the Dionysian:

> Man is no longer artist, he has become a work of art: all nature's artistic
> powers reveals itself here, amidst shivers of intoxication, to the highest,
> most blissful satisfaction of the primordial unity. *Das Eine.*[98]

The folly or scandal of the cross distinguishes Christianity from much
natural religion. How can we glimpse of the majesty of God in the bizarre
man of sorrows? In Nietzsche we have the identification of the true self with
the Divine: Christ as Dionysus. At the time of *The Birth of Tragedy* Nietzsche
was doubtless still influenced by the Romantic-Christian legacy of Christ
and Dionysus in figures like Schelling or Hölderlin. There were traces in his
early thought of that view of the great Christian feast of thanksgiving as an
encountering with the strange liberating, wine-bearing deity of suffering
and renewal. The mystery of this encounter cannot be reduced to some
ritualistic mechanism. As Erasmus says of Christian communion:

> Although the ritual is not to be despised, nevertheless it is, in itself, of
> little profit, even harmful, unless it bring nearer that which is spiritual
> — especially that which is represented by these visible signs. What is
> represented is the death of Christ. Mortal men, having tamed, destroyed
> and as it were, buried their bodily passions, ought to imitate this death,
> so that they may rise again 'to newness of life', able to be 'one with in'
> and 'one with each other'. These are the things which the pious man
> does; these are the things he practises. The crowd, on the contrary,
> believe that the sacrifice consist in being near altars — as close as
> possible — hearing their yelling voices and gazing upon other ritual
> trivialities. Not in such things alone, which we only put forward as

---

98 Nietzsche. (1999) *Birth of Tragedy*, Geuss and Spiers (eds.). Cambridge: Cambridge
    University Press, p. 18.

examples, but quite simply in all his life, the pious man flees from those things which are akin to the body, and is caught up towards the things which are eternal, invisible and spiritual.[99]

In this passage Erasmus is drawing upon the Origenistic distinction between "spiritual" and "somatic" Christianity. In the Eucharist the communicant becomes one with other Christians and with God. The soul is raised above itself in this union with the glorified and indwelling Christ. The Church, on the Erasmian view, is properly viewed as a domain of Divine indwelling. As in St. Paul: "The Spirit itself beareth witness with our spirit, that we are children of God and if children, then heirs of God and joint heirs with Christ" (Rom. 8.16).

But the participation in the Divine is not an automatic or mechanical process. There is a purging of the soul required if it is to see aright if it can see with reverence the created order as Divine gift, a world animated by the Divine presence. This will not be unveiled to a carnal or even superstitious soul. Roger Scruton mirrors the sentiments of Erasmus when he observes that

> the Eucharist reminds us that this renewal is an inward thing — a repossession of freedom. And with freedom comes *agape*, the strange and transforming ability to give . . . In the Christian view the Eucharist is described as 'these gifts', gifts that represent the original gift of himself that Christ made on the cross.[100]

We might even employ an analogy from wine drinking. There is something odd about the solitary consumption of a fine wine. The enjoyment of superb wine is genuinely enhanced by the awareness of the simultaneous pleasure shared by one's companions. It is puzzling why, since this pleasure is not merely the communal merriment of the alehouse nor the curiosity about the workings of *forum internum* of another conscious agent.

Love is the acknowledgment of a unity behind our surface distinction — our separateness as individuals. Our strictly "individual" nature is that which is divided or separated; "individual" being cognate with the Latin verb dividere, divisus. The Christian Banquet emphases our communion with other persons, human and Divine, as the basis for a life renewed and the imagination regenerated. Through the regenerate imagination it can be seen with joy that the essence of reality as grounded in Divine love is revealed and realized in love. As Herbert says:

> Love is that liquor sweet and most Divine,
> Which my God feels as blood, but I, as wine.[101]

99   Screech, *Ecstacy and the Praise of Folly*, p. 117.
100 Scruton, Roger. (2009) *I Drink Therefore I Am: A Philosopher's Guide to Wine*. London; New York: Continuum, p. 107.
101 Herbert. (1957) "The Agonie," in *The Metaphysical Poets*, Helen Gardner (ed.). Harmondsworth: Penguin, p. 118.

The "Quire-Musick of the Temple" and the Heavenly Banquet

A broken A L T A R, Lord, thy servant reares,
Made of a heart, and cemented with teares:
Whose parts are as thy hand did frame;
No workmans tool hath touch'd the same.
A H E A R T alone
Is such a stone,
As nothing but
Thy pow'r doth cut.
Wherefore each part
Of my hard heart
Meets in this frame,
To praise thy Name;
That, if I chance to hold my peace,
These stones to praise thee may not cease.
O let thy blessed S A C R I F I C E be mine,
And sanctifie this A L T A R to be thine.[1]

Sacrifice is an occasion of joy in many archaic societies since it is the time of the feast and the celebration. The Temple represents the epiphany of the Divine to the human soul and the joy of the holy festival: Henry Corbin has described the image of the Temple as it develops from Ezekiel's vision of the departure of the Sheckinah from the First Temple to Hellenic Judaism and later Cabbalistic and Christian mystical accounts of the spiritual Temple and the Shiite hermeneutics of the Temple. Margaret Barker's paradigm-shifting work on the Temple sources of Christian theology has illumined the central role of Temple imagery in Christian theology and the theory of correspondence between earthly and heavenly that underlies it. All that God creates is capable of having a sacramental role. The sacrament is not to be understood as extrinsic or nonessential to the profane: reveals the real nature of all being as created. Because of the likeness between created and uncreated, the Divine exists in creatures potentially. Maistre's reliance upon the Cambridge Platonists, especially Cudworth, is explored. Both rely upon a theory of correspondence between the physical cosmos and the Divine mind, and the sacramental dimension of idea of the Christian Eucharist is explored. We conclude with considerations about the dimension of sacrifice as feast and from reflections of John Smith about the "sober ecstasy" as

---

1   Herbert, George. (1991) "The Altar," in *The Complete English Poems*, John Tobin (ed.). Harmondsworth: Penguin, p. 23.

induced by the music of the Temple.

An unlikely admiration?

Let us imagine Count Joseph de Maistre, at his house in Chambéry. It is September 22, 1792. The Revolutionary army is descending upon Chambéry. Among the few books he can rescue from his library, Maistre takes the two weighty volumes of *The True Intellectual System of the Universe*, the magnum opus of the Cambridge Platonist Ralph Cudworth (1617–1688), Regius Professor of Hebrew and sometime Master of Clare College and Christ's College, Cambridge. With this work Maistre escapes the marauding French army until he reaches the Val d'Aosta. The Terror and the subsequent conquests transformed Maistre's perception of the Revolution radically from initial favor to implacable opposition. Yet this episode in the early career of Maistre indicates a continuity of esteem for the great Cambridge Platonist. In his major work, *St Petersburg Dialogues; or, Conversation on the Temporal Government of Providence* (*Soirées de Saint Pétersbourg*) Maistre refers to "*Le célèbre Cudworth.*" In the sixth dialogue he attacks Locke's empiricism:

> We should therefore assume, with the greatest of men, that we naturally have intellectual ideas that have not come to us by the senses, and that the contrary opinion offends good sense as well as religion.[2]

Against Locke, Maistre quotes a fine company of great authors from Pythagoras to Malebranche. Cudworth is part of this "*bonne compagnie.*" Against the Lockean empiricism lauded by the Voltaire and philosophes, Maistre appeals to an epistemological innatism that he wishes to defend as a part of a *philosophia perennis*. In one striking passage Maistre appeals to Cudworth for his demonstration of the truth of innatism:

> I read somewhere that the celebrated Cudworth, disputing one day with one of his friends on the origin of ideas, said to him: Please take a book from my library, the first that comes to hand, and open it at random. The friend picked up Cicero's De Officiis and opened it at the beginning of the first book and read ALTHOUGH a year ago, etc. That is enough, replied Cudworth, tell me how you could have acquired the idea of ALTHOUGH from the senses. The argument is excellent under a simple form Man cannot speak, he cannot articulate the least element of his thought, he cannot say AND, without refuting Locke.[3]

---

2   Maistre, J. M. (1993) *St Petersburg Dialogues; or, Conversations on the Temporal Government of Providence*. Montreal: McGill-Queen's University Press, p. 185.

3   *J'ai lu que le célèbre Cudworth, disputant un jour avec un des ses amis sur l'origin des Idées, lui did, Prenez, je vous prie, un livre dans ma bibilothèque, le premier qui se présentera sous votre main, et ouvrez le l'ami tomba sur les Offices de Cicéron au commencement du premier livre: «QUOIQUE depuis un an, etc. — C'est assez, reprit Cudworth: dites-moi de grâce comment vous avez pu acquérir par les sens l'idée de QUOIQUE. L'argument était excellent sous une*

It is a curious passage and it is not at all obvious where Maistre found this anecdote. But it reflects a rather puzzling interest. Maistre is the fount of "Throne and Altar" conservativism, an eloquent gentleman philosopher in exile, firing salvoes at the monstrous rationalism of revolutionary France. Cudworth is a donnish figure, a writer of dense and learned tomes, a man who advised Cromwell and was no opponent of the Commonwealth. Cudworth was also a theologian. He was part of that group known as the latitudinarians or men of latititude. This was a term of insult applied to those liberally minded churchmen who were neither supporters of the Laudian reforms nor happy with the dogmas of the Puritans. Thus we have the strange phenomenon of a (proto-) ultramontane Roman Catholic quoting with reverence the English latitudinarian!

And the puzzle deepens. In his *Eclaircissement sur les Sacrifices* Joseph de Maistre refers positively to "*la dissertation de Cudworth, de vera coeñoe Domini*, cap. 1, n VII", at the end of the *Systema intellectuale universum*. The first paragraph of the text is an account of the "Grand Errour of the Papists" — that is to say, an attack upon Tridentine position of the Mass as a sacrifice offered to God.

Cudworth's early work

In 1630, Cudworth was admitted to Emmanuel College and was elected Fellow in 1639. In 1642 he published his first work, *A Discourse Concerning the True Notion of the Lord's Supper*. In the same year he published *The Union of Christ and the Church*. It would seem that the reputation he gained with these works secured his appointment to Clare College.

A cursory reading of the Cudworth reveals a view of Eucharist as a meal, whereas Maistre seems to assume the Catholic view of the Mass as sacrifice. How odd to find Maistre, stalwart anti-Gallican and intransigent advocate of papal authority, praising a work that seems, *prima facie*, a piece of erudite, if rather pallid, Protestant polemic! Yet if we look more closely at the text, we can see reasons for a deep affinity between the fiercely reactionary Savoyard and the Cambridge latitudinarian. We find a commitment to Christian sacramental practice based upon an ontology of participation. It is interesting that Maistre should show such sympathy for Cudworth despite their apparently different theological inclinations. The reason for this lies in the very similar Platonic metaphysics. Maistre writes of Cudworth's *Lord's Supper*: "This curious text directly refutes Heynes's ideas, and will be found completely in agreement with Hebraic theories, according to which the shedding of blood constitutes the essence of sacrifice."[4]

In *A Discourse Concerning the True Notion of the Lord's Supper*, Cudworth

---

forme très simple: l'homme ne peut parler, il ne peut articuler le moindre élément de sa pensée; il ne peut dire ET, sans réfuter Locke. » Les Soirees de Saint-Petersbourg, p. 629.

4   *Ce text curieux refute directement les idees de Heyne, et se trouve parfaitement d'accord avec les hebraiques, suivant lesquelles l'effusion du sang constitue l'essence du sacrifice.* Maistre, St Petersbourg, p. 378.

wants to explain the source of the error of the Eucharist as a gift to God: "Pure Falsehood is pure Non-Entity, and could not subsist alone by it self, wherefore it always twines up together with some truth,"[5] Furthermore,

> because it is not enough in any Discourse, as *Aristotle* well observeth in his *Ethics*, to confute an error, unless we can also show . . . The Cause of that Errot; Having thus discovered The *True Notion of the Lord's Supper*, we may easily from hence discern also, How that mistake grew up, and that by the degeneration of this Truth, There is a Sacrifice in the Lord's Supper Symbolically, but not there as Offered up to God, but Feasted on by us; and so not a Sacrifice but a Sacrificial Feast: Which beganne too soone to be misunderstood.[6]

The nineteenth-century theologian Tulloch observed of the *A Discourse Concerning the True Notion of the Lord's Supper* and *The Union of Christ and the Church* that they contain a strong philosophical dimension:

> The subjects handled in these early tracts are directly religious; but it is their philosophical more than their religious tendency which interests us . . . His mind instinctively seeks the root of religion and morality — their ultimate basis in the laws and principles of human nature.[7]

Tulloch is right. And it is this interest in the laws and principles of human nature that links Cudworth to Maistre.

Sacrifice and making sacred

The author of the New Testament book of Hebrews claims, in ch. 9, v. 22, that atonement requires the shedding of blood. The claim was presumably uncontroversial for Christians or contemporary pagans. Yet for the secular modern mind, the assumption that blood is required seems at best question begging, at worst barbaric. Maistre provides a startling meditation upon this in his principle of "*Régénération dans le sang*" (regeneration through blood). The world is an "*Autel immense où tout ce qui vit doit être immole sans fin sans mesure, sans relâche jusqu'à la consommation des chose, jusqu'à la mort de la mort.*"[8] Maistre is fascinated by the problem of sacrifice. Hence the relationship of mosaic sacrifice to Christ's atonement is a matter of enormous importance for him. Is sacrifice a Divinely instituted practice or a sign of human frailty and superstition? The latter is the position

---

5 Cudworth. (1642) *A Discourse Concerning the True Notion of the Lord's Supper.* London, p. 2.
6 Cudworth, *A Discourse*, p. 55f.
7 Tulloch, John. (1874) *Rational Theology and Christian Philosophy in England in the Seventeenth Century* (2nd edn.), 2 vols. Edinburgh: William Blackwood, 2, p. 202.
8 The entire earth, perpetually steeped in blood, is nothing but an immense altar on which every living thing must be immolated without end, without restraint, without respite, until the consummation of the world, until the extinction of evil, until the death of death. Maistre, *St Petersburg Dialogues*, p. 217.

maintained by leading Enlightenment figures. For Maistre no theology of the vicarious expiation of sin can work without a sense of the Divine institution of the ritual of sacrifice, among the pagans as well as among the Hebrews. Thus Maistre's question about Primitive sacrifices is: do they express a principle of expiation or merely a human sense of dependence and responsibility/obligation. Many distinguished thinkers in the English seventeenth century, alongside Cudworth, reflected upon this issue. One of the greatest, the eminent Cambridge man in its most glorious age, John Spencer (1630–1693), Master of Corpus Christi (1667–1693) and younger contemporary of Cudworth, thought sacrifices were gifts that expressed both longing for Divine favor and expressing submission. Spencer, an authority on Hebrew, was the author of *De Legibus Hebraeorum Earum Rationibus* (1685), and became a frequent source used by deists.[9] The Socinians thought that propitiatory sacrifices were merely ceremonial and lacking any moral or spiritual dimension. The great German philologist Heyne's (1729–1812) theory was that sacrifice was essentially an offering. Maistre sees David Hume (1711–1776) as pursuing a similar position when he represents sacrifice as an exemplification of the irrational fear at the basis of religious belief. Maistre opposes Cudworth on sacrifice to Hume *"dans sa vilaine Histoire naturelle de la religion"*:

> Hume, in his odious Natural History of Religion, adopted this same ideas from Heyne and embittered it in his own way: "A sacrifice," he says, "is conceived as a present; and any present is delivered to the deity by destroying it and rendering it useless to men; by burning whatever is solid, pouring out the liquid, and killing the animate, For want of a better way doing him service, we do ourselves injury; and fancy that we thereby express, at least, the heartiness of our good will and adoration. Thus our mercenary devotion deceives ourselves, and imagines it deceives the deity."[10]

Maistre observes that "this acrimony explains nothing." Cudworth argues that sacrifice is constituted by both "expiation and feasting."[11]

The breaking of the bread and offering of wine among Christians is linked to the Last Supper of Christ before his passion and crucifixion. Margaret Barker has emphasized that the Eucharist, or thanksgiving in English, is the core of Christian worship and yet its roots are opaque.[12] The Synoptic Gospels present the Eucharist as founded by Christ at the Last Supper, itself a Passover meal (Mk. 14.14, 16; Lk. 22.7, 8, and so forth). The paschal supper was a reminiscence of the Lamb that was killed and the

---

9 Champion, J. A. I. (1992) *The Pillars of Priestcraft Shaken: The Church of England and Its Enemies, 1660–1730, Cambridge Studies in Early Modern British History*. Cambridge: Cambridge University Press, ch. 5; Assmann, Jan. (1997) *Moses the Egyptian: The Memory of Egypt in Western Monotheism*. Cambridge, MA; London: Harvard University Press.

10 Maistre, *St Petersburg Dialogues*, p. 373.

11 Cudworth, *A Discourse*, p. 62.

12 Barker, Margaret. (2007) *Temple Themes in Christian Worship*. London: T&T Clark, pp. 167–219.

blood sprinkled — in memory of the night when this enabled the Israelites to escape death. In John's Gospel we do not find the Eucharist and the Last Supper is held before Passover. St. John seems to deny that the Last Supper was the Passover meal (Jn. 13.1, 18.28, 19.14), and John places it 24 hours earlier (or is using a different calendar). John's version of the events, of course, has the symbolic appeal of making Jesus, as the Lamb of God, die at the same time as the Passover lambs were being sacrificed. Most scholars now deny that the Last Supper was in fact a Passover meal.[13] First, leaven bread is used: ἄρτος (*artos*). Second, there are considerable problems with the dating of the Passover. Third, there is no reference to Lamb. Fourth, the *Didache*, the ancient anonymous guide for early Christians, makes no mention of Passover. But Cudworth is determined to present "The Paschall Feast" as the paradigm of the Lord's supper:

> [O]nely this difference arising in the Parallel, that because those *Legal Sacrifices* were but Types and Shadowes of the true *Christian Sacrifice*, they were often repeated and renewed, as well as the *Feasts* that were made upon them: but now the True *Christian Sacrifice* being come, and offered up once for all, never to be repeated; we have therefore no more Typical *Sacrifices* left among us but onely the *Feasts upon the* True *Sacrifice* still Symbolically continued, and often repeated, in reference to that ONE GREAT SACRIFICE, which is always as present in Gods sight and efficacious, as if it were but now offered up for us.[14]

Cudworth insists that the Lord's Supper is a Feast upon a Sacrifice that is analogous to the legal sacrifices of the Jews. He thus employs a typological argument. The legal sacrifices were "types and shadows" of the sacrifice of Christ. And the Jews joined feasting with the sacrifice. The Eating of the Sacrifice is an "appendix" to all sacrifices — hence the analogous Christian practice of feasting upon that which has been sacrificed. This insistence upon the correspondence between the sacrifices of the Hebrews and pagans and Christ's own sacrifice is the core of Cudworth's account. He refers to the Middle Platonist Plutarch's account of the "Aegyptian Fables of Isis and Osiris" as providing "certaine weake appearances and glimmerings of Truth."[15] The tearing asunder of Osiris by Typhon is typological figuring of Christ. Indeed, the *Isis and Osiris* of Plutarch is an important source for Maistre that represents a pagan intimation of the sacrifice of Christ.[16]

Cudworth also discusses parallels from Homeric and Platonic sources and from Virgil. And here he makes explicit his Platonic inheritance. Maistre is interested in this because Cudworth emphasizes the sacrificial nature of

13 Barker, *Temple Themes in Christian Worship*, p. 167ff.
14 Cudworth, *Lord's Supper*, pp. 15–16.
15 Cudworth. (1642) *The Union of Christ and the Chuch, in a Shadow*, London, printed for Richard Bishop, p. 2.
16 Lieb, Michael. (1994) *Milton and the Culture of Violence*. Ithaca, NY; London: Cornell University Press; Maistre, *St Petersburg Dialogues*, pp. 41, 126, 340.

Christ's death and the participation of believers in that sacrifice. Rather than crass attempts to bribe the deity, sacrifice is part of a Divine economy that can be evinced in the practices of the Jews and the heathens and which finds its culmination in the sacrificial death of Christ — hence Cudworth's concern to show the legitimacy of the link with the Passover Festival in *Christus consummator*. The Christian sacrifice can symbolize the sacrificial energy that finds expression in much human culture. Anthropology and revelation touch. Christ is a way of seeing the invisible world. He is the great High Priest who opens the veil of the Temple and reveals the Divine essence. As the bood stained Logos, he opens the heavens.

The *Banquet* and the language of the mysteries

In his *Symposium* or *Banquet*, Plato uses the language of the mysteries to express the intellectual quest for the Divine.[17] Hence the language of the ideas was rooted in the mystery cults.[18] Via this mediation of Plato and Philo, the Fathers used the language of the ideas to express the meaning of the Christian Eucharist.[19] Thus we should not think of the Christian Fathers merely plundering the language of the mysteries. They are employing a tradition of thought about the vision of God that has employed mystery language.[20] The Lord's Supper is not merely a feasting but it represents the renewed covenant between God and man, a "Federall Rite between God and us."

> The Apostle . . . dehorts the Corinthians from Eating the Feasts upon Idoll-Sacrifices, which are a parallel to the Feast upon the Christian Sacrifice, in the Lord's Supper, Because this was to have *Fellowship*, and *Federall Communion with devils*; the Things that the Gentile sacrifice, they sacrifice to Devils, and not to God, and I would not Brethren that you should have Fellowship (or COMMUNION, . . .) with Devils.[21]

Cudworth also states: "Therefore, as to Eate the Body and Blood of Christ in the Lords [sic] Supper, is to be made partake of his Sacrifice offered up to God for us, as to Eate of the Jewish Sacrifices of the law was to partake in the legall sacrifices themselves: So to eate of things offered up in Sacrifice to Idols, was to be made partakers of the Idoll-Sacrifices: And therefore was unlawful."

17   Smith, D. E. (2003) *From Symposium to Eucharist: The Banquet in the Early Christian World.* Minneapolis, MN: Fortress Press.
18   Festuguiere, A. J. (1932) *L'ideal religieux des grec et l'Evangile.* Paris: J. Gabalda.
     Ysebaert, J. (1962) *Greek Baptismal Terminology: Its Origins and Early Development.* Nijmegen: Dekker, p. 161.
19   Louth, Andrew. (2007) *The Origins of the Christian Mystical Tradition: From Plato to Denys* (2nd edn.). Oxford: Oxford University Press.
20   See Louth, *Origins of the Christian Mystical Tradition.*
21   Cudworth, *A Discourse*, p. 54.

The word Paul uses is κοινωνία and has the basic sense of sharing. The word was derived from Greek classical literature, and conveys the meaning of an interior union or communion. It can mean friendship, companionship, or matrimony, but in Plato it means fellowship with the Divine (in *Gorgias* 508 or *Laws* X 903). Cudworth is drawing upon a natural point of contact between Platonic language of participation and the Christian mysteries.

Paul provides the only two descriptions of the Lord's Supper (1 Cor. 11.20) among early Christians: in his letters to the Galatians and the Corinthians, he uses the language for his Christ mysticism — spiritual kinship and a mutual sharing in things invisible and spiritual (perhaps Ancient Dionysiac rites). This fellowship and communion of believers with Christ is contrasted with the communion with devils at the pagan altars: "You cannot partake of the table of the Lord and the table of demons" (1 Cor. 10.21). Cudworth remarks:

> If there to Eate the Sacrifice of Devils be to have *Federall Communion* with those Devils, to whom it was offered, then to Eate of the Sacrifice of Christ, once offered up to God, in the Lord's Supper, is to have *Federall Communion* with God.[22]

The bread and wine are the instruments of Christ's presence. Paul does not tell us how this participation occurs but is emphatic about its reality.

> The Eating of Gods Sacrifices was a FEDERALL RITE, between God and those that offered them, according to the Custome of the Ancients, and especially in those Orientall Parts, to confirm and Ratify their Covenenants, by Eating and Drinking together.[23]

What is, according to Cudworth, the false and The Right Notion? His answer is that the Lord's Supper is not an "oblatio sacrificii," "but as Tertullian excellently speaks; PARTICIPATIO SACRIFICII: Not the *Offering of Something up to God upon an Altar*, but the *Eating of Something which comes from God's Altar* and is set upon Our Tables."[24] Cudworth's metaphysics is a theory of correspondences: The Lord's Supper is a Feast upon a Sacrifice that is analogous to the legal sacrifices of the Jews. The legal sacrifices were "Types and Shadowes."[25] This language is reminiscent of Plotinus. He distinguishes between *tupos* and *phantasma* as the difference between an image that participates in the noetic realm and an illusion.[26] This distinction becomes essential for the symbolism of many Christian Platonists. The lower relation does not merely illustrate the higher, but is, in fact, its

22   Cudworth, *A Discourse*, p. 70.
23   Cudworth, *A Discourse*, p. 56.
24   Cudworth, *A Discourse*, p. 55.
25   Cudworth, *A Discourse*, p. 16.
26   Emilsson, E. K. (1988) *Plotinus on Sense-Perception: A Philosophical Study.* Cambridge: Cambridge University Press, p. 108ff. See Hedley, Douglas. (2008) *Living Forms of the Imagination.* London: T&T Clark.

Divinely constituted *tupos* or shadow of the higher.

> As the Platonist used to say concerning spiritual and material things
> . . . That material things are but Ectypall Resemblances and imitations
> of spiritual things, which were the First, Primitive, and Archetypal
> Beings.[27]

Cudworth proceeds to quote the German humanist and Cabbalist Johannes
Reuchlin (1455–1522): "God often prints the same seal on severall matters."
Interestingly, Cudworth quotes Bacon approvingly as part of the *philosophia
perennis*, with his references to *"Parallela Signacula* and *Symbolizantes
Schematismos."* This idea, Cudworth claims, was known to the Hebrews;
it was "the true foundation of all their CABALA," "secret and mystical
Divinity . . . almost wholly built on this one foundation".[28] This foundation
is "That everything which is below, hath some Root above"[29] means that
there is, for Cudworth, no absolute opposition between creation and its creative principle, but rather an infinite gradation within which the supreme
good diffuses itself (*bonum diffusivum sui* as Aquinas puts it). Cudworth's
polemics against Hobbes and Maistre's analysis of the Enlightenment
philosophes both rest upon a similar critique of a nominalist opposition
between thought and Being. Both Cudworth and Maistre are defending
the ancient *Ordo* structure of a classical metaphysical world, where God
is both the efficient and final cause of the universe and where ethics and
religion are placed with the process of *exitus* and *reditus* of the cosmos to
its Divine source and telos: a structure that Cudworth identifies explicitly
with a Platonic legacy.

> And certain it is that *Plato* in all this, did thinke there was contained
> some Mystical meaning concerning the Nature of Divine Love, either as
> *Ficinus* or *Leo Hebraeus* allegorize it, or else perhaps more simply thus,
> That Man in his first Estate being united with God, and one with him,
> afterward Sinning was divorced from him, and sunk down quite into the
> Body, but so as that by Divine Love he might still recover himselfe, and
> so by degrees work up himself again unto God, and be made perfectly
> one with him . . .[30]

For Cudworth in his *The Union of Christ and the Church* this becomes the
basis for a sacramental view of marriage:

> God having framed the excellent plot of the Gospel and therein contin-
> ued the mystical union between Christ and the Church, delighted to
> draw some shadowings and adumbrations of it here below, and left the
> seal of that truth upon these material things, that so it might print the

---

27 Cudworth. (1642) *The Union of Christ and the Church: In a Shadow.* London, 1642 p. 3.
28 Cudworth, *Union*, p. 3.
29 Cudworth, *Union*, p. 6.
30 Cudworth, *Union*, p. 23.

same stamp and idea.[31]

Shadow is *skia,* in Greek, a word often liked with *tupos.* The author of the book of Hebrews affirms that the earthly sanctuary is "a copy (*hupodeigma*) and shadow (*skia*) of the heavenly sanctuary" (Heb. 8.5). He reinforces this principle of correspondence between the earthly and heavenly quoting Exod. 25.40: "For when Moses was about to erect the tent, he was instructed by God, saying, 'See that you make everything according to the pattern (tupos) which was shown you on the mountain.'"

In his *Elucidation on Sacrifices* (*l'Éclaircissement sur les sacrifices*), Joseph de Maistre insists upon sacramental continuity between the spiritual and material elements of the universe, and man and world. Speaking of his favorite theologian, Origen, he writes:

> It is in this immense scope that Origen envisaged the effect of the great sacrifice. "But this theory," he said, belongs to celestial mysteries, which is what the apostle himself desclared to us when he told us: that it was necessary, therefore, that the copies of the heavenly realities should be cleansed by this; but the heavenly realities themselves require better sacrifices than these . . . the lamb alone could take upon himself the sins of the whole world etc.[32]

The focus of Origen's theology of sacrifice is very much a meditation upon the heavenly reality in relation to its copy and shadow (Heb. 8.5): that Christ's sacrificial work is principally before the throne of the Father.[33] For Philo and Clement of Alexandria, sacrifice represents the soul's itinerary to God. For Clement:

> The altar, then, that is with us here, the terrestial one, is the congregation of those who devote themselves to prayers, having as it were one common voice and one mind . . . Now breathing together is properly said of the church. For the sacrifice of the Church is the word breathing incense from holy souls, the sacrifice and the whole mind being at the same time unveiled to God.[34]

The word "sacrament" was used in the Latin to translate μυστήριόν (*mysterion*) — that is, a secret or veiled reality, revealed only to initiates. Philip Sherrard in his fine little book *The Sacred in Life and Art* notes that the word "*sacramentum*" has a forensic nature that limits its power to convey the Greek. In the earliest Christian tradition *sacramentum* or *mysterion* applied to anything that mirrors the Divine.[35] The two most significant *mysteria* in

31 Cudworth, *Union*, p. 4.
32 Maistre, Joseph de. (2007) "Eclaircissement sur les sacrifices," in Pierre Glaudes (ed.), *Œuvres*. Paris: R. Laffont, p. 382.
33 Daly, R. J. (1972) "Sacrifice in Origen," *Studia Patristica 9 Texte und Untersuchungen* 108: Berlin, pp. 125–9.
34 Clement, *Stromata*, 7.6.
35 See Bouyer, L. (1956) "Mysterion" in Plé, A. (ed.) *Mystery and Mysticism: A Symposium*.

Christian life are the Baptism and Eucharist. But from Cudworth's view-point, Reformation debates about the number of sacraments are potentially misleading. All that God creates is capable of having a sacramental role. The sacrament is not to be understood as extrinsic or nonessential to the profane. The sacrament reveals the real nature of all being as created. Because of the likeness between created and uncreated, the divinity lies in creatures in potentiality.[36]

Cudworth claims the rejection of the Roman Catholic view of marriage as one of the seven sacraments produced the neglect of the "mystical" notion (that which today we associate with the Orthodox Church). In order to explain the "mystical" idea of it, Cudworth expounds Paul's letter to the Ephesians, 5.22-33.

> [T]he Apostle in these words doth not onely suppose a bare Similitude between the union of Man and Wife by Marriage, and the mystical union of Christ and Church, and thence compare them together, as there is a Similitude between the Kingdome of Heaven and a Grain of Mustard seed: But he makes one to be a *Reall Type* of the other, and the other an *Archetypal* Copy, according to which, that was limmed and drawn out.

The sacrament is only necessary because the divided state of creation — not by virtue of its purportedly profane or non-sacred nature but because of its separated and estranged condition. The sacrament is the proleptic overcoming of this state of alienation.

The sacramental system requires exactly the balance between the tran-scendent and the immanent that we find in Cudworth: if one emphasizes the transcendent too strongly, then the world is marked by the absence of the sacred. Stress too strongly the immanence of the Divine, and the sacramental becomes redundant.

Cudworth objects to the idea that a sacramental object may be turned into some occult or totemic object, distinct from the rest of the created order. The sacrament is rather the means of reintegration through the spiritual eye that recalls or remembers (*anamnesis*) the primordial Divine order of being. Mankind is not composed of "*maîtres et possesseurs*" of nature, but is participating in the process of the making sacred.

The Jerusalem Temple

The God of the philosophers is worshiped in the Jerusalem Temple. Cudworth was Regius Professor of Hebrew and deeply indebted to the Temple tradition.[37] As Regius Professor, he gave lectures in Cambridge

---

London: Blackfriars, pp. 18–32.
36 Sherrard, Philip. (1990) *The Sacred in Life and Art*. Ipswich: Golgonooza, p. 25.
37 Tulloch, *Rational Theology and Christian Philosophy in England in the Seventeenth Century*, p. 205. Cf. Conway, Anne (1996) *The Principles of the Most Ancient and Modern Philosophy*, Allison Coudert and Taylor Corse (eds.). Cambridge: Cambridge University Press, pp. viii–xxii.

on the subject of the Jerusalem Temple. Maistre was a mason for a long period of his life and clearly many of his core tenets derive from this period. The Platonic legacy behind the thought of both Cudworth and Maistre is uncontroversial. But theirs is also a deeply biblical approach. Cudworth is fascinated by the "Tabernacle or Temple, being thus as a House for God to Dwell in visibly"[38] and understood this as "a speciall Type of Gods future Dwelling in Christ's humane nature, which was the TRUE SHECHINAH."[39] As we shall see, the Cabbalistic language is telling.

Our understanding of the significance of parallelism between heaven and earth in the letter to the Hebrews has been immensely enriched by the research of Margaret Barker. In her paradigm shifting work on the context of Christian origins, she argues that the traditions of the preexilic Jerusalem Temple, its symbols and rituals, provide the key to much that is mysterious in the New Testament. Her work is based on reconstructing the influence of the First Temple cult from the Old Testament and from apocalyptic materials, fragments from the Dead Sea Scrolls, early Christian documents. Her argument is that, notwithstanding the exile and the establishment of the second Temple, the First Temple tradition with it strong royal and prophetic dimension, rather a subterranean but potent force within Hebrew religion until it emerged in apocalyptic groups such as the Essences or the Christians. She argues that Christian imagery and practice go back to the Day of Atonement, described in Leviticus. Though Leviticus provides details of the ritual (although transposed from the original Temple setting into the desert), but this has to be complemented through reconstructing the mythic-theological component not contained in Leviticus.

On the Day of Atonement the priest went alone into the Holy of Holies and sprinkled blood, then blood was sprinkled outside and on the altar. Though Leviticus describes the rituals in the desert and with a tent, Barker argues persuasively that the actual context of the ritual was the First Temple. She stresses three aspects of the ancient Temple ritual. First, that blood was seen to represent the atoning power of life (not death!). The blood represents life. Second, the atonement ritual expressed the restoration of creation through life. Finally, the theocentric dimension is important. The blood or life is sprinkled first in the Holy of Holies and then beyond the curtain onto the altar. It represented a movement of God bestowing life on creation.

Barker also emphasizes the fact that the three autumn festivals of New Year, Day of Atonement, and Tabernacles were part of a royal cult, and linked to a festival of royal enthronement and seasonal renewal. Texts like Isaiah 40–55 and certain Psalms suggest a royal setting and Barker conjectures that the atonement rite would have been performed by the monarch, suggesting that the Suffering Servant is derived therefrom. For Barker, the Philippians servant figure in St. Paul and Lk. 24.26-7 presents the vision of Jesus suffering in order to be glorified and thus fulfilling scripture is a

---

38   Cudworth, *A Discourse*, p. 63.
39   Cudworth, *A Discourse*, p. 62.

sign of early Christians using the ancient royal pattern of atonement. The dramatic language of Revelation or Hebrews reflects this ancient atonement pattern in which the priest/monarch represents the Divine atoning and casting out evil, healing and re-ordering of creation.

But when Christ appeared as a high priest of the good things that have come, then through the greater and more perfect tent (not made with hands — that is, not of this creation), he entered once for all into the holy place, taking not the blood of goats and bulls but his own blood, thus securing an eternal redemption (Heb. 9.11-12).

Therefore, how does the blood of Christ secure forgiveness and redemption? His sacrifice is embedded in the practice of ritual atonement with analogies in the practices of the pagans as well as among the Hebrews. His physical death on the cross was part of a Divinely instituted pattern, part of a cosmic process of expiation and reconciliation. In ch. 9 of the letter to the Hebrews, it is argued:

> Thus it was necessary for the copies [hupodeigma] of the heavenly things to be purified with these rites [animal sacrifices], but the heavenly things themselves with better sacrifices than these. For Christ has entered, not in a sanctuary made with hands, a copy [antitupos] of the true one [alethinos], but into heaven itself, now to appear in the presence of God in our behalf.[40]

Because of this "we have confidence to enter the [heavenly] sanctuary by the blood of Jesus" (Heb. 10.19).[41]

In the Hindu tradition, the Temple is the sacred place where chaos of the scattered world is reintegrated. In the letters to the Hebrews we find a similarly cosmic dimension to the Temple. Distinct from economic images of saturation as redemption or forensic images of salvation; Christ's work is a cultic and cosmic sacrifice. Christ is the High Priest who gives himself once and for all mankind in the Temple that represents all creation.

Margaret Barker has shown how the Cabbalistic and Masonic traditions kept much of the ancient Temple tradition and its imagery alive. Much of that which seems "Platonic" in both Cudworth and Maistre is equally "Hebraic" in this sense of the Temple tradition. Blood in the atonement rituals is construed as life not death, and the atoning power of blood came from the principle of life. "For the life of the flesh is in the blood; and I have given it for you the altar to make atonement for your souls for it is the blood that makes atonement by reason of the life" (Lev. 17.11). Maistre insists quite rightly upon the proper symbolism of blood: he speaks of "The vitality of blood, or rather the identity of blood and life, being posed as a fact that antiquity never doubted."[42] Cudworth is adamant about this dimension of St. Paul's mystical Christology:

40   Heb. 9.23-4.
41   See the work of Hofius, Otfried (1972) *Der Vorhang vor dem Thron Gottes*. Mohre Siebeck: Tübingen.
42   Maistre, *St Petersburg Dialogues*, p. 358.

Which he doth illustrate, First from a Parallel Rite, in Christian Religion. Where the Eating and the Drinking of the Body and Blood of Christ, offered up to God on the Crosse for us, in the *Lords Supper*, is a Reall Communication in his Death and Sacrifice, ver 16. The cup of blessing which we blesse, is it not the Communion of the blood of Christ?[43]

The preexilic Temple represented heaven and earth, the Divine throne, the paradise garden and the rest of the created order. Sprinkled blood was seen as a means of removing the influence of sin on creation. The process was theocentric in that the blood or life was transferred from the Divine to the world in order to remove sin.[44]

Let us recall that both Cudworth and Maistre are operating with the Christian Platonic *exitus/reditus* scheme. They do not view salvation in narrow personal terms. It is a process of *paideia* through Christ. It resonates with the ancient Temple themes of the renewal of the cosmos as creation rather than being a narrowly forensic re-ordering of the relationship between God and man. The secret kinship of all mankind, the "incomprehensible unity, the necessary basis of substitution" is the foundation of the idea of sacrifice as reversing merit, sinners being regenerated by the good.[45] This culminates in the final subjection of all to God. All human history is thus tending towards this final culmination in unity with God. In the fallen state of the current world, history is the scheme of Providence's temporal rule, and the sufferings of the innocent and the righteous are part of a return of the cosmos to God. Thus the Divine *paideia* is also a process of sorrow and suffering, a via *purgativa*, but it is primarily by means by which God can appeal to mankind's freedom to become participate in Christ and become coworkers in the redemption of the created order. Cudworth shares this redemption as participation in the new creation inaugurated by Christ's atoning work: "Christ as the logos or true Word of God — in respect of the Creation of the whole world, which was made out of that Ideall Fecundity which was in him: which might be better applied to him, in respect of the Church."[46] Thus believers are members of Christ's Body but this is not "to be understood as the derivation of any material substance . . . but by the Effluxe and communication of his Spirit. For the Church is nothing else but Christus *explicatus*."[47] The making sacred (*sacra facere!*) of the Christian life, the living sacrifice, is the making explicit of that which is implicit since creation.

Ezekiel's mysterious vision of the Sheckinah was pivotal for Henry Corbin's work on the speculative significance of image of the Temple in contemplative Neoplatonic thought with Christian, Jewish and Islamic theology that culminate, in his eyes, in the Shi'ite hermeneutics of the Temple. This is because Ezekiel's vision is that of a heavenly archetype,

43 Cudworth, *A Discourse*, p. 53.
44 Barker, Margaret. (1995) *On Earth as It Is in Heaven: Temple Symbolism in the New Testament*. Edinburgh: T&T Clark.
45 Maistre, *St Petersburg Dialogues*, p. 301.
46 Cudworth, *Union*, p. 27.
47 Cudworth, *Union*, p. 28.

paradise itself, a city, that is ultimately transcendent. The new Temple is seen as preexisting in its celestial archetype. And, of course, Ezekiel's message is about the founding of Divine dominion. This tradition of the Temple re-imagined exerted a prodigious impact upon Apocalyptic literature.

Philo's attempt to explicate the hidden meaning of the Temple, in particular, is momentous. Philo thinks of the Jerusalem Temple as the only genuine earthly Temple. Yet corresponding to the idea of the unique Temple of the one God is the idea of the temple of the soul and the temple of the physical cosmos. In his account of the Temple, Corbin employs the Coleridgean-Schellingian concept of the tautegory.[48] That is, the tautegory does not hide that which it symbolizes (as some "other") but discloses through itself or, rather, corresponds enigmatically with its transcendent referent. For Corbin, the imagery of the Temple within the traditions of the book, or the so-called Abrahamic traditions, depends upon this Platonic correspondence between the noetic and the physical cosmos.

In Avicenna's recital of *Hayn ibn Yaqzan* the angel is asked whence he comes: He says I come from the Temple. The Arabic designates the Jerusalem Temple but meant is the celestial Temple. It is this New Temple, between the noetic cosmos and the sensory world. Ibn Arabi's use of the Temple motif has been discussed by Henri Corbin in his *"L'imagination creatrice dans la soufisme d'Ibn Arabi."* Here Corbin sees Ibn Arabi as a decisive exponent of the idea of the domain of intellectual images, which is also the Temple that is a world between (*barzakh*) — at the meeting place of two seas.[49] The beginning of history is the exile — this commences with the destruction of the Temple. The exiled Sheckinah is the sum of all human suffering as alienated from the Divine.[50]

Meister Eckhart seeks to define the highest sphere of the soul, its "'knowledge by way of the intellect' through the imagery of the Temple." The soul's noetic capacity, *Vernunftlichkeit*, is its pure thought.[51] Eckhart says:

> When we grasp God in his being, we grasp him in his courtyard, since Being is his courtyard. Where is he truly except in his Temple, in which

---

48   See Hedley, *Living Forms of the Imagination*, pp. 121ff, 140ff.

49   Corbin. (1969) *Creative Imagination in the Sufism of Ibn 'Arabi*. Princeton University Press. (Reissued in 1998 as *Alone with the Alone*), p. 277ff.

50   The rock — the place of the sacrifices of Adam, Cain and Abel, Noah, Abraham — is the same rock. The holy rock is also the place where Jacob slept, dreaming of the ladder between heaven and hell, during which the angels descended and ascended (Genesis 28). This place is seen as the gateway to a higher world. All the vicissitudes of actual temples Solomon 586 BC–AD 70 of Second Temple are moments in the basic catastrophe and the rebuilding part of the restoration of the cosmos. And the Temple of JHWH though destroyed, returns spiritualized.

51   Quoted by Corbin, Eckhart *Die deutschen Werke*, Quint (ed.). Stuttgart: Kohlhammer, p. 150. "Vernunftlichkeit ist der temple gotes. Niergen wonet got eigentlicher dan in sinem temple, in vernuenflicheit, als der ander meister sprach, daz got ist ein vernuenflicheit, diu da lebet in sin aleines bekantnisse, in im selber aleine blibende, da in nie niht engeuorte, wan er aleine da ist in siner stilheit. Got in sin selbes bekanntnisse bekennet sich selben in im selben." See also McGinn. (1986) *Meister Eckhart, Teacher and Preacher*. New Jersey: Paulist, p. 28.

He shines in holiness. Reason is 'the Temple of God'. Nowhere does God dwell more truly than in his Temple, in Reason. As that other Master says God is that Reason that lives in knowledge solely of itself, only remaining in itself, where nothing as touched Him, since he is alone in all peace. God knows in self-knowledge himself as He is.[52]

It is the soul that is the locus of spiritual worship. Eckhart develops the idea of the temple in his sermon on Mt. 21.12. The soul's rank that is based upon the *imago Dei* and it is necessary to fend off the traders from the Temple:

For this reason God wants this temple cleared, that He may be there all alone. This is because this temple is so agreeable to Him, because it is so like Him and He is so comfortable in this Temple when He is alone there.[53]

Music, feast, and celebration: the "Quire-Musick of the Temple"

One may ask what is the relevance of these great dead philosophers to present pressing concerns? Plato's Athenian in the *Laws* 653 argues that the gods felt compassion for the suffering and misery of human beings. As a result they instituted festivals as a means of alleviating this suffering. Apollo, Dionysus, and the muses were given as companions in these festivals for the reconstitution of humanity. This passage from Plato's *Laws* is used by Joseph Pieper in his little, but bold, book *Leisure: The Basis of Culture*. His critique of the Soviet German Democratic Republic is savage, if now rather dated. It must have seemed paradoxical, however, to extol leisure amidst the ruins of post–Second World War Germany at the dawn of the *Wirtschaftswunder*. Pieper, nevertheless, insisted that the Christian concept of sacrifice is emphatically not a form of gloomy and puritanical renunciation. He writes:

The Christian conception of sacrifice is not concerned with the suffering involved qua suffering, it is not primarily concerned with the toil and the worry and with the difficulty, but with salvation, and with fullness of being, and thus ultimately with the fullness of happiness.[54]

52 Eckhart, Wenn wir Gott im Sein nehmen, so nehmen wir ihn in seinem Vorhof, denn das Sein ist sein Vorhof, in dem er wohnt. Wo ist denn aber in seinem Temple, in dem er als heilig ergalnzt. Vernuft ist 'der Temple Gottes'. Nirgends wohnt Gott eigentlicher als in seinem Tempel, in der Vernunft, wie jener andere Meister sagte: verharrend dort, wo ihn nie etwas beruhrt hat; denn da ist er allein in seiner Stille. Gott erkennt im Erkennen seiner selbst sich selbst in sich selbst. Meister Eckhart. (1958) *Die deutschen Werke*. Stuttgart: Kohlhammer, p. 464.
53 Meister Eckhart. (1998) *Sermons and Treatises*, M.O'C. Walshe (trans. and ed.). Shaftesbury: Element, vol. 1, p. 55.
54 Pieper, Joseph. (1963) *Leisure, the Basis of Culture*. New York: Random House, p. 32.

Philosophically, we need not simply the observation and exact classification of physical phenomena, but the imaginative *interpretation* of mankind's relation to physical nature and to the Godhead. The Real must be considered in relation to these two worlds: the noumenal and phenomenal. Theologically we wish to add to this the appeal to the imagination regenerate. In which case, we can agree with Pieper that

> [t]he Christian cultus, unlike any other, is at once a sacrifice and a sacrament. In so far as the Christian cultus is a sacrifice held in the midst of the creation which is affirmed by this sacrifice of the god man – every day is a feast day.[55]

At the core of the celebration of the festival is Divine worship. This has been part of Western philosophy for millennia. Marcus Aurelius, for example, wished primarily "To worship and bless the gods, and to do good to men" in his *Meditations* (5.33, 6). Hegel liked to play on the etymology of the German words "Thought" (*Denken*) and "Devotion" (*Andacht*) because for him philosophical thought is ultimately devotion. The "Philosophy of Religion" culminates in the cult (*Kultus*).

The most eloquent of the Cambridge Platonists, John Smith (1618–1652), Fellow of Queens' College, Cambridge, developed such an idea of the feast of contemplation and the ecstasy of the soul in true worship in ch. 9 of the "Discourse on Prophecy" in his *Select Discourses*. Smith emphasizes the fact of the school or "Colledge" context of prophecy. He notes:

> [A]nciently many were trained so up in a way of School discipline, that they might become *Candati Prophetiae*, and were as Probationers to these Degrees which none but God himself conferr'd on them. Yet while they heard others *prophesie*, there was sometime an *afflatus* upon them also, their Souls as it were sympathizing (like *Unisons* in Musick) with the souls of those which were touched by the Spirit.[56]

The musical analogy continues in this passage about the disciples of the Prophets:

> [F]or it is probably that the *Prophesies* there spoken of were *Anthems divinely dictated*, or *Doxologies* which such elegant strains of Devotion and Phansie as might also excite and stir up the Spirits of the Auditors: As often we find that any admirable Discourses, in which there is a chearful and free flowing forth of a rich Phansie in an intelligible, and yet extraordinary, way, are apt to beget a symbolizing qualitie of Mind in a stander-by.[57]

55 Pieper, *Leisure: The Basis of Culture*, p. 63.
56 Smith, John. (1660) *Select Discourses*. Cambridge. Reprint New York and London: Garland (1978), p. 252.
57 Smith, *Select Discourses*, p.252.

It may not be unduly fanciful to envisage Smith as reflecting, in part at least, upon his own context in Queens'. When he reflects upon the "Quire-Musick of the Temple," Smith is also drawing upon his own college context, and especially the tradition of college evensong. In arguing that "Musick was greatly advantageous to the Prophets and Holy men of God."[58] Smith may be engaging indirectly in a contemporary debate in mid-seventeenth-century England about church music.[59] John Milton offers an interesting analogy of a deep Platonic interest in spiritual music.[60]

One of Smith's main objectives is to distinguish between true and false enthusiasm. Smith speaks of a "sober kind of Ecstasies" as when Plotinus was found with his soul "separated from his Body."[61] This is a phrase that Smith could find in Plotinus as connected with the "erotic" Intellect (in *Ennead* VI 7 35). Indeed, Smith can speak of the Divine knowledge that, as Plotinus speaks, makes us "amorous of Divine beauty, beautifull and lovely; and this Divine Love and Purity reciprocally exalts Divine Knowledge".[62] Smith could find the notion of sober intoxication in late Antiquity, given in Latin as *ebria sobrietas* — the major source is probably Philo and Origen — which was used to designate the encounter between man and God.[63] Seventeenth-century English thought is replete with reference to the idea that music can elevate the soul to the vision of God.

> Now, Divine air ! now is his soul ravished !
> Is it not strange that sheeps' guts should hale
> Souls out of men's bodies?[64]

These lines from Shakespeare reflect a trajectory of speculation about music ravishing the soul and taking it out of the body into communion with the Divine. Or one might reflect upon Lorenzo's speech in the *Merchant of Venice* concerning "touches of sweet harmony," whereby:

> Such harmony is in immortal souls,
> But whilst this muddy vesture of decay
> Doth grossly close in it, we cannot hear it.[65]

58 Smith, *Select Discourses*, p. 240.
59 Finney, G. L. (1943) "'Organical musick' and ecstacy." *Journal of the History of Ideas*, 7: 272–92.
60 Wilson, A. N. (1983) *The Life of John Milton*. Oxford: Oxford University Press. I owe this point to James Vigus.
61 Smith, *Select Discourses*, p. 100.
62 Smith, *Select Discourses*, p. 20.
63 See Daniélou, Jean. (1953) *Platonisme Et Théologie Mystique: Essai Sur La Doctrine Spirituelle De Saint Grégoire De Nysse* (new edn.). Paris; Aubier: Éditions Montaigne, p. 292. Lewy, Hans. (1929) "Sobria ebrietas," *Untersuchungen zur Geschichte der antiken Mystik*. Giessen: Topelmann.
64 Shakespeare, W. *Much Ado*, 2.3.60–62.
65 Shakespeare, *Merchant of Venice*, 5.1, 55ff.

King David was, of course, a musician (see 1 Samuel 16). Hebrew poetry, prophesy, and music coalesce for Smith in the Psalms. Smith discusses the idea of the *Spiritus sanctus* or the prophetic level beneath that of Moses or the Prophets strictly, but, of the *Hagiographi*:

> [We] may see the Reason why Musical instruments were so frequently used by the Prophets, especially the Hagiographi; which indeed seems to be nothing else but that their Minds mights be thereby put into a *more composed, liberal and cheerful temper*, and so the *better disposed* and *fitted* for the transportation of the Prophetical Spirit.[66]

Smith claims here that the cheerfulness of spirit that is conducive to true prophecy — as opposed to the craze and melancholy that fosters prophetic delusion and false enthusiasm — may be seen in relation to those great songs of scripture, the Psalms. Smith notes 1 Chronicles 25 on "rapt and Divine Poems at the Sound of the Quire-Musick of the Temple." Another famous place we find for this purpose is 1 Samuel 10, "which . . . cannot mean any less then *Divine Poetrie*, and a composure of Hymns excited by a Divine energy inwardly moving the Mind."[67]

Milton writes in his "At a Solemn Music":

> Blest pair of sirens, pledges of heaven's joy,
> Sphere-borne harmonious sisters, Voice, and Verse,
> Wed your Divine sounds, and mixed power employ
> Dead things with inbreathed sense able to pierce,
> And to our high-raised phantasy present,
> That undisturbed song of pure concent,
> Ay sung before the sapphire-coloured throne
> To him that sits thereon
> With saintly shout, and solemn jubilee,
> Where the bright seraphim in burning row
> Their loud uplifted angel trumpets blow,
> And the cherubic host in thousand choirs
> Touch their immortal harps of golden wires,
> With those just spirits that wear victorious palms,
> Hymns devout and holy psalms
> Singing everlastingly.[68]

Interestingly, Milton speaks of "our high-raised phantasy" as the mode of the ascent of the soul to the throne of God. In these lines we have a reference to the Temple tradition in the likeness of a throne in the form of sapphire stone in Ezekiel 1.26. One can note also the tradition of holy rapture and ecstasy through music. Milton is drawing on a late Renaissance tradition in

---

66   Smith, *Select Discourses*, p. 249.
67   Smith, *Select Discourses*, p. 249.
68   Milton. (1971) *Complete Shorter Poems*, John Carey (ed.). London: Longman, pp. 162–4.

which the soul could be separated from the body through music. Richard Hooker, discussing the Psalms, observes that: "There is also that carrieth as it were into ecstasies, filling the mind with an heavenly joy and for the time in a manner severing it from the body."[69] Sir Thomas Browne attacks those who "declaim against Church-Musick." Music is, he insists, "an Hieroglyphical and shadowed lesson of the whole World, and creatures of God."[70] The power of music, for Browne, is derived from God and leads to "a profound contemplation of the First Composer."[71]

As a Fellow of Queens', Smith would doubtless have known evensong at which the Psalms would be sung: "that a fine gentle . . . Tranquillitie ushered in (so that) the soul might be better disposed for the Divine breathings of the Prophetical Spirit."[72] The *Select Discourses* are sermons preached in the turbulent and violent age of the English Civil War. The poetry and the music of the sung Psalms, Smith suggests, should create a mood conducive for receptivity of the Divine Spirit.

The *Select Discourses* of John Smith were published 8 years after his death in 1652. Their publication in the same year as the appearance of Henry More's *The True Mystery of Godliness* in 1660 may be of some significance with the Restoration of the Church of England and the monarchy. For a Platonist, the "mystery" of godliness is a not brute inexplicable fact but a higher truth expressed in a lower medium. The Restoration of the Church of England meant the reestablishment of theater and liturgy in England, and the vision of a moderate like Smith may have been thought a salutary work at that time.[73]

The relationship between the Cambridge Platonists and their Neoplatonic sources is not clear. We know that Henry More read the Elizabethan Platonic poet Spenser and then came to Plotinus as a young man at Cambridge. In Smith we seem to have the Arabic-Jewish Neoplatonic tradition coming into fruitful converse with perhaps the greatest artistic legacy of Platonism in England of the Elizabethan period: Shakespeare.

Joy

The Christian Eucharist is literally a meal of thanksgiving. This word is cognate with the word *chara* for joy. Wine, as Scruton observes, is an apt way to express the joy of the awareness of communion with the Divine.[74] Christ's use of the breaking of the bread and sharing of wine in order to predict his sufferings was obviously linked in the Hellenistic world with

---

69 Hooker, *Ecclesiastical Polity*, 5.38. Quoted by Finney, "'Organical musick' and ecstacy," p. 155.
70 Browne, Thomas. (1844) *Religio Medici*, Geoffrey Keynes (ed.). London: Longman, Brown, Green, & Longmans, 2. 9. Quoted by Finney, "'Organical musick' and ecstacy," p. 161.
71 Browne, *Religio Medici*, 2. 9. Quoted by Finney, "'Organical musick' and ecstacy," p. 161.
72 Smith, *Select Discourses*, p. 251.
73 I am grateful to Sarah Hutton for this suggestion.
74 Scruton, *I Drink Therefore I Am: A Philosopher's Guide to Wine*, p. 169.

Dionysus — and, indeed, with the mystery cult of Ceres and Proserpine.

A Christian theist has a motive for sacrifice in joy. Before Dante invokes Apollo to flay him like Marsyas, he produces a paean to the beauties of the cosmos as revealing

> The glory of Him who moves all things penetrates the universe and shines in one part more and in another less.

> *La Gloria di colui che tutto move*
> *per L'universo penetra e risplende*
> *in una parte più e meno altrove.*[75]

This joy seems, incidently, seems to be a central aspect of Christ's own ministry. Philosophically, if the world is seen in sacramental terms, and articulated with the Platonic eloquence of William James: "the bare assurance that this natural order is not ultimate but a mere sign of vision, the external staging of a many-storied universe, in which spiritual forces have the last word and are eternal."[76] The thought of the brute contingency of the world, the fact that its existence is a mystery and its nonexistence is just as possible as its existence, is a primordial motor of philosophical speculation. From Plato and Aristotle's claim that philosophy begins in wonder to the Stoic adamant rejection: *nil admirari!* As William James observed: "Every generation will produce its Job, its Hamlet, its Faust, or its Sartor Resartus."[77]

This joy is grounded in the awareness of the world as bodying forth the goodness of God, albeit imperfectly. I wish to argue that the world stands for or re-presents the Deity through a resemblance. Since it is caused by God, it shares in God's being and not merely his intentions. If God is absolute perfection, self-subsistent existence, the world expresses this perfection in an inferior mode. On such a view, the world is a domain of intrinsic value. It is the idea of reality as a gift proceeding from Divine love and goodness; *bonum diffusivum sui*. Joy is linked to the perception of the world as enchanted — a created domain and having its ground in a transcendent personal being, rather than being meaningless and impersonal.

Self-sacrifice is employed by the mystics in various traditions as expressing the intuition that the love of God is the source of great practical energy. Sacrifice is to become an instrument of the Divine.

It is the joy evoked by the sense of the spirit that "impels all thinking things and rolls through all things" that provides the parameters for any genuinely religious theory of sacrifice. If personality is either a construction or a contingent emergent property, and if the universe is an impersonal order, it is very hard see the religious emotional reactions of love or

---

75   Dante, Alighieri. (1939) "Paradiso," in John D. Sinclair (trans.) *The Divine Comedy of Dante Alighieri*. Oxford: Oxford University Press, p. 19.

76   James, W. (1956) *The Will to Believe*. New York: Longmans, Green, & Co., p. 56.

77   James, *Will to Believe*, p. 75.

gratitude as having any meaning. This, rather than any crude reciprocal exchange provides the foundation for Christian ethics.

This hardly coheres with the Promethean rights culture of a society in which citizens have strict and equal entitlements, in which the injustice of the world is dismantled as a task of government, that utopian project which found lucid and forceful expression in John Rawls and his work *A Theory of Justice*. Such a secular theory ignores what the atheistic Schopenhauer calls the "guilt of existence," but it also rejects any sense of redemption. Such is the spirit excoriated by Wordsworth:

> The world is too much with us; late and soon
> Getting and spending, we lay waste our powers;
> Little we see in Nature that is ours;
> We have given our hearts away, a sordid boon![78]

There is a view of sacrifice that a Christian theist can welcome: embracing suffering within the good news of creation and salvation. Parents make great sacrifices for children. This is, doubtless, in part biology and attributable to certain psychological factors. The joy that a child generates provides the parent with the energy and drive to sustain the sleeplessness, anxiety, expense, and so forth. This joy is akin to wonder. Fénelon and the Christian mystics tended to emphasize this joy that does not expect reward.

Religion has its dark and crude aspects, but it envinces the remarkable power of inspiration. The view of human agency propounded by Hobbes of Bentham is far too restricted in its hedonistic psychology. The interests and attachments of human beings extends far beyond rational calculation of utilities. There are bonds and attachments, interests and duties which cannot be categorised in terms of, or reduced to, the rational self interest of particular agents. The capacity of religion to provide goals of contemplation that really inspire is a crucial counter instance to such a crudely mechanistic psychology. Great sacrifices and altruistic endeavours can ensue from the attempt to realise the Divine love on earth. If one considers the lives of Wilberforce, Gandhi or Luther King, for example, the contemplative vision provided the basis for their social reforms. Contemplation is the prerequisite and source of much efficacious social reform, not its enemy.

As we have argued, the Divine goodness requires Divine self-sacrifice. The historical passion of Jesus Christ is the sacrament or representation of this primordial sacrifice. Christian theism can reject the bogus unities of naturalism or pantheism. The first excludes anything that cannot be accommodated the verifiable data of the laboratory — the unity of a naturalism like, say, that of Hobbes, or the unity of pantheism that describes all phenomena as mere modifications of one true substance, as, say, Spinoza. Both of these unities cannot explain our sense of freedom, and the related senses of responsibility, guilt: consciousness of responsibility, and a fractured existence, one of dissonance and death. Yet this sense of real evil and

---

78 Wordsworth, "World is too Much". *The Complete Poetical Works*, p.206

suffering is combined with the conviction in the ultimate goodness of the
cosmos. The law of the universe is not that of meaningless suffering and
destruction but, rather, redemption through suffering, culminating in the
victory over sin and death. As a great bard observes:

> Then is there mirth in heaven
> When earthly things made even
> Atone together.[79]

Feast

It is sometimes observed that the primary sense of sacrifice is the feast. For
the Greeks, if not for the ancient Semites, this was not a provision of food
for the Gods.[80] This sense of sacrifice has little to do with renunciation but,
rather, the feast and the festival. Joseph Pieper writes:

> The origin of the arts in worship, and of leisure derived from its celebra-
> tion, is given in the form of a magnificent mythical image: man attains
> his true form and his upright attitude "in festive companionship with
> the Gods."[81]

The sacred aspect of culture: as Vico and Maistre stressed, there is no
civilization without an altar. The festival furnishes that ecstasy described
so eloquently by John Smith or the exalted mood founded on the sense
of the Divine presence: "something more deeply interfused." The festival
yoking Dionysus, Apollo, and the muses is the affirmation and celebration
of the identity of value and existence rather than the diremption of the two
by Classical empiricism. Morality is based upon freedom, one might say,
with Kant. Such freedom is liberty not license, grounded in values and laws
not the arbitary *sponte sua*. Futhermore, one might insist with Plato, that
freedom, properly understood, is grounded in reason. The ends of reason
are beauty, truth, and goodness. The justification of the university is not
the development of intelligence in any narrow sense but the shaping of the
whole personality. If Mathew Arnold is correct that

> we are here as on a darkling plain
> Swept with confused alarms of struggle and flight
> Where ignorant armies clash by night.[82]

then only an enervating pessimism and inertia can ensue. Dedication presupposes a clear idea of what *ought* to be. We can only dedicate ourselves

---

79   Shakespeare, *As You Like It*, 5.4.
80   Hughes, D. (1936) *Culture and Sacrifice*, Thomas Hutchinson and Rev. Ernest de
     Selincourt (eds.). Oxford: Oxford University Press, p. 11.
81   Pieper, *Leisure: The Basis of Culture*, p. 61.
82   Arnold, M. (1979) "Dover Beach," in *The Complete Poems*, K and M Allott (eds.). London:
     Longman, p. 257.

to an ideal if we can envisage it clearly. It helps to believe that we are not "our own," but our lives are gifts and that we have a duty to aspire to virtue and goodness. In Pindar's words:

> Creatures of a day! What is a man?
> What is he not? A dream of a shadow
> Is our mortal being. But when there comes to men
> A gleam of splendour given of heaven,
> Then rests on them a light of glory
> And blessed are their days.[83]

In education, the cultivation of that part of mankind that is kindled upon the Divine altar. As Hölderlin writes:

> Like the bright day that shines on human kind
> And with a light of heavenly origin
> All things obscure and various gathers in,
> Is knowledge, deeply granted in mind.[84]

> *Als wie der Tag die Menschen hell umscheinet*
> *Und mit dem Lichte, das den Höhn entspringet,*
> *Die dämmernden Erscheinungen vereinet,*
> *Ist Wissen, welches tief der Geistigkeit gelinget.*[85]

A life dedicated is a life consecrated. Christianity teaches the serious calling to life of more than a cheerful busy-ness. St. Paul says: "I beseech you, by the mercies of God, that ye present your bodies a living sacrifice, holy and acceptable to God, which is your reasonable service." This living sacrifice, a consecration of the self for God and for others is replacing the sacrifices of the old covenant and its rites. This is to become a proper temple of the Divine.

83 Pindar. (1972) "Pythian 8," in *The Odes of Pindar*, Geoffrey S. Conway (trans.). London: Dent, p. 144.
84 Hölderlin, Friedrich, *Poems and Fragments*, Michael Hamburger (trans.). Cambridge: Cambridge University Press, p. 585.
85 Hölderlin, F. (1943–85) *Sämtliche Werke: Grosse Stuttgarter Ausgabe*, F. Beissner and A. Beck (eds.), 3 vols. Stuttgart: Cotta, p. 360.

Epilogue

O my noble Friends, slaughter this cow,
If you wish to raise up the spirit of insight.
I died to being mineral and was transformed
I died to vegetable growth
and attained to the state of animals.
I died from animality and became Adam:
Why then should I fear?
When have I become less by dying
Next I shall soar and lift up my head
among the angels
Yet I must escape from even that
Angelic state:
everything is perishing except his Face
Once again I shall be sacrificed, dying to the angelic
I shall become that which could never be imagined-
I shall become nonexistent
Nonexistence sings its clear melody
Truly, unto Him shall we return.[1]

Is the symbolic imaginary, familiar to many through deeply sacrificial hymns of Wesley, a perverse fantasy or opening a dimension of truth, the drama of salvation, that otherwise may be obscured by the familiar? If ritual be the "slow deposit" of the imaginative apprehension of life, the ritual of the Eucharist is poorly understood in mechanical-scholastic terms or by trying to demythologize the unsavory or archaic dimensions.[2] I was once asked to preach in a large and beautiful church (of the Church of North India) in Calcutta, India. I gave my short address and enjoyed the convivial meeting after the service. My sense of composure and delight in this Anglican church in Southeast Asia was to be abruptly challenged. After tea, my host ushered me to the nearby Kali Temple, where I saw a large goat and a kid sacrificed by a half-naked, pot-bellied priest wielding a huge knife. It was an ugly scene in the crowded temple; but I had the sense of experiencing a primordial rite. Immediately afterward I was taken by my Indian host to see the dying station of Mother Theresa, where I saw young destitute patients dying of AIDS-related illnesses. There were many

---

1 Rumi, Mathnawi, 3.3900–06, quoted in *The Pocket Rumi*, Kabir Helminski (ed.). Boston: Shambhala (2008), pp. 195–6.
2 Langer, S. (1957) *Philosophy in a New Key*. Cambridge: MA: Harvard, pp. 45, 157.

young European volunteers among the nurses. I felt much more deeply disturbed by the dying station than what I had witnessed at the temple, but it was equally as shocking. I still remember my sense of awkwardness in the face of the devotion and self-sacrifice of those working at the station. Though in English we use the word sacrifice for both cases, is there any real link between the two? How can the horrid and brutal primal rite have any relationship to the self-offering of the nurses and nuns I saw? Mother Theresa deliberately placed her dying station next to this pagan temple, just as the ancient Christians both distanced themselves from and transformed the ancient language and practices of sacrifice, the making holy. Perhaps Mother Theresa wanted to highlight the contrast between Christian love and the grim Kali. But perhaps we should not lose sight of the link between the two. After all, Dionysus was not expunged by Christian theology and the wine god survived through the Renaissance to Hölderlin and beyond in the wake of the "pale Galilean." I do not wish to hold to the *prisca theologia* in the strict form of Ficino or Cudworth, but I do wish to hold to certain common structures in human experience are recapitulated in *Christus consummator*.

In one of his last works, Hans Blumenberg asked how is it possible for the modern listener to be moved by Bach's *St Matthew Passion* (BVW 244)?[3] Bach's musical narrative of the Last Supper, arrest, and execution of Christ is a simply structured (recitative with *aria* and *arioso*) but superlative musical drama, using Matthew 26–27. The work emerged through a very creative rapport with the librettist Christian Friedrich Henrici, known as Picander.[4] The *St Matthew Passion* was performed in Leipzig on a few occasions from 1727 to 1742 and then forgotten until Felix Mendelssohn performed a version of it in 1829 in Berlin. It thus had its greatest impact in a world that was becoming increasingly deaf to its message. After the cataclysmic shock of biblical criticism and philosophical challenges of the Enlightenment, how can the modern listener be moved by the narrative of Christ's sacrificial death, which is explicitly that of a lamb offered for slaughter? Or be moved at the end of the first half by words like "Oh Man, weep for your great sin!" (O Mensch, bewein dein' Sünde groß).

During the ultimate chorale, the chorus sings "tear me from my fears/ thorough your fear and pain." One might say that to understand the dramatic power of the Passion one only need appeal to *purely* ethical and human responses to the sufferings of the protagonist. One can leave the religious dimension out of consideration. One might argue that Bach's poignant presentation of the sham trial, the betrayal by friends, the loneliness of Christ in the garden can generate the sympathy of the hearer for universal aspects of human suffering.[5] Yet this argument leaves out an important dimension: that of the religious imaginary redemptive suffering.

It is a moot point whether one can legitimately divorce any discrete

---

3   Blumenberg, Hans. (1988) *Matthauspassion*. Frankfurt am Main: Surkamp.
4   Butt, John. (2010) *Bach's Dialogue with Modernity Perspectives on the Passions*. Cambridge: Cambridge University Press.
5   John Rutter has expressed this view to me.

experience from its interpretative framework. Most hearers of Bach's masterpiece bring with them some knowledge, even if implicit or barely articulated, of the narrative of redemptive suffering that Bach/Picander constructed. The music of the drama is reinforcing the grip of the narrative upon the imagination.[6] The point of that narrative is precisely that Christ is not *any* man but, rather, the redeemer who can bear the guilt of humanity. The pattern has it roots in primordial sacrificial cults, in the apotheosis of the tragic hero through the mystery plays to Bach's great work. This is an archetypal dimension to this imaginative structure. As we have seen earlier, there are good reasons why the sufferings of Dionysus could be rekindled in medieval mystery plays about Christ's passion. But, as with the tragic hero, affections generated by the *St Matthew Passion* remain explicitly "more" than simple empathy with the human condition when, in the concluding chorale, the chorus sings "tear me from my fears/ through your own fear and pain".

As Blumenberg insists, there is a paradox of reception (das der nichts erfahrt, der noch nichts erfahren hat). One cannot experience what is not already (in some sense) familiar. What is there in the tale of Adam's sin and Christ's sacrifice that still resonates in the wake of Christendom?

We have been concerned with a particular symbol, that of sacrifice, and a particular symbolic narrative of salvation. We are appealing to a distinction between appearance and reality and the principle of levels of reality mediated through the symbolic.

Of course, the language of sacrifice has been appallingly abused. Contemporary Christian culture shudders at language of the early Church — *sanguis martyrum semen christianorum*! Doubtless part of Girard's immense impact has been connected to his critique of the idea of sacrifice, which has particularly appealed to Christians. The deeper problem is the blindness to the relevance of the symbolic and the significance of different levels of meaning from the vulgar and literal to the sacred and figurative. If religion is based on the superstitious attempt to manipulate the gods and sacrifice its ubiquitous organ, then the critiques of sacrifice are well founded. But if that story is true, then the root of religion is the cruel phantasy of the unregenerate ego. All the higher forms of religion, from Hinduism to Christianity and Islam, see the point of sacrifice in the transformation of the crude selfish ego, the source of division and strife, into a vehicle of Divine love. Sacrifice of self becomes the realization of self through the assimilation to Divine. As in Plato, the practice of death becomes, at the same time, transformation into the image of God.

Sacrifice is not merely an artificial "construct" of human culture: it has roots in human prehistory and myth. Equally, the rationalistic account of sacrifice as primitive bargaining device is also inadequate. The idea of sacrifice exhibits the natural and legitimate human sense of the sacred dimension of life. Here I think Plato, Kant, and Maistre are better guides than sociopolitical pragmatists like Detienne. Sacrifice traditionally concerns usually a relation to gods or a god. The holy is both destructive and

---

6 See Cottingham, John. (2005) *The Spiritual Dimension*. Cambridge: Cambridge University Press, p. 80f.

life-giving. Its ritual forms often reflect or point to the violent sacrifice that pervades the animal kingdom and human culture: the threat of death and the violent origins of cultures. Yet it also points to mankind's abiding desire for renewal: to "make sacred" and participate in the very source of life. Religious thinkers, from Vico to Maistre and Girard, know that society is not a product of human contract, but is grounded in pre-contractual obligations. If the sceptic sees religious sacrifice as the outcome of crude quasi-economic reciprocal exchange, this is belied by the spiritual construal of sacrifice as grounded in altruism. If the sceptic is correct that apparent sacrificial altruism can be performed by an enlightened egoist, it does not mean that egoism is the *source* of altruism. Considered and intentional self-sacrifice is intelligible – see the idea of the just war or drastic revision in energy consumption. The withers of psychological hedonism are wrung by the persisting grip of the sacrificial. More deeply, the modern critics of the idea of sacrifice have worked with the assumption that civilisation emerges out of economic, ecological or biological forces. We have followed Vico in seeing civilisation as the invention of the human mind or imagination: human culture is founded through altar and Temple.

The plurality of sacrifice imagined holds together the different levels of the cruel, the archaic, the sublimity of altruism and the inspiration of love. We have explored the persistence of the inherited imaginary of the atavistic and mythological realm of sacrificial savagery, together with sublimated dimension of making sacred and the release of divine energy through kenotic self-sacrifice. This is perplexing for those empiricists who see imagination exclusively as the capacity to generate fiction or illusion. If we recognise the imaginative encounter with reality as an unavoidable aspect of human cognition, however, then this *apparent* paradox is resolved. We have explored Maistre's sense of the antinomies of human existence as glassy enigmas that bespeak and reveal a transcendent resolution. Not just religion and politics, but even war, juridicial punishment, or even the practices of science itself, are distinctively human rituals with an inalienable sacrificial-symbolic component. Since the world is neither a collection of neutral facts nor a kaleidoscope of our projected fancies, we require the creative contemplation of the imagination to discern those distinctive realities which cannot be designated as literal and value free 'facts', but equally cannot be merely figurative embellishments. While such enigmas remain perplexing for the naturalist, for the theist they are mysteries that point to the spiritual reality that pervades and sustains the physical cosmos.

Bibliography

Allen, M. J. B. (1981) *Marsilio Ficino and the Phaedran Charioteer*. Berkeley: University of California.

Armenteros, Carolina. (2008) "Revolutionary violence and the end of history: the divided self in Francophone thought, 1762–1914," in Carolina Armenteros, Tim Blanning, Isabel DiVanna, and Dawn Dodds (eds.), *Historicising the French Revolution*. Newcastle: Cambridge Scholars.

Assmann, Jan. (1997) *Moses the Egyptian: The Memory of Egypt in Western Monotheism*. Cambridge, MA; London: Harvard University Press.

Baeumer, M. L. (1976) "Nietzsche and the tradition of the Dionysian," in James O. Flahery and Timothy F. Sellner (eds.), *Studies in Nietzsche and the Classical Tradition*. Chapel Hill: University of North Carolina.

Bainton, R. (1979) *Christian Attitudes to Peace and War: A Historical Survey and Critical Reevaluation*. Nashville, TN: Abingdon Press.

Barker, Margaret. (1995) *On Earth as It Is in Heaven: Temple Symbolism in the New Testament*. Edinburgh: T&T Clark.

Barker, Margaret. (2007) *Temple Themes in Christian Worship*. London: T&T Clark.

Barthelet, P. (2005) *Les Dossiers*. Paris: Editions L'Age d'Homme.

Behler, Ernst. (1988) "Nietzsche, Marx und die Deutsche Romantik," in *Studien Zur Romantik Und Zur Idealistischen Philosophie*. Paderborn: Schoening.

Beierwaltes, W. (1985) *Denken des Einen: Studien zur Neuplatonischen Philosophie und Ihrer Wirkungsgeschichte*. Frankfurt: Klostermann.

Benz, E. (1950) "Der Gekreuzigte Gerechte Bei Plato, Im Neuen Testament und in Der Alten Kirche." *Akademie der Wissenschaften und Literature in Mainz*, 12: 1–46.

Benz, E. (1950) *Die abendländische Sendung der östlich-orthodoxen Kirche: Die russische Kirche und das abendländische Christentum im Zeitalter der Heiligen Allianz*.

Berlin, Isaiah. (1953) *The Hedgehog and the Fox: An Essay on Tolstoy's View of History*. New York: Simon & Schuster.

Blackburn, S. (1998) *Ruling Passions: A Theory of Practical Reasoning*. Oxford: Clarendon Press.

Bradley, F. H. (1927), *Ethical Studies*, Oxford: Clarendon.

Bradley, Owen. (1999) *A Modern Maistre: The Social and Political Thought of Joseph de Maistre*, European Horizons. Lincoln; London: University of Nebraska Press.

Bregman, Jay. (1982) *Synesius of Cyrene, Philosopher–Bishop, Transformation of the Classical Heritage*. Berkeley; London: University of California Press.

Bremer, Dieter. (1993) "Don Juan and Faust: *Mythische Figurationen Neuzeitlichen Bewusstseins*" *Arcadia*, 28, 1. 12–13.

Breslauer, Daniel. (1980) "Philosophy and imagination: the politics of prophecy in the view of Moses Maimonides." *Jewish Quarterly Review*, 70, 3 (January): 153–71.

Brown, David. (2007) *God and Grace of Body: Sacrament in Ordinary*. Oxford: Oxford University Press.

Browne, Thomas. (1844) *Religio Medici*, Geoffrey Keynes (ed.). London: Longman, Brown, Green, & Longmans.

Brudholm, Thomas. (2008) *Resentment's Virtue: Jean Améry and the Refusal to Forgive, Politics, History, and Social Change*. Philadelphia, PA: Temple University Press.

Bruno, G. (2004) *Eroici furori*, Rome-Bari: Laterza

Bungay, Stephen. (1984) *Beauty and Truth: A Study of Hegel's Aesthetics*. Oxford: Clarendon.

Burkert, Homo Necans. (1972) *Homo Necans: Interpretationen Altgriechischer Opferriten und Mythen*. Berlin: De Gruyter. *Homo Necans: The Anthropology of Ancient Greek Sacrificial Ritual and Myth*. Peter Bing (trans.). Berkeley: University of California. 1983.

Butler, Joseph. (1913) *Sermons Preached at the Rolls Chapel*. London: Macmillan.

Buxton, R. (2001) *Oxford Readings in Greek Religion*. Oxford: Clarendon.

Caird, E. (1883) *Hegel* (Edinburgh: Blackwood & Sons).

Cannon, G. H. (1970) *The Letters of Sir William Jones*, vol. 2. Oxford: Clarendon.

Cannon, G. H. (1990) *The Life and Mind of Oriental Jones: Sir William Jones, the Father of Modern Linguistics*. Cambridge: Cambridge University Press.

Carter, C. (2003) *Understanding Religious Sacrifice: A Reader*. London and New York: Continuum.

Champion, J. A. I. (1992) *The Pillars of Priestcraft Shaken: The Church of England and Its Enemies, 1660–1730, Cambridge Studies in Early Modern British History*. Cambridge: Cambridge University Press.

Chrysakopoulou, Sylvana. (2003) *Théologie versus physique dans la poésie présocratique de Xénophane à Empedocle*. Paris: Sorbonne.

Clark, S. R. L. (1986) *The Mysteries of Religion: An Introduction to Philosophy through Religion, Philosophical Introductions*. Oxford: Blackwell.

Clayton, Philip. (2000) *The Problem of God in Modern Thought*. Grand Rapids, MI; Cambridge: Eerdmans.

Clement. (1919) *Exhortation to the Greeks*. London: Loeb.

Coleridge, Samuel Taylor. (1984) *Biographia Literaria; or, Biographical Sketches of My Literary Life and Opinions*, James Engell and Walter Jackson Bate (eds.). Princeton, NJ: Princeton University Press.

Conway, Anne. (1996) *The Principles of the Most Ancient and Modern Philosophy*, Allison Coudert and Taylor Corse (eds.). Cambridge: Cambridge University Press.

Cooper, Ian. (2008) *The Near and Distant God Poetry, Idealism and Religious Thought from Hölderlin to Eliot*. Oxford: Legenda.

Corbin, Henry. (1998) *Alone with the Alone, Creative Imagination in the Sufism of Ibn Arabi*. Princeton, NJ: Bollingen.

Croce, Benedetto, and Collingwood, R. G. (1913) *The Philosophy of Giambattista Vico*. London: H. Latimer.

Cudworth, Ralph. (1647) *A Sermon Preached before the House of Commons*, March 31.

Cudworth, R. (1996) "A treatise of freewill," in Hutton (ed.), *A Treatise Concerning Eternal and Immutable Morality*. Cambridge: Cambridge University Press.

Daly, R. J. (1972) "Sacrifice in Origen," *Studia Patristica 9 Texte und Untersuchungen* 108: Berlin.

Dalferth. (1993) *Jenseits von Mythos und Logos: Die christologische Transformation der Theologie* Freiburg: Herder.

Daniélou, Jean. (1953) *Platonisme et théologie mystique: essai sur la doctrine spirituelle de Saint Grégoire de Nysse* (new edn.). Paris; Aubier: Éditions Montaigne.

Dante, Alighieri. (1939) "Purgatorio" in *The Divine Comedy of Dante Alighieri*. Oxford: Oxford University Press.

Dante, Alighieri. (1939) "Paradiso," in John D. Sinclair (trans.), *The Divine Comedy of Dante Alighieri*. Oxford: Oxford University Press.

Davidson, Herbert A. (1979) "Maimonides' secret position on creation," in Isadore Twersky (ed.), *Studies in Medieval Jewish History and Literature*. Cambridge, MA: Harvard University Press, viii.

Davidson, Herbert A. (1992) *Alfarabi, Avicenna, and Averroes, on Intellect: Their Cosmologies, Theories of the Active Intellect, and Theories of Human Intellect*. New York; Oxford: Oxford University Press.

Dawkins, Richard. (1976) *The Selfish Gene*. Oxford: Oxford University Press.

Dennett, Daniel C. (1991) *Consciousness Explained*. London: Penguin.

Dermenghem, Emile. (1946) *Joseph de Maistre Mystique*. Paris: La Colombe.

Dörrie, Henrich. (1956) "That a highest power wishes to teach mankind through suffering." *Leid und Erfahrung: Die Wort und Sinn–Verbindung . . . im griechischen Denken, Akademie der Wissenschaften und der Literatur, Abhandlung der Geistes und Sozialwissenschaftlichen Klasse,* 5: 1–41, 36.

Dostoevsky, Fyodor. (1991) *Crime and Punishment*, David McDuff (trans.). Harmondsworth: Penguin Books.

Du Bois Marcus, Nancy. (2001) *Vico and Plato, Emory Vico Studies*. New York: P. Lang.

Durkheim, Emile. (1976) *The Elementary Forms of the Religious Life*, Joseph Ward Swain. London: George Allen & Unwin.

Eckhart, Meister. (1955) *Die deutschen und Lateinischen Werk*. J. Quint (ed. and trans.). Munich: C. Hanser.

Eckhart, Meister. (1996) *Sermons and Treatises*, M. O'C Walshe (ed.). Shaftesbury: Watkins.

Ehrenreich, Barbara. (1997) *Blood Rites: The Origins and History of the Passions of War*. New York: Henry Holt.

Eliade, M. (2009) *Yoga, Immortality and Freedom*. Princeton, NJ: Princeton University Press.

Emilsson, E. K. (1988) *Plotinus on Sense-Perception: A Philosophical Study*. Cambridge: Cambridge University Press.

Engell, James. (1981) *The Creative Imagination: Enlightenment to Romanticism*. Cambridge, MA: Harvard University Press.

Ericson, E. E. (1991) *The Apocalyptic Vision of Mikhail Bulgakov's The Master and Margarita*. Lewiston, SA: Mellon.

Faguet, Émile. (1898) *Politiques et moralistes du dix–neuvième siècle*. Paris: Société Française d'imprimerie et de Librairie.

Feldman, B. and Richardson, R. D. (1975) *The Rise of Modern Mythology, 1680–1860*. Bloomington: Indiana University Press.

Festuguière, A. J. (1932) *L'ideal religieux des grec et l'Evangile*. Paris: Gabalda.

Feuerstein, G. (1974) *Introduction to the Bhagavad Gita: Its Philosophy and Cultural Setting*. London: Rider.

Findlay, J. N. (1967) *The Transcendence of the Cave: Gifford Lectures Given at the University of St Andrews, December 1965–January 1966*. London: Allen & Unwin.

Finlan, M. (2007) *Options on Atonement in Christian Thought*. Collegeville, MN: Liturgical Press.

Finney, G. L. (1947) "'Organical musick' and ecstacy" *Journal of the History of Ideas*, 7: 272–92.

Foley, H. P. (1985) *Ritual Irony: Poetry and Sacrifice in Euripides*. Ithaca, NY: Cornell.

Foot, Philippa. (1990) "Locke, Hume, and modern moral theory: a legacy of seventeenth and eighteenth century philosophies of mind," in G. S. Rousseau (ed.), *The Languages of Psyche: Mind and Body in Enlightenment Thought*. Berkley: University of California Press.

Foucault, M. (1975) *Surveiller et Punir*. Paris: Gallimard.

Foucault, M. (1977) *Discipline and Punish: The Birth of the Prison*. London: Allen Lane.

Foucault, M. (1984) *Histoire de la sexualité: Le souci de soi*. Paris: Gallimard.

Foucault, M. (1989) *Philosophe, Rencontre Internationale*. Paris 9.10.11. Janvier 1988. Jean Claude Milner, Paul Veyne, Francois Veyne, and Francois Wahl (eds.). Paris, Seuil.

Frank, Manfred. (1982) *Der Kommende Gott: Vorlesungen Über Die Neue Mythologie*. Frankfurt am Main: Suhrkamp.

Freud, S. (1961) *Civilization and its Discontents*. New York: Norton.

Garrett, Don., "Spinoza's ethical theory,", in Don Garrett, *Cambridge Companion to Spinoza*. Cambridge: Cambridge University Press, 267–314.

Gibbon, Edward. (1993) *The Decline and Fall of the Roman Empire*, 6 vols. H. R. Trevor-Roper (ed.). London: David Campbell.

Girard, R. (1996) "Nietzsche versus the crucified," in James Williams (ed.), *The Girard Reader*. New York: Crossroad Herder, pp. 243–61.

Girard, R. (2005) *Violence and the Sacred*. London: Continuum.

Girard, René, Oughourlian, J-M., Lefort, G., Bann, S., and Metteer, M. (1987) *Things Hidden since the Foundation of the World*. Stanford, CA: Stanford University Press.

Girard, R., de Castro Rocha, J. C., and Antonello, P. (2007) *Evolution and Conversion: Dialogues on the Origins of Culture*. London: Continuum.

Goethe, J. W. V. (1987) *Werke. Weimarer Ausgabe in 143 Bänden*. München: Deutscher Taschenbuch Verlag.

Graevenitz, Gerhart von. (1987) *Mythos: Zur Geschichte Einer Denkgewohnheit*. Stuttgart: Metzler.

Hadot, P. (1995) *Philosophy as a Way of Life*, M. Chase (trans.). Oxford: Blackwells.

Harnack, A. (1990) *Lehrbuch der Dogmengeschichte*, I. Tübingen: Mohr Siebeck.

Harris, H. S. (1972) *Hegel's Development: Towards the Sunlight (1770–1801)*. Oxford: Clarendon Press.

Hebblethwaite, Brian. (1989) "Mackinnon and the problem of evil," in Kenneth Surin (ed.), *Christ, Ethics and Tragedy: Essays in Honour of Donald Mackinnon*. Cambridge: Cambridge University Press, pp. 131–45.

Hedley, Douglas. (2008) *Living Forms of the Imagination*. London: T&T Clark.

Hedley, Douglas, and Hebblethwaite, Brian. (2006) *The Human Person in God's World: Studies to Commemorate the Austin Farrer Centenary*. London: SCM Press.

Heesterman, J. C. (1993) *The Broken World of Sacrifice: An Essay in Ancient Indian Ritual*. Chicago: University of Chicago Press.

Hegel. (1977) *Phenomenology of Spirit*, A.V. Miller (trans.). Oxford: Oxford University Press.

Hegel, G. W. F. (1953) *Reason in History*, R. S. Hartmann (trans.). New York: Liberal Arts Press.

Heidegger, Martin. (1950) *Holzwege*. Frankfurt am Main: V. Klostermann.

Hengstermann, C. (2010) "The 'Dignity of God's Image': Origen's Metaphysics of Man," in *Natur und Normativität*. Münster: Lit Verlag.

Henninger, Joseph. (1987) "Sacrifices," in Mircea Eliade (ed.), *Encyclopedia of Religion*. New York: Macmillan, pp. 557.

Henrichs, A. (1980) "Changing Dionysiac identities," in E. P. Sanders and Ben F. Meyer (eds.), *Jewish and Christian Self-Definition*. London: SCM Press.

Henrichs, A. (1984) "Loss of self, suffering, violence: the modern view of Dionysus from Nietzsche to Girard." *Harvard Studies in Classical Philology*, 88: 205–40.

Heyman, George. (2007) *The Power of Sacrifice: Roman and Christian Discourses in Conflict*. Washington, DC: Catholic University of America Press.

Hick, J. (1994) "Is the doctrine of atonement a mistake?" in A. G. Padgett (ed.), *Reason and the Christian Religion: Essays in Honour of Richard Swinburne*. Oxford: Clarendon.

Hillman, J. (1975) "Plotino, Ficino and Vico," in *Loose Ends*. Dallas: Spring Publications, pp. 146–69.

Hiltebeitel, A. (1976) *The Ritual of Battle: Krishna in the Mahabharata*. Ithaca, NY: Cornell.

Hobbes, T. (1958) *Leviathan*. Oxford: Clarendon Press.

Hofius, Otfried (1972) *Der Vorhang vor dem Thron Gottes*. Tübingen: Mohr Siebeck.

Hogh-Oleson, Henrik. (2006) "The Sacrifice and the reciprocity–programme in religious rituals and in man's everyday interactions." *Journal of Cognition and Culture*, 6, 3–4: 499–519.

Homer. (1961) *Iliad*. 18.107–110. R. Lattimore (trans.). Chicago: University of Chicago Press.

Hughes, D. (2007) *Culture and Sacrifice: Ritual Death in Literature and Opera*. Cambridge: CUP.

Hume, D. (1979) *Enquiry Concerning Principle of Morals*. Oxford: Clarendon.

Hume, D. (1993) *Principal Writings on Religion Including Dialogues Concerning Natural Religion and the Natural History of Religion*, J. C. A. Gaskin (ed.). Oxford: Oxford University Press.

Hume, David. (1998) "On the standard of taste," in Stephen Copley and Andrew Edgar (eds.), *Selected Essays*. Oxford: Oxford University Press, pp.133–54.

Hume, D., Nidditch, P. H., and Selby-Bigge, L. A. (1978) *A Treatise of Human Nature*. (2nd edn.). Oxford: Clarendon Press.

Hutton, Sarah. (1983) "The prophetic imagination: a comparative study of Spinoza and the Cambridge Platonist, John Smith," in C. de Deug (ed.), *Spinoza's Political and Theological Thought*. Amsterdam: North Holland Publishing, pp. 73–81.

Jakob, Michael. (2005) *Paesaggio e letteratura, giardini e paesaggio*. Firenze: Leo S. Olschki.

James, W. (1956) *The Will to Believe*. New York: Longmans, Green, & Co.

Jung, C. G. (1963) *Memories, Dreams, Reflections*, Aniela Jaffé, Richard Winston, and Clara Winston (eds.). London: Collins and Routledge & Kegan Paul.

Jung, C. G. (1986) *Jung: Selected Writings*, Anthony Storr (ed.). London: Fontana Press.

Justin Martyr. (2003) *Dialogue with Trypho*, 69.2. T. B. Falls (trans.). Washington, DC: Catholic University of America.

Kalsched, Donald. (1996) *The Inner World of Trauma: Archetypal Defenses of the Personal Spirit*. London: Routledge.

Kamper. (1981) *Zur Geschichte der Einbildungskraft*. München: Hanser.

Kant, Immanuel. (1951) *Critique of Judgement* (2nd edn.), J. H. Bernard (trans.). New York: Hafner.

Kant, Immanuel. (1981) *The Moral Law; or, Kant's Groundwork of the Metaphysic of Morals*, H. J. Paton (trans.). London: Hutchinson.

Kant, Immanuel. (1982) *Critique of Pure Reason*, Norman Kemp Smith (trans.). London: Macmillan.

Kant, Immanuel. (1998) *Religion within the Boundaries of Mere Reason and Other Writings*, Allen W. Wood and George Di Giovanni (eds.). Cambridge: Cambridge University Press.

Kant, Immanuel. (2004) *Critique of Practical Reason*, Mary J. Gregor (ed.). Cambridge: Cambridge University Press.

Kaplan, Lawrence. (1977) "Maimonides on the Miraculous Element in Prophecy." *Harvard Theological Review*, 70: 233–56.

Kerényi, Karl (1976) *Dionysos: Archetypal Image of Indestructible Life*, Ralph Manheim (ed.). London: Routledge & Kegan Paul.

Kierkegaard, Søren Aabye. (1974) *Fear and Trembling and The Sickness unto Death*, W. Lowrie (trans.). Princeton, NJ: Princeton University Press.

Klawans, Jonathan. (2006) *Purity, Sacrifice and the Temple: Supercessionism in the Study of Ancient Judaism*. Oxford: Oxford University Press.

Knowles, Dudley (ed.). (1990) *Explanation and its Limits*. Cambridge: Cambridge University Press.

Kobusch, T. (1980) "Die Philosophische Bedeutung des Kirchenvaters Origenes." *Theologische Quartalschrift*, 165: 9–31.

Kolakowski, L. (1988) *Metaphysical Horror*. Oxford: Blackwell.

Körner, J. L. (1990) *Caspar David Friedrich and the Subject of Landscape*. New Haven: Yale University Press.

Latacz, Joachim. (1994) "Fruchtbares Agernis: Nietzsches Geburt der Tragoedie und die graezistishce Trageoedienforschung," in J. Latacz (ed.), *Erschliessung der Antike. Kleine Schriften zur Literatur der Griechen und Romer*. Teubner: Stuttgart, pp. 469–98.

Le Brun, Jacques. (2002) *Le pur amour de platon à lacan*. Paris: Seuil.

Leslie, John. (1979) *Value and Existence*. Oxford: Basil Blackwell.

Lieb, Michael. (1994) *Milton and the Culture of Violence*. Ithaca, NY; London: Cornell University Press.

Lilla, Mark (1993). *G.B. Vico: The Making of an Anti-Modern*. Cambridge, MA; London: Harvard University Press.

Longinus. (1927) "On the Sublime," in *Aristotle: The Poetics; Longinus: On the Sublime; Demetius: On Style*. London: William Heinemann.

Lorenz, Konrad. (1967) *On Aggression*, Marjorie Latzke (trans.). London: Methuen & Co.

Louth, Andrew. (2007) *The Origins of the Christian Mystical Tradition: From Plato to Denys* (2nd edn.). Oxford: Oxford University Press.

Lucas, J. R. (1994) "Reflections on the atonement," in A. G. Padgett (ed.), *Reason and the Christian Religion: Essays in Honour of Richard Swinburne*. Oxford: Clarendon.

MacIntyre, A. (1981) *After Virtue*. London: Duckworth.

Mack, Burton. (1987) "Introduction: religion and ritual," in Walter Burkert, René Girard, Jonathan Z. Smith, and Robert Hamerton-Kelly (eds.), *Violent Origins: Ritual Killing and Cultural Formation*. Stanford, CA: Stanford University Press, pp. 1–70.

Mackie, J. (1982) "Retribution: a test for ethical objectivity." *Criminal Justice Ethics*, Winter/Spring: 3–10.

Mackinnon, D. (1974) *The Problem of Metaphysics*. Cambridge: Cambridge University Press.

Maimonides, Moses. (1963) *The Guide of the Perplexed*, 2 vols., Shlomo Pines (trans.). Chicago: University of Chicago Press.

Maistre, Joseph de. (2007) "Considérations Sur La France," in Pierre Glaudes (ed.), *Œuvres*. Paris: R. Laffont.

Maistre, Joseph de. (2007) "Les Soirées De Saint–Pétersbourg," in Pierre Glaudes (ed.), *Œuvres*. Paris: R. Laffont.

Maistre, Joseph de. (2007) "Eclaircissement Sur Les Sacrifices," in Pierre Glaudes (ed.), *Œuvres*. Paris: R. Laffont.

Maistre, Joseph de (1993) *St Petersburg Dialogues; or, Conversations on the Temporal Government of Providence*. Montreal: McGill-Queen's University Press.

Maistre, Joseph de. (1994) *Considerations on France*, Richard Lebrun (trans.). Cambridge: Cambridge University Press.

Mali, Joseph. (1992) *The Rehabilitation of Myth: Vico's "New Science."* Cambridge: Cambridge University Press.

Mascaró, Juan. (2003) *The Bhagavad Gita.* Harmondsworth: Penguin.

McClymond, Kathryn. (2008) *Beyond Sacred Violence: A Comparative Study of Sacrifice.* Baltimore, MD: Johns Hopkins University Press.

McKenzie, D. F. (1970) "A Cambridge playhouse of 1638," in *Renaissance Drama*, vol. 3, pp. 263–72

Menn, Stephen Philip. (1998) *Descartes and Augustine.* Cambridge: Cambridge University Press.

Miller, Cecilia. (1993) *Giambattista Vico: Imagination and Historical Knowledge.* Basingstoke: Macmillan.

Miltchyna, Vera. (2001) "Joseph de Maistre in Russia," in Richard Lebrun (ed.), *Joseph de Maistre's Life, Thought and Influence: Selected Studies.* Montreal: McGill-Queen's University Press.

Milton, John. (1644: London; New York: Eragny, 1904) *Areopagitica: A Speech for the Liberty of Unlicenc'd Printing.* London.

Moore, Greg. (2002) *Nietzsche, Biology and Metaphor.* Cambridge: Cambridge University Press.

Münch, M. M. (1981) *Joseph-Daniel Guigniaut et sa Traduction de la Symbolique de Creuzer*, Interférences. Rennes: L'Institut de Littérature Générale et Comparée de L'U.E.R. Litterature, Université de Haute Bretagne.

Murphy, Jeffrie. (2003) *Getting Even.* Oxford: Oxford University Press.

Nehemas, A. (1998) *The Art of Living: Socratic Reflections from Plato to Foucault.* Berkeley: University of California.

Nietzsche, Friedrich. (1999) *Birth of Tragedy*, Geuss and Spiers (eds.). Cambridge: Cambridge University Press, p. 18.

Nietzsche, Friedrich. (2003) *Writings from the Late Notebooks.* Cambridge: Cambridge University Press.

Newman, John Henry. (1985) *An Essay in Aid of a Grammar of Assent*, I. T. Ker (ed.). Oxford: Clarendon Press.

Nicholas of Cusa. (1998) "De Beryllo," in Jasper Hopkins (trans.), *Nicholas of Cusa: Metaphysical Speculations: Six Latin Texts.* Minneapolis, MN: A. J. Banning Press.

Osborn, Eric Francis. (2001) *Irenaeus of Lyons.* Cambridge: Cambridge University Press.

Otto, Rudolf. (1928) *The Idea of the Holy: An Inquiry into the Non-Rational Factor in the Idea of the Divine and Its Relation to the Rational* (revised edn.), John W. Harvey (trans.). London: Oxford University Press.

Ovid. (1977) *Metamorphoses* (3rd edn.), Frank Justus Miller and G. P. Goold (eds.). *Loeb Classical Library.* London: W. Heinemann.

Pailin, David. (1981) 'Abraham and Isaac: A Hermeneutical Problem Before Kierkegaard' in *Kierkegaard's Fear and Trembling: Critical Appraisals*, Robert L. Perkins (ed.). Alabama: University of Alabama, pp. 10–42.

Pascal, Blaise. (1976) *Pensées*, Philippe Sellier (ed.). Paris: Mercure de France.

Peetz, Siegbert. (1988) *Die Wiederkehr im Unterschied: Ernst von Lasaulx.* Freiburg: Alber.

Peuckert, Will–Erich. (1948) *Die Grosse Wende; Das Apokalyptische Saeculum und Luther. Geistesgeschichte und Volkskunde.* Hamburg: Claassen & Goverts.

Pinkard, T. (1996) *Hegel's Phenomenology: The Sociality of Reason.* Cambridge: Cambridge University Press.

Plato, and Lee, H. D. P. (1987) *The Republic* (2nd edn.). Harmondsworth: Penguin.

Plotinus. (1989) *Enneads*, (revised edn.) Paul Henry, Hans-Rudolf Schwyzer, and A. H. Armstrong (eds.). London: W. Heinemann.

Plutarch. (1959) "Isis and Osiris," Frank Cole Babbitt (trans.). *Moralia*, vol. 5. London: W. Heinemann.

Pranchère, Jean-Yves. (2001) "The Persistence of Maistrian thought," in Richard Lebrun (ed.), *Joseph De Maistre's Life, Thought and Influence: Selected Studies.* Montreal: McGill-Queen's University Press, pp. 290–325.

Puttfarken, Thomas. (2005) *Titian & Tragic Painting: Aristotle's "Poetics" and the Rise of the Modern Artist.* New Haven, CT; London: Yale University Press.

Radhakrishnan S. (1929) *Indian Philosophy* (revised edn.). London: George Allen.

Rahner, Hugo. (1963) *Greek Myths and Christian Mystery.* London: Burns & Oates.

Rahner, Hugo. (1971) *Greek Myths and Christian Mystery*, E. O. James and Brian Battershaw (eds.). New York: Biblo & Tannen.

Rahner, Hugo. (1990) "The Christian mystery and the pagan mysteries," in Joseph Campbell (ed.), *The Mysteries*. Princeton, NJ: Bollingen.

Rogers, S. R. (1991) "Christian adaptations of Euripidean themes in Clement of Alexandria's Protrepticus and Stromata," (doctoral disseration). Catholic University of America.

Rohls, Jan. (1987) *Theologie Und Metaphysik: Der Ontologische Gottesbeweis und Seine Kritiker*. Gütersloh: Mohn.

Rudd, Anthony. (1993) *Kierkegaard and the Limits of the Ethical*. Oxford: Clarendon Press.

Rumi, Mathnawi. (2008), quoted in *The Pocket Rumi*, Kabir Helminski (ed.), Boston: Shambhala, pp. 195–6.

Rust, George (1661) *A Letter of Resolution Concerning Origen and the Chief of his Opinions London*.

Ryle, Gilbert. (1949) *The Concept of Mind*. Harmondsworth: Penguin.

Schellenberg, J. L. (1993) *Divine Hiddenness and Human Reason, Cornell Studies in the Philosophy of Religion*. Ithaca, NY; London: Cornell University Press.

Schelling, F. W. J. (1989) *The Philosophy of Art*, D. Stott (trans.). Minneapolis: University of Minnesota.

Schelling, F. W. J. (1996) *On University Studies*. E. S. Morgan and N. Guterman (trans.). Athens: Ohio University Press.

Schockenhoff, Eberhard. (1990) *Zum Fest Der Freiheit: Theologie Des Christlichen Handelns Bei Origenes*. Mainz: Grünewald.

Screech, M. A. (1980) *Ecstacy and the Praise of Folly*. London: Duckworth.

Scruton, Roger. (2004) *Death Devoted Heart: Sex and the Sacred in Wagner's Tristan Und Isolde*. Oxford: Oxford University Press.

Scruton, Roger. (2009) *Beauty*. Oxford: Oxford University Press.

Scruton, Roger. (2009) *I Drink Therefore I Am: A Philosopher's Guide to Wine*. London; New York: Continuum.

Seneca, Lucius Annaeus. (1961) *Ad Lucilium Epistulae Morales*, 3 vols., Richard M. Gummere (trans.). *Loeb Classical Library*. London: William Heinemann.

Shakespeare, W. (1987) *The Complete Oxford Shakespeare*. Oxford: Oxford University Press.

Sherrard, Philip. (1990) *The Sacred in Life and Art*. Ipswich: Golgonooza.

Smith, D. E. (2003) *From Symposium to Eucharist: The Banquet in the Early Christian World*. Minneapolis, MN: Fortress Press.

Smith, J. (1660) *Select Discourses*, Cambridge. Reprint New York and London: Garland, 1978.

Spinoza. (1996) *Ethics*, Curley, E. M. (trans.) London: Penguin.

Stone, Harold Samuel. (1997) *Vico's Cultural History: The Production and Transmission of Ideas in Naples, 1685–1750, Brill's Studies in Intellectual History*. Leiden: Brill.

Strenski, Ivan. (2003) *Theology and the First Theory of Sacrifice*. Leiden: Brill.

Stroumsa, Guy G. (2005) *La Fin Du Sacrifice: Les Mutations Religieuses De L'antiquité Tardive*. Paris: Odile Jacob.

Swinburne, Richard. (1989) *Responsibility and Atonement*. Oxford: Clarendon Press, 1989.

Taliaferro, C. C. and Teply, A. J. (2004) *Cambridge Platonist Spirituality*. Mahwah, NJ: Paulist Press.

Tanner, M. (1994) "Morals in fiction and fictional morality." *Proceedings of the Aristotelian Society*, 68: 27–66, 53.

Taylor, Charles. (1989) *Sources of the Self: The Making of Modern Identity*. Cambridge: Cambridge University Press.

Taylor, Charles. (1995) *Philosophical Arguments*. Cambridge, MA; London: Harvard University Press.

Taylor, Charles. (2007) *A Secular Age*. Cambridge, MA: Belknap Press of Harvard University Press.

Traherne, Thomas. (1927) *Centuries of Meditations*. London: Dobell.

Tulloch, John. (1872) *Rational Theology and Christian Philosophy in England in the Seventeenth Century* (2nd edn.), 2 vols. Edinburgh: William Blackwood.

Upanishads. (2008) Olivelle, Patrick (trans.). Oxford: OUP.

Verene, Donald Phillip. (1981) *Vico's Science of Imagination*. Ithaca, NY: Cornell University Press.

Vico, Giambattista. (1999) *New Science: Principles of the New Science Concerning the Common Nature of Nations* (3rd edn.), David Marsh (trans.). London: Penguin.

Vico, Giambattista. (2004) *La Scienza Nuova*. Milan: Rizzoli.

Walker, D. P. (1972) *The Ancient Theology: Studies in Christian Platonism from the Fifteenth to the Eighteenth Century*. London: Duckworth.

Walker, D. P. (2000) *Spiritual & Demonic Magic from Ficino to Campanella* (new edn.). Stroud: Sutton.

Walton, Kendall. (1990) *Mimesis as Make Believe: On the Foundations of the Representational Arts*. Cambridge, MA: Harvard University Press.

Walton, Kendall. (1994) "Morals in fiction and fictional morality I." *Proceedings of the Aristotelian Society*, Suppl. 68: 27–50.

Weil, S. (1995) *Gravity and Grace*. London: Routledge.

Westcott, B. F. (1891) *Essays in the History of Religious Thought in the West*. London; New York: Macmillan.

Westcott, B. F. (1886) *Christus Consummator: Some Aspects of the Work and Person of Christ in Relation to Modern Thought (Sermons)*. London: &c.: Macmillan.

Whichcote, B. (1930) *Dr Whichcote's Aphorisms*. London: Elkin Mathews & Marrot.

Whitehead, A. N. (1961) *Adventures of Ideas*. New York: Collier-Macmillan, p. 25.

Whitehead, A. N. (1967) *Adventures in Ideas*. New York: The Free Press, p. 25.

Williams, Bernard A. O. (1973) "Personal identity and individuation," in *Problems of the Self: Philosophical Papers, 1956–1972*. Cambridge: Cambridge University Press, pp. 1–18.

Williamson, G. S. (2004) *The Longing for Myth in Germany: Religion and Aesthetic Culture from Romanticism to Nietzsche*. Chicago, IL; London: University of Chicago Press.

Wilson, A. N. (1983) *The Life of John Milton*. Oxford: Oxford University Press.

Wilson, J. E. (1996) *Schelling und Nietzsche: Zur Auslegung Der Frühen Werke Friedrich Nietzsches*, Monographien Und Texte Zur Nietzsche-Forschung. Berlin: Walter de Gruyter.

Wind, Edgar. (1980) *Pagan Mysteries in the Renaissance* (2nd edn.). Oxford: Oxford University Press.

Wolfson, Harry Austryn. (1973) "Maimonides on the internal senses," in *Studies in the History of Philosophy and Religion*, 2 vols. Cambridge, MA: Harvard University Press.

Wordsworth, William. (1970) *The Prelude*, Stephen C. Gill (ed.). Oxford: Clarendon.

Wright, I. R. (1986) "An early stage at Queens'." *Magazine of the Cambridge Society*, pp. 74–83.

Wynn, Mark. (2009) *Faith and Place: An Essay in Embodied Religious Epistemology*. Oxford: Oxford University Press.

Wyss, Edith. (1996) *The Myth of Apollo and Marsyas in the Art of the Italian Renaissance: An Inquiry into the Meaning of Images*. Newark: University of Delaware Press.

Yolton, John W. (1991) *Locke and French Materialism*. Oxford: Clarendon Press.

Ysebaert, J. (1962) *Greek Baptismal Terminology: Its Origins and Early Development*. Dekker: Nijmegen.

Index of Names

Index of Subjects

Made in the USA
Las Vegas, NV
28 January 2021